CORPORATE ATTRIBUTION IN PRIVATE LAW

Looking at key questions of how companies are held accountable under private law, this book presents a succinct and accessible framework for analysing and answering corporate attribution problems in private law. Corporate attribution is the process by which the acts and states of mind of human individuals are treated as those of a company to establish the company's rights, duties, and liabilities. But when and why are acts and states of mind attributed in private law?

Drawing on a wide range of material from across the disparate areas of company law, agency law, and the laws of contract, tort, unjust enrichment, and equitable obligations, this book's central argument is that attribution turns on the allocation and delegation of the company's own powers to act. This approach allows for a much greater and clearer understanding of attribution. A further benefit is that it shows attribution to be much more united and coherent than it is commonly thought to be. Looking at corporate attribution across the broad expanse of the common law, this book will be of interest to lawyers across the common law world, including the United Kingdom, Australia, Canada, and Singapore.

Volume 41 in the series Hart Studies in Private Law

Corporate Attribution in Private Law

Rachel Leow

•HART•
OXFORD • LONDON • NEW YORK • NEW DELHI • SYDNEY

HART PUBLISHING

Bloomsbury Publishing Plc

Kemp House, Chawley Park, Cumnor Hill, Oxford, OX2 9PH, UK

1385 Broadway, New York, NY 10018, USA

29 Earlsfort Terrace, Dublin 2, Ireland

HART PUBLISHING, the Hart/Stag logo, BLOOMSBURY and the Diana logo are trademarks of Bloomsbury Publishing Plc

First published in Great Britain 2022

A catalogue record for this book is available from the British Library.

A catalogue record for this book is available from the Library of Congress

ISBN: HB: 978-1-50994-135-3
ePDF: 978-1-50994-137-7
ePub: 978-1-50994-136-0

Typeset by Compuscript Ltd, Shannon

FOREWORD

This book explores a central aspect of the law relating to companies that presents perplexing legal problems not least in private law. Given that a company is a legal person but not a human being, how does one work out how central legal concepts that naturally apply to humans, whether concerned with knowledge or action, should be applied to companies? This is the issue of attribution. How and when should one attribute to a company, human states of mind and conduct?

One traditional approach (the 'directing mind and will' approach) was to identify particular individuals, who were sufficiently high up in a company or who had sufficient control within a company, and to treat their minds and conduct as the mind and conduct of the company. But in the leading modern case of *Meridian Global Funds Management Asia Ltd v Securities Commission* [1995] UKPC 5, [1995] 2 AC 500, Lord Hoffmann, giving the advice of the Privy Council, downplayed the 'directing mind and will' approach. Instead he suggested that there were various rules of attribution and that the appropriate rule to be applied depended, crucially, on the context: in other words, attribution turned on the legal rule with which one was concerned and, more specifically, the purpose of that rule.

The central thesis of this book is that, contrary to those approaches, the correct and simpler analysis – at least in English private law which is here being focussed on – is that attribution of acts and knowledge to a company depends on the allocation and delegation to particular groups or individuals of the company's powers to act. Put another way, it is the internal organisation of powers within a company that dictates the answer to the attribution conundrum. This approach is explored, and its ramifications rigorously set out, across the main areas of private law, especially contract, tort and unjust enrichment and whether common law or equity. The approach provides the reader with new insights across the spectrum of attribution including, for example, agency in the making of contracts by companies and vicarious liability in tort for the conduct of companies.

Perhaps the most pressing and difficult attribution problem of all is how to deal with attribution of acts or knowledge where the company is seeking to enforce duties owed to it. The leading case on this issue is *Bilta UK Ltd v Nazir* [2015] UKSC 23, [2015] 2 WLR 1168 which is carefully assessed in chapter 7; and the central thesis of the book is applied to indicate that, even if arriving at the correct result, as in *Bilta*, the courts have been using more complex reasoning than necessary.

Rachel Leow has worked tirelessly on this issue of attribution for many years (during and after completing her PhD on this subject) and has refined her thinking through presentations of her views at conferences and seminars across the common law world. Readers are therefore being treated to the culmination of countless hours of dedicated research and thought. The end product is a fine testimony to her labours. Adopting a traditional 'interpretive' methodology, which pays very close attention to the case law, she writes in a clear and concise style that brings to life and simplifies what might otherwise seem highly complex and dry legal detail.

While not everyone will agree with the author's proposed solution, or the insights that, she argues, follow from it, everyone interested in this fascinating area of the law – whether as judges, practitioners, academics or students – will benefit from reading this book.

Andrew Burrows
September 2021

ACKNOWLEDGEMENTS

This book has been a long time in the making. It is the very distant descendant of a PhD thesis submitted to the University of Cambridge in 2017. I am grateful to my doctoral supervisor, Sarah Worthington, and doctoral advisor, Nick McBride, for their encouragement and helpful feedback during the PhD, when I was still in the early stages of the project.

In the years since, my thinking on attribution has evolved substantially. Although the earlier thesis and this book are on the same topic, they are in many respects wholly different. During the long period of revision and rewriting, I incurred many more debts to friends, colleagues, and others who generously offered support, encouragement, and critical comments. It would be impossible to thank all who have contributed. However, special thanks are owed to Elise Bant, Michael Bridge, Lord Andrew Burrows, Joshua Getzler, Amy Goymour, Birke Häcker, Jason Neyers, Francis Reynolds, Robert Stevens, William Swadling, Graham Virgo, and Stephen Watterson. I am especially grateful to Lord Burrows, who very kindly agreed to write a foreword for the book after the final manuscript had been submitted.

Drafts of several chapters were presented at different venues, including the Obligations VIII conference, the Oxford Obligations Discussion Group, the Cambridge Private Law Centre, the LSE Private Law Forum, the McGill Global Seminars in Private Law Theory series, and the Melbourne/UWA Obligations Group Annual Conference 2020. I would like to thank the organisers of these events for allowing me to speak, and the participants for their very helpful feedback.

Generous financial support from the National University of Singapore made it possible to embark on this project, and later to bring it to completion. Many thanks are also owed to my colleagues at the law faculty who provided support and advice. I would also like to thank my research assistants for proofreading final drafts of the manuscript. I gratefully acknowledge the generous financial support from NUS grant WBS R-241-000-171-133.

The wonderful team at Hart Publishing have helped make this book a reality. Their enthusiasm for the project was infectious. I am especially grateful to Sinead Moloney and Sasha Jawed, who were always at hand to answer any questions I had. They took care of the publication process with remarkable efficiency.

Above all, this book would never have been completed without the support and encouragement of my family, especially my husband, Timothy Liau. He has been my biggest supporter from the start. From teaching me about Hohfeld, to pointing me to literature on group agency, to bearing a greater share of household tasks, it is impossible to fully detail how vital his contributions have been to this project coming to fruition. Through many ups and downs, changes of jurisdiction, several degrees, and a pandemic, he has uncomplainingly borne with the difficulties of living with a distracted and frazzled author. I am truly in his debt.

CONTENTS

PART II
APPLICATION

PART III
DIFFICULT PROBLEMS

TABLE OF CASES

United Kingdom Cases

Australian Cases

Canadian Cases

New Zealand Cases

Singaporean Cases

Hong Kong Cases

US Cases

TABLE OF STATUTES

United Kingdom Legislation

Legislation from Other Jurisdictions

1

Introduction

Companies are artificial legal persons. They lack a physical body and a mind of their own. Unable to act or think 'immaculately',[1] they must act and think through human persons. The acts and states of mind of those human persons are then regarded as the company's. This process is known as 'corporate attribution'. As Lord Walker NPJ explained in *Moulin Global Eyecare Trading Ltd v Commissioner of Inland Revenue*:

> Attribution means, in this context, the process of legal reasoning by which the conduct or state of mind of one or more natural persons (that is, human beings) is treated as that of a non-natural person (that is, a company) for the purpose of determining the company's legal liability or rights in civil proceedings (in particular, its liability or rights in contract, in tort or for unjust enrichment) or its criminal liability.[2]

Although attribution has existed for as long as companies have, when and why attribution is available remains highly controversial. For proof, one only needs to examine the voluminous case law, much of it recent. In England and Wales, the House of Lords and Supreme Court have repeatedly grappled with this question over the last decade.[3] Judges at first instance and in the Court of Appeal regularly face attribution problems. Nor is this limited to England and Wales; the same phenomenon can be seen across the Commonwealth.[4] Keeping pace with the

[1] J Payne, 'Corporate Attribution and the Lessons of Meridian' in PS Davies and J Pila (eds), *The Jurisprudence of Lord Hoffmann: A Festchrift for Leonard Hoffmann* (Oxford, Hart Publishing, 2015).

[2] *Moulin Global Eyecare Trading Ltd v Commissioner of Inland Revenue* [2014] HKCFA 22, (2014) 17 HKCFAR 218 [61].

[3] Eg *Stone & Rolls Ltd (in liquidation) v Moore Stephens* [2009] UKHL 39, [2009] 1 AC 1391; *Bilta (UK) Ltd (in liquidation) v Nazir* [2015] UKSC 23, [2015] 2 WLR 1168; *Singularis Holdings Ltd v Daiwa Capital Markets Europe* [2019] UKSC 50, [2020] AC 1189. Concerning vicarious liability, whose relevance to attribution is discussed in Ch 4, see also *Various Claimants v Catholic Child Welfare Society* [2012] UKSC 56, [2013] 2 AC 1; *Cox v Ministry of Justice* [2016] UKSC 10, [2016] AC 660; *Mohamud v WM Morrison Supermarkets plc* [2016] UKSC 11, [2016] 2 WLR 821; *WM Morrison Supermarkets plc v Various Claimants* [2020] UKSC 12, [2020] AC 973; *Barclays Bank plc v Various Claimants* [2020] UKSC 13, [2020] AC 973.

[4] *Moulin Global* (n 2); *HKSAR v Luk Kin Peter Joseph* [2016] HKCFA 81, (2016) 19 HKCFAR 619; *Ho Kang Peng v Scintronix Corp Ltd* [2014] SGCA 22, [2014] 3 SLR 329; *Ong Bee Chew v Ong Shu Lin* [2017] SGHC 285, [2019] 3 SLR 132; *Red Star Marine Consultants Pte Ltd v Personal Representatives of Satwant Kaur d/o Sardara Singh* [2019] SGCA 76, [2020] 1 SLR 115. See also, in Australia, *Director of Public Prosecutions Reference No 1 of 1996* [1998] 3 VR 352, (1997) 96 A Crim R 513; *Director General, Department of Education and Training v MT* [2006] NSWCA 270, (2006) 67 NSWLR 237, 44; *Commonwealth Bank v Kojic* [2016] FCAFC 186 [97]–[99].

profusion of case law is an explosion in academic commentary.[5] But a succinct and accessible account of when and why acts and states of mind can be attributed in private law is still lacking.

The lack of such an account can be fairly ascribed to the impact of attribution's leading case, *Meridian Global Funds Management Asia Ltd v Securities Commission*.[6] A true landmark, *Meridian* was the first to develop the terminology of attribution and to identify categories of attribution rules. Today, it is most closely associated with a highly context-specific approach to attribution.[7] On this view, when and why acts and states of mind are attributed varies; an act or state of mind attributed for one purpose may not be for another. Judicial statements to this effect are not difficult to find. Expressing this point of view most strongly was Lord Hoffmann NPJ in the Hong Kong Court of Final Appeal, who said that:

> [The question before the court] suggests that there are uniform common law principles by which one will attribute acts, knowledge, states of mind etc to the company. In my opinion it cannot be too strongly emphasised that there are no such 'common law principles'. The authorities since *Meridian* … and in particular the more recent cases of *Moulin Global Eyecare Trading Ltd v Commissioner of Inland Revenue* (2014) 17 HKCFAR 218 and *Bilta (UK) Ltd (in liquidation) and others v Nazir and Ors (No 2)* [2016] AC 1 make it clear that in every case the criteria for attribution must be such as will give effect to the purpose and policy of the relevant substantive rule, whether that rule is contained in a statute or the common law.[8]

If these statements are correct, working out attribution rules across private law would be a mammoth task of enormous complexity. Myriad factors might require consideration. Attribution rules could vary depending on the doctrine requiring attribution, the remedy sought, the type of company to whom the act or knowledge is to be attributed, the company's solvency, and countless other variables. The prospects for producing a succinct and accessible account of attribution in private law appear correspondingly dim.

The book aims to show that attribution is not so complicated or difficult after all. It offers the first ever book-length account of when and why attribution is available

[5] See eg E Ferran, 'Corporate Attribution and the Directing Mind and Will' (2011) 127 *LQR* 239; P Watts, 'Illegality and Agency Law: Authorising Illegal Action' [2011] *Journal of Business Law* 213; P Watts, 'Principals' Tortious Liability for Agents' Negligent Statements – Is "Authority" Necessary?' (2012) 128 *LQR* 260; E Lim, 'A Critique of Corporate Attribution: "Directing Mind and Will" and Corporate Objectives' (2013) *Journal of Business Law* 333; E Lim, 'Attribution in Company Law' (2014) 77 *MLR* 794; Payne (n 1); S Worthington, 'Corporate Attribution and Agency: Back to Basics' (2017) 133 *LQR* 118; P Watts, 'The Acts and State of Knowledge of Agents as Factors in Principals' Restitutionary Liability' (2017) *LMCLQ* 386; P Watts, 'Attribution and Limitation' (2018) 134 *LQR* 350; E Lim, 'Attribution' in W Day and S Worthington (eds), *Challenging Private Law: Lord Sumption on the Supreme Court* (Oxford, Hart Publishing, 2020).

[6] *Meridian Global Funds Management Asia Ltd v Securities Commission* [1995] UKPC 5, [1995] 2 AC 500.

[7] For just a sampling of some key cases, see *Moulin Global* (n 2) [41]; *Bilta* (n 3) [20] (Lord Neuberger), [41] (Lord Mance), [92] (Lord Sumption), [201] (Lords Toulson and Hodge); *Singularis* (n 3) [34]. See Ch 2 below.

[8] *HKSAR v Luk* (n 4) [41].

in private law. Drawing on a wide range of material from across the disparate areas of company law, agency law, and the laws of contract, tort, unjust enrichment, and equitable obligations, its central argument is that attribution turns on the allocation and delegation of the company's own powers to act.

I. The Central Argument

Over the past two decades, *Meridian* has garnered virtually unanimous support. Likewise, the context-specific approach associated with it has been widely endorsed. The picture is one of apparent harmony. But problems surface on closer reflection. While all agree that context is important, what context is relevant? There is little agreement here. While some regard attribution as turning on the source or the type of the right being enforced,[9] others rely on the purpose and policy of the claim as the key feature for attribution.[10] A third approach considers all features relevant to the factual or legal context.[11] Other variants undoubtedly exist. These accounts share a common theme: they regard attribution as turning, either partially or wholly, on features concerning the right being enforced or the claim by which it is enforced. We might call these 'right-sided' features.

The central argument of this book is that attribution turns not on 'right-sided' features, but on the allocation and delegation of the company's powers to act. Justifications must fit the thing to be justified. True of other subjects of justification, this is equally true for attribution. Reasons for attribution must fit attribution's form. Attribution involves treating *this* act or knowledge of *this* individual as that of *this* company. It thus concerns the connection between act or knowledge, individual, and the company. Reasons given for attribution must fit this form, connecting act or knowledge, individual, and company in a single normative sequence. This explains why accounts focusing on 'right-sided' features miss the mark: these right-sided features are external to the connection between act or knowledge, individual, and the company. They do not fit attribution's form. Equally, the same objection can be made to accounts which regard attribution as turning on who the least-cost-avoider is.[12] Concerned with improving economic efficiency, they too do not fit attribution's form.

This connection is found in the company's allocation and delegation to human individuals of its own powers to act. As a legal person, the company comes into existence with its own powers. Those powers can be allocated to different groups

[9] Most prominently by Peter Watts, eg Watts, 'Attribution and Limitation' (n 5) 350.

[10] Eg *Bank of India v Morris* [2005] EWCA Civ 693, [2005] BCC 739 [111]–[112] (Mummery LJ), affirming [2004] EWHC 528 (Ch), [2004] BCC 404 [121] (Patten J); *Lebon v Aqua Salt Co Ltd* [2009] UKPC 2, [2009] BCC 425; *Red Star Marine Consultants* (n 4) [42]–[43] (Judith Prakash JA, Tay Yong Kwang JA, and Steven Chong JA).

[11] Eg *Moulin Global* (n 2) [113] (Lord Walker).

[12] Eg A Griffiths, *Contracting with Companies* (Oxford, Hart Publishing, 2005).

or individuals through the company's constitution. Most commonly, powers to act are allocated to the board of directors and shareholders in general meeting. These groups, or others allocated the company's powers, can then delegate those powers throughout the corporate hierarchy to chief officers, managers, and rank-and-file employees. When these allocated or delegated powers are exercised, the company's own powers to act are exercised. The company acts personally. This involves no legal fiction, only the application of ordinary legal concepts.

On this account, the attribution of acts thus turns on four questions: (i) does the company have the power to act? (ii) was the power allocated or delegated to the person doing the act? (iii) was the power exercised within its scope? (iv) was the power properly exercised? A similar analysis applies to the attribution of knowledge. The attribution of knowledge turns on whether the knowledge-holder was allocated or delegated the company's powers and that the knowledge was material to those powers.

The account presented here is an interpretive one. Like other interpretive accounts, it 'aim[s] to enhance understanding of the law … by revealing an intelligible order in the law, so far as such an order exists'.[13] This intelligible order is to be found by showing how features of the law are best explained.[14] In line with interpretive theories generally, the account here has good fit with the current law, is largely transparent in reflecting the reasoning of judges for reaching their conclusions, and provides a normatively attractive account of the doctrine.

II. Advantages

This account offers important advantages; three are focused on here.

First, it provides a simple, user-friendly framework which can be used to analyse and answer difficult attribution problems. As the many recent attribution cases indicate, courts often face difficulty in deciding whether acts or knowledge can be attributed. As Jackson LJ said about the key decision of *Bilta (UK) Ltd (in liquidation) v Nazir*,[15] '[t]he length and multiplicity of the different analyses in those passages do not make life easy for practitioners and judges dealing with attribution issues on a day-to-day basis'.[16] The same is true of attribution more generally. Many questions remain unanswered. Can acts be attributed to establish negligent driving? Battery? When is knowledge attributed to establish defences against a company? When are acts attributed in restitutionary claims?

[13] SA Smith, *Contract Theory* (Oxford, Clarendon Press, 2004) 5.

[14] Eg Smith, ibid 5; A Beever and C Rickett, 'Interpretive Legal Theory and the Academic Lawyer' (2005) 68 *MLR* 320, 325.

[15] (n 3).

[16] *Howmet Ltd v Economy Devices Ltd & others* [2016] EWCA Civ 847, [2016] BLR 555 [71].

The account presented here provides these answers, and the framework to at least make a start on others. The attribution of acts turns on the company's powers to act, their allocation and delegation, scope, and proper exercise. The attribution of knowledge likewise turns on whether that knowledge was material to the powers allocated or delegated to the knowledge-holder. Conversely, if attribution turns on context, with attendant difficulties as to what context means, these questions become even more difficult to answer.

Second, it presents a non-fictional account of attribution. As shown in Chapter 2, it is often assumed that attribution is only a fictional deeming process, necessitated by the prior legal fiction of the company.[17] In other words, attribution merely involves artificially treating acts and mental states as the company's though they are not.[18] But if only a deeming rule, attribution possesses no natural limits. In tort law, Robert Stevens once recognised this problem:

> [W]hilst some sort of rules for the attribution of acts are essential, this does not tell us what the detailed content of those rules ought to be ... What is the correct approach? How many players should a team of footballers contain? Five? Eight? Eleven? Twenty? It is important to know who counts as a member of the team, but there are different ways in which rational rules can be formulated. Whilst some answers may be demonstrably wrong (eg one-a-side, 90-a-side), there may be no single demonstrably right answer.[19]

But the approaches taken to attribution have been remarkably consistent over decades and across common law jurisdictions. This suggests a shared common intuition that there are right answers to attribution. The account advanced here presents a way to vindicate that intuition.

This account also suggests that attribution has deeper normative significance. In line with recent valuable new work on group agency, it suggests that attributed acts are largely intentional acts done by companies as agents, used here in a philosophical sense to refer to beings with capacity for action. This is important as capacity to act as an agent is often regarded as a necessary precondition to holding the actor responsible for the act, whether morally or otherwise.

Third, the very possibility of formulating an account of when and why attribution is available suggests that attribution is more unified than commonly thought to be. At first sight, attribution appears highly disparate. Doctrines governing it appear loosely dispersed across far-flung islands of company law, agency law, and the law of obligation, with little to bridge the gap between them. But this image is inaccurate. Although applying to many different areas, attribution has its own internal logic. United by the central idea of the allocation and delegation of the

[17] Eg *Meridian* (n 6) 506.

[18] Eg Payne (n 1) 368. For similar approaches, see analogies between companies and human owners of businesses who are in the South of France or the grouse moors, eg *Standard Chartered Bank v Pakistan National Shipping Corpn (Nos 2 and 4)* [2002] UKHL 43, [2003] 1 AC 959 [23] (Lord Hoffmann); *PCW Syndicates v PCW Reinsurers* [1996] 1 WLR 1136 (CA).

[19] R Stevens, *Torts and Rights* (Oxford, Oxford University Press, 2007) 267.

company's own powers, the rules of attribution form a coherent body across different areas of private law. Attribution's unity has importance going beyond mere conceptual tidiness. It might suggest that attribution in other contexts might work similarly. The account here may thus have insights for corporate attribution in other contexts, and attribution to other actors, including local authorities, universities, even the Crown.

III. Scope

This book examines attribution to companies in private law. It is a book on corporate attribution. It is not a book on corporate *liability* generally. It is therefore beyond the scope of the book to examine the different ways and reasons why companies may incur liability in private law. The aim is to provide an account of when and why acts and some states of mind are attributed to the company.

The book has two key focal points: companies and private law. A 'company' here refers to a company incorporated by registration in England and Wales under the Companies Act 2006 and its predecessors. Attribution to unincorporated business vehicles[20] or other incorporated legal persons[21] falls outside its scope. The reason for this is simple: the company incorporated by registration is undoubtedly the most used business vehicle today, and a familiar figure in reported litigation. This suggests that attribution to registered companies is where a systematic account of attribution of attribution is most needed, as well as where there is the richest source material from which to develop it.

As to 'private law', the book focuses here on one branch of private law, the law of obligations. This includes three areas which are uncontroversially regarded as part of private law: contract law, tort law, and the law of unjust enrichment or restitution. Some aspects of equitable liability are also examined, particularly in attributing knowledge, and further discussion of equity's attribution rules can be found elsewhere.[22] Space constraints mean that not every private law doctrine can be considered. Although focusing on corporate attribution in private law, the account here may have some important insights for attribution to other actors or in other areas of law.[23] These are considered at the end of the book.

[20] Such as general partnerships under the Partnership Act 1890.

[21] Such as limited liability partnerships under the Limited Liability Partnership Act 2000, or public bodies established by Acts of Parliament.

[22] R Leow, 'Equity's Attribution Rules' (2021) 15 *Journal of Equity* 35.

[23] Compare with the literature on corporate attribution in the criminal law. For a brief sampling, see eg B Fisse and J Braithwaite, *Corporations, Crime and Accountability* (Cambridge, Cambridge University Press, 1993); CMV Clarkson, 'Kicking Corporate Bodies and Danning Their Souls' (1996) 59 *MLR* 557; GR Sullivan, 'The Attribution of Culpability to Limited Companies' (1996) 55 *CLJ* 515; N Cavanagh, 'Corporate Criminal Liability: an Assessment of the Models of Fault' (2011) 75 *Journal of Criminal Law* 414; C Wells, *Corporations and Criminal Responsibility*, 2nd edn (Oxford, Oxford University Press, 2001); J Gobert and M Punch, *Rethinking Corporate Crime* (London, Butterworths, 2003); A Pinto and M Evans, *Corporate Criminal Liability*, 2nd edn (London, Sweet & Maxwell, 2008).

Reasons of space necessitate focus on one core jurisdiction: English law. However, references are frequently made to other common law jurisdictions. As approaches to attribution in different common law jurisdictions often have much in common, the analysis offered in this book will also be of interest to lawyers across the common law world, including the United Kingdom, Australia, Canada, New Zealand, and Singapore.

IV. Outline

The book is divided into three parts.

Part I comprises a single chapter, Chapter 2. It introduces attribution and sets out orthodox approaches to when and why attribution is available. Identifying problems with these orthodox accounts, it advances a new account of attribution under which attribution turns on the internal allocation and delegation of the company's own powers to act under the company's constitution. When these powers are properly exercised by those to whom they have been allocated or delegated, the company acts personally. This provides a useful analytical framework for the attribution of acts. It shows that the attribution of acts turns on four questions: (i) did the company have the power to do the act? (ii) was the power allocated or delegated to the group or individual purporting to do the act? (iii) was the power exercised within its scope? (iv) was the power properly exercised? The account advanced also suggests that attribution has a deeper normative basis than commonly thought, generally identifying intentional acts done by the company as a group agent.

This analysis is then developed in Part II, comprising Chapters 3–6. Chapters 3, 4, and 5 concern the attribution of acts, while Chapter 6 considers the attribution of knowledge.

Chapter 3 examines the attribution of acts in contract formation, where agency analysis dominates. It is argued that while agency analysis is appropriate in analysing contracting by subordinate agents, it is less so when analysing contracting by the board of directors, shareholders in general meeting, or those to whom powers have been allocated directly under the company's constitution. It argues that it is preferable to focus on the allocation and delegation of the company's powers instead. The chapter then shows that in both cases, the attribution of acts turns on the four questions identified in Chapter 2. It also explains the role of other routes to liability, including the indoor management rule, apparent authority, and statutory deeming provisions.

Chapter 4 turns to attributing acts in tort law, a surprisingly difficult topic. It is not clear whether tort law has rules attributing acts at all. While some might point to the well-known doctrine of vicarious liability, orthodoxy holds that it attributes only liability and not acts. This chapter shows that, although hidden, tort law does have rules attributing acts. Before 1956, those rules were found in the doctrine of 'vicarious liability', which then attributed acts. After 1956, vicarious liability changed. It became a doctrine attributing liability. This did not mean that acts could no longer be attributed in tort law after 1956. They still could be, on the same basis as before, albeit no longer under the banner of 'vicarious liability'. It is shown that attribution in tort also turns on the allocation and delegation of the company's powers.

Chapter 5 moves on to unjust enrichment, in some respects a relatively new subject. It focuses on what is generally accepted to be unjust enrichment's core case: mistaken payments. Prominent commentators have recently argued that attribution rules in restitutionary claims are wider than those in contract or tort claims. This chapter challenges these views, arguing that attribution rules here are no different from those in other branches of private law. Again, they turn again on the company's allocation of its powers to act. Three situations are considered: (i) where the company mistakenly pays another money; (ii) where the company induces a mistaken payment to be made; and (iii) where the company receives mistaken payments.

Chapter 6 moves on to attributing knowledge. It is suggested that while attributing acts requires connecting act, individual, and company, attributing knowledge goes one step further. Knowledge, act, individual, and company must all be connected. It is argued that knowledge will be attributed where two conditions are met: the knowledge must be possessed by a person allocated or delegated the company's powers to act, and that knowledge must be material to the exercise of those powers. This is explained by the function of knowledge in private law. The test is then illustrated with reference to cases of knowing receipt, dishonest assistance, deceit, and statutory liability.

The basic framework in place, Part III then turns to two more complicated attribution problems in Chapters 7 and 8.

Previous chapters considered when and why acts and knowledge could be attributed to a company to establish its duties and liabilities. Chapter 7 addresses a different problem: when can acts and knowledge be attributed to the company when it is enforcing duties owed to it? This question has proven highly problematic, necessitating no less than three visits to the ultimate appellate court in England and Wales within a decade. The chapter argues that the same rules of attribution which are used to establish the company's duties and liabilities should also be applied when the company is enforcing duties owed to it. This 'both ways' test is the same as that in contributory negligence. However, even if the act or knowledge is attributed, the company's claim will not necessarily fail; the effect of attribution depends on the substantive rule of law in question. This argument is then illustrated with reference to contributory negligence, consent, clean hands, conspiracy, estoppel by acquiescence, and illegality, before important recent cases are evaluated.

Chapter 8 moves on to the problem of aggregation. Previous chapters examined the attribution of acts or knowledge of a single individual. But companies are frequently large, complex organisations. Many different individuals may act for it or possess different states of knowledge at the same time. This chapter addresses the difficult question of when the act of one individual can be aggregated together with the knowledge of another so that the company is responsible for the combined effect of those acts and knowledge. It argues that aggregation of A1's knowledge and A2's act is only possible where A1, possessing the knowledge, (i) knows or suspects that A2 will do the act, and (ii) intends that A2 does the act.

Chapter 9 draws together the core arguments of the book and suggests some further implications. If attribution is not 'right-sided' but turns on the connection between act or knowledge, individual, and company, then there is no reason in principle why the account should be limited to private law. It appears equally applicable to attribution in other areas of law, such as criminal law. Furthermore, the account may also be applicable to other artificial legal persons, such as the Crown. Some of these implications are explored in greater detail. Although developed in the context of corporate attribution in private law, the analysis offered in this book may have far-reaching implications for other areas of law as well.

PART I

Foundations

2

Attribution as Allocated and Delegated Powers

When and why are acts and states of mind attributed to companies? This is a difficult question, generating much litigation.[1] Ever since the leading decision of *Meridian Global Funds Management Asia Ltd v Securities Commission*,[2] it has been widely accepted that when and why acts and states of mind are attributed turns on the context.[3] All agree that context is important, but there is little agreement on what context counts. Some focus on the purpose and policy of the substantive rule requiring attribution. Others focus on the source or type of the right which is being enforced. A third, more expansive, approach admits into consideration all the factual and legal background.

These approaches regard attribution as turning primarily on the right being enforced or the claim by which it is enforced. We might call them 'right-sided' approaches. But right-sided approaches miss the mark. They do not justify attribution, the thing to be justified. Attribution involves treating *this* act of *this* individual as *this* company's. The reason for doing so must link act, individual, and company.

[1] Eg *Stone & Rolls Ltd (in liquidation) v Moore Stephens* [2009] UKHL 39, [2009] 1 AC 1391; *Bilta (UK) Ltd v Nazir* [2015] UKSC 23, [2015] 2 WLR 1168; *Singularis Holdings Ltd v Daiwa Capital Markets Europe* [2019] UKSC 50, [2020] AC 1189. Concerning vicarious liability, whose relevance to attribution is discussed in Ch 4 below, see also *Various Claimants v Catholic Child Welfare Society* [2012] UKSC 56, [2013] 2 AC 1; *Cox v Ministry of Justice* [2016] UKSC 10, [2016] AC 660; *Mohamud v WM Morrison Supermarkets plc* [2016] UKSC 11, [2016] 2 WLR 821; *WM Morrison Supermarkets plc v Various Claimants* [2020] UKSC 12; *Barclays Bank plc v Various Claimants* [2020] UKSC 13. In the Privy Council, see *Lebon v Aqua Salt Co Ltd* [2009] UKPC 2, [2009] BCC 425; *Julien v Evolving TecKnologies and Enterprise Development Co Ltd* [2018] UKPC 2, [2018] BCC 376.

[2] *Meridian Global Funds Management Asia Ltd v Securities Commission* [1995] UKPC 5, [1995] 2 AC 500.

[3] See eg E Ferran, 'Corporate Attribution and the Directing Mind and Will' (2011) 127 *LQR* 239; P Watts, 'Illegality and Agency Law: Authorising Illegal Action' (2011) *Journal of Business Law* 213; P Watts, 'Principals' Tortious Liability for Agents' Negligent Statements – Is "Authority" Necessary?' (2012) 128 *LQR* 260; E Lim, 'A Critique of Corporate Attribution: "Directing Mind and Will" and Corporate Objectives' (2013) *Journal of Business Law* 333; E Lim, 'Attribution in Company Law' (2014) 77 *MLR* 794; J Payne, 'Corporate Attribution and the Lessons of Meridian' in PS Davies and J Pila (eds), *The Jurisprudence of Lord Hoffmann: A Festschrift for Leonard H Hoffmann* (Oxford, Hart Publishing, 2015); S Worthington, 'Corporate Attribution and Agency: Back to Basics' (2017) 133 *LQR* 118; P Watts, 'The Acts and State of Knowledge of Agents as Factors in Principals' Restitutionary Liability' [2017] *LMCLQ* 386; P Watts, 'Attribution and Limitation' (2018) 134 *LQR* 350; E Lim, 'Attribution' in W Day and S Worthington (eds), *Challenging Private Law: Lord Sumption on the Supreme Court* (Oxford, Hart Publishing, 2020).

Right-sided approaches do not provide this link. They also generate other problems. Their adoption appears to stem from a persistent view that attribution is a purely fictional deeming process.

This chapter advances a non-fictional account of attribution which connects act, individual, and company. It argues that attribution turns on the internal allocation and delegation of the company's own powers to act under the company's constitution. When these powers are properly exercised by those to whom they have been allocated or delegated, the company acts personally. This involves no legal fiction, only the application of ordinary legal concepts.

Two immediate payoffs of this account follow. First, it provides a useful framework for resolving attribution questions about acts across private law. It turns on four central questions: (i) did the company have the power to do the act? (ii) was that power properly allocated and, if necessary, delegated to an individual or group who did the act? (iii) did the act fall within the scope of the power? (iv) was the power properly exercised? We turn to the attribution of knowledge and other states of mind in Chapter 6. A merit of this approach is that it is consistent with the hierarchy of attribution rules set out in *Meridian*. Second, it suggests that attribution has a deeper normative basis than commonly thought. It generally identifies intentional acts done by the company as a group agent.

I. *Meridian Global Funds Management Asia Ltd v Securities Commission*

For many decades, the best-known approach for determining how companies acted through human individuals was the 'directing mind and will' approach. Departing from it, *Meridian* developed the idea of attribution and identified three sets of attribution rules. Today, *Meridian* is closely associated with a highly context-specific approach towards attribution.

A. 'Directing Mind and Will'

Prior to *Meridian*, it was commonly thought that acts and states of mind could only be attributed to a company where they were done or possessed by the company's 'directing mind and will'.[4] This test traces its lineage to *Lennard's Carrying Co Ltd v Asiatic Petroleum Co Ltd*, where a ship carrying oil caught fire, resulting in its cargo being totally lost.[5] The shipowner, Lennard's Carrying Company Ltd, sought

[4] Even after *Meridian*, this language is still sometimes used, eg *Stone & Rolls Ltd* (n 1); *Bellman v Northampton Recruitment Ltd* [2018] EWCA Civ 2213; *FCA v Avacade Ltd (in liquidation)* [2020] EWHC 1673 (Ch) [403].

[5] *Lennard's Carrying Co Ltd v Asiatic Petroleum Co Ltd* [1915] AC 705 (HL) 713.

to establish a statutory defence to claims for the loss of cargo put on board the ship, which required it to show that the loss happened 'without his actual fault or privity'.[6] In explaining how the statute could apply to a company, Viscount Haldane LC explained that:

> A corporation is an abstraction. It has no mind of its own any more than it has a body of its own; its active and directing will must consequently be sought in the person of somebody who for some purposes may be called an agent, but who is really the directing mind and will of the corporation, the very ego and centre of the personality of the corporation.[7]

In *Lennard's Carrying Co*, the shipowner thus needed to show that the loss happened without the 'actual fault or privity' of the company's directing mind and will. They could not do so. Mr Lennard, 'the person registered in the ship's register and designated as the person to whom the management of the vessel was entrusted', knew of the ship's faults.[8] An inference could be drawn that he was the company's directing mind and will.[9] As this inference was not rebutted, Mr Lennard's acts and states of mind could thus be attributed to the company.[10] The defence therefore failed.

Lennard's Carrying Co explained that the 'directing mind and will' would be the 'life and soul of the company',[11] his actions 'the very action of the company itself'.[12] He or she would be the embodiment of the company.[13] The 'directing mind and will' approach was expanded on by Denning LJ in characteristically vivid terms:

> A company may in many ways be likened to a human body. It has a brain and nerve centre which controls what it does. It also has hands which hold the tools and act in accordance with directions from the centre. Some of the people in the company are mere servants and agents who are nothing more than hands to do the work and cannot be said to represent the mind or will. Others are directors and managers who represent the directing mind and will of the company, and control what it does. The state of mind of these managers is the state of mind of the company and is treated by the law as such.[14]

The test was later applied elsewhere in private law[15] and also in criminal law.[16]

[6] Merchant Shipping Act 1894 (57 & 58 Vict c 60), s 502.
[7] *Lennard's Carrying Co* (n 5) 713.
[8] ibid.
[9] ibid 713–14.
[10] ibid 714.
[11] ibid.
[12] ibid.
[13] Eg *Trevor Ivory Ltd v Anderson* [1992] 2 NZLR 517 (NZCA) 520 (Cooke P).
[14] *HL Bolton Engineering Co Ltd v TJ Graham & Sons Ltd* [1957] 1 QB 159 (CA) 172.
[15] Eg *El Ajou v Dollar Land Holdings plc* [1994] BCC 143 (CA); *Stone & Rolls* (n 1).
[16] Eg *DPP v Kent and Sussex Contractors Ltd* [1944] KB 146 (KB); *R v ICR Haulage Ltd* [1944] KB 551 (Ct of Crim Appeal); *Tesco Supermarkets v Nattrass* [1972] AC 153 (HL) 170–71 (Lord Reid), 180 (Lord Morris), 187 (Viscount Dilhorne); *Attorney General's Reference (No 2 of 1999)* [2000] 2 Cr App R 207, [2000] QB 796; *R v St Regis Paper Company Ltd* [2011] EWCA Crim 2527, [2012] 1 Cr App R 14; *Serious Fraud Office v Barclays plc* [2018] EWHC 3055 (QB); *R v Varley* [2019] EWCA Crim 1074.

One problem was that this approach suggested that only the acts or states of mind of sufficiently senior individuals of the company could be regarded as the company's.[17] But this did not fit what courts did in practice.[18] In *Lennard's Carrying Co* itself, Lennard was identified as the directing mind and will because he had authority over part of the company's business, though not general decision-making authority for all of it. In *El Ajou v Dollar Land Holdings*,[19] a director was identified as the directing mind and will of the company for a particular transaction because he 'committed the company to the transaction as an autonomous act which the company adopted by performing the agreement'[20] even though he did not have ultimate decision-making authority for that particular transaction. Foreshadowing *Meridian*, Hoffmann LJ recognised in *El Ajou* that '[t]he authorities show clearly that different persons may for different purposes satisfy the requirements of being the company's directing mind and will'.[21] Lord Walker, sitting in the Hong Kong Court of Final Appeal, eventually concluded that '[t]o refer instead to "the relevant responsible director or employee", or some such expression, would be less arresting but a good deal more accurate'.[22]

A second problem would soon be highlighted by *Meridian*. The 'directing mind and will' approach rested on contested assumptions about the nature of a company. It explicitly adopted an anthropomorphic approach[23] which sought to identify a human person as the embodiment of the company.[24] Drawing analogies with the human body, judges sought to identify different people as the company's 'brains' and 'hands'.[25] But these rough metaphors were unlikely to satisfy proponents of either of the two main theories of corporate personality, the 'fiction' and 'real' theories. Fiction theorists regarded companies as legal fictions, 'mere creation[s] of the law'.[26] To them, direct analogies with human persons might not always be appropriate.[27] They might argue, as Ross Grantham did, that such analogies should be 'driven by the practical need to extend such rules to the company', and 'shaped by the policy and purpose of the particular rule at issue'.[28] Conversely, 'real'

[17] Ferran (n 3) 242.
[18] *Moulin Global Eyecare Trading Ltd v Commissioner of Inland Revenue* [2014] HKCFA 22, (2014) 17 HKCFAR 218 [67].
[19] *El Ajou* (n 15) 159–60.
[20] ibid 160.
[21] ibid 159.
[22] *Moulin Global* (n 18) [67].
[23] Ferran (n 3) 239.
[24] *Lennard's Carrying Co* (n 5) 713.
[25] Eg *Bolton Engineering* (n 14) 172 (Denning LJ); *Cassidy v Ministry of Health* [1951] 2 KB 343 (CA) 360 (Denning LJ).
[26] *Trustees of Dartmouth College v Woodward* (1819) 17 US (4 Wheat) 518 (US Sup Ct) 636 (Marshall CJ). See also *Welton v Saffery* [1897] AC 299 (HL) 305 describing a registered company as an 'artificial creature'.
[27] HLA Hart, 'Definition and Theory in Jurisprudence' in *Essays in Jurisprudence and Philosophy* (Oxford, Oxford University Press, 1983).
[28] R Grantham, 'Commentary on Goddard' in C Rickett and R Grantham (eds), *Corporate Personality in the 20th Century* (Oxford, Hart Publishing, 1998) 68.

theorists[29] regarded a group like a company as 'a living organism and a real person, with body and members and a will of its own',[30] existing independently of the law.[31] They too would likely have been uncomfortable with the 'directing mind and will': its blunt anthropomorphism did not seem to accurately represent a distinctive *group* personality.[32]

B. The Idea of Attribution

It was against this background that *Meridian* was decided. In a magisterial speech, Lord Hoffmann rejected the 'directing mind and will' approach, introduced the idea of attribution, and identified different categories of attribution rules.

Meridian's facts were straightforward. Meridian Global Funds Management Asia Ltd was an investment management company. Its chief investment officer, Koo, and senior portfolio manager, Ng, were secretly embroiled in a scheme to take over a New Zealand company. They concocted a plan to raise the necessary financing by using Meridian to acquire shares in the target company, making Meridian a substantial shareholder of the target. Section 20 of the New Zealand Securities Amendment Act 1988 provided that every person who became a substantial shareholder of a public company came under a duty to disclose its substantial shareholding once it knew, or ought to know, of its substantial shareholding. No disclosure was made. The New Zealand Securities Commission brought proceedings against Meridian for non-compliance with the Act.

Koo and Ng knew of the company's substantial shareholding. Could their knowledge be attributed to the company under the statute? Yes, said the New Zealand Court of Appeal. Koo's knowledge could be attributed because he was the company's directing mind and will.[33] Koo had once been Meridian's managing director.[34] Although replaced by a new managing director, Koo continued buying and selling securities in the same way as before.[35] Through Koo's knowledge, Meridian came under a duty to disclose, which it had breached.

[29] Developed by Otto von Gierke, brought into prominence in England by FW Maitland, see FW Maitland, 'Introduction' in O Gierke, *Political Theories of the Middle Age*, transl FW Maitland (Cambridge, Cambridge University Press, 1900) xx. See further WM Geldart, 'Legal Personality' (1911) 27 *LQR* 90; F Hallis, *Corporate Personality* (London, Oxford University Press, 1930). See now E Micheler, 'Company Law – A Real Entity Theory' (April 2021), available at https://papers.ssrn.com/sol3/papers.cfm?abstract_id=3783696.

[30] Maitland, ibid xxv–xxvi.

[31] FW Maitland, 'Moral Personality and Legal Personality' in D Runciman and M Ryan (eds), *Maitland: State, Trust and Corporation* (Cambridge, Cambridge University Press, 2003) 68.

[32] C Wells, *Corporations and Criminal Responsibility*, 2nd edn (Oxford, Oxford University Press, 2001) 84.

[33] *Meridian Global Funds Management Asia Ltd v Securities Commission* [1994] 2 NZLR 291 (NZCA).

[34] *Meridian* (n 2) 505.

[35] ibid.

On appeal to the Privy Council, Lord Hoffmann delivered the unanimous advice of the Board. He affirmed the Court of Appeal's decision, concluding that Koo's knowledge could be attributed, but he took a different route to this result.

Lord Hoffmann began by introducing the idea of attribution, which he saw as connected to the company's separate legal personality:

> A company exists because there is a rule (usually in a statute) which says that a *persona ficta* shall be deemed to exist and to have certain of the powers, rights and duties of a natural person. But there would be little sense in deeming such a *persona ficta* to exist unless there were also rules to tell one what acts were to count as acts of the company. It is therefore a necessary part of corporate personality that there should be rules by which acts are attributed to the company. These may be called 'the rules of attribution'.[36] (emphasis added)

Lord Hoffmann then identified three categories of attribution rules: primary rules; general rules; and special rules of attribution.[37] Primary rules of attribution will generally be found in the company's constitution or in general company law.[38] Examples include the rule that 'for the purpose of appointing members of the board, a majority vote of the shareholders shall be a decision of the company'[39] or that 'the decisions of the board in managing the company's business shall be the decisions of the company'.[40] These are supplemented with general rules of attribution – the rules of agency.[41] They are 'general' rules because they also apply equally to human persons, while the primary rules do not. In some exceptional cases, neither of these two categories provide an answer, but the court may conclude that the substantive rule of law ought to apply to companies.[42] The court must then formulate a special rule of attribution, asking, '[w]hose act (or knowledge, or state of mind) was *for this purpose* intended to count as the act etc of the company?'[43] In doing so, the court has to take into account the language of the rule (if it is a statute), its content, and policy.[44]

Just as in judgments in public law,[45] contractual interpretation,[46] and tax law,[47] Lord Hoffmann saw the key issue in *Meridian* as 'one of construction rather than

[36] ibid 506 (italics added).
[37] ibid 506–507.
[38] ibid.
[39] See eg Model Articles for Public Companies, Model Art 20; Model Articles for Private Companies Limited by Shares, Model Art 17, which will apply to limited companies unless the company registers its own articles of association: Companies Act 2006, s 18.
[40] *Multinational Gas and Petrochemical Co v Multinational Gas and Petrochemical Services Ltd* [1983] Ch 258 (CA), cited at *Meridian* (n 2) 506.
[41] ibid.
[42] ibid.
[43] ibid 507.
[44] ibid.
[45] A Young, 'Lord Hoffmann and Public Law: TV Dinner or Dining at the Savoy?' in PS Davies and J Pila (eds), *The Jurisprudence of Lord Hoffmann: A Festschrift in Honour of Lord Leonard Hoffmann* (Oxford, Hart Publishing, 2015), especially 126–30.
[46] Eg *Investors Compensation Scheme Ltd v West Bromwich Building Society* [1998] 1 WLR 896 (HL) 912–13; *Chartbrook Ltd v Persimmon Homes Ltd* [2009] UKHL 38, [2009] 1 AC 1101. See further PS Davies, 'The Meaning of Commercial Contracts' in Davies and Pila (n 45).
[47] J Freedman, 'Lord Hoffmann, Tax Law and Principles' in Davies and Pila (n 45).

metaphysics'.[48] He downplayed the importance of the 'directing mind and will' test, explaining it simply as a special rule of attribution, fashioned for the particular statute in *Lennard's Carrying Co*.[49]

In *Meridian* itself, Lord Hoffmann fashioned a special rule of attribution. He identified the policy of the statute as being 'to compel, in fast-moving markets, the immediate disclosure of the identity of persons who become substantial security holders in public issuers'.[50] Whose knowledge should be attributed? To Lord Hoffmann, the answer was:

> Surely the person who, with the authority of the company, acquired the relevant interest. Otherwise the policy of the Act would be defeated. Companies would be able to allow employees to acquire interests on their behalf which made them substantial security holders but would not have to report them until the board or someone else in senior management got to know about it. This would put a premium on the board paying as little attention as possible to what its investment managers were doing. Their Lordships would therefore hold that upon the true construction of section 20(4)(e), the company knows that it has become a substantial security holder when that is known to the person who had authority to do the deal. It is then obliged to give notice under section 20(3).[51]

Thus, Koo's knowledge could be attributed to Meridian, who then owed a duty to give notice. Since notice had not been given, the duty was breached.[52]

C. *Meridian*'s Impact: Context-Specificity

Meridian's legacy has endured. Endorsed by English courts at all levels,[53] followed by courts across the Commonwealth[54] and with influential academic supporters,[55]

[48] *Meridian* (n 2) 511.
[49] ibid 509.
[50] ibid 511.
[51] ibid.
[52] ibid.
[53] Eg *Re Josi Group v Walbrook Insurance Co Ltd* [1996] 1 WLR 1152 (CA); *PCW Syndicates v PCW Reinsurers* [1996] 1 WLR 1136 (CA); *Arab Bank plc v Zurich Insurance* [1998] CLC 1351 (QB); *AG's Reference (No 2 of 1999)* (n 16); *Re Odyssey (London) Ltd v OIC Run Off Ltd* [2001] Lloyd's Rep IR 1 (CA); *Crown Dilmun v Sutton* [2004] EWHC 52 (Ch), [2004] 1 BCLC 468; *Man Nutzfahrzuege AG v Freightliner Ltd* [2005] EWHC 2347 (Comm); *Bank of India v Morris* [2005] EWCA Civ 693, [2005] BCC 739; *KR v Royal & Sun Alliance* [2006] EWCA Civ 1454; *Mohammad Jafari-Fini v Skillglass Ltd* [2007] EWCA Civ 261; *Safeway Stores Ltd v Twigger* [2010] EWCA Civ 1472, [2011] 2 All ER 841; *R v St Regis* (n 16); *Hawksford Trustees Jersey Ltd v Stella Global UK Ltd* [2012] EWCA Civ 55; *Bilta* (n 1); *Howmet Ltd v Economy Devices Ltd* [2016] EWCA Civ 847, [2016] BLR 555; *R v A Ltd* [2016] EWCA Crim 1469; *Singularis* (n 1); *Bilta (UK) Ltd (in liquidation) v Natwest Markets plc* [2020] EWHC 546 (Ch).
[54] *Director of Public Prosecutions Reference No 1 of 1996* [1998] 3 VR 352, (1997) 96 A Crim R 513 (Sup Ct of Victoria); *Director General, Department of Education and Training v MT* [2006] NSWCA 270, (2006) 67 NSWLR 237, 44; *Commonwealth Bank v Kojic* [2016] FCAFC 186 [97]–[99] (Federal Court of Australia); *Lebon* (n 1); *Julien* (n 1); *Moulin Global* (n 18); *HKSAR v Luk Kin Peter Joseph* [2016] HKCFA 81, (2016) 19 HKCFAR 619; *Ho Kang Peng v Scintronix Corpn Ltd* [2014] SGCA 22, [2014] 3 SLR 329; *Ong Bee Chew v Ong Shu Lin* [2017] SGHC 285, [2019] 3 SLR 132; *Red Star Marine Consultants Pte Ltd v Personal Representatives of Satwant Kaur d/o Sardara Singh* [2019] SGCA 76, [2020] 1 SLR 115.
[55] See generally references at n 3, especially Ferran (n 3); Lim, 'A Critique of Corporate Attribution' (n 3); Lim, 'Attribution in Company Law' (n 3); Payne (n 3); Worthington (n 3).

it has garnered enormous support. Although initially best-known for its rejection of the directing mind and will test and for establishing the three categories of attribution rules, *Meridian* has more recently been associated with a context-specific approach to attribution.

Citing *Meridian*, ultimate appellate courts and academic commentators alike have repeatedly echoed the importance of context. Sitting in the Hong Kong Court of Final Appeal, Lord Walker recognised that '[o]ne of the fundamental points to be taken from *Meridian* is the importance of context … in any problem of attribution'.[56] In *Bilta v Nazir*, Lord Mance reiterated that '[a]s Lord Hoffmann made clear in *Meridian Global*, the key to any question of attribution is ultimately always to be found in considerations of context or purpose'.[57] In his view, the question is: 'whose act or knowledge or state of mind is for the purpose of the relevant rule to count as the act, knowledge or state of mind of the company?'[58] These views were echoed by Lady Hale, sitting in the Supreme Court in *Singularis Holdings Ltd v Daiwa Capital Markets Europe Ltd*.[59] She criticised the Court of Appeal for attributing 'whatever the context and purpose of the attribution in question',[60] agreeing with *Bilta* that 'the answer to any question whether to attribute the knowledge of the fraudulent director to the company is always to be found in consideration of the context and the purpose for which the attribution is relevant'.[61] Similar endorsements can be found throughout the Commonwealth.[62] The voluminous academic literature, a veritable cottage industry in its own right, is virtually unanimous in its support for the importance of context.[63]

All agree that context is important. But what context counts? At least three approaches might be identified from the literature.

The first approach focuses on the purpose and policy of the substantive rule requiring attribution, as in *Meridian* itself. *Bank of India v Morris* provides another example.[64] The Bank of India received deposits from the BCCI group on terms that the money was to be paid to one of BCCI's creditors. But these transactions were circular: the money would eventually be returned to BCCI. Their aim was to give the false impression that BCCI's debts were being serviced. Six such transactions occurred. After the BCCI group collapsed, its liquidators sought to make the bank contribute to BCCI's assets, arguing that it had 'knowingly [been] a party to the carrying on of the business of BCCI with intent to defraud creditors or for any other fraudulent purpose' under section 213 of the Insolvency Act 1986.

[56] *Moulin Global* (n 18) [41].
[57] *Bilta* (n 1) [41].
[58] ibid.
[59] (n 1).
[60] ibid [33].
[61] ibid [34].
[62] Eg *Lebon* (n 1); *Moulin Global* (n 18); *HKSAR v Luk* (n 54); *Ho Kang Peng* (n 54); *Ong Bee Chew* (n 54); *Red Star* (n 54).
[63] See generally references at n 3.
[64] (n 53).

The bank officer who entered the transactions for the bank knew that the transactions had no legitimate purpose. Could his knowledge be attributed to the bank under section 213? The Court of Appeal held that it could. Mummery LJ relied on section 213's policy, which he identified as 'the compensation of those who have suffered loss as a result of the fraudulent trading'.[65] He concluded that the purpose of the section would be defeated if only senior management's knowledge could be attributed.[66] Conversely, attributing the officer's knowledge would promote its purpose. Other similar examples exist.[67]

A second approach, defended most strongly by Peter Watts, locates the relevant context in the nature and the source of the right being enforced.[68] Watts argues that one approach applies to 'rights and obligations that ultimately turn on the intentions of a drafter or of the parties to a transaction, as opposed to being sourced from general common law'.[69] While attribution in the former category requires 'those intentions, albeit objectively determined, to be assessed each time before the question of attribution is resolved',[70] attribution in the latter category does not. On this account, attribution rules in contract differ from those in restitutionary claims.[71] The former turns on the intentions of the parties, while the latter does not. A third, different set of attribution rules might apply to some, but not all torts.[72] On this approach, it might even be said that a separate set of attribution rules applies to attribution in equitable claims, since the nature and source of equitable rights may differ from that of common law rights.[73]

A third, expansive approach admits into consideration all matters concerned with the 'factual and statutory background [and] also the nature of the proceedings in which the question arises'.[74] The Singapore Court of Appeal recently endorsed such an approach, saying that 'the court must consider both the legal and factual context of the case'.[75] This meant consideration of the legal rule requiring attribution,[76] whether the company was in insolvent liquidation,[77] and whether remedies awarded would fall into a wrongdoer's hands.[78]

[65] ibid [111].

[66] ibid [112]. See also the first instance judgment in *Bank of India v Morris* [2004] EWHC 528 (Ch), [2004] BCC 404 [121] (Patten J), reaching a similar conclusion.

[67] Eg *KR* (n 53); *Jafari-Fini* (n 53); *Hawksford* (n 53); *Lebon* (n 1); *Bilta* (n 1); *Singularis* (n 1).

[68] Watts, 'Attribution and Limitation' (n 3) 350.

[69] ibid.

[70] ibid.

[71] Watts, 'The Acts and State of Knowledge' (n 3).

[72] Watts suggests that torts which require an assumption of responsibility might more appropriately follow the contractual approach: Watts, 'Principals' Tortious Liability' (n 3).

[73] Disagreeing, see R Leow, 'Equity's Attribution Rules' (2021) 15 *Journal of Equity* 35.

[74] *Moulin Global* (n 18) [113] (Lord Walker). See also Payne, 'Corporate Attribution and The Lessons of Meridian' (n 3) 375, appearing to suggest a similar approach.

[75] *Red Star* (n 54) [40].

[76] ibid [42].

[77] ibid [44].

[78] ibid [43], [47]–[48].

All three approaches regard attribution as turning on 'right-sided features': features concerning the right to be enforced or the claim by which it is enforced. Though varying as to which right-sided features are relevant and whether other features are also relevant, we might fairly call them 'right-sided' approaches. Other variants may also exist.

II. Problems with Existing Approaches

Existing 'right-sided' approaches miss the mark. They do not justify the thing to be justified: attribution. Attribution involves treating *this* act or state of mind of *this* individual as that of *this* company. It concerns the single thread connecting act or state of mind, individual, and the company. Reasons for attribution must fit this form. But right-sided approaches do not. They also generate other problems, making attribution unnecessarily controversial, creating unacceptable uncertainty, and creating inconsistency in the law, risking its rationality.

A. Justification

Justification must fit the thing to be justified.[79] In private law, this idea was made prominent by Ernest Weinrib, who emphasised private law's bilateral structure. As Weinrib explained, '[a] finding of liability [in private law] always relates a particular plaintiff to a particular defendant … Given the relational nature of liability, the reasons [given for liability] must themselves be relational'.[80] For Weinrib, only bilateral reasons can justify private law rights.[81] Other important private law scholars have since endorsed similar views.[82] A prominent supporter of such views, Robert Stevens, has similarly argued that law's 'form dictates the kinds of substantive reasons that can justify it'.[83] As duties of right are owed to other people, 'this

[79] R Stevens, 'Private Law and the Form of Reasons' in A Robertson and J Goudkamp (eds), *Form and Substance in the Law of Obligations* (Oxford, Hart Publishing, 2019); B McFarlane, 'Form and Substance in Equity' in Robertson and Goudkamp, ibid; B McFarlane and R Stevens, 'What's Special about Equity? Rights about Rights' in D Klimchuk et al (eds), *Philosophical Foundations of the Law of Equity* (Oxford, Oxford University Press, 2020); T Liau, 'Standing in Private Law' (DPhil thesis, University of Oxford, 2020); T Liau, 'Privity: Rights, Standing, and the Road Not Taken' (2021) 41 *OJLS* 803. See also E Weinrib, *The Idea of Private Law*, rev edn (Oxford, Oxford University Press, 2012) Ch 5; E Weinrib, *Corrective Justice* (Oxford, Oxford University Press, 2012) 13–15, 18–20.

[80] Weinrib, *Corrective Justice*, ibid 1–2.

[81] Weinrib, *Corrective Justice* (n 79) 2–3, 19, Ch 6; Weinrib, *The Idea of Private Law* (n 79) 125, 142–44; E Weinrib, 'Correctively Unjust Enrichment' in R Chambers et al (eds), *Philosophical Foundations of the Law of Unjust Enrichment* (Oxford, Oxford University Press, 2009).

[82] See references at n 79.

[83] Stevens, 'Private Law and the Form of Reasons' (n 79) 119. See also McFarlane and Stevens, 'What's Special About Equity? Rights about Rights' (n 79) 192.

form imposes a constraint upon the kind of reasons that can, as a matter of justice, justify them. They must be reasons that tie this particular right-holder to this particular duty-bearer. They must be reasons that are bilateral in form, applying to both parties.'[84]

Similarly, in justifying attribution, the focus should be on attribution's structure. The attribution of acts concerns the connection between act, individual, and company. When we attribute, we are treating *this* act of *this* individual as that of *this* company. The reason for attribution must fit this relational structure. It must simultaneously link act, individual, and company. A similar analysis is true for the attribution of states of mind.[85]

The importance of this connection is revealed by cases where it is missing. What if a stranger's acts or states of mind are sought to be attributed to the company? No case has suggested that attribution would be possible. Here the problem is the missing connection between company and individual; nothing links them together.

In some other cases there may be a connection between the company and individual, but even there not all acts are attributable. Some acts are personal or private: eating a pastry at home, having a nap, or doing CrossFit in one's leisure time. The same is true of knowledge. An employee's knowledge of his children's favourite foods, of mathematical principles learnt at school, or of his own family disputes, is likewise personal, with no connection to the company which employs him. As Sir WM James LJ said in *Re Marseilles Extension Railway Co*, '[i]s it to be imputed to the banking company that they have knowledge of everything a director knows about his own private affairs? Such a proposition seems to be most unreasonable.'[86] These acts and knowledge are unrelated to the company; they too are not attributable. In these examples, while there is a connection between act or state of mind and individual, and another connection between individual and company, there is no single thread linking the three together.

Right-sided accounts, however, do not provide a justification which fits attribution's structure. The source or type of the right being enforced, or the purpose and policy of the rule requiring attribution, are features external to the connection between act or state of mind, individual and company. The source or type of the right may justify the shape and scope of the right, but it has little to say on attribution, a separate concept. Similarly, the purpose and policy of the substantive rule might justify that rule, but it again has nothing to say on the connection between act, individual, and company. The same objection might be made about accounts of attribution which seek to improve economic efficiency overall by attributing acts or mental states in a way which minimises transaction costs.[87] Such approaches likewise do not fit attribution's structure.

[84] Stevens, 'Private Law and the Form of Reasons' (n 79) 124. See also R Stevens, 'The Unjust Enrichment Disaster' (2018) 134 *LQR* 574.
[85] See further Ch 6 below.
[86] *Re Marseilles Extension Railway Co* (1871–72) LR 7 Ch App 161 (CA) 170.
[87] Eg A Griffiths, *Contracting with Companies* (Oxford, Hart Publishing, 2005).

The same point might be made from a different angle. Perhaps the greatest modern taxonomist of English private law, Peter Birks, emphatically stressed the importance of mapping the law. Taxonomy, he explained, 'changes nothing, but it promotes understanding'.[88] Drawing on *Justinian's Institutes*, Birks described a modern scheme of English private law as follows: 'the whole law is either public or private; private law is about the persons who bear rights, the rights which they bear, and the procedures by which those rights are realised'.[89] In this scheme, rights and obligations are two sides of the same coin: when an obligation – a duty – is owed by one to another, the latter has a right.[90] Obligations may be divided again by the 'events' which generate them: consent, wrongs, unjust enrichment, and a residual miscellany.[91] In this map, companies belong in the law of persons.[92] So too does attribution, which is the means by which a company's corporate personality can be realised in the world. With this map, it can be observed that attribution, belonging to the law of persons, belongs in an entirely different part of the map from rights and obligations. Justifications for one concept, in one part of the map, are misplaced when used to justify another concept in a different part of the map.

The inadequacies of right-sided approaches are revealed when applied. Consider first approaches focusing on the source and type of the right. Even if we identify the source of a right as agreement-based, this seems wholly external to the necessary connection between act, individual, and company. The former tells us little about the latter. It is not clear how the source of the right can tell us when or why to attribute.

A different problem arises if the focus is instead on the purpose and policy of the rule requiring attribution. In *Meridian*, Lord Hoffmann identified the relevant policy as 'ensuring disclosure of substantial shareholdings in fast-moving markets'.[93] But promoting this policy seems to lead to the wrong result in some cases. It would suggest that attribution is possible even if there is no connection between knowledge, individual, and company. Thus, the policy could justify attributing the knowledge of even a stranger to the company. The same is true of *Bank of India v Morris*, where the identified policy of providing compensation for loss[94] would be better achieved if the knowledge of anyone in the world could be attributed, not just the authorising bank officer. Even when courts rely on the purpose and policy of the rule requiring attribution, they formulate narrower rules where the necessary connection is present. In both *Meridian* and *Bank of India*, the rule formulated was that the knowledge of individuals with authority to enter

[88] P Birks, 'Equity in the Modern Law' (1996) 26 *University of Western Australia Law Review* 1, 1.
[89] P Birks, 'Definition and Division: A Meditation on Institutes' in P Birks (ed), *The Classification of Obligations* (Oxford, Clarendon Press, 1997) 9.
[90] ibid 17.
[91] P Birks, *Introduction to the Law of Restitution*, rev ed (Oxford, Clarendon Press, 1989) 28–55; P Birks, *Unjust Enrichment*, 2nd edn (Oxford, Oxford University Press, 2005) 24–28.
[92] A Burrows (ed), *English Private Law* (Oxford, Oxford University Press, 2013).
[93] *Meridian* (n 2) 511.
[94] *Bank of India* (n 53) [112].

the transaction was attributable.[95] The purposes and policies identified thus do not justify the rule adopted. These problems continue to be present in the third and widest approach to attribution, where attribution turns on these right-sided features as well as others.

B. Unnecessary Controversy

Right-sided approaches also suffer from another weakness. Tying attribution to right-sided features mires attribution in contentious debates about the purposes, policies, or sources of rights. Attribution then becomes unnecessarily controversial.

Identifying the purpose and policy of a common law rule may not be simple. Requiring courts to take a stance on a rule's purpose and policy as a precursor to attribution creates unnecessary controversy over attribution. For example, it has been suggested that knowing receipt is a wrong akin to conversion based on interference with another's rights in property,[96] a fault-based equitable wrong concerning inconsistent dealing,[97] or that it involves two claims, one of which is based on unjust enrichment.[98] Yet others argue that a knowing recipient is a genuine trustee held accountable for what he does with the trust assets,[99] or who is subject to claims for breach of trust.[100] There is no shortage of controversy over the doctrine's purpose or policy. Illegality provides another example. Is it a rule of public policy, requiring the court to consider the purpose of the prohibition which was transgressed and other relevant policies?[101] Or is it based on the internal coherence of the law?[102] Or something else?[103] Where the purpose and policy of a rule are hotly contested, attempting to build attribution rules on top of that purpose or policy will be fraught with controversy.

Legitimate disagreements also exist about the source or type of a right. Recall that Watts has suggested that torts which require an assumption of responsibility might use contractual attribution rules.[104] But the concept of an assumption of

[95] *Meridian* (n 2) 511; *Bank of India* (n 53).

[96] L Smith, 'Unjust Enrichment, Property and the Structure of Trusts' (2000) 116 *LQR* 412.

[97] W Swadling, 'The Nature of "Knowing Receipt"' in PS Davies and J Penner (eds), *Equity, Trusts and Commerce* (Oxford, Hart Publishing, 2017).

[98] P Birks, 'Receipt' in P Birks and A Pretto (eds), *Breach of Trust* (Oxford, Hart Publishing, 2002); Lord Nicholls, 'Knowing Receipt: The Need for a New Landmark' in WR Cornish et al (eds), *Restitution: Past, Present and Future* (Oxford, Hart Publishing, 1999).

[99] C Mitchell and S Watterson, 'Remedies for Knowing Receipt' in C Mitchell (ed), *Constructive and Resulting Trusts* (Oxford, Hart Publishing, 2010).

[100] R Chambers, 'The End of Knowing Receipt' (2016) 2 *Canadian Journal of Comparative and Contemporary Law* 1.

[101] *Patel v Mirza* [2016] UKSC 42, [2017] AC 467 [101]; A Burrows, 'Illegality after Patel v Mirza' (2017) *Current Legal Problems* 55; A Burrows, 'A New Dawn for the Law of Illegality' in S Green and A Bogg (eds), *Illegality after Patel v Mirza* (Oxford, Hart Publishing, 2018).

[102] *Patel v Mirza*, ibid [230]–[233].

[103] Eg F Wilmot-Smith, 'Illegality as a Rationing Rule' in Green and Bogg (n 101).

[104] Watts, 'Principals' Tortious Liability' (n 3); Watts, 'Attribution and Limitation' (n 3).

responsibility has itself generated considerable academic disagreement. At one end, some scholars regard it as essentially meaningless, reflecting another concept,[105] or even 'a discredited fiction'.[106] At another, others hold it out as a 'meaningful and distinctive basis of legal obligation',[107] an important source of rights.[108] Whether one ought to apply contractual rules of attribution in assumption of responsibility cases will be affected by one's position on that concept. Similarly, suggestions that the 'law of torts' may have different attribution rules from the 'law of restitution' again raises controversial issues: what is the relationship between 'restitution' and 'unjust enrichment'?[109] Between restitution and property?[110] And what is included in the 'law of torts'? Do equitable wrongs fall within it?[111]

These examples illustrate the danger in anchoring attribution to contested features of private law. Attribution may be mired in unnecessary controversy, opening it to avoidable objections.

C. Inconsistency and Self-Contradiction

A third problem is that right-sided approaches accept that an act or state of mind may be attributed to the company for one purpose but not another. This creates inconsistency, possibly even self-contradiction.

In *Bilta*, multiple members of the Supreme Court stressed that the question was whether the act or knowledge could be attributed to the company *for this purpose*.[112] The same point is reiterated in academic commentary. A representative view is Worthington's statement that

> An individual within the corporate structure may act, or intend or know a wide variety of things, but these will not count as the company's actions, intentions or knowledge for all purposes. Generalisations are impossible; context is all.[113]

Accepting this creates further paradoxes. In principle, it suggests that whether a representation can be attributed to a company may depend on whether attribution

[105] A Robertson and J Wang, 'The Assumption of Responsibility' in K Barker et al (eds), *The Law of Misstatements: 50 Years on from Hedley Byrne v Heller* (Oxford, Hart Publishing, 2015); C Witting, 'What are We Doing Here? The Relationship Between Negligence in General and Misstatements in English Law' in Barker et al, ibid.

[106] B Hepple, 'Negligence: The Search for Coherence' (1997) *Current Legal Problems* 69, 87–88.

[107] D Nolan, 'Assumption of Responsibility: Four Questions' (2019) *Current Legal Problems* 123.

[108] R Stevens, *Torts and Rights* (Oxford, Oxford University Press, 2007) 10–11.

[109] Birks, *Unjust Enrichment* (n 91) 21–28.

[110] Compare Birks, *Unjust Enrichment* (n 91) 28–38; A Burrows, *The Law of Restitution* (Oxford, Oxford University Press, 2011) Ch 8; G Virgo, *The Principles of the Law of Restitution* (Oxford, Oxford University Press, 2015) Chs 21–22; R Grantham and C Rickett, 'Property Rights as a Legally Significant Event (2003) 62 *CLJ* 717.

[111] Eg J Edelman, 'Equitable Torts' (2002) 10 *Torts Law Journal* 64.

[112] (n 1) [20] (Lord Neuberger), [41] (Lord Mance).

[113] Worthington, 'Back to Basics' (n 3) 124.

is sought to rescind a contract, to establish the company's tortious liability for deceit, or to require the company to make restitution of mistaken payments induced by the representation. The rules requiring attribution may have different purposes, the rights being enforced certainly have different sources, and the factual and legal contexts of the three claims are different. But it is difficult to see why attribution's availability should differ across the three cases once attribution's structure is borne in mind. Attribution concerns the connection between act, individual, and company. This connection is the same across each of the three scenarios. If attribution is possible in some of these scenarios but not others, the law would be taking inconsistent positions on the same problem. By giving different answers to the same question, it could even be said that the law is contradicting itself, saying that an act or state of mind both is and is not the company's.

The problem of inconsistency and self-contradiction has come to the fore in a series of prominent recent cases concerning the intersection between attribution and illegality starting from *Stone & Rolls v Moore Stephens*.[114] In these cases, a company's director uses the company to perpetuate frauds. The director's acts and states of mind can be attributed to the company to determine its duties and liability.[115] But can they be attributed under the illegality doctrine to establish that the company was party to illegal conduct, so that its claims against the director or other parties would fail? Recent cases suggest that even though attribution may be available in the former category, it may not be in the latter categories. Lord Hoffmann NPJ's statement in *HKSAR v Luk Kin Peter Joseph* illustrates the prevailing school of thought:

> The fact that the knowledge or state of mind of, say, a director, must be attributed to a company for the purpose of one rule (for example, imposing liability on the company to a third party) does not mean that his knowledge or state of mind must be attributed to the company for the purpose of a different rule (for example, imposing liability on the director for defrauding the company).[116]

The same problem of inconsistency is clear. One question is asked, but two (or more) different answers are given.

The inconsistency goes even deeper. *Bilta* and *Singularis* accept that the directors' acts and states of mind may not be attributed to the company to establish the company's illegality where it is bringing claims against those directors[117] or third parties[118] for their breach of duties. But the first instance decision in *Singularis*,[119]

[114] (n 1).
[115] See eg in the *Stone & Rolls* litigation, *Komercni Banka AS v Stone and Rolls Ltd* [2002] EWHC 2263 (Comm).
[116] (n 54).
[117] *Bilta* (n 1).
[118] *Singularis* (n 1).
[119] *Singularis Holdings Ltd (in liquidation) v Daiwa Capital Markets Europe Ltd* [2017] EWHC 257 (Ch).

as well as other cases, accept that those very same acts and states of mind might be attributed to establish the company's contributory negligence.[120] Thus, even when the company is enforcing duties owed to it, different answers to attribution's availability are given. These inconsistencies diminish the rationality and coherence of the legal system.

D. Uncertainty

The very existence of the multiplicity of current approaches also results in uncertainty. Although all are clear that context is important, there is no uniformity as to what context is relevant. Some focus on the purpose and policy of the rule requiring attribution, others on the source and type of the right, while yet others consider these features as well as others. These approaches will not always lead to the same outcome.

But uncertainty generates rule of law concerns. The rule of law is a virtue the law should possess.[121] It requires that those subject to the law can tell what the law is in advance.[122] Otherwise, they cannot use the law to guide their actions.[123] In Raz's own words:

> [I]f the law is to be obeyed it must be capable of guiding the behaviour of its subjects. It must be such that they can find out what it is and act on it. This is the basic intuition from which the doctrine of the rule of law derives.[124]

III. A Fictional View of Attribution

Why then have right-sided approaches been adopted? At first sight, it appears surprising that leading accounts of *corporate* attribution focus on features external to the company. A likely reason is that judges and commentators view attribution as merely a fictional deeming rule, necessitated by the legal fiction of the company.[125]

Recall Lord Hoffmann's statement in *Meridian* that:

> Any proposition about a company necessarily involves a reference to a set of rules. A company exists because there is a rule (usually in a statute) which says that a persona ficta shall be deemed to exist and to have certain of the powers, rights and duties of a

[120] *Daniels v Anderson* (1995) 15 ACSR 607, [1995] PNLR 727 868, 878 (NSWCA) (Clarke and Sheller JJA); *Barings plc v Coopers & Lybrand* [2003] EWHC 1319 (Ch), [2003] PNLR 34 [961]–[964]. See further Ch 7 below.

[121] J Raz, 'The Law's Own Virtue' (2019) 39 *OJLS* 1.

[122] J Raz, *The Authority of Law: Essays on Law and Morality* (Oxford, Oxford University Press, 1979) 213–14.

[123] ibid 217.

[124] ibid 214.

[125] I owe thanks to discussions with Frederick Wilmot-Smith for this point.

> natural person. *But there would be little sense in deeming such a persona ficta to exist unless there were also rules to tell one what acts were to count as acts of the company.*[126] (emphasis added)

Later, Lord Hoffmann continued to emphasise the same point:

> Any statement about what a company has or has not done, or can or cannot do, is necessarily a reference to the rules of attribution (primary and general) as they apply to that company. Judges sometimes say that a company 'as such' cannot do anything; it must act by servants or agents. This may seem an unexceptional, even banal remark and of course the meaning is usually perfectly clear. But a reference to a company 'as such' might suggest that there is something out there called the company of which one can meaningfully say that it can or cannot do something. *There is in fact no such thing as the company as such, no ding an sich, only the applicable rules.* To say that a company cannot do something means only that there is no one whose doing of that act would, under the applicable rules of attribution, count as an act of the company.[127] (emphasis added)

These statements view the company as a legal fiction, with attribution rules an extension of that fiction.[128] Lord Hoffmann's statement that there was no such thing as a company 'as such' clearly disapproved of 'real' theories of corporate personality in favour of their chief rival, the 'fiction' theory.

This was a bold move. No shortage of literature on corporate personality exists.[129] Fiction theories come in many variants. They range from 'concession' theories which emphasise the role of the state in permitting companies to exist[130] to the modern variant put forward by neoclassical law and economics corporate law scholars,[131] which sees the company as a legal fiction serving as a 'nexus of contracts':[132] a focal point for mediating the relationships of those who associate voluntarily with the company: management, shareholders, and creditors.[133]

[126] *Meridian* (n 1) 506.

[127] ibid 506–507.

[128] See similarly Payne (n 3) 361.

[129] For a brief sampling, see eg Maitland (n 29), AW Machen Jr, 'Corporate Personality' (1911) 24 *Harvard LR* 253; WM Geldart, 'Legal Personality' (1911) 27 *LQR* 90; J Dewey, 'The Historic Background of Corporate Legal Personality' (1926) 35 *Yale LJ* 655; M Radin, 'The Endless Problem of Corporate Personality' (1932) 32 *Columbia LR* 643; F Hallis, *Corporate Personality* (Oxford, Oxford University Press, 1930); M Wolff, 'On the Nature of Legal Persons' (1938) 54 *LQR* 494; Hart, 'Definition and Theory in Jurisprudence' (n 27).

[130] For a modern version of a 'concession' theory, see S Watson, 'The Corporate Legal Person' (2019) 19 *Journal of Corporate Law Studies* 137.

[131] Who focus on what they see as a central aim of corporate law to reduce ongoing costs of organising business through the corporate form, by facilitating coordination between participants and reducing 'agency costs': R Coase, 'The Nature of the Firm' (1937) 4 *Economica* 386; A Alchian and H Demsetz, 'Production, Information Costs and Economic Organization' (1972) 62 *American Economic Review* 777; MC Jensen and WH Meckling, 'Theory of the Firm: Managerial Behavior, Agency Costs and Ownership Structure' (1976) 3 *Journal of Financial Economics* 305. See also R Kraakman et al, *The Anatomy of Corporate Law: A Comparative and Functional Approach*, 3rd edn (Oxford, Oxford University Press, 2017) 2.

[132] F Easterbrook and D Fischel, *The Economic Structure of Corporate Law* (Cambridge, Harvard University Press, 1991).

[133] Coase, 'Nature of the Firm' (n 131); Jensen and Meckling, 'Theory of the Firm: Managerial Behavior, Agency Costs and Ownership Structure (n 131) 310; E Fama, 'Agency Problems and the Theory of the Firm' (1980) 88 *Journal of Political Economy* 288, 289.

By contrast, the strongest form of the 'real' theory, stemming from Otto von Gierke, emphasised the company's personality and group-will of its own, which it thought was created independently of the law.[134] More modern variants have emerged, stressing that a group is something different from the individuals that comprise it. As Dicey once said, 'When a body of 20 or 2000 or 200,000 men bind themselves together to act in a particular way for some common purpose, they create a body which, by no fiction of law but from the very nature of things, differs from the individuals of whom it is constituted.'[135] A significant body of work has developed, arguing that some groups, including companies, may be intentional agents.[136] Put simply, this means that 'the members act jointly with the purpose of achieving shared goal according to some common beliefs, thereby functioning as a coherent, uniform unit'.[137]

Viewing attribution as fictional creates its own problems. On a fictional view of attribution, there may be no right answer to when and why we attribute. In Stevens's words,

> Whilst some sort of rules for the attribution of acts are essential, this does not tell us what the detailed content of those rules ought to be … What is the correct approach? How many players should a team of footballers contain? Five? Eight? Eleven? Twenty? It is important to know who counts as a member of the team, but there are different ways in which rational rules can be formulated. Whilst some answers may be demonstrably wrong (eg one-a-side, 90-a-side), there may be no single demonstrably right answer.[138]

As Stevens's example demonstrates, attribution has no fixed content if it is only fictional. To give it some boundaries, commentators and courts have thus sought to anchor attribution to right-sided or other features to explain when and why attribution is available.

There is a way out. Happily, it requires neither definitive resolution of long-standing disputes about corporate personality nor the inappropriate reliance on right-sided features. Only the application of ordinary concepts to companies is required. As Lord Hoffmann recognised, one result of the company's separate legal personality is that the company becomes eligible to bear rights, owe duties, and possess powers.[139] Whether this personality is 'fictional' or 'real' is not particularly helpful in this context.[140] The crucial point is that ordinary concepts applicable to

[134] See text to n 29.

[135] AV Dicey, 'The Combination Laws as Illustrating the Relation between Law and Public Opinion in England during the 19th Century' (1904) 16 *Harvard LR* 511, 513.

[136] See most prominently C List and P Pettit, *Group Agency: The Possibility, Design, and Status of Corporate Agents* (Oxford, Oxford University Press, 2011).

[137] R Tuomela, *Social Ontology: Collective Intentionality and Group Agents* (Oxford, Oxford University Press, 2013) 22; List and Pettit, ibid, 20.

[138] Stevens (n 108) 267.

[139] *Meridian* (n 2) 506.

[140] See similarly HLA Hart, 'Definition and Theory in Jurisprudence' (n 27); Dewey, 'The Historic Background of Corporate Legal Personality' (n 129) for doubts over the usefulness of theories of corporate personality.

human persons become potentially applicable to companies. Like human persons, companies possess an array of powers which they may exercise. When a company exercises them, it acts personally. This involves no legal fiction.[141] It just requires the application of tools that the law already has; tools it has had all along.

IV. A Non-Fictional Account of Attribution

This section advances a non-fictional account of attribution, connecting act, individual, and company. It locates the key to attribution in the exercise of the company's own powers to act. The process of incorporation creates the company's separate legal personality and endows the company with powers for carrying out its stipulated purposes. These powers are allocated and delegated through the company's constitutional documents to groups or individuals. When they are exercised, the company acts personally. This is not a fiction; it just is how the company acts.

A. Incorporation

Legal personality under English law does not convey a fixed set of rights, duties, and powers.[142] A company with separate legal personality may owe and possess different duties and rights than another incorporated legal person, such as a trade union registered under a different statute.[143] In *Bumper Development Corpn Ltd v Metropolitan Police Commissioner*, Purchas LJ approved of the statement that '[artificial] persons, being the arbitrary creations of the law, may be of as many kinds as the law pleases'.[144] The rights, duties, and powers of each legal person must be examined independently.

Companies incorporated by registration are incorporated under the relevant Companies Acts, which set out the process for and identify some consequences of incorporation. Successive rounds of Companies Acts have been passed since general incorporation became available in 1844[145] with the latest being the Companies Act 2006 (the 2006 Act). Under the 2006 Act, one or more persons must subscribe to a memorandum stating that they wish to form a company under

[141] For a prominent definition, see L Fuller, 'Legal Fictions' (1930) 25 *Illinois LR* 363, 369.

[142] See also V Kurki, *A Theory of Legal Personhood* (Oxford, Oxford University Press, 2019).

[143] J Armour, 'Companies and Other Associations' in Burrows (n 92); *cf* statements sometimes made that a person has 'the ordinary attributes of legal personality', eg *Clark v University of Lincolnshire and Humberside* [2000] 3 All ER 752 (CA) 756 (Sedley LJ), or a person who possesses the 'powers normally attendant on legal personality': *National Union of General and Municipal Workers v Gillian* [1946] KB 81 (CA) 86 (Scott LJ).

[144] *Bumper Development Corpn Ltd v Metropolitan Police Commissioner* [1991] 1 WLR 1362 (CA) 1371–72.

[145] Joint Stock Companies Act 1844 (7 & 8 Vict 1 c 110).

the Act, agree to become members, and if the company has share capital, to take at least one share each.[146] The memorandum of association must then be delivered to the Registrar with an application for registration, along with other documents about the company's name, proposed address, proposed officers, and so on.[147] If the Registrar is satisfied that the requirements of the Act have been complied with, he will register the documents,[148] and issue a certificate that the company is incorporated.[149] This process thus integrates both the facilitative machinery of the state and the bottom-up private initiative of would-be incorporators: it is neither purely public nor purely private.[150]

From that date, a new legal person, the company, is created, separate from its members.[151] Other consequences follow: the members of a company have limited liability (if a limited liability company is created),[152] the company itself has the ability to hold property,[153] the company can sue and be sued in its own name, and enjoys perpetual succession. The company also becomes eligible to bear rights, duties, and possess powers.

B. The Importance of the Company's Powers

Of these, perhaps the most important for our purposes are the company's powers, which can be sorted into two: legal powers; and ordinary powers.

Uncontroversial examples of legal powers include powers to contract, make wills, and transfer property. Defining a legal power, however, is more difficult. One well-known attempt by Hohfeld defined a legal power as the ability to change a person's legal relations with another by performing an act which was under the volitional control of the actor.[154] However, as is well-known, this definition is too wide. Some acts may be under the volitional control of the actor, and when performed, change the actor's legal relations with another, but they would not normally be thought of as the exercise of a legal power. One example is where A hits B, exercising her volitional control to do so. Through the act, A's legal relations with B are changed, since A now comes under new duties, for example to compensate

[146] Companies Act 2006 (CA 2006), s 7(1), s 8.

[147] CA 2006, s 9.

[148] CA 2006, s 14.

[149] CA 2006, s 15.

[150] E Orts, *Business Persons – A Legal Theory of the Firm* (Oxford, Oxford University Press, 2013) 14–27.

[151] *Salomon v A Salomon & Co Ltd* [1897] AC 22 (HL). See now CA 2006, s 16(1).

[152] See H Hansmann and R Kraakman, 'The Essential Role of Organizational Law' (2000) 110 *Yale LJ* 387.

[153] Eg *Macaura v Northern Assurance Co Ltd* [1925] AC 619 (HL) 626 (Lord Buckmaster), 630 (Lord Sumner), 633 (Lord Wrenbury); *Short v Treasury Commissioners* [1948] 1 KB 116 (CA) 122 (Evershed MR).

[154] Eg WN Hohfeld, 'Some Fundamental Legal Conceptions as Applied in Judicial Reasoning' (1913) 23 *Yale LJ* 16; WN Hohfeld, 'Fundamental Legal Conceptions as Applied in Judicial Reasoning' (1919) 26 *Yale LJ* 710.

the victim.[155] Similarly, Raz gives the example of someone moving house within his volitional control.[156] This might bring about changes in the house-mover's legal relations with another, such as coming under new obligations to pay council tax to the destination's local authority. Again, this seems to fall within Hohfeld's definition, but is not normally thought to involve the exercise of a legal power.

A more precise definition of a legal power has thus been proposed: a person has a legal power where he has the ability to change his legal relations with another by performing an act under his volitional control, where the change in legal relations is brought about by the manifestation of intention to achieve that change.[157] This definition excludes the problematic cases of hitting another and house-moving. In both cases, the change in legal relations is brought about regardless of any manifested intention to bring about that change. Thus, a company's exercise of legal powers to contract brings about contractual duties and rights owed as against counterparties to the contract; exercises of legal powers to assume responsibility for statements create duties to take care in statement-making;[158] exercising powers to create new security rights confer on the security-holder new rights he did not previously have.

As the examples of hitting another and house-moving suggest, legal powers do not exhaust the field of an actor's abilities to do acts which bring about changes in legal relations. These latter abilities have sometimes been described as 'physical powers'[159] or 'ordinary powers';[160] I adopt the latter term here. Like legal powers, ordinary powers may bring about a change in the company's legal relations; unlike legal powers, the change results without the power-holder manifesting intention to bring about that change. Other examples of ordinary powers include powers to make statements,[161] drive vehicles,[162] or take possession of property.[163] Exercises

[155] Which legal relations are changed is controversial, compare S Smith, 'Duties, Liabilities and Damages' (2012) 125 *Harvard Law Review* 1727; S Smith, 'A Duty to Make Restitution' (2013) 26 *Canadian Journal of Law and Jurisprudence* 157; SA Smith, *Rights, Wrongs, and Injustices: The Structure of Remedial Law* (Oxford, Oxford University Press, 2019); S Steel and R Stevens, 'The Secondary Legal Duty to Pay Damages' (2020) 136 *LQR* 283; T Liau, 'Standing in Private Law' (DPhil thesis, University of Oxford, 2020).

[156] J Raz, 'Voluntary Obligations and Normative Powers' (1972) 46 *Proceedings of the Aristotelian Society* 59, 81.

[157] L Lindahl and D Reidhav, 'Legal Power: The Basic Definition' (2017) 30 *Ratio Juris* 158, 170–71, and see similarly C Essert, 'Legal Powers in Private Law' (2015) 21 *Legal Theory* 136. For a similar idea, see A Halpin, 'The Concept of a Legal Power' (1996) 16 *OJLS* 129, who locates the relevant feature in the person's decision to bring about the change. But this is under-inclusive, as often a mere decision alone is not enough to bring about the exercise of the power: see eg Lindahl and Reidhav, 160.

[158] *Hedley Bryne and Co Ltd v Heller and Partners Ltd* [1964] AC 465 (HL); *Williams v Natural Life Health Foods Ltd* [1998] 1 WLR 830 (HL).

[159] Halpin, 'Concept of a Legal Power' (n 157) 138.

[160] A Perry, 'The Crown's Administrative Powers' (2015) 131 *LQR* 652, 664 (in the context of the Crown's administrative powers).

[161] Eg *Williams* (n 158); *Colonial Mutual Life Assurance Society Ltd v Producers and Citizens Co-operative Assurance Company of Australia Ltd* [1931] HCA 53, (1931) 46 CLR 41.

[162] Eg *Limpus v London General Omnibus Co* (1862) 1 H&C 526 (Ct of Exchequer); *Rose v Plenty* [1976] 1 WLR 141 (CA).

[163] Eg *Armory v Delamirie* (1722) 1 Stra 505 (KB); *Parker v British Airways Board* [1982] QB 1004 (CA).

of these powers may generate new rights and duties in the power-holder, whether primary (in the case of taking possession), or secondary, from breach of primary duties.[164]

C. The Source of the Company's Powers: The Constitution

Like many other aspects of the internal affairs of a company, a registered company's powers are derived either expressly or implicitly from the company's constitution. As *Gower's Principles of Modern Company Law* observes, the extent to which the company's internal affairs can be regulated by the constitution is a 'remarkable feature of British company law'.[165] Its importance has historical roots, tracing back to alternative legal structures attempting to mimic the effects of incorporation before the availability of general incorporation. One example was the deed-of-settlement company, essentially a partnership with partnership property settled on trust. A deed of settlement would be entered into by all the members of the deed-of-settlement company to govern the management and use of the company's assets – the modern precursor of the constitution.

Although the constitution consists of the memorandum of association, articles of association and certain special resolutions or agreements between shareholders,[166] in many cases the company's powers will be found in the memorandum of association, the articles, or both. Powers were often expressly listed in an 'objects clause' to avoid falling foul of the 'ultra vires' rule, which required companies to list the purposes for which the company could be used.[167] Where these powers were expressly included, the position was clear. But powers might not always be expressly listed, yet the ability to do those acts was at least important for the company to go out in the world and pursue the objects for which it had been created. As Buckley LJ emphasised in *Re Horsley & Weight Ltd*:

> It does not follow, however, that any act which is not expressly authorised by the memorandum is ultra vires the company. Anything reasonably incidental to the attainment or pursuit of any of the express objects of the company will, unless expressly prohibited, be within the implied powers of the company ... it is the practical need to imply the power in order to enable the company effectively to pursue its authorised objects which justifies the implication of the power.[168]

This confirmed that companies had implied powers to do any act which was reasonably incidental to the achievement or pursuit of any of its express objects,

[164] *Photo Production Ltd v Securicor Transport Ltd* [1980] AC 827 (HL).
[165] PL Davies and S Worthington, *Gower's Principles of Modern Company Law*, 10th edn (London, Sweet & Maxwell, 2016) para 3–13.
[166] CA 2006, s 17.
[167] *Ashbury Railway Carriage and Iron Company (Ltd) v Riche* (1874–75) LR 7 HL 653.
[168] *In re Horsley & Weight Ltd* [1982] Ch 442 (CA) 448.

unless such an act was expressly prohibited.[169] Both legal and ordinary powers might be expressly or impliedly conferred.

D. Allocation and Delegation of the Company's Powers

The company's constitution plays a critical role not just in identifying and defining the scope of the company's powers, but also in allocating them to groups or individuals. As Lord Diplock explained in *Tesco Supermarkets v Nattrass*:[170]

> [A] corporation incorporated under the Companies Act 1948 owes its corporate personality and its powers to its constitution, the memorandum and articles of association. The obvious and the only place to look to discover by what natural persons its powers are exercisable, is in its constitution …
>
> In my view, the question: what natural persons are to be treated in law as being the company for the purpose of acts done in the course of its business, including the taking of precautions and the exercise of due diligence to avoid the commission of a criminal offence, is to be found by identifying those natural persons who by the memorandum and articles of association or as a result of action taken by the directors, or by the company in general meeting pursuant to the articles, are entrusted with the exercise of the powers of the company.[171]

At least since *Automatic Self-Cleansing v Cunninghame*, the company's constitution effected a constitutional division of the company's powers, allocating them to different groups or individuals.[172] Where powers are allocated to the board of directors, the board of directors is not merely the agent of the shareholders, and so the latter cannot pass resolutions directing the directors on how to exercise their powers[173] unless the articles so provide.[174] Instead, as *John Shaw & Sons (Salford) Ltd v Shaw* explains,

> A company is an entity distinct alike from its shareholders and its directors. Some of its powers may, according to its articles, be exercised by directors, certain other powers may be reserved for the shareholders in general meeting. If powers of management are vested in the directors, they and they alone can exercise these powers. The only way in which the general body of the shareholders can control the exercise of the powers vested by the articles in the directors is by altering their articles, or, if opportunity arises under the articles, by refusing to re-elect the directors of whose actions they disapprove.[175]

[169] See also *In re Lee, Behrens & Co Ltd* [1932] 2 Ch 46 (Ch) 51–52.

[170] (n 16).

[171] ibid 199–200.

[172] *Automatic Self-Cleansing v Cunninghame* [1906] 2 Ch 34 (CA). See also *Quin & Axtens v Salmon* [1909] 1 Ch 311 (CA).

[173] *Automatic Self-Cleansing*, ibid 42–43 (Collins MR), 45 (Cozens-Hardy LJ).

[174] Eg Model Articles for Private Companies Limited by Shares, Model Art 4; Model Articles for Public Companies, Model Art 4.

[175] *John Shaw & Sons (Salford) Ltd v Shaw* [1935] 2 KB 113 (CA) 134 (Greer LJ).

Powers are commonly divided between the board of directors and shareholders in general meeting.[176] The Model Articles allocate the company's powers to manage the company's business to the board of directors, with the remaining powers allocated to the shareholders, subject to statute.[177] But there is considerable flexibility. Companies may depart from this scheme, sometimes radically. In *Lee v Lee's Air Farming*, the articles of a 'one-man company' allocated very extensive powers to a single individual.[178]

Even if the company's powers were not allocated to an individual directly under the company's constitution, they may be delegated to that individual by someone empowered to do so.[179] A good illustration of this process was offered in *Base Metal Trading Ltd v Shamurin*,[180] where the board delegated its powers to a managing director, Shamurin. In assessing whether Shamurin had the power to enter futures contracts for the company, Arden LJ, as she was then, explained:

> The relevant question was whether Mr Shamurin was given that power in accordance with the company's constitution. The power to run the business of [the company] was in the usual way conferred on the board of directors. We are told that Yuri and Mr Shamurin [the two shareholders and directors of the company] agreed that Mr Shamurin should be the managing director of the company. Article 99 of the company's articles provides that the managing director shall have any of the powers of the board conferred on him by the directors ... It is for Mr Shamurin to show that the power to enter such contracts was within the powers conferred on him by the board of directors.[181]

The same analysis applies to a vast array of the company's other powers, including its ordinary powers. Typically allocated to the board, the company's ordinary powers, such as powers to make representations to banks, may then be delegated in the first instance to a chief executive officer, then delegated to a chief financial officer, and again successively delegated to senior managers, junior managers, and eventually to rank-and-file employees.

[176] Eg Companies Act 2006, Sche 3; Model Articles for Public Companies, Model Arts 3 and 4.
[177] Eg allocating power to make certain decisions to the shareholders in general meeting.
[178] *Lee v Lee's Air Farming* [1961] AC 12 (PC) 15.
[179] In this sense, delegation is agency. The delegate has powers to exercise the delegator's powers: see R Leow 'Understanding Agency: A Proxy Power Definition' (2019) 78 *CLJ* 99. In *Northern Land Council v Quall* [2020] HCA 33, Nettle and Edelman JJ regarded agency and delegation as involving different concepts. In their view, while agency involves one person acting for another so that the former's acts are attributed to the latter, delegation 'in a strict or precise sense' refers to someone who acts on his own behalf and in his own name: at [77], see also [81]–[84]. While delegation can be used in the latter sense, it is not so clear that delegation should always be given this meaning. The issue in that case was whether the Council could delegate performance of its functions of certifying applications for registration of indigenous land use agreements to its CEO. All members of the High Court of Australia agreed that it could, but while the majority adopted the language of delegation, Nettle and Edelman JJ preferred the language of agency.
[180] *Base Metal Trading Ltd v Shamurin* [2004] EWCA Civ 1316, [2005] 1 WLR 1157.
[181] ibid [81].

The allocation and delegation of a company's powers overlaps to some extent with an agency law analysis. Could it be said that the allocation and delegation of a company's powers is simply an application of agency law principles?[182] This depends on what one means by 'agency', a difficult question.[183] I suggest three reasons why it is preferable to focus on an allocation and delegation of the company's powers, rather than seeking to fit the entirety of attribution into 'agency law'. First, while agency is apt to describe delegation, a respectable body of opinion indicates that the groups whom the company's powers are allocated should be regarded as the company's organs, not merely its agents.[184] It is thus doubtful whether an agency analysis can accurately capture all instances of attribution. Second, an agency analysis might lead some to conclude prematurely that the analysis cannot apply to some areas of law, such as tort, and perhaps aspects of the law of restitution. This would hamper efforts to produce a unified account of corporate attribution in private law. Third, an agency analysis might import other disputed consequences, suggesting, for example, that the shareholders in general meeting owe fiduciary duties.[185] Focusing on the allocation and delegation of the company's powers thus avoids unnecessary baggage, paving the way for the account's wider application.

When individuals or groups exercise the powers allocated or delegated to them, they exercise the company's own powers. The company acts personally. This provides a non-fictional way to understand attribution. We attribute *this* act of *this* individual to *this* company because this individual has exercised the company's powers which were allocated or delegated to him. The creation, allocation, and delegation of the company's powers in the company's constitution is given effect to for the same reasons that we recognise companies: a combination of the bottom-up efforts of incorporators and the facilitative machinery of registration, provided by the state.

E. Consistency with *Meridian*

A merit of this view is that it is very largely consistent with the well-known hierarchy of attribution rules identified by *Meridian*. Lord Hoffmann's analysis contemplated that the primary rules were at the top of the hierarchy, followed by the general rules, and only then by the special rules.[186] As Lord Hoffmann explained, the combination of the primary rules, usually specified in the company's constitution

[182] Eg P Watts and F Reynolds (eds), *Bowstead & Reynolds on Agency*, 22nd edn (London, Sweet & Maxwell, 2020) para 1-028.

[183] Compare R Leow, 'Understanding Agency: A Proxy Power Definition' (n 183); R Leow, 'Two Kinds of Agency' (2019) 93 *Supreme Court Law Review* 383; F Reynolds and CH Tan, 'Agency Reasoning – A Formula or a Tool?' [2018] *Singapore Journal of Legal Studies* 43.

[184] *Gower's* (n 165) para 7-4. See Ch 3 below.

[185] As argued for by E Lim, *A Case for Shareholder Fiduciary Duties in Common Law Asia* (Cambridge, Cambridge University Press, 2019).

[186] *cf* Worthington, 'Back to Basics' (n 3) 125.

or general company law, and the general rules of attribution (agency rules) would usually provide the answer to attribution questions. Special rules were only required in 'exceptional cases'.[187] This hierarchy of rules continue to be applied by some courts, demonstrating their traction.[188] Perhaps the reason why this hierarchy has been overlooked in favour of a general context-specific approach is that it was not clear why we had it.

The allocation and delegation of the company's powers provides the answer. The primary rules' focus is the allocation of the company's powers and decision-making by the groups or persons to whom powers have been allocated. These powers can then be delegated to other groups or individuals using the law's general tools for delegation to others: agency rules. The primary rules are primary because they have logical priority: they deal with the analytically prior question of to whom the company's powers have been allocated. The general rules, dealing with their delegation, can only come after the powers have been allocated.

This account places considerations of purpose and policy of the substantive rule in the appropriate place. Ordinarily, it is unnecessary to consider the purpose and policy of the rule of private law in attributing acts. Apparent exceptions might be found in interpreting statutes or other written instruments, such as contracts, trusts, or wills.[189] For example, a contract may provide that a company must make disclosure to a counterparty when information had 'come to the attention' of the company,[190] or it might exclude liability for the company's 'deliberate act or omission'.[191]

Purpose and policy might be appropriately considered here, but this is because prevailing approaches to interpretation require consideration of these factors.[192] Statutory interpretation requires the court to search for the meaning of the statutory language, having regard to the purpose that the statute was intended to have.[193] The court should consider not just the literal meaning of the words in interpreting the statute, but also the legislative purpose in enacting the statute[194] and the mischief that it was intended to address.[195] Similarly, interpreting a provision in a contract, trust, or will may also require consideration of

[187] *Meridian* (n 2) 507.

[188] Eg *Sandham t/a Premier Metals Leeds v Commissioners for HMRC* [2019] UKFTT 0218 (TC) [213], but see also *Sandham t/a Premier Metals Leeds v Commissioners for HMRC* [2020] UKUT 193 (TCC).

[189] See eg *Bowstead & Reynolds on Agency* (n 181) paras 1-028–1-029.

[190] Eg *Jafari-Fini* (n 53).

[191] Eg *KR* (n 53).

[192] See also *Bowstead & Reynolds on Agency* (n 181) para 1-028.

[193] *IRC v McGuckian* [1997] 1 WLR 991 (HL) 999: 'Where there is no obvious meaning of a statutory provision the modern emphasis is on a contextual approach designed to identify the purpose and to give effect to it.' See also *MacNiven (HM Inspector of Taxes) v Westmoreland Investments Ltd* [2001] UKHL 6, [2001] 2 WLR 377 [6]; *Barclays Mercantile Business Finance Ltd v Mawson (Inspector of Taxes* [2004] UKHL 51, [2005] 1 AC 684 [28].

[194] Similarly in Australia see eg *Bropho v Western Australia* [1990] HCA 24, (1990) 171 CLR 1; *CIC Insurance Ltd v Bankstown Football Club Ltd* [1997] HCA 2, (1997) 187 CLR 384.

[195] *CIC* ibid 408.

available background context,[196] going beyond the literal meaning of the words used.[197] It is the approach to interpretation, not attribution, which requires consideration of context, purpose, and policy. However, even in these cases the importance of purpose and policy should not be overstated; the general law of attribution will usually be followed.[198] Only rarely will the parties or legislators have intended that the company's acts or knowledge to have a different meaning in private law.

V. The Account Applied

One immediate payoff is that this account of attribution provides a helpful analytical framework to determine questions of attribution. If attribution turns on the allocation and delegation of the company's powers, any question of attribution of acts turns on four questions: (i) did the company have the power to do the act? (ii) was that power properly allocated and, if necessary, delegated to an individual or group who did the act? (iii) did the act fall within the scope of the power? (iv) was the power properly exercised? The attribution of knowledge requires a further question, whether the knowledge of the individual was material to acts which he had the company's power to do. We consider knowledge in Chapter 6.

A. The Company's Powers

The first question is whether the company had the power to do the relevant act. As we have already seen, the company will have whatever powers are expressly provided for under in its constitution.[199] Companies may also have implied powers to do all acts necessary and expedient to achieve their purposes.[200] Companies were once required to set out their objects, but today this is no longer required under the Companies Act 2006. Unless a company chooses otherwise, it will have unlimited objects.[201] Companies with unlimited objects will have very wide powers. Companies with limited objects will have correspondingly restricted powers.

[196] *Investors Compensation Scheme* (n 46) 912. See also *Chartbrook* (n 46); *Rainy Sky SA v Kookmin Bank* [2011] UKSC 50, [2011] 1 WLR 2900. For trust deeds and wills: *Brynes v Kendle* [2011] HCA 26, (2011) 243 CLR 253.

[197] *Investors Compensation Scheme* (n 46) 913.

[198] Eg *Meridian* (n 2); *Bank of India* (n 53).

[199] This is so even if the power is described as an object, see eg *In re German Date Coffee Co* (1882) 20 Ch D 169 (CA); *Introductions Ltd v National Provincial Bank Ltd* [1970] Ch 199 (CA).

[200] *In re Horsley & Weight Ltd* (n 168) 448 (Buckley LJ).

[201] CA 2006, s 31(1).

B. Allocation and Delegation

Second, were the company's powers properly allocated to the individual or group whose acts are sought to be attributed?

The process of registration ensures that from the very moment that the company is incorporated, it comes into existence already with at least a rudimentary allocation of its powers. If the company provides its own articles, allocation of its powers follows what has been provided for. If not, default articles (the Model Articles, formerly found in Table A of the Companies Acts) are provided and apply to the extent that they are not excluded by articles registered by the company.[202] Unless the company's articles stipulate otherwise, and subject to statute,[203] the Model Articles provide that the company's powers will be allocated to and divided between the board of directors and shareholders in general meeting.[204] The Model Articles also stipulate default procedures for board and general meeting decision-making.[205] Additionally, the application for registration requires the incorporators to provide a statement of the company's intended officers, including directors,[206] and its initial shareholdings.[207] Once incorporated, the company comes into existence with its powers already allocated to groups and with specified individuals making up membership of these groups.

Once allocated, the company's powers may then be delegated to other individuals or groups. For example, the board may wish to delegate powers to enter remuneration contracts to a remuneration committee,[208] or may wish to delegate many of its powers of management to executives, led by a chief executive officer, with the board retaining a largely supervisory role.[209] To do so successfully, the board, like any other individual or group wishing to delegate, must have the powers it wishes to delegate. It must also have the power to delegate those powers. Not all powers may be delegable: certain decisions may be reserved for certain groups under the articles.[210] If either is lacking, then the delegation is a nullity.[211] Attempts by the delegate to exercise the power will also be null and void.[212]

[202] CA 2006, s 20.

[203] Certain powers are allocated to the shareholders in general meeting, eg alteration of the company's articles: CA 2006, s 21; issuance of shares: CA 2006, s 549; disapplication of pre-emption rights to shares: CA 2006, ss 569–573; decisions to reduce share capital: CA 2006, s 641; decisions to wind up company voluntarily: Insolvency Act 1986, s 84.

[204] Model Articles of Private Companies Limited by Shares, Model Art 3; Model Articles of Public Companies, Model Art 3.

[205] Model Articles for Private Companies Limited by Shares, Model Arts 7–16 (directors' decision-making), 37–47 (shareholders' decision-making); Model Articles for Public Companies, Model Arts 7–19 (directors' decision-making), 28–40 (shareholders' decision-making).

[206] CA 2006, s 9(4)(c), s 12.

[207] CA 2006, s 9(4)(a), s 10.

[208] Eg *Guinness plc v Saunders* [1990] 2 AC 663 (HL).

[209] Gower's (n 165) paras 14-3–14-4, 14-9–14-10.

[210] Eg *Guinness* (n 207) 686–87 (Lord Templeman).

[211] *Guinness* (n 207).

[212] ibid.

Courts will carefully assess to whom the company's powers have been allocated and then delegated in practice, not simply on paper. Anyone working in an organisation of reasonable size will quickly learn that organisational decision-making may not be accurately reflected by the formal corporate hierarchy. Sometimes this is intentional, with individuals wishing to wield great control over the company's affairs without formal responsibility.[213] Or practices may develop organically over time. A long-serving secretary, formally delegated only limited powers, may in practice wield enormous power. The board of directors may dispense with formal meetings in favour of decision-making over tennis; senior executives may habitually give instructions to subordinates over the water-cooler; a lazy manager may be bypassed, and his instructions ignored. Difficulties of proof aside, informality should not pose additional conceptual difficulty. It is well-accepted that allocation, and especially delegation, may take place informally. Unanimous decision-making by the board[214] or shareholders,[215] may be valid even if the procedures for calling of meetings are not met, subject to restrictions.[216] Powers are typically delegable without the performance of formalities at common law. The complexity of real-world organisational decision-making may make fact-finding more complex, but the underlying inquiry remains the same.

Crucially, the search for the person(s) to whom the company's powers have been allocated or delegated applies regardless of whether the question of attribution arises in contract, tort, unjust enrichment, or equity. In corporate contracting, courts have always construed the company's memorandum of association and articles carefully to determine whether the individual or group had the power to do the act.[217] Whether the power was properly delegated to the individual is also a question that courts focus on in analysing whether the individual had actual authority to do the act. In tort, whether the individual was allocated the company's power to do the act is similarly material. The cases focus on whether the acts done by the individual were authorised or not. They might be specifically authorised, as where the board of directors directs an individual to do something that constitutes a tort.[218] Or the individual might be given the power to do a class of acts,

[213] Eg the 'shadow director', a person with those instructions the directors may be accustomed to act: CA 2006, s 251.

[214] *Re Bonelli's Telegraph Co* (1871) LR 12 Eq 246 (Ch); *Charterhouse Investment Trust Ltd v Tempest Diesels Ltd* (1885) 1 BCC 99544 (Ch); *Runciman v Walker Runciman plc* [1993] BCC 223 (QB) 230; *Hunter v Senate Support Services Ltd* [2004] EWHC 1085 (Ch).

[215] Often named the 'Re Duomatic' principle after *Re Duomatic* [1969] 2 Ch 365 (Ch) 373 (Buckley J). See further *Parker and Cooper Ltd v Reading* [1926] Ch 975 (Ch); *Multinational Gas* (n 40) 268–69 (Lawton LJ); *In re Oceanrose Investments Ltd* [2008] EWHC 3475 (Ch), [2009] Bus LR 947; *Ciban Management Corpn v Citco (BVI) Ltd* [2020] UKPC 21, [2021] AC 122.

[216] Eg the shareholders must consent: *EIC Services Ltd v Phipps* [2003] EWHC 1507 (Ch), [2003] BCC 931 (reversed on a different point: [2004] EWCA Civ 1069, [2005] 1 WLR 1377), and the transaction must not involve relevant dishonesty: *Re Duomatic*, ibid 372; *Bowthorpe Holdings Ltd v Hills* [2002] EWHC 233 (Ch), [2003] 1 BCLC 226.

[217] Eg *Rolled Steel Products (Holdings) Ltd v British Steel Corpn* [1986] Ch 246.

[218] *Mill v Hawker* (1873–74) LR 9 Ex 309 (Ct of Exch).

such as making representations,[219] collecting and delivering goods,[220] or moving vehicles.[221] In what is regarded as unjust enrichment's core case, the mistaken payment of money, the question might be whether the individual was allocated the company's power to make payments,[222] to give instructions to banks to effect payments,[223] or to receive money for the company.[224] If the individual purported to do an act which he did not have the power to do, his act cannot be attributed to the company.[225]

C. Scope

The third question is whether the act done by the individual was within the scope of the power allocated to him.

If the act done is outside the scope of the power, then the purported exercise of the power will be void; that act then cannot be attributed to the company. If an individual has the power to enter contracts for loans under £1 million and he tries to exercise a power to enter into contracts for a loan of £5 million, he is acting outside the scope of the power. Similarly, if the individual only has power to enter a 12-month charter of a ship but purports to enter a three-year charter, then this too is void.[226] The same analysis applies equally to claims in tort and unjust enrichment. If an individual has power to make statements to certain clients, but instead does so to other clients, he acts outside the scope of his power.[227] Conversely, if he has power to receive money for the company and he so receives, then his acts in receiving the money will be attributed to the company, even if the money was not deposited into the company's bank accounts.[228]

Two sets of rules superficially appear to attribute acts on a wider basis than suggested above: apparent authority and vicarious liability. However, on closer analysis, neither of them attributes acts. Apparent authority is a type of estoppel by representation, while present-day vicarious liability attributes liability, not actions. They are dealt with in Chapters 3 and 4 respectively.

[219] *Colonial Mutual Life* (n 161).
[220] *Rose v Plenty* [1976] 1 WLR 141 (CA).
[221] *London County Council v Cattermoles (Garages) Ltd* [1953] 1 WLR 997 (CA).
[222] *Barclays Bank Ltd v W J Simms Son & Cooke (Southern) Ltd* [1980] QB 677 (QB).
[223] *Agip (Africa) Ltd v Jackson* [1991] Ch 547 (CA).
[224] *Thompson v Bell* (1854) 10 Exch 10; 156 ER 334 (Ct of Exch).
[225] Eg *Russo-Chinese Bank v Li Yau Sam* [1910] AC 174 (PC) (claim failed because individual did not have power to receive money from the company's customers).
[226] *Armagas Ltd v Mundogas SA* [1986] AC 717 (CA) 726–27 (Goff LJ), approved [1986] AC 717 (HL) 777 (Lord Keith).
[227] *Kooragang Investments Pty Ltd v Richardson & Wrench Ltd* [1982] AC 462 (PC).
[228] Eg *Thompson v Bell* (n 223).

D. Proper Exercise

Finally, even if an individual was properly allocated a power and attempted to exercise it within its scope, was that exercise proper?

Where the individual is allocated the company's legal powers to act, a condition precedent to the successful exercise of the power is implied. In *General Assembly of Free Church of Scotland v Lord Overtoun*, Lord Lindley said: 'I take it to be clear that there is a condition implied in this as well as in other instruments which create powers, namely that the powers shall be used bona fide for the purposes for which they are conferred.'[229] In *Hopkins v TL Dallas Group Ltd*, Lightman J again reiterated the same point: 'the grant of actual authority should be implied as being subject to a condition that it is to be exercised honestly and on behalf of the principal.'[230] The test is subjective, in that the individual must intend to exercise it honestly in what he believes to be the interests of the principal.[231]

The rationale for this condition is not difficult to find. As Lionel Smith has observed,

> When one person acquires the authority to make decisions *on behalf* of another person, there is a partial transfer of autonomy. One person is now authorised to act, not just in a way that *affects* another person, but rather *for* that other person. And it is part of the logic of acting *for* another person that there is only one right way to do it: you must do it in the way that you think is best for that other person.[232]

The same is true when one is acting *as* another person, as where one exercises the company's powers to act.

Many illustrations exist in private law. It clearly applies in contract law, where an individual is entering into contracts on behalf of the company. In *Hopkins*, the deputy managing director of companies in the Dallas Group signed letters on behalf of the companies undertaking to pay large sums of money to a third party, TTB, in exchange for TTB supplying goods and finances to one of TTB's customers, Malik. These undertakings were for Malik's benefit, not the benefit of the Dallas Group companies.[233] As a result, the managing director did not successfully exercise the company's power, so that the company was not bound to any contract with TTB unless apparent authority existed.

[229] *General Assembly of Free Church of Scotland v Lord Overtoun* [1904] AC 515 (HL) 694.

[230] *Hopkins v TL Dallas Group Ltd* [2004] EWHC 1379 (Ch), [2005] 1 BCLC 543 [88], citing *Lysaght Bros & Co v Falk* [1905] HCA 7, (1905) 2 CLR 421.

[231] P Watts, 'Actual Authority: The Requirement for an Agent Honestly to Believe that an Exercise of Power is in the Principal's Interests' [2017] *Journal of Business Law* 269, 274.

[232] L Smith, 'Fiduciary Relationships: Ensuring the Loyal Exercise of Judgement on Behalf of Another' (2014) 130 *LQR* 608, 613.

[233] (n 229) [91].

The same rule applies to what some regard as unjust enrichment claims[234] where the company exercises powers to transfer its property to a recipient. In *Clark v Cutland*, a director misappropriated money from the company[235] by paying himself unauthorised remuneration and other benefits and then paying them into a pension trust. It was held that the company had not authorised either of these payments and could recover them from the director. Similarly, in *Re Hampton Capital Ltd*, the company Hampton received monies from an investor, Tolent, through the dealings of its controller, Mayweather.[236] Acting on Mayweather's instructions, Hampton's sole shareholder and director made payments on behalf of Hampton to third parties. It was accepted that these payments were equivalent to monies that had been stolen from Hampton. It was held that the dissipated funds had been paid away for Mayweather's own benefit and not for Hampton's benefit. Hampton thus had a personal claim against the recipients for the value of those funds.

The same rule also applies to a company's ordinary powers. But what counts as proper exercise may be different between legal powers and ordinary powers. As we will see, the main illustrations of ordinary powers are in tort law, where the cases suggest that the test is whether the individual intended to act adversely to the company's interests. If he did, then the exercise is improper, but if not, it is proper. This small difference might be explicable by the difference between legal and ordinary powers. No manifestation of intention to change legal relations is necessary to exercise ordinary powers. Many acts exercising ordinary powers may thus be done without any specific intention, especially those done carelessly. Taking this into account, the requirement of proper exercise is less demanding, permitting attribution of acts exercising ordinary powers unless they are intentionally done against the company's interests.

VI. Attribution as Identifying Intentional Acts

An account based on the allocation and delegation of the company's powers may have further implications. It also suggests that attribution reflects acts done by companies as intentional actors – as 'group agents'. This is important because some prominent accounts of private law suggest that an actor's capacity for intentional acts is a necessary condition for him to owe duties and hold rights in private law.[237] Yet others see capacity for agency as necessary for the actor to be held responsible, whether morally or otherwise.[238] The allocation and delegation of the company's

[234] C Mitchell et al, *Goff & Jones on the Law of Unjust Enrichment*, 9th edn (London, Sweet and Maxwell, 2016) paras 8-58–8-66.

[235] *Clark v Cutland* [2003] EWCA Civ 810, [2004] 1 WLR 783.

[236] *Re Hampton Capital Ltd* [2015] EWHC 1905 (Ch).

[237] Eg Weinrib, *The Idea of Private Law* (n 79) 24.

[238] List and Pettit, *Group Agency* (n 136) Ch 7.

powers help explain how companies can meet these requirements. In turn, it helps emphasise how attributed acts can be said to be truly the company's, not just a legal fiction.

A. Group Agency

Group agency theorists argue that groups, including companies, may be able to satisfy the conditions for agency.[239] Here, 'agency' is used in the sense used in philosophy of action, referring to a being with the capacity for action, rather than the legal concept of agency. List and Pettit identify three criteria for agency: the agent has 'representational states' depicting how things are in the environment; 'motivational states' specifying how it requires things to be in the environment; and the capacity to process its representational and motivational states, leading it to intervene where the environment fails to match a motivation.[240] In other words, the agent must be able to form intentions and goals, and take action motivated by those intentions and goals.[241]

The idea of group agency has intuitive appeal. In law and in ordinary life, it is observable that statements about groups are often not straightforwardly reducible to statements about the aggregate of their members. As Hart pointed out many years ago, the statement 'Smith & Co Ltd conveyed property to Smith' is not equivalent to 'All of Smith & Co Ltd's members conveyed property to Smith'.[242] In ordinary life, Peter French gives the example of the statement, 'The American people were responsible for the Vietnam War'.[243] This again, is not straightforwardly reducible to the statement, 'All Americans were responsible for the Vietnam War', which would include even Americans who had refused to serve in the army or objected to the war efforts. The same may be true of statements about moral duties. Another example, identified by Stephanie Collins, comes from an editorial in *The Observer*, where it was suggested that 'surely we can all agree that Britain has a moral duty to provide safe harbour to more people fleeing conflicts'.[244] This exhortation again seems to regard the moral duty as owed by the group itself, rather than by each and every member of the group.

[239] List and Pettit, *Group Agency* (n 136).

[240] ibid 20.

[241] For similar views, see additionally PA French, *Collective and Corporate Responsibility* (Columbia, Columbia University Press, 1984); R Tuomela, *Social Ontology: Collective Intentionality and Group Agents* (Oxford, Oxford University Press, 2013). For related work on shared or joint intentions, see also Tuomela, *Social Ontology*, and see also J Searle, 'Collective Intentions and Actions' in P Cohen et al (eds), *Intentions in Communication* (Cambridge, MIT Press, 1990); M Gilbert, *On Social Facts* (London and New York, Routledge, 1989); M Gilbert, *Joint Commitment: How We Make the Social World* (Oxford, Oxford University Press, 2013); and contrast M Bratman, *Faces of Intention* (Cambridge, Cambridge University Press, 1999); M Bratman, *Shared Agency: A Planning Theory of Acting Together* (Oxford, Oxford University Press, 2014).

[242] Hart, 'Definition and Theory in Jurisprudence' (n 27) 41.

[243] French, *Collective and Corporate Responsibility* (n 239) 18.

[244] S Collins, *Group Duties: Their Existence and their Implications for Individuals* (Oxford, Oxford University Press, 2019) 1.

This is not to say that all groups will be group agents. Consider, for example, all the people who happen to be present in a shopping centre at 9am on a Thursday. Their membership of 'persons present in a shopping centre at 9am on a Thursday' is merely a matter of happenstance. Such 'groups' might be described as 'collections'[245] or 'aggregates'.[246] It is widely accepted that they will not satisfy the conditions for group agency: members of the group do not form intentions and act together, and the identity of this 'group' cannot survive changes in membership.[247]

To qualify as a group agent, the group must be able to generate and maintain rational group-level intentions, beliefs, and goals. This is typically done through decision-making procedures which will work, broadly, to incorporate beliefs and preferences, processing them to produce decisions.[248] Collins, speaking of a similar type of group which she calls 'collectives', explains that a collective is constituted by agents that are united under a rationally operated group-level decision-making procedure that can attend to moral considerations.[249] As she explains, the collective will be at least partly constituted by agents, who will be united by a decision-making procedure. In the most general terms, a decision-making procedure takes in beliefs and preferences, processing them to produce decisions. This procedure may include many sub-procedures, including informal, tacit, and even vague procedures that could be subsumed under notions of the group's 'culture'.[250] Rational operation of this decision-making procedure requires that current decisions follow from current beliefs and preferences, and broadly accord with past beliefs, preferences, and decisions, incorporating new evidence which had arisen since those past beliefs, preferences, and decisions were arrived at.[251]

B. Companies as Group Agents

Many companies will indeed meet the conditions for group agency. In fact, List and Pettit identify companies as 'paradigm examples of instrumentally rational group agents',[252] which:

> pursue the financial welfare of their shareholders as their common purpose, at least on common lore, and exhibit the characteristics of agency in full dress … Shareholders, directors, managers and workers combine, often in subsidiary units, to ensure that they pursue the overall goals of their corporations according to a single body of representations.[253]

[245] List and Pettit (n 136) 31.
[246] French, *Collective and Corporate Responsibility* (n 239) 19–26.
[247] French, *Collective and Corporate Responsibility* (n 239) 19–26; List and Pettit (n 136) 31.
[248] Collins (n 242) 11–14. See, similarly, List and Pettit (n 136) 36–37.
[249] Collins (n 242) 11.
[250] ibid.
[251] ibid.
[252] List and Pettit (n 136) 40.
[253] ibid.

As Collins points out, having group-level decision-making procedures is a typical way in which groups can generate and maintain group-level intentions, beliefs, and goals. These decision-making processes are a key feature of companies. From the very moment of their incorporation, companies come into existence with a scheme setting out how their powers are, or can be, allocated and delegated. They also possess processes for decision-making, which are often very detailed. Typically, the company's powers are first allocated to primary decision-making bodies, typically the board of directors and shareholders in general meeting. Decision-making processes are specifically provided for: quorum requirements, rules on voting procedures, and whether decision-making is to be done unanimously, by simple majority, or some other standard. When members vote, their individual inputs go into and generate a group decision – a decision of the group, even if it is one that individual members disagree with. Through delegation, the company's decision-making processes can also be dispersed throughout different individuals or groups within the corporate hierarchy. Again, there may be specified procedures for decision-making in these cases. All this might be called, as Peter French did, the company's 'corporate internal decision structure'.[254] Actions can then be authorised, again as part of the decision-making process, to ensure that the company's decisions can be implemented. These acts, produced through the company's group-level decision-making processes, can thus be described as the company's intentional acts. They are acts done by the company as a group agent.

The account of attribution here suggests that attribution is of greater normative significance than is often assumed. In companies with decision-making procedures such as those described earlier, attribution generally identifies the company's intentional acts – the acts which are motivated by the company's own intentions, beliefs, and goals. Some limited exceptions may exist, such as one-man companies with a single director and shareholder. Although a company, there is only one human individual present, and no group at all. As it is not a group at all, it cannot be a group agent.

This analysis is important because some prominent accounts of private law, such as some corrective justice accounts, are premised on actors in private law having capacity for intentional acts.[255] For example, in his account of private law as a species of corrective justice, Ernest Weinrib highlights the idea of 'personality', which 'refers to the capacity for purposive agency that forms the basis for the capacity for rights and duties in private law'.[256] In his view, personality 'as the capacity for purposiveness contains the indispensable conditions for the ascription of responsibility for the effects of one's action'.[257] Without the capacity for

[254] French, *Collective and Corporate Responsibility* (n 239) 39.

[255] Eg Weinrib, *Corrective Justice* (n 79) 23–25. See also Weinrib, *The Idea of Private Law* (n 79) 127–29.

[256] Weinrib, *The Idea of Private Law* (n 79) 24.

[257] ibid 25.

purposive or intentional actions, an actor cannot come under private law duties or possess rights. This is borne out by some extent to English law: no act is committed, and thus no tort of trespass to land is committed, where an actor is thrown onto land by another person or enters the land 'in an effective state of automatism'.[258] Yet others emphasise the role of agency in holding agents responsible.[259] This account of attribution helps show how companies can meet the requirements of agency and thus be consistent with these accounts of private law, or more widely, responsibility. It also emphasises, from a different perspective, that attribution is not merely a fictional deeming process.

VII. Conclusion

If attribution is viewed as purely fictional, there may be no right answer to when and why we attribute. To avoid this outcome, leading accounts have sought to anchor attribution to features external to the connection between act, individual, and company, resulting in difficulties.

The aim of this chapter was to indicate a new route forward. Attribution is not a fiction. It involves only the application of ordinary concepts to the company. Like human persons, companies possess powers. These powers are allocated and delegated to individuals or groups through the company's constitution throughout the corporate hierarchy.

The attribution of acts thus turns on four questions: (i) did the company have the power? (ii) was the power allocated, and if necessary, delegated to the individual or group doing the act? (iii) was the act within the scope of the power? (iv) was the power properly exercised? The next three chapters show how this analysis is already implicitly adopted when attributing acts in contract law (Chapter 3), tort law (Chapter 4), and unjust enrichment (Chapter 5). This account might also suggest that attribution of acts has deeper normative significance than is often assumed, identifying the company's intentional acts.

[258] *Network Rail Infrastructure Ltd v Conarken Group Ltd* [2010] EWHC 1852 (TCC) [65]. See generally James Goudkamp, *Tort Law Defences* (Oxford, Hart Publishing, 2013) 48–49.
[259] List and Pettit, *Group Agency* (n 136) Ch 7.

PART II

Application

3

Attribution of Acts in Contract

This chapter, the first of three considering the attribution of acts, examines attribution in contract. It focuses on the area where issues have arisen most prominently: contract formation. The dominant analysis here is that of agency law, supplemented by statute. As Hannigan states, attribution problems 'are limited in respect of contract … where agency and statute (in the case of contracts) … provide the answers to questions of whose acts are the acts of the company for the purpose of liability'.[1]

But agency's applicability to all corporate contracting is controversial. Widely accepted in analysing contracting by subordinate agents, its use in analysing contracting by the board of directors or shareholders in general meeting remains disputed. Using agency analysis in the latter case is problematic: it relies on contested definitions of agency, is difficult to square with the incorporation process, and may import unwanted consequences.

In this chapter, I argue that attribution in corporate contracting is better analysed as turning on the allocation and delegation of the company's powers to act. Attribution thus turns on four questions: (i) did the company have the power to do the act? (ii) was that power allocated or delegated to the individual acting? (iii) was the power exercised within its scope? (iv) was the power properly exercised? This analysis incorporates the advantages of agency analysis but not its difficulties. The chapter shows how the considerable case law already implicitly adopts this analysis, by examining a wide range of cases ranging from those on the *ultra vires* doctrine to those found in agency law and fiduciary law. An important payoff is to show how a wide variety of different flaws in corporate contracting at common law and in equity are analysed. Attribution is then further distinguished from three other routes to the company's liability: the indoor management rule; statutory deeming provisions; and apparent authority.

I. Agency Analysis

Orthodoxy suggests attribution in corporate contracting turns on agency analysis. This is particularly clear where subordinate agents – those below the level of the

[1] B Hannigan, *Company Law*, 5th edn (Oxford, Oxford University Press, 2018) para 4-2.

board or general meeting – are concerned. But this analysis is controversial in contracting by the board of directors or shareholders in general meeting. Analysing the board or general meeting as the company's agents raises four problems: it rests on contested definitions of agency, seems inconsistent with the incorporation process, might suggest that individual members of the board or general meeting are agents, and might indicate that the board or general meeting are fiduciaries of the company.

A. Contracting by Subordinate Agents

It is widely accepted that agency analysis is used to analyse corporate contracting by subordinate agents. Although earlier implicit acceptance of agency analysis could be observed,[2] perhaps the best-known modern authority is *Freeman & Lockyer v Buckhurst Park Properties.*[3] Mr Kapoor, a property developer who formed the defendant company, instructed the claimant architect firm to do work on the Buckhurst Park Estate. The claimants executed the work but were not paid. The question was whether Kapoor's acts in contracting with the claimant architects could be attributed to the company. If so, the company would owe contractual duties to the architects which could be enforced.

The Court of Appeal unanimously concluded that Kapoor's acts could be attributed: he acted as de facto managing director with the power to contract. The leading speech was delivered by Diplock LJ, who straightforwardly regarded the person acting for the company as an agent:

> This [case] makes it necessary to inquire into the state of the law as to the ostensible authority of officers and servants to enter into contracts on behalf of corporations … We are concerned in the present case with the authority of an agent to create contractual rights and liabilities between his principal and a third party whom I will call 'the contractor'.[4]

In statements now regarded as authoritatively setting out general agency law principles,[5] Diplock LJ explained the differences between two types of authority which the agent might have: actual authority and apparent authority.[6] While actual authority is based on the principal's consent to the agent acting for him,[7] apparent

[2] See eg *JC Houghton v Nothard, Lowe and Wills Ltd* [1928] AC 1 (HL); *Morris v Kanssen* [1946] AC 459 (HL); *Rama Corpn Ltd v Proved Tin & General Investments Ltd* [1952] 2 QB 147 (QB).

[3] *Freeman & Lockyer v Buckhurst Park Properties* [1964] 2 QB 480 (CA).

[4] ibid 502.

[5] P Watts and F Reynolds (eds), *Bowstead & Reynolds on Agency*, 22nd edn (London, Sweet & Maxwell, 2020) paras 3-003 (actual authority), 3-004 (apparent authority).

[6] *Freeman* (n 3) 502–504.

[7] ibid 502–503.

authority is based on an estoppel by representation.[8] If the principal represents to the counterparty that the agent has authority to act and the counterparty reasonably relies on this representation, the principal is estopped from denying the truth of his representation.[9] Diplock LJ regarded agency principles as applying to persons acting for companies, subject only to two differences. As he explained:

> In applying the law as I have endeavoured to summarise it to the case where the principal is not a natural person, but a fictitious person, namely, a corporation, two further factors arising from the legal characteristics of a corporation have to be borne in mind. The first is that the capacity of a corporation is limited by its constitution …; the second is that a corporation cannot do any act, and that includes making a representation, except through his agent.[10]

After *Freeman*, if not before, agency analysis became the dominant way to analyse corporate contracting by subordinate agents. Used in numerous leading cases,[11] its use is so unexceptional that courts rarely even question its applicability. Academic commentators, too, wholeheartedly endorse application of agency principles when analysing contracting by subordinate agents. The leading English company law text, *Gower's Principles of Modern Company Law*, considers corporate contracting by the board and general meeting separately from contracting by subordinate agents, using straightforward agency analysis for the latter.[12] In another text, it is explained that 'for the purposes of making a company a party to legal relationships such as contracts, the legal concept of agency is used to establish whose acts are to be attributed to the company'.[13] One of *Gower's* authors, Sarah Worthington, regards the two main issues in corporate contracting as the company's capacity, dealt with by *ultra vires*,[14] and the authority of individuals to act for the company, dealt with by agency.[15]

[8] ibid 503.
[9] ibid 503.
[10] ibid 504.
[11] Some notable cases include *Hely-Hutchinson v Brayhead* [1968] 1 QB 549 (CA) 583 (Lord Denning); *Egyptian International Foreign Trade Co v Soplex Wholesale Supplies Ltd (The Raffaella)* [1985] 2 Lloyds LR 36 (CA) 39-43 (Browne-Wilkinson LJ); *Armagas Ltd v Mundogas SA* [1986] AC 717 (CA) 728–32 (Goff LJ), affirmed [1986] AC 717 (HL) 777–79 (Lord Keith); *First Energy (UK) Ltd v Hungarian International Bank Ltd* [1993] BCC 533 (CA) 540 (Steyn LJ); *Hopkins v TL Dallas Group Ltd* [2004] EWHC 1379 (Ch), [2005] 1 BCLC 543 [87] (Lightman J); *Kelly v Fraser* [2012] UKPC 25, [2013] 1 AC 450 [10]; *Akai Holdings Ltd v Kasikornbank Public Co Ltd* [2010] HKCFA 64, [2011] 1 HKC 357 [41]–[43] (Lord Neuberger NPJ); *East Asia Co Ltd v PT Satria Tirtatama Energindo* [2019] UKPC 30 [39]–[43].
[12] PL Davies and S Worthington, *Gower's Principles of Modern Company Law*, 10th edn (London, Sweet & Maxwell, 2016) paras 7-4–7-5, 7-16.
[13] D French, *Mayson, French and Ryan on Company Law*, 36th edn (Oxford, Oxford University Press, 2019) 610.
[14] See Section II.A below.
[15] S Worthington, *Sealy & Worthington's Text, Cases, & Materials in Company Law*, 11th edn (Oxford, Oxford University Press, 2016) 90–93.

B. Contracting by the Board of Directors or Shareholders in General Meeting

But the use of agency analysis is disputed in respect of contracting by the board or shareholders in general meeting. Some regard agency analysis as applicable, but others argue that the board or general meeting, as the company's 'organs', are in a distinct position.

The view that agency analysis is generally applicable to solving all non-statutory attribution problems has been defended most ably by the distinguished agency scholar, Peter Watts. The leading agency text, *Bowstead & Reynolds on Agency*, of which Watts is an editor, argues that:

> A company (as with other corporations) can operate only through individuals, but in relation to the rules of the common law (including equity) the rules of agency and vicarious liability suffice to enable a company to be held liable and entitled in respect of acts performed, and the states of mind held, by its agents and employees in the same way as a human principal.[16]

Watts draws considerable support from the influential statement of Lord Diplock in *Tesco Supermarkets Ltd v Nattrass*:

> A corporation is an abstraction. It is incapable itself of doing any physical act or being in any state of mind. Yet in law it is a person capable of exercising legal rights and of being subject to legal liabilities which may involve ascribing to it not only physical acts which are in reality done by a natural person on its behalf but also the mental state in which that person did them. In civil law, apart from certain statutory duties, this presents no conceptual difficulties. Under the law of agency the physical acts and state of mind of the agent are in law ascribed to the principal, and if the agent is a natural person it matters not whether the principal is also a natural person or a mere legal abstraction. *Qui facit per alium facit per se: qui cogitat per alium cogitat per se.*[17]

Although *Tesco* is a criminal case, Watts regards the references to agency as applying equally to corporate contracting.[18]

More specifically, Watts has also argued that the board is an agent of the company. As Watts argues:

> … at the level of definition it is difficult to see how directors, whether acting individually or collectively as the board, can be extracted from the concept of agent. Hence, the board meets the standard definition of agency, namely a person or persons on whom has been conferred a mandate to alter a principal's legal position in relation to third parties.[19]

[16] *Bowstead & Reynolds* (n 5) para 1-028.

[17] *Tesco Supermarkets Ltd v Nattrass* [1972] AC 153 (HL) 198–99.

[18] Subject to the caveat that for duties resulting from drafting, whose acts or states of mind were intended to be attributed turns on construction: P Watts, 'Attribution and Limitation' (2018) 134 *LQR* 350, 350; *Bowstead & Reynolds* (n 5) para 1-028.

[19] P Watts, 'Directors as Agents – Some Aspects of Disputed Territory' in D Busch et al (eds), *Agency Law in Commercial Practice* (Oxford, Oxford University Press, 2016) para 7-08.

He further points to several old cases as evidence,[20] where directors have been described as agents[21] or where it is emphasised that companies must act through the agency of others.[22]

But against this, a notable body of contrary opinion exists. A view is that the board and general meeting are not merely the company's agents, but are the company's 'organs'. This view is by no means heterodox; it commands some powerful support. *Gower's*, the leading English company law text, accepts it. As its authors explain, 'Where the board or the shareholders collectively act, they constitute the company, i.e. they act *as* the company. They are not its agents'.[23] Similarly, for Susan Watson, directors have a dual role, depending on whether they are acting individually or acting as part of the board. While directors acting individually are acting as the company's agents, this is not true when acting as a member of the board. 'When directors are acting collectively as part of the board, they are not the agents of the company'.[24]

C. Problems with Applying Agency Analysis to the Board or General Meeting

The distinction between 'organs' and 'agents' originated from German law, where it carried important practical consequences. Under German law, the organs' powers and capacity were unlimited and could not be restricted by another corporate organ.[25] These consequences do not seem to follow in English law. Even *Gower's*, for example, accepts that the powers of the company's organs can be limited by the company's constitution, and that the company's constitution can divide up the company's powers between those organs.[26] But whether the board or general meeting are analysed as agents of the company still matters, albeit differently than in German law.

Applying agency analysis to the board or general meeting might be problematic for four reasons. First, whether agency analysis is apt here turns partly on one's definition of agency, a contested issue. Second, on common definitions, agency analysis appears inconsistent with the incorporation process. Third, it might

[20] ibid para 7-09.

[21] Citing *Aberdeen Railway v Blaikie* (1854) 1 Macq 461 (HL); *Ferguson v Wilson* (1866) LR 2 Ch App 77 (Ch) 89.

[22] Citing *Yarborough v The Bank of England* (1812) 16 East 6 (KB) 7, 104 ER 991; *Citizens Life Assurance Co Ltd v Brown* [1904] AC 423 (PC) 426.

[23] *Gower's* (n 12) para 7-4.

[24] S Watson, 'Conceptual Confusion: Organs, Agents and Identity in the English Courts' (2011) 23 *Singapore Academy of Law Journal* 762. See also S Watson, 'How the Company Became an Entity: A New Understanding of Corporate Law' [2015] *Journal of Business Law* 120, 139.

[25] V Edwards, *EC Company Law* (Oxford, Oxford University Press, 1999) 35; C Gerner-Beurle and M Schillig, *Comparative Company Law* (Oxford, Oxford University Press, 2019) 196.

[26] *Gower's* (n 12) para 7-5.

suggest that individual members of the board or the general meeting are agents. Finally, it might lead to the unjustified importation of other incidents of agency, such as fiduciary duties.

i. Contested Definitions

Whether the board or general meeting is the company's agent turns at least partly on one's definition of agency.[27] Defining agency is not easy. The concept of agency itself has been described by *Bowstead & Reynolds* as 'peculiarly troublesome'.[28] Recall Watts' argument that 'the board meets the standard definition of agency, namely a person or persons on whom has been conferred a mandate to alter a principal's legal position in relation to third parties'.[29] A standard definition of agency focuses on three features: the agent's ability to act for the principal; the voluntarily created nature of the relationship; and the relationship being fiduciary.[30] But it has been suggested that it might still be apt to describe relationships as ones of agency even where the agent cannot bind the principal,[31] as with estate or canvassing agents,[32] or if the agent owes no fiduciary duties,[33] with irrevocable agency a possible example.[34]

ii. The Process of Incorporation

On most common definitions of agency, the agent's mandate or power to act for the principal must be conferred *by the principal*. As Lord Cranworth said in *Pole v Leask*, 'No one can become the agent of another person except by the will of that other person'.[35] Similarly, Bowstead & Reynolds state that 'Agency is the fiduciary relationship which exists betweeen *two persons, one of whom expressly or impliedly manifests assent that the other should act on his behalf* so as to affect his legal relations with third parties …'.[36] Arguably the core case of agency, powers of attorney

[27] See eg WA Seavey, 'The Rationale of Agency' (1920) 29 *Yale LJ* 859; FE Dowrick, 'The Relationship of Principal and Agent' (1954) 17 *MLR* 24; *Bowstead & Reynolds* (n 5) paras 1-001–1-003; F Reynolds and CH Tan, 'Agency Reasoning – A Formula or A Tool?' [2018] *Singapore Journal of Legal Studies* 43; R Leow, 'Understanding Agency: A Proxy Power Definition' (2019) 78 *CLJ* 99.

[28] *Bowstead & Reynolds* (n 5) para 1-002.

[29] Watts, 'Some Aspects of Disputed Territory' (n 19) para 7-08.

[30] See eg *Bowstead & Reynolds* (n 5) para 1-001; *UBS AG (London Branch) v Kommunale Wasserwerke Leipzig GmbH* [2017] EWCA Civ 1567 [91].

[31] See *Bowstead & Reynolds* (n 5) paras 1-003-1-004, 1-020. See further Reynolds and Tan (n 27) 47.

[32] *Bowstead & Reynolds* (n 5) para 1-020; Reynolds and Tan (n 27) 48.

[33] *UBS AG (London Branch) v Kommunale Wasserwerke Leipzig GmbH* [2017] EWCA Civ 1567 [83]–[84], [92]; *Eze v Conway* [2019] EWCA Civ 88 [39]; *Pengelly v Business Mortgage Finance 4 plc* [2020] EWHC 2002 (Ch) [30]–[35], appealed on other grounds: *Wood v Commercial First Business Ltd* [2021] EWCA Civ 471.

[34] Eg *Angove's Pty Ltd v Bailey* [2016] UKSC 47, [2016] 1 WLR 3179, especially [9]. See further Reynolds and Tan (n 27) 49–51.

[35] *Pole v Leask* (1863) 33 LJ Ch 155.

[36] *Bowstead & Reynolds* (n 5) para 1-001.

demonstrate that the agent's consent is unnecessary for the creation of the agency relationship.[37] What is important is the principal's manifestation of will that the other be his agent.[38] Cases where this requirement is omitted are well-known as problematic. If examples are necessary, the wife's power to act as her husband's agent is one,[39] and *Watteau v Fenwick*[40] another.

But are the board or general meeting's powers conferred by the company? It seems not. To assert so would be inconsistent with the incorporation process. Once incorporated, the company comes into existence as a new legal person. From that moment, it is imbued with powers to act, which are (typically, under default rules) already distributed to the board or general meeting. The distribution of powers is governed by the company's constitution, which is likewise constituted as the company's constitution during the incorporation process. In other words, prior to incorporation, no company exists. After incorporation, the company exists, with its powers already allocated to the board and general meeting. There is thus no moment where the company as a person exists before the company's constitution. It is therefore difficult to see how the board or general meeting's powers can be delegated to them *by the company*, when both come into existence simultaneously.[41] Conferring powers requires that the conferrer exists before the alleged conferral occurs. As the company comes into existence at the same time as its allocation of powers, this casts doubt on an agency analysis.

iii. Individual Members as Agents

Third, agency analysis might suggest that individual members of the board or general meeting are, by virtue of membership of the board or general meeting alone, automatically also the company's agents. Some accounts of corporate contracting appear to suggest this. For example, *Bowstead & Reynolds* describes directors on a board as 'co-agents',[42] suggesting that a director may have the power to act for his company solely by virtue of his role as a director.

But there is long-standing authority to the contrary. In *Re Marseilles Extension Railway*, Mellish J firmly stated that: 'a director is simply a person appointed to act as one of a board, with power to bind the company when acting as a board, but having otherwise no power to bind them'.[43] More recently, Arden LJ (as she was then) affirmed this in *Base Metal Trading Ltd v Shamurin*, explaining that:

> The articles did not confer on Mr Shamurin any spontaneous executive power of his own. As an ordinary director, with no power of the board delegated to him, he would

[37] *Bowstead & Reynolds* (n 5) para 1-006.
[38] ibid.
[39] Eg *Manby v Scott* (1660) 1 Lev 4, 2 Sm LC 417; *Bowstead & Reynolds* (n 5) para 3-044.
[40] *Watteau v Fenwick* [1893] 1 QB 346 (QB).
[41] Leow (n 27) 105.
[42] *Bowstead & Reynolds* (n 5) para 1-028. See also Watts, 'Some Aspects of Disputed Territory' (n 19) paras 7.04, 7.08.
[43] *Re Marseilles Extension Railway* (1871) LR 7 Ch App 161 (CA).

only be able to carry out functions on behalf of the company collectively with the other director.[44]

These statements make clear that individual directors are not automatically the company's agents simply by being members of a board. In that capacity, they cannot bind the company except when acting collectively with other members of the board. Considering the position of a single shareholder may be particularly helpful. If a member of the board was automatically the company's agent, able to act alone for the company, a single shareholder ought to be able to do so as well. But this view is properly rejected.[45] A shareholder, as such, cannot act for the company.

There are two main reasons why individual directors are typically described by cases as agents. First, individual directors were often analogised to trustees or agents to justify their owing fiduciary duties to the company.[46] Here, directors are described as agents only for a limited purpose. Second, particularly in smaller companies in England and Wales, individual directors are often delegated substantial powers and are thus agents by virtue of this process. For example, managing directors of English companies are typically members of the board as well as the company's chief executive officer.[47] The latter role may carry substantial powers, but those powers come from their being delegated to the director,[48] not simply because the managing director is a board member.[49]

iv. Fiduciary Duties and Other Incidents of Agency

Finally, agency analysis might import other unwanted consequences. For instance, it might suggest that other standard incidents of agency, such as fiduciary duties, ought to apply to the board or general meeting.

Agency relationships are generally thought to be fiduciary in nature,[50] though exceptions of course exist.[51] Who owes fiduciary duties, the scope of such duties and why they arise remains contentious.[52] But a good statement of widely accepted

[44] *Base Metal Trading Ltd v Shamurin* [2004] EWCA Civ 1316, [2005] 1 WLR 1157 [81].

[45] Eg E Lim, *A Case for Shareholder Fiduciary Duties in Common Law Asia* (Cambridge, Cambridge University Press, 2019) 143–44.

[46] Eg *Aberdeen Railway* (n 21).

[47] Eg *Hely-Hutchinson* (n 11) 560.

[48] See eg *Smith v Butler* [2012] EWCA Civ 314, [2012] BCC 645.

[49] Eg *Biggerstaff v Rowatt's Wharf Ltd* [1896] 2 Ch 93 (CA) 97; *Hely-Hutchinson* (n 11) 560.

[50] Eg *Bowstead & Reynolds* (n 5) para 1-001.

[51] See especially *Angove's* (n 34) [6]–[9] (irrevocable agency); *Eze v Conway* [2019] EWCA Civ 88 [39]–[48].

[52] See eg AW Scott, 'The Fiduciary Principle' (1949) 37 *California LR* 539, 540; LS Sealy, 'Fiduciary Relationships' (1962) 20 *CLJ* 69; P Finn, *Fiduciary Obligations* (Sydney, Law Book Co, 1977); JC Shepherd, *The Law of Fiduciaries* (Toronto, Carswell, 1981); P Finn, 'The Fiduciary Principle' in TG Youdan (ed), *Equity, Fiduciaries and Trusts* (Toronto, Carswell, 1989); R Flannigan, 'The Fiduciary Obligation' (1989) 9 *OJLS* 285; M Conaglen, *Fiduciary Loyalty: Protecting the Due Performance of Non-Fiduciary Duties* (Oxford, Hart Publishing, 2010); J Edelman, 'When Do Fiduciary Duties Arise?' (2010) 126 *LQR* 302; L Smith, 'Fiduciary Relationships: Ensuring the Loyal Exercise of Judgement on

principles was set out in the leading case of *Bristol and West Building Society v Mothew*, where Millett LJ said that:

> A fiduciary is someone who has undertaken to act for or on behalf of another in a particular matter or circumstances which give rise to a relationship of trust and confidence. The distinguishing obligation of a fiduciary is the obligation of loyalty … This core liability has several facets. A fiduciary must act in good faith; he must not make a profit out of his trust; he may not act for his own benefit or the benefit of a third person without the informed consent of his principal.[53]

This statement highlights two relatively uncontroversial aspects of a fiduciary's duties: first, the duty to not to act in conflict of interest,[54] and second, the duty not to make an unauthorised profit out of the fiduciary relationship.[55]

As discussed above, agency analysis might lead to the conclusion that individual members of the general meeting are agents. If this is so, then individual members might owe fiduciary duties. A case has been made for this very conclusion.[56] But this does not seem to reflect the law. Courts have repeatedly emphasised that individual shareholders can generally vote on whatever way they want, subject to certain minimal constraints which we will turn to later. As *Pender v Lushington* explains, this is because the voting rights of individual shareholders are 'rights of property':

> when men exercise their rights of property, they exercise their rights from some motive adequate or inadequate, and I have always considered the law to be that those who have the rights of property are entitled to exercise them, whatever their motives may be for such exercise.[57]

The matter was decisively settled by *North-West Transportation Co Ltd v Beatty*.[58] Shareholders in general meeting approved a bye-law passed by the directors that the company should purchase a steamer ship from James Beatty, one of its directors and shareholders. Beatty and two associates, who were also shareholders and directors, together held a majority of the company's shares. They voted to approve the sale. The approval could not have been obtained without their votes. Although

Behalf of Another' (2014) 130 *LQR* 608; L Smith, 'Parenthood is a Fiduciary Relationship' (2020) 70 *University of Toronto LJ* 395, 401–18.

[53] *Bristol and West Building Society v Mothew* [1998] Ch 1 (CA) 18.

[54] Eg *Aberdeen Railway* (n 21); *Erlanger v New Sombrero Phosphate Co* (1877–78) LR 3 App Cas 1218 (HL); *Re Cape Breton Co* (1885) 29 Ch D 795 (CA); *North-West Transportation Co v Beatty* (1887) 12 App Cas 589 (PC); *Burland v Earle* [1902] AC 83 (PC); *Transvaal Lands Co v New Belgium (Transvaal) Land and Development Co* [1914] 2 Ch 488 (CA); *Boardman v Phipps* [1967] 2 AC 46 (HL); *Hilton v Barker Booth and Eastwood (a firm)* [2005] UKHL 8, [2005] 1 WLR 567.

[55] Eg *Bray v Ford* [1896] AC 44 (HL) 51 (HL); *Keech v Sandford* (1726) Sel Cas King 61, 25 ER 223; *Chan v Zacharia* [1984] HCA 36, (1984) 154 CLR 178; *Regal (Hastings) Ltd v Gulliver* [1967] 2 AC 134 (HL); *Boardman* (n 54).

[56] Lim (n 45) 156; E Lim and J Lowry, 'Reconsidering the Rule on Shareholders' Exercise of Voting Powers' [2020] *Journal of Business Law* 645, 653–57.

[57] *Pender v Lushington* (1877) 6 Ch D 70 (Ch) (Jessel MR).

[58] (n 54).

the majority voted in a position of conflict of interest, the Privy Council readily concluded that the general meeting had validly exercised its powers to approve the purchase, explaining that:

> great confusion would be introduced into the affairs of joint stock companies if the circumstances of shareholders, voting in that character at general meetings, were to be examined, and their votes practically nullified, if they also stood in some fiduciary relation to the company … it was within the competency of the shareholders at the meeting of the 16th to adopt or reject it. In form and in terms they adopted it by a majority of votes, and the vote of the majority must prevail, unless the adoption was brought about by unfair or improper means.[59]

No such unfairness or impropriety was found. Rather, this was simply 'a pure question of policy' on which 'differences of opinion' were to be expected and upon which the majority ought to prevail.[60] In the Privy Council's view, 'to reject the votes of the defendant upon the question of the adoption of the bye-law would be to give effect to the views of the minority, and to disregard those of the majority'.[61] If agency analysis was applied to individual shareholders, it might lead to the conclusion that these individual shareholders are fiduciaries. This would be contrary to the law's long-standing approach.

In summary, analysing the board or general meeting as the company's agents may create unnecessary problems. Doing so requires engaging with contested definitions of agency. On most common definitions of agency, agency analysis also appears inconsistent with the incorporation process. Applying agency analysis may also create avoidable misunderstandings about the role of individual members of the board or general meeting, and may suggest inappropriate implications about the applicability of fiduciary duties. This suggests that we should not use agency law as the sole analytical framework for attributing acts in contract formation.

II. Contracting by the Board or Shareholders in General Meeting

If not agency, then what? It is argued that attribution turns on the allocation of the company's own powers to act, and thus on four questions: (i) what powers the company has, (ii) to whom they are allocated, (iii) their scope, and (iv) their proper exercise. Of these, the last is most difficult, spanning a wide range of possible flaws across the common law/equity divide. Discussion first commences with the historically important *ultra vires* rule before addressing each of the four questions.

[59] ibid 600.
[60] ibid 601.
[61] ibid 601.

A. The *Ultra Vires* Doctrine and the Company's Powers

It is impossible to commence any discussion of corporate contracting without mentioning a doctrine which was historically very significant: the *ultra vires* rule. Early companies' legislation required that companies included a statement of their objects (an objects clause) in their memorandum of association. In the leading case, *Ashbury Railway Carriage and Iron Company (Ltd) v Riche*, the House of Lords held that the company's objects set out the only purposes for which the company could be used (the *ultra vires* rule).[62] The objects thus had a positive and a negative dimension. Positively, the objects identified the ambit and extent of power given to the company by law. Negatively, it stated that 'nothing shall be done beyond that ambit, and that no attempt shall be made to use the corporate life for any other purpose than that which is so specified'.[63] As the Court of Appeal recently explained,

> The *ultra vires* doctrine … does not exist at common law. it is entirely the consequence of statutory limitations. Apart from individuals under a disability (minors and individuals lacking mental capacity), the common law imposes no limits as to the capacity of legal persons … [t]he position is different as regards companies and other bodies corporate created by or pursuant to statute. By creating or authorising the creation of a corporation for defined purposes, a statute limits the capacity of the corporation to those purposes.[64]

If the company attempted to pursue an object outside the list, it would have no capacity to do so, and in principle that act would be 'void' – a nullity.

The *ultra vires* rule was widely criticised. Infringements could be technical and inadvertent. It sometimes operated harshly, prejudicing third parties dealing with the company in good faith. The Cohen Report 1945 deprecated it, saying that it provided 'illusory protection for the shareholders and yet may be a pitfall for third parties dealing with the company', and concluding that it 'serves no positive purpose but is, on the other hand, a cause of unnecessary prolixity and vexation'.[65]

Despite statutory amendment being mooted for decades in the UK,[66] reform only occurred in 1972 when the UK became a member of the European Union and became bound to implement the EC First Company Law Directive[67] into domestic law.[68] Article 9 of the First Directive required that acts done by organs

[62] *Ashbury Railway Carriage and Iron Company (Ltd) v Riche* (1874–75) LR 7 HL 653 (HL).

[63] ibid 670 (Lord Cairns). See also 678 (Lord Chelmsford), 684 (Lord Hatherley). See also *In David Payne & Co Ltd* [1904] 2 Ch 608 (Ch) 612 (Buckley J).

[64] *Ukraine v Law Debenture Trust Corpn plc* [2018] EWCA Civ 2026, [2019] 2 WLR 655 [67], [70].

[65] *Report of the Committee on Company Law Amendment (Cohen Report 1945)* (Cmd 6659) para 12.

[66] Eg Cohen Report 1945, ibid, and the *Report of the Company Law Committee (Jenkins Report 1962)* (Cmd 1749).

[67] Directive 68/151/EEC (9 March 1968), Art 9.

[68] European Communities Act 1972, s 9.

of the company bind the company even if those acts were outside the objects of the company, though Member States could provide that the company would not be bound if the third party knew or could not have been unaware that the act was outside those objects. Its first implementation in section 9 of the European Communities Act 1972 was problematic,[69] requiring successive reforms, with the latest implementation found in the Companies Act 2006.

Today, the 2006 Act no longer requires companies to set out their objects. A company's objects are unrestricted unless its articles specifically restrict its objects.[70] Even if a company restricts its objects, '[t]he validity of an act done by a company shall not be called into question on the ground of lack of capacity by reason of anything in the company's memorandum'.[71] The *ultra vires* doctrine has thus effectively been largely abolished for non-charitable companies incorporated by registration,[72] unless companies expressly limit their objects. As we will see below, *ultra vires* left significant marks on the law, and some of the problems previously hidden under its banner are only now starting to be resolved.

B. Identifying the Company's Powers to Contract

Putting *ultra vires* to one side, the first question which cases implicitly ask is: does the company have powers to do the act? In corporate contracting, we are typically asking whether the company has powers to make offers and acceptances to another, or otherwise come to agreement with a counterparty.

This requirement can be observed from cases which expressly search for whether the company had power to do the act allegedly done by it. In *Re Bonelli's Telegraph Co*,[73] the directors sold the company's telegraph business to the government. In deciding whether the company was bound, the court inquired into the company's articles to identify the powers the directors had, which must be powers the company itself had. The company's articles made clear that the directors had 'the entire power over all the affairs of the company', and 'are at liberty to buy, to lease, or sell, all or any part of the estate, assets, interests, and effects of the

[69] Amongst other problems, it left unchanged the requirement that the memorandum must contain an objects clause, did not alter the duty of the directors to act within the scope of the clause, and arguably left open the raising of *ultra vires* by a third party as a defence against the company: see JH Farrar and DG Powles, 'The Effect of Section 9 of the European Communities Act 1972 on English Company Law' (1973) 36 *MLR* 270; JC Collier and LS Sealy, 'European Communities Act 1972 – Company Law' (1972) 32 *CLJ* 1.

[70] CA 2006, s 31(1).

[71] CA 2006, s 39. This provision is identical to s 35(1) of the Companies Act 1985 (CA 1985), as amended by s 108 of the Companies Act 1989. The 2006 Act does not reproduce the rest of the amended s 35, which provided that acting outside the company's objects still had some consequences, eg members could bring proceedings to restrain a company from doing an act which would be beyond the company's objects.

[72] For charitable companies, see CA 2006, s 42.

[73] *Re Bonelli's Telegraph Co* (1871) LR 12 Eq 246 (Ch).

company'.[74] They acted within the scope of this power in selling the telegraph business.[75] Similarly, in *Rolled Steel Products (Holdings) Ltd v British Steel Corpn*, the claimant company had guaranteed the indebtedness of another company, Scottish Steel, to the latter's creditor.[76] Was the guarantee void? The Court of Appeal first answered this question by examining the company's powers. It concluded that the company was expressly empowered under its articles to 'lend and advance money or give credit to such persons, firms, or companies and on such terms as may seem expedient, and in particular to customers of and others having dealings with the company'.[77] It thus had powers to enter guarantee contracts.

A company's powers may be expressly or impliedly conferred. Examples of the former are seen above, where the company's constitution expressly provides for such powers. Alternatively they may also be implied. Powers will be implied where the implied power is 'reasonably incidental to the attainment or pursuit of the express objects of the company'.[78] Thus, in *Taunton v Royal Insurance Co*, it was held that an insurance company had implied powers to pay losses not within those they had insured against, though not expressly provided for.[79] Such powers were incidental to carrying on the company's business. The same reasoning applied in *Hampson v Price's Patent Candle Co*, where the company had implied powers to make gratuitous payments to their employees after a good year.[80] Likewise, in *Henderson v Bank of Australasia*, the company had implied powers to pay pensions to widows of ex-employees; doing so would encourage others to pursue employment with the company.[81]

The company's powers were historically bound up together with the *ultra vires* rule, though conceptually distinct. *Ultra vires* had two important implications for the company's powers. First, efforts to escape the rule led to a widespread practice where the company's powers were extensively listed in objects clauses. Although strictly unnecessary[82] and deprecated by judges,[83] it was extremely common for the company's powers to be expressly conferred. Second, the *ultra vires* rule also affected the implication of powers. As indicated above, the test focuses on whether the implied power is reasonably incidental to the attainment or pursuit of the objects. The wider the company's objects, the wider its implied powers. After the 2006 Act, unlimited objects became possible, suggesting the possibility that companies could have very expansive, perhaps even nearly unlimited, powers.

[74] ibid 256.
[75] ibid 257–58.
[76] *Rolled Steel Products (Holdings) Ltd v British Steel Corpn* [1986] Ch 246 (CA).
[77] ibid 289.
[78] *In re Horsley & Weight Ltd* [1982] Ch 442 (CA) 448.
[79] *Taunton v Royal Insurance Co* (1864) 2 H&M 135, 71 ER 413.
[80] *Hampson v Price's Patent Candle Co* (1876) 45 LJ Ch 437 (Court of Equity).
[81] *Henderson v Bank of Australasia* (1889) 40 Ch D 170 (Ch).
[82] *In re Horsley & Weight* (n 78).
[83] Eg *Cotman v Brougham* [1918] AC 514 (HL) 522–23 (Lord Wrenbury); *Rolled Steel* (n 76).

C. Allocating the Company's Powers to Contract

Once the company's powers are identified, the next inquiry is: to whom have they been allocated?

The board was once regarded as the agent of the shareholders in general meeting, allowing the latter to pass resolutions to control decisions made by the former. Ever since *Automatic Self-Cleansing Filter Syndicate Co v Cunninghame*, the position has changed. It is clear that the board is not simply the agent of the shareholders in general meeting.[84] Instead, the company's constitution effects a constitutional division of the company's powers between different bodies, most commonly the board of directors and shareholders in general meeting.[85] As *Manson v Curtis*, a well-known decision of the Court of Appeals of New York, explains, these powers are *allocated* to the board and general meeting:

> In corporate bodies, the powers of the board of directors are, in a very important sense, original and undelegated. The stockholders do not confer, nor can they revoke those powers. They are derivative only in the sense of being received from the state in the act of incorporation. The directors convened as a board are the primary possessors of all the powers which the charter confers, and like private principals they may delegate to agents of their own appointment the performance of any acts which they themselves can perform. The recognition of this principle is absolutely necessary in the affairs of every corporation whose powers are vested in a board of directors.[86]

A common division, seen in the current Model Articles, is to allocate powers of management of the company's business to the board of directors, with all other powers allocated to the shareholders in general meeting,[87] subject to powers reserved for the general meeting under statute.[88] As we will see below, 'powers of management' typically include a wide range of powers to contract with customers, suppliers, financiers, and more.

But this default allocation is just that: default. Alternatives are surely possible. In *Lee v Lee's Air Farming*, Mr Lee was appointed the company's sole governing director, capable of exercising all the powers and authorities and discretions vested in the directors generally, as well as 'all the powers of the company which are not by statute required to be exercised by the company in general meeting'.[89] Another

[84] *Automatic Self-Cleansing Filter Syndicate Co v Cunninghame* [1906] 2 Ch 34 (CA).

[85] See also *Quin & Axtens v Salmon* [1909] AC 442 (HL); *John Shaw & Sons (Salford) Ltd v Shaw* [1935] 2 KB 113 (CA).

[86] *Manson v Curtis* 119 NE 559, 562 (1918).

[87] *Model Articles for Private Companies Limited by Shares*, Model Art 3; *Model Articles for Public Companies*, Model Art 3.

[88] See eg alteration of the company's articles: CA 2006, s 21; issuance of shares: CA 2006, s 549; disapplication of pre-emption rights to shares: CA 2006, ss 569–573; decisions to reduce share capital: CA 2006, s 641; decisions to wind up company voluntarily: Insolvency Act 1986, s 84.

[89] *Lee v Lee's Air Farming* [1961] AC 12 (PC) 15.

interesting variation is found in *John Shaw & Sons (Salford) Ltd v Shaw*, where the company had eight directors, of which three were 'permanent' directors and the remaining five were 'ordinary' directors.[90] The articles were amended to provide that the ordinary directors had no right to vote in respect of – nor any control over – the company's financial affairs, and 'with regard to the management of the company's business they shall have only such rights of voting and such control over the management as may from time to time be conferred upon them by the permanent directors'.[91] Finally, in *Guinness plc v Saunders*, the power to award special remuneration to directors of the company was allocated to the board,[92] replacing the default allocation to the general meeting under the default articles.[93]

If the power to enter a specific class of contracts is allocated to the board of directors or general meeting then, for it to be exercised, the board or general meeting must act collectively to successfully exercise it. Collective action procedures are generally regulated by the constitution and supplemented by the Companies Act. For instance, the Model Articles provide that board decision-making must take place by majority decision at a board meeting,[94] or alternatively by directors' written resolution for public companies.[95] Shareholder decision-making may be conducted at general meetings,[96] with voting conducted by a show of hands[97] unless a poll is demanded,[98] but may also be conducted informally.[99] Requirements as to quorum,[100] when directors are disqualified from voting,[101] or any other conditions as to notice are also provided in the Model Articles. These requirements in the Model Articles will apply subject to any contrary indication in the company's constitution.[102]

[90] (n 85).
[91] ibid 116–17.
[92] *Guinness plc v Saunders* [1990] 2 AC 663 (HL) 686.
[93] ibid.
[94] *Model Articles for Public Companies*, Model Art 7; *Model Articles for Private Companies Limited by Shares*, Model Art 7.
[95] *Model Articles for Public Companies*, Model Art 7.
[96] *Model Articles for Public Companies*, Model Art 28; *Model Articles for Private Companies Limited by Shares*, Model Art 37.
[97] *Model Articles for Public Companies*, Model Art 34; *Model Articles for Private Companies Limited by Shares*, Model Art 42.
[98] *Model Articles for Public Companies*, Model Arts 34, 36–37; *Model Articles for Private Companies Limited by Shares*, Model Arts 42 and 44.
[99] *Re Duomatic* [1969] 2 Ch 365 (Ch) 373 (Buckley J); *Parker and Cooper Ltd v Reading* [1926] Ch 975 (Ch); *Multinational Gas and Petrochemical Co v Multinational Gas and Petrochemical Services Ltd* [1983] Ch 258 (CA) 268–69 (Lawton LJ); *In re Oceanrose Investments Ltd* [2008] EWHC 3475 (Ch), [2009] Bus LR 947; *Ciban Management Corpn v Citco (BVI) Ltd* [2020] UKPC 21, [2021] AC 122.
[100] Board: *Model Articles for Private Companies Limited by Shares*, Model Art 11; *Model Articles for Public Companies*, Model Art 10. General meeting: *Model Articles for Private Companies Limited by Shares*, Model Art 38; *Model Articles for Public Companies*, Model Art 30.
[101] Board: *Model Articles for Private Companies Limited by Shares*, Model Art 14; *Model Articles for Public Companies*, Model Art 16.
[102] Eg *Quin & Axtens* (n 85).

Exceptionally, it may be possible for the board or general meeting to make an informal unanimous decision.[103] *Re Bonelli's Telegraph Co* took the first step, concluding that the board need not assemble under one roof to decide provided that 'the persons whose concurrence is necessary to give validity to the act did so concur, with full knowledge of all that they were doing, in my opinion the terms of the law are fully satisfied'.[104] Over a century later, it was possible to say: 'That directors, provided they act unanimously, can act informally appears clearly established'.[105] Indeed, unanimity can be established on the basis of even informal acquiescence by other board members.[106]

D. Scope

Like the company's other powers, to whom powers to contract have been allocated and their scope turn on construction of the company's constitution, particularly the articles. The constitution is a contract between the company and its members inter se,[107] albeit a special kind.[108] In principle, ordinary principles of construction of contractual agreements should apply,[109] subject to the caveat that courts are more hesitant to conclude that the constitution has a content substantially different from that which a reader might have reasonably understood.[110]

At the highest level of generality, the Model Articles allocate the company's 'powers of management' to the board. This would generally include extensive powers to contract, whether with suppliers, customers, financiers, or others. More specifically, the constitution may expressly allocate powers to make certain contracts, such as to pay directors remuneration,[111] to the board of directors. There is considerable flexibility: certain powers may be allocated even to a sub-set of the board, such as a remuneration committee, or as in the *Shaw* case, to 'permanent' directors.[112]

[103] *Model Articles for Private Companies Limited by Shares*, Model Arts 7–8, confirming the common law position: *Re Bonelli's* (n 73); *Charterhouse Investment Trust Ltd v Tempest Diesels Ltd* (1985) 1 BCC 99544 (Ch); *Runciman v Walker Runciman plc* [1993] BCC 223 (QB) 230; *Hunter v Senate Support Services Ltd* [2004] EWHC 1085 (Ch).

[104] *Re Bonelli's* (n 73) 258.

[105] *Runciman* (n 103) 230.

[106] *Charterhouse* (n 103).

[107] Now CA 2006, s 33, confirming eg *Hickman v Kent or Romney Marsh Sheepbreeders Association* [1915] 1 Ch 881 (Ch).

[108] *Gower's* (n 12) paras 3-18–3-32.

[109] Eg *Investors Compensation Scheme Ltd v West Bromwich Building Society* [1998] 1 WLR 896 (HL).

[110] *Scott v Frank F Scott (London) Ltd* [1940] Ch 794 (CA) (no rectification); *Bratton Seymour Service Co Ltd v Oxborough* [1992] BCLC 693 (CA) (implication of terms); *Re Coroin Ltd* [2011] EWHC 3466 (Ch), affirmed [2012] EWCA Civ 179, [2012] BCC 575.

[111] *Guinness* (n 92).

[112] (n 85) 116–17.

Likewise, restrictions may be imposed. As Browne-Wilkinson LJ noted in *Rolled Steel*, 'due regard must be paid to any express conditions attached to or limitations on powers contained in a company's memorandum'.[113] For example, in *Irvine v Union Bank of Australia*, the articles limited the directors' power to borrow, providing that such power 'should not exceed in the aggregate as an existing debt at the same time one-half of the then actually paid-up capital'.[114] In *Shaw*, the permanent directors argued that they were entitled to authorise the starting of proceedings on behalf of the company as part of their exclusive powers. Slesser LJ explained that 'It therefore becomes necessary to examine in some detail what powers are so given to the permanent directors to the exclusion of the ordinary directors'.[115] Turning on construction, these problems may not have a clear answer. While Slesser LJ concluded that the permanent directors had no power to authorise the starting of proceedings without the ordinary directors, Greer LJ reached the opposite conclusion.[116]

Where the board or general meeting act outside the scope of their powers to contract, they fail to successfully exercise the power. No contract is formed by that act alone,[117] leaving aside ratification[118] and other doctrines.[119]

E. Proper Exercise

Perhaps the most difficult questions concern the proper exercise of the power. A preliminary problem is classification: is it part of scope, or a distinct inquiry? Arguments and authority for both positions can be found.[120] Space precludes detailed consideration of this question; no position is taken on it. For present purposes, the two flaws are kept analytically separate for clarity.

Even with classificatory problems left aside, others exist. One is complexity. Many flaws might exist: the power-holder might be acting dishonestly, against what they believed to be the company's interests, for an improper purpose, or may have acted carelessly or in conflict of interest.[121] Distinct flaws have not always been kept apart. Some have been unhelpfully referred to as *ultra vires* ones, a practice

[113] (n 76) 295.
[114] *Irvine v Union Bank of Australia* (1877) 2 App Cas 366 (PC) 372.
[115] (n 85) 139.
[116] ibid 132–33 (Greer LJ).
[117] *Irvine* (n 114).
[118] ibid 373–79 (no ratification).
[119] See Section IV below.
[120] Part of scope: P Sales, 'Use of Powers for Proper Purposes in Private Law' (2020) 136 *LQR* 384, 394; but see against: *Howard Smith v Ampol Petroleum* [1974] AC 821 (PC) 834; *Hillsdown Holdings v Pensions Ombudsman* [1996] Pens LR 427 (QB) [62]; *Pitt v Holt* [2013] UKSC 26, [2013] 2 AC 108 [60] (Lord Walker); *Eclairs Group Ltd v JKX Oil & Gas plc* [2015] UKSC 71, [2015] Bus LR 1395, [30] (Lord Sumption); RC Nolan, 'Controlling Fiduciary Power' (2009) 68 *CLJ* 293, 299.
[121] See eg J Payne and D Prentice, 'Company Contracts and Vitiating Factors Developments in the Law on Directors' Authority' [2005] *LMCLQ* 447.

that ought not be continued.[122] Another exacerbating factor is the common law/equity jurisdictional divide. While some flaws were recognised at common law, others were recognised only in equity, complicating efforts to provide a unified analysis.

These flaws can be divided into three categories. In the first two, the lack of good faith and improper purposes, the flaw means the power is not successfully exercised. The third category comprises cases where, despite some flaw in the exercise of the power, the power was successfully exercised; the flaw constitutes only a breach of duty.

i. Lack of Good Faith

First, like the company's other legal powers, its powers to contract can only be successfully exercised where exercised in good faith. As Lindley MR (as he was then) explained in *Allen v Gold Reefs of West Africa*, good faith, or bona fides, is a condition precedent to the successful exercise of the power:

> the power conferred by [the Companies Act on the company to alter its articles] must, like all other powers, be exercised subject to those general principles of law and equity which are applicable to all powers conferred on majorities and enabling them to bind minorities. It must be exercised, not only in the manner required by law, but also bona fide for the benefit of the company as a whole, and it must not be exceeded. These conditions are always implied, and are seldom, if ever, expressed.[123]

Several years later he was able to say, now as Lord Lindley, that:

> I take it to be clear that there is a condition implied in this as well as in other instruments which create powers, namely, that the powers shall be used bona fide for the purposes for which they are conferred.[124]

These cases concerned the amendment of existing contracts rather than the formation of fresh ones, but the point is general.

While 'good faith' may have different meanings in different contexts, here it seems to require that the power must be exercised in furtherance of what the power-holder honestly believes to be the company's interests.[125] Evidence from

[122] *Charterbridge Corpn v Lloyds Bank Ltd* [1970] Ch 26 (Ch) describing as *ultra vires* a guarantee made by a director to benefit himself rather than the company, though the company's articles gave it the power to 'secure or guarantee by mortgage'.

[123] *Allen v Gold Reefs of West Africa* [1900] 1 Ch 656 (CA) 671.

[124] *General Assembly of Free Church of Scotland v Lord Overtoun* [1904] AC 505 (HL) 695.

[125] See eg R Nolan and M Conaglen, 'Good Faith: What Does it Mean for Fiduciaries and What Does It Tell Us About Them?' in E Bant and M Harding (eds), *Exploring Private Law* (Cambridge, Cambridge University Press, 2010) 331. See similarly JE Penner, 'Trustees and Agents Behaving Badly: When and How is "Bad Faith" Relevant?' in P Miller and M Harding (eds), *Fiduciaries and Trust: Ethics, Politics, Economics, and Law* (Cambridge, Cambridge University Press, 2020): bad faith involves breaching the trust, confidence, or faith one person has reposed in another.

different sources can be found. Where the general meeting seeks to exercise powers to amend the company's articles, numerous cases, including *Allen v Gold Reefs*, use the test that the majority must be acting in what they believe to be the best interests of the company.[126] Similarly, where the board exercises powers to allot shares, it was stressed that the powers of the board have a 'built-in' 'implied' limitation[127] that they are 'to be exercised bona fide in the best interests of the company'.[128] The cases emphasise that the 'ultimate question must always be whether in truth the issue was made honestly in the interests of the company',[129] with the onus being on he who challenges the action to establish otherwise.[130] Good faith and acting 'honestly in the interests of the company' are often used interchangeably in this context, suggesting that they bear the same meaning. As Dixon J explained in *Peter's American Delicacy Co Ltd v Heath*, '[t]he reference to "benefit as a whole" [in 'bona fide for the benefit of the company as a whole'] is but a very general expression negativing purposes foreign to the company's operations, affairs and organizations'.[131]

Examples where the board or general meeting lacked good faith are not easy to find, and most occur outside the contractual realm. In *Re Halt Garage (1964) Ltd*,[132] power to award remuneration was purportedly exercised in favour of a director even after she fell ill and took no part in the company's business. They were described as *ultra vires* and hence could be recovered by the company. A better analysis would be that the payments were recoverable by the company because the company had not successfully exercised its powers to validly award remuneration to the director. Similarly, the law on theft in criminal law emphasises that shareholders cannot validly consent to the appropriation of the company's assets for their own purposes.[133] In *Prest v Petrodel Resources Ltd*, Lord Sumption confirmed this, saying that 'not even [the sole shareholder or whole body of shareholders] can validly consent to their own appropriation of the company's assets for purposes which are not the company's'.[134] This must be because such acts could not plausibly be for the benefit of the company and were not in good faith.

[126] *Brown v British Abrasive Wheel Co* [1919] 1 Ch 290 (Ch) 296; *Sidebottom v Kershaw, Leese and Co Ltd* [1920] 1 Ch 154 (CA) 165; *Dafen Tinplate Co v Llanelly Steel Co* [1920] 2 Ch 124 (Ch); *Shuttleworth v Cox Brothers Ltd* [1927] 2 KB 9 (CA); *Harlowe's Nominees Pty Ltd v Woodside (Lakes Entrance) Oil Co NL* [1968] HCA 37, (1968) 121 CLR 483, 493. This test is not easy to apply when dealing with intra-company constituencies, see eg *Greenhalgh v Ardene Cinemas* [1951] Ch 286 (CA); *Mills v Mills* [1938] HCA 4, 60 CLR 150, 164; *Gambotto v WCP Ltd* [1995] HCA 12, 182 CLR 432.

[127] *Bamford v Bamford* [1970] Ch 212 (Ch) 235.

[128] *Bamford* ibid; *Australian Metropolitan Life Assurance Co Ltd v Ure* [1923] HCA 29, (1923) 33 CLR 199; *Richard Brady Franks Ltd v Price* [1937] HCA 42, (1937) 58 CLR 112; *Ngurli Ltd v McCann* [1953] HCA 39, (1953) 90 CLR 425; *Harlowe's Nominees* (n 126).

[129] *Harlowe's Nominees* (n 126) 494.

[130] *Richard Brady Franks* (n 128); *Hindle v John Cotton Ltd* (1919) 56 SLR 625 (HL).

[131] *Peter's American Delicacy Co Ltd v Heath* [1939] HCA 27, (1939) 61 CLR 457, 512.

[132] *Re Halt Garage (1964) Ltd* [1982] 3 All ER 1016 (Ch).

[133] *Re Attorney-General's Reference (No 2 of 1982)* [1984] QB 624 (CA); *R v Gomez* [1993] AC 442 (HL) 496–97.

[134] *Prest v Petrodel Resources Ltd* [2013] UKSC 34, [2013] 3 WLR 1 [41], citing *Belmont Finance Corpn Ltd v Williams Furniture Ltd* [1979] Ch 250 (CA).

As a condition precedent to the power's successful exercise, lack of good faith means the power has not been successfully exercised. For powers to contract, this indicates that no contract has been formed.[135] Although sometimes described as 'void', legal consequences may still follow from the purported exercise.[136] For example, legal title may pass and restitutionary claims may also lie against the recipient, though the precise analysis of and justification for recovery is controversial.[137]

ii. Improper Purposes

The second requirement is that powers must be exercised for proper purposes.[138] Judicial authority can be found in the passages earlier on the lack of good faith and in the old equitable doctrine of 'fraud on a power'.[139]

This requirement is conceptually distinct from good faith. The leading case of *Howard Smith v Ampol Petroleum* confirms that the board may be exercising their powers for improper purposes even though they are acting in what they honestly believe to be the interests of the company.[140] As *JKX v Eclairs Group* also explained while discussing *Hogg v Cramphorn*,[141] '[t]he company's interest was an additional and not an alternative test for the propriety of a board resolution'.[142] As *Hutton v West Cork Railway Co* recognised,

> Bona *fides* cannot be the sole test, otherwise you might have a lunatic conducting the affairs of the company, and paying away its money with both hands in a manner perfectly *bonâ fide* yet perfectly irrational.[143]

While the requirement is easy to state, it is much less easy to identify what purposes are proper.[144] It is generally accepted that the starting point is the source of the company's powers, whether the articles of association,[145] or statute.[146] From there, three principles can be identified.

[135] Subject to doctrines later, see Section V.

[136] For discussion of similar points in pension trusts, see C Mitchell and J Hudson, 'Legal Consequences of the Flawed Exercise of Pension Scheme Powers' in S Agnew et al (eds), *Pensions: Law, Policy and Practice* (Oxford, Hart Publishing, 2020).

[137] Some argue that recovery is based on 'unjust enrichment', but even then, different reasons for restitution have been suggested. See eg A Burrows, *The Law of Restitution* (Oxford, Oxford University Press, 2011) (ignorance); R Chambers and J Penner, 'Ignorance' in S Degeling and J Edelman (eds), *Unjust Enrichment in Commercial Law* (Sydney, Lawbook Co, 2005) ('want of authority'); J Edelman and E Bant, *Unjust Enrichment*, 2nd edn (Oxford, Hart Publishing, 2012) (policy-motivated reasons).

[138] For directors, confirmed now by CA 2006, s 171(a).

[139] Eg *Lane v Page* (1754) Amb 233, 27 ER 155 (Ch); *Aleyn v Belchier* (1758) 1 Eden 132 28 ER 634 (Ch); *Duke of Portland v Topham* (1864) XI HL Cas 32, 11 ER 1242 (HL); *Vatcher v Paull* [1915] AC 372 (HL). Equating it with proper purposes, see *JKX* (n 120) [15] (Lord Sumption).

[140] *Howard Smith* (n 120) 834.

[141] *Hogg v Cramphorn* [1967] Ch 254 (Ch).

[142] *JKX* (n 120) [16].

[143] *Hutton v West Cork Railway Co* (1883) 23 Ch D 654 (CA) 671 (Bowen LJ).

[144] Eg *Gower's* (n 12) para 16-27.

[145] *Howard Smith* (n 120) 835, 837.

[146] *JKX* (n 120) [31].

First, the exercise of a power will be improper if done to alter the constitutional division of powers between the board and shareholders in general meeting.[147] The leading case is *Howard Smith*, where the board exercised powers to allot new shares to prevent a takeover. This involved contracting: the allotment of new shares bound the new shareholders to the constitutional contract with the company and other shareholders.[148] As the Privy Council explained, the constitution divides powers between the board and general meeting. It would therefore be improper for the board to circumvent this division by allotting shares to alter the composition of the general meeting.[149] Entering a poison-pill agreement to prevent a takeover bid would be similarly objectionable.[150] Entering an agreement which obliged the company to allot shares was also improper where the contract was made to avoid a takeover bid.[151]

It is also improper for the board to exercise powers for the purpose of affecting the general meeting's decision-making. In *JKX*, the board issued notices restricting certain shareholders from exercising voting rights. This was improper as the notices were issued to prevent those shareholders from affecting the outcome of a forthcoming general meeting.[152] Likewise, boards act improperly where, to affect the general meeting's decision-making, they fail to give notice to hostile shareholders,[153] fix the general meeting for a time when they know hostile shareholders are unable to attend,[154] or make calls to disqualify hostile shareholders at a general meeting.[155]

Second, in Australia, though not in England, shareholders exercise their powers improperly where they alter articles to allow the majority shareholder to expropriate the minority's shares.[156] Shares are property, so their expropriation could only be justified in 'exceptional circumstances'.[157] While English courts accept that amendment of the company's articles is subject to implied limitations, they generally seem more hesitant to conclude that the power to amend was improperly exercised as long as it was exercised for the benefit of the company as a whole.[158] But doubts might rightly be expressed about that test.[159] Some

[147] Where there is less of a strict separation between board and general meeting, as with private companies, then this principle applies less strongly. See eg *Smith v Fawcett* [1942] Ch 304 (CA).
[148] CA 2006, s 33.
[149] *Howard Smith* (n 120) 837.
[150] The facts of *Criterion Properties plc v Stratford UK Properties LLC* [2004] UKHL 28, [2004] 1 WLR 1846 (refusing summary judgment and ordering the matter to trial).
[151] *Teck Corpn Ltd v Millar* (1972) 33 DLR (3d) 288 (BCSC).
[152] *JKX* (n 120) [41].
[153] *Re OS3 Distribution Ltd* [2017] EWHC 2621 (Ch), [2019] 1 BCLC 736.
[154] *Cannon v Trask* (1875) LR 20 Eq 669 (Ch).
[155] *Anglo-Universal Bank v Baragnon* (1881) 45 LT 362 (CA), cited in *JKX* (n 120) [16].
[156] *Gambotto* (n 126).
[157] ibid [28].
[158] Eg *Allen v Gold Reefs* (n 123); *Shuttleworth v Cox Brothers and Co (Maidenhead) Ltd* [1927] 2 KB 9 (CA); *Greenhalgh v Ardene* (n 126); *Rights & Issues Investment Trust Ltd v Style Shoes Ltd* [1965] Ch 250 (Ch).
[159] *Citco Banking Corpn NV v Pusser's Ltd* [2007] UKPC 13, [2007] BCC 205.

of these amendments may only be 'for the purpose of regulating the rights of shareholders in matters in which the company as a corporate entity has no interest, such as the distribution of dividends or capital or the power to dispose of shares'.[160] It was rightly pointed out by Dixon J in *Peter's American Delicacy* that:

> To say that the shareholders forming the majority must consider the advantage of the company as a whole in relation to such a question seems inappropriate, if not meaningless, and at all events starts an impossible inquiry. The 'company as a whole' is a corporate entity consisting of all the shareholders.[161]

Similarly, in *Mills v Mills*, Latham CJ said that:

> The question which arises is sometimes not a question of the interest of the company at all, but a question of what is fair as between different classes of shareholders. Where such a case arises some other test than that of the 'interests of the company' must be applied.[162]

Third, for other powers, the proper purpose is likely to be what the power-holder believes to be the company's interests. As *Australian Metropolitan Life Assurance* explains, the 'power is entrusted to them for the benefit and protection of the Company and should only be exercised for those purposes'.[163] Thus, gratuitous payments were upheld where made for the company's business, whether to encourage prospective employees,[164] support research relevant to the company's activities,[165] or secure future profits.[166] But they were not where remuneration was paid to a director who rendered no services,[167] or where there were outright attempts by shareholders to transfer themselves the company's assets directly[168] or indirectly.[169] This reasoning may also explain why certain wrongs are said to be 'un-ratifiable' by the general meeting:[170] the defaulting directors and shareholders would be acting for improper purposes if they ratified wrongs they did to the company, effectively expropriating the company's assets.[171]

Acting for proper purposes generally is a condition precedent to the power's successful exercise, whether in contracting or elsewhere.[172] Imminent exercises

[160] ibid [18].
[161] (n 131) 512.
[162] (n 126) 164.
[163] (n 128) 206.
[164] n 82. See also n 81.
[165] *Evans v Brunner Mond & Co Ltd* [1921] 1 Ch 359 (Ch).
[166] *Taunton* (n 79) 138.
[167] *Re Halt Garage* (n 132).
[168] *Menier v Hooper's Telegraph Works* (1874) LR 9 Ch App 350 (CA); *Re Attorney-General's Reference (No 2 of 1982)* (n 133); *R v Gomez* (n 133) 496–97.
[169] Eg *Belmont Finance* (n 134).
[170] Contrast *Daniels v Daniels* [1978] Ch 406 (Ch) and *Pavlides v Jensen* [1956] Ch 565 (Ch).
[171] Eg *Cook v Deeks* [1916] 1 AC 554 (PC); *Daniels* ibid.
[172] *Allen v Gold Reefs* (n 123) 671; *General Assembly* (n 124) 695, but note CA 2006, s 171 ('Duty to act within powers'). One test for whether a claim is a breach of duty is to consider whether that claim generates secondary rights to damages: J Edelman, 'Equitable Torts' (2002) 10 *Torts Law Journal* 64, but there is little evidence that proper purposes or fraud on a power ever do.

of powers for improper purposes can be restrained by injunction.[173] If, however, attempts to exercise the power have already occurred then – in principle– purported exercises are a nullity: they do not bring about the change in legal relations intended,[174] subject to one historical jurisdictional kink. Proper purposes developed from the equitable doctrine of fraud on a power[175] but, historically, equity could not impose conditions precedent to the successful exercise of statutory powers or powers arising from title to property.[176] It thus appears that in the latter cases, the exercise of the power is valid, but can be set aside, subject to laches and bars to rescission.[177] But this kink might be criticised.[178]

iii. Breaches of Duty

Other flaws in exercising powers may constitute only breaches of duty. Consider the failure to exercise reasonable care and skill,[179] a breach of duty. The standard remedy is compensation for loss,[180] but the power's exercise remains unaffected.

More complicated are conflicts of interest[181] and receiving unauthorised profits.[182] Once, these flaws might have been regarded as going to a lack of power,[183] but today they are typically described as fiduciary duties, breach of which gives rise to various remedies, including accounts of profits,[184] compensation for loss,[185] and constructive trusts.[186] But the cases indicate that the power has been successfully exercised. Where the board contracts on behalf of the company with one of its directors in a conflict of interest, the remedy is not that the contract is a nullity, but rather that the company can set aside the contract[187] subject to bars to rescission, amongst other remedies.

[173] *Ashburton Oil NL v Alpha Minerals NL* [1971] HCA 5, (1971) 123 CLR 614.

[174] *Cloutte v Storey* [1911] 1 Ch 18 (Ch) 30–32; J Hudson, 'One Thicket in Fraud on a Power' (2019) 39 *OJLS* 577.

[175] Eg *JKX* (n 120) [15].

[176] *Cloutte* (n 174) 30–32; Hudson (n 174).

[177] *Cloutte* (n 175) 30–32.

[178] *Abacus Trust Co (Isle of Man) v Barr* [2003] Ch 409 (Ch) [31] (Lightman J); *Pitt* (n 120) [62]. For one reform suggestion, see M Ashdown, *Trustee Decision-Making: The Rule in Re Hastings Bass* (Oxford, Oxford University Press, 2015) Ch 9.

[179] At common law: *Re City Equitable Fire Insurance Co* [1925] Ch 407 (CA); *Norman v Theodore Goddard* [1991] BCLC 1027 (Ch); *Re D'Jan of London Ltd* [1994] 1 BCLC 561 (Ch); now see CA 2006, s 174.

[180] *Gower's* (n 12) para 16-20. See also CA 2006, s 178(2).

[181] Eg *North-West* (n 54); *Aberdeen Railway* (n 21); *Regal (Hastings)* (n 55); at statute: CA 2006, s 175.

[182] Eg *Reading v Attorney General* [1951] AC 507 (HL). See also CA 2006, s 176.

[183] Sometimes described as 'disabilities', see eg *Tito v Waddell (No 2)* [1977] Ch 106 (Ch) 248. See similarly Smith, 'Fiduciary Relationships: Ensuring the Loyal Exercise' (n 52).

[184] Eg *Murad v Al-Saraj* [2005] EWCA Civ 959.

[185] Eg *Swindle v Harrison* [1997] PNLR 641 (CA); *Gwembe Valley Development Co Ltd v Koshy (No 3)* [2003] EWCA Civ 1048, [2004] 1 BCLC 131.

[186] *Attorney General for Hong Kong v Reid* [1994] 1 AC 324 (PC); *FHR European Ventures LLP v Cedar Capital Partners LLC* [2014] UKSC 45, [2015] AC 250.

[187] Eg *Re Cape Breton* (n 54) 808 (Bowen LJ), 811 (Fry LJ); *Transvaal Lands* (n 54) 595; *Hely-Hutchinson* (n 11) 585–86 (Lord Denning MR), 589 (Lord Wilberforce), 594 (Lord Pearson).

III. Contracting by Subordinate Agents

Not all decision-making in corporate contracting will be taken by the board or general meeting. Indeed, outside very small companies, most corporate contracting is likely to be conducted by more junior individuals in the corporate hierarchy. As we have already seen, agency analysis is widely used here to analyse contracting by subordinate agents. Although using slightly different language, agency analysis mirrors perfectly the idea of delegation and exercise of the company's powers.

A. The Company's Powers

The paradigmatic way in which a principal may be bound by its agents' acts is through the doctrine of 'actual authority', where the principal confers authority on the agent to act on his behalf.[188]

Although agency law typically uses the language of 'authority', it is widely acknowledged that 'authority' takes the form of a legal power.[189] It has recently been argued that the core idea of agency, focusing on actual authority, is best understood as involving a 'proxy power': a power in the agent to exercise the principal's legal powers.[190] This analysis helps explain the animating idea behind agency: through the agent, the principal can 'expand his legal personality in space'.[191] In the words of the Latin maxim, *qui facit per alium, facit per se* – he who acts through another, acts himself.[192] The principal's own powers are exercised through the agent. Thus, the principal acts personally, albeit through the body of another.

A pre-requisite for the agent to act for the principal is thus that the principal himself possesses the powers which he is seeking to confer on the agent. Where the principal lacks those powers, the agent cannot exercise them for him.[193] The orthodox analysis of actual authority thus presupposes that the company has the powers sought to be delegated. It is an implicit requirement.

B. Delegation of Powers: Actual Authority

The conferral of authority is a 'unilateral juristic act'[194] by the principal on the agent. The principal confers authority, a power, to the agent for the latter to act on

[188] *Freeman* (n 3) 502–503.
[189] Eg *Bowstead & Reynolds* (n 5) para 1-001; Seavey (n 27) 860–61; Dowrick (n 27) 37–38.
[190] Leow (n 27).
[191] PH Winfield, *Principles of Contract*, 13th edn (London, Stevens & Sons, 1950) 45; Leow (n 27) 114.
[192] Leow (n 27) 108–109.
[193] Leow (n 27) 110–11.
[194] JL Montrose, 'The Basis of the Power of an Agent in Cases of Actual and Apparent Authority' (1938) 16 *Can Bar Review* 757, 769–70; W Müller-Freienfels, 'Legal Relations in the Law of Agency: Power of Agency and Commercial Certainty' (1964) 13 *Am J Comp L* 193, 203.

his behalf. Another way of describing this is as delegation: the principal delegates powers to the agent.

As Diplock LJ explained in *Freeman*, actual authority applies equally to corporate principals, subject to the qualifications that a company's capacity may be limited by its constitution and that a corporation cannot do any act except through a human individual.[195] Thus, a corporate principal must confer 'actual authority' through persons themselves with the actual authority (ie power) to do so. This then leads to the question: who will have the actual authority to confer actual authority? Answering this requires us to go further up the corporate hierarchy. This iterative process ultimately ends at those allocated powers to do so under the constitution.[196]

Looking at this process from the other direction, those allocated the company's powers, such as the board, may delegate those powers to subordinate agents, sometimes through successive rounds of delegation, giving the latter 'actual authority'. As the 'proxy power' analysis explains, these subordinate agents have powers to exercise the principal's own powers. When delegates exercise those powers, they exercise the company's own powers. They act as the company. The company thereby acts personally. The same phenomenon as with the exercise of *allocated* powers is at work, albeit at one or more removes. This analysis holds through successive rounds of delegation.

At this juncture, we might briefly contrast actual authority with 'apparent' or 'ostensible' authority. A fuller discussion of the latter appears at the end of the chapter. It suffices for now to say that apparent authority is created where the principal represents to a third party that the agent has authority to act on his behalf. Under English law, it is a species of estoppel, estopping the principal from denying the agent's lack of authority.[197] The agent is not involved in this relationship and may even be unaware of it. An agent acting with apparent authority does not exercise the principal's powers. As an estoppel, apparent authority's effect is asymmetrical, creating no new rights in the principal, but enabling rights to be asserted against him.[198]

C. Scope

An agent's delegated power includes both express and implied actual authority.

Express actual authority, as the name suggests, refers to authority expressly conferred on the agent. A principal may appoint shop assistants to sell goods,

[195] *Freeman* (n 3) 504.
[196] *Freeman* (n 3) 505.
[197] *Freeman* (n 3) 503; *Kelly v Fraser* (n 11) [17]; *Industrial and Commercial Bank of China Ltd v Ambani* [2019] EWHC 3436 (Comm) [82]; *East Asia* (n 11) [42], [88].
[198] *Bowstead & Reynolds* (n 5) para 8-012.

instruct them to market products to a potential customer, or task a manager to obtain a bank loan. The agent will have express actual authority to contract to sell goods to customers, make representations to potential customers, and enter into loan agreements respectively.

Additionally, an agent will also have implied actual authority to do whatever is necessary for, or ordinarily incidental to, the effective execution of his express authority.[199] The shop assistant, expressly given authority to sell goods at the shop till, will have implied actual authority to enter the shop premises. Without that implied actual authority, she cannot perform her expressly authorised tasks. If appointed to a position, then the agent will have implied authority to do acts that a person in that position would ordinarily have.[200] In *Hely-Hutchinson v Brayhead*, it was accepted that the managing director of a company has wide authority to make decisions for the company in its ordinary course of business.[201] A company secretary, though once possessing very limited authority,[202] is now 'an officer of the company with extensive duties and responsibilities',[203] with significant implied authority derived from that position.[204]

The scope of an agent's delegated power is fact specific. Evidence about how the company is run in practice will frequently be necessary.[205] This may lead to the conclusion that a deputy managing director with responsibility for the marine department and to resolve outstanding insurance claims had no authority to raise funds by financing trading by third parties, as in *Hopkins v TL Dallas Group*.[206] Similarly, on the facts, in *Armagas Ltd v Mundogas SA*, a 'chartering manager and vice-president of transportation' had no actual authority to conclude three-year ship charters.[207] Some agents may only have power to negotiate contracts, but not to approve them.[208] Yet others may have authority only to communicate the company's authorisation, but not to authorise.[209]

199 *Bowstead & Reynolds* (n 5) para 3-022.

200 *Law Debenture Trust Corpn plc v Ukraine* [2018] EWCA Civ 2026, [2019] QB 1121 [79]. Sometimes called 'usual' authority and not always clearly distinguished from apparent authority, but now see *Hely-Hutchinson* (n 11) 583.

201 *Hely-Hutchinson* (n 11) 584 (Lord Denning MR). See also *Rimpacific Navigation Inc v Daehan Shipbuilding Co Ltd* [2009] EWHC 2941 (Comm), [2010] 2 Lloyds Rep 236.

202 *George Whitechurch Ltd v Cavanagh* [1902] AC 117 (HL) 124; *Ruben v Great Fingall Consolidated* [1906] AC 439 (HL) 443 (Lord Loreburn LC), 444 (Lord Macnaghten).

203 *Panorama Developments (Guildford) Ltd v Fidelis Furnishing Fabrics Ltd* [1971] 2 QB 711 (CA) 716 (Lord Denning MR).

204 ibid 716–17 (Lord Denning MR).

205 Eg *British Bank of the Middle East v Sun Life Assurance Co of Canada (UK) Ltd* [1983] 2 Lloyds LR 9 (HL); *The Raffaella* (n 11).

206 *Hopkins v TL Dallas Group* [2004] EWHC 1379 (Ch), [2005] 1 BCLC 543 [90].

207 (n 11) 731.

208 Eg *Armagas* (n 11); *Hawksford Trustees Jersey Ltd v Stella Global UK Ltd* [2012] EWCA Civ 55; *Krakowski v Eurolynx Properties Ltd* [1995] HCA 68, 183 CLR 563.

209 *The Raffaella* (n 11); *Armagas* (n 11); *First Energy* (n 11); *Kelly v Fraser* (n 11).

D. Good Faith and Proper Purposes

Like the board or general meeting, individual agents must exercise their powers in good faith and for proper purposes. But while the two requirements are distinct for the board and general meeting, the same test is used for both in the case of subordinate agents.

i. Good Faith and Proper Purposes

In the context of subordinate agents, good faith and proper purposes both seem to come down to the same thing: the agent must act honestly and in what he believes to be the best interests of the principal. The leading case is *Hopkins v TL Dallas Group*, where Lightman J explained that:

> The grant of actual authority to an agent will not normally include authority to act for the agent's benefit rather than that of his principal and therefore, without agreement, the scope of actual authority will not include this. The grant of actual authority should be implied as being subject to a condition that it is to be exercised honestly and on behalf of the principal: *Lysaght Bros & Co Ltd v. Falk* (1905) 2 CLR 421.[210]

Hopkins has since been repeatedly endorsed.[211] Similar statements pre-date it.[212] Consistently with the cases discussed earlier, the powers delegated to the agent are subject to a condition precedent that they are to be exercised honestly and on behalf of the principal. As Watts points out,

> This idea does in practice rest on an implication, since it is not in the nature of human relations for one proposing to employ the services of another to spell out that the purpose of the conferral of powers is that they should be exercised for the benefit of the former. But that purpose goes without saying.[213]

Some illustrations can be provided. If a deputy managing director of an insurance company gives onerous undertakings on the company's behalf to make substantial payments, where these payments benefited only either or both the deputy managing director and a third party, the implied condition is not satisfied.[214] Similarly,

[210] (n 206).

[211] *Lexi Holdings (in administration) v Pannone & Partners* [2009] EWHC 2590 (Ch) [75]; *Credit Agricole Corporate and Investment Bank v Ahmad* [2010] EWHC 3968 (QB) [33], [35]; *Re Capitol Films Ltd (in administration)* [2010] EWHC 2240 (Ch) [54]; *GHLM Trading Ltd v Maroo* [2012] EWHC 61 (Ch) [171]; *Relfo Ltd (in liquidation) v Varsani* [2012] EWHC 2168 (Ch) [86]; *Newcastle International Airport Ltd v Eversheds LLP* [2012] EWHC 2648 (Ch) [91].

[212] *Lysaght Bros & Co Ltd v Falk* [1905] HCA 7, (1905) 2 CLR 421, 439; *Heinl v Jyske Bank (Gibraltar) Ltd* [1999] 1 Lloyd's Rep Bank 511 (CA).

[213] P Watts, 'Actual Authority: The Requirement for an Agent Honestly to Believe that an Exercise of Power is in the Principal's Interests' [2017] *Journal of Business Law* 269; *cf* S Worthington, 'Corporate Attribution and Agency: Back to Basics' (2017) 133 *LQR* 118, 132–39.

[214] *Hopkins* (n 206) [87]–[91].

in *Akai Holdings*, Akai's executive chairman and chief executive officer, Ting, entered agreements with the Thai Farmers Bank on behalf of Akai under which the bank lent US$30m to a third party, Singer, in exchange for onerous obligations from Akai to repay the loan and security over shares owned by Akai. Ting was also chairman and director of Singer. It was accepted that Ting lacked actual authority to enter those agreements on behalf of Akai because he had been acting dishonestly.[215]

But at one time this rule was not so clear. Two important cases seemed to stand against it. The first is *Hambro v Burnand*.[216] Burnand, a member of Lloyd's, was given written authority to act for the five defendants in underwriting insurance policies. Acting under that authority, he underwrote guarantee policies in the defendants' names, which were to be used as security for loans advanced to a company, Henry Gaze & Sons, of which Burnand was a director. It was argued that the defendants were not bound by the policies as Burnand was acting for his own interests and thus lacked authority. This view was rejected by the Court of Appeal. The leading judgment of Collins MR emphasised that:

> It would be impossible, as it seems to be, for the business of a mercantile community to be carried on, if a person dealing with an agent was bound to go behind the authority of the agent in each case, and inquire whether his motives did or did not involve the application of the authority for his own private purposes'.[217]

This principle was later adopted in the second case, a decision of Millett J in *Macmillan Inc v Bishopsgate Investment Trust plc*.[218] One of the cases following the Maxwell group's collapse, it concerned shares transferred by Mr Maxwell, the head of the group, from Macmillan. Maxwell had formal authority from a board resolution to transfer those shares but did so to enable money to be raised for his own purposes and against the interests of Macmillan.[219] Millett J concluded that:

> under the law of Delaware Mr. Maxwell's signature of the share transfers was duly authorised notwithstanding his fraudulent purpose. Like English law, Delaware law recognises the distinction between want of authority and abuse of authority .... In particular, I am satisfied that under Delaware law as under English law: 'an act of an agent within the scope of his actual or apparent authority does not cease to bind his principal merely because the agent was acting fraudulently and in furtherance of his own interests:' see *Bowstead on Agency*, 15th ed. (1985), p. 279, art. 74.[220]

Relying on these cases, Sarah Worthington has argued that cases where the agent acts dishonestly or against what he believes to be the principal's interests involve

[215] *Akai* (n 11) [10], and before the Hong Kong Court of Appeal, see [2009] HKCA 286, [2010] 3 HKC 153, [43]–[50].
[216] *Hambro v Burnand* [1904] 2 KB 10 (CA).
[217] ibid 20, citing in support *Bryant, Powis & Bryant, Ld v Quebec Bank* [1893] AC 170 (PC); *President of the Westfield Bank v Cornen* 37 NYR (10 Tiff) 322.
[218] *Macmillan Inc v Bishopsgate Investment Trust plc* [1995] 1 WLR 978 (Ch).
[219] ibid 984.
[220] ibid 984.

only the abuse of authority, not the want of authority.[221] Amongst other points, Worthington argues that *Hopkins* 'muddles two quite different contexts' in applying rules that operate as between principal and agent to that between principal and third parties, cannot explain cases involving breaches of fiduciary duty, is difficult to apply, and makes an analysis of apparent authority unworkable.[222]

These points have been refuted by Peter Watts, who accepts that there was some potentially misleading wording in *Bowstead & Reynolds* which could be taken to suggest that the agent only had actual authority when his acts actually benefited the principal.[223] Once clarified, most objections concerning its application and problems created fall away.[224] Objections concerning the breach of fiduciary duty cases are persuasively countered by Watts, who points out that these cases do not involve the agent acting against the principal's interests.[225] Finally, as Watts points out, it is well-established that actual authority turns on the principal-agent relationship, while it is apparent authority which deals with the third party.[226] His view thus involves no muddling of contexts, while, conversely, Worthington's does.

There is no conceptual difficulty with an implied condition precedent to the exercise of actual authority. Such condition requires justification, but that justification is easily found in the idea that 'it is part of the logic of acting for another person that there is only one right way to do it: you must do it in the way that you think is best for that other person'.[227] The idea of good faith and proper purposes is built into the relationship itself. Justifying the lack of such requirements, it is suggested, is more difficult than justifying their existence.

What then of *Hambro* and *Macmillan*? As to *Macmillan*, it might be put to one side, since Millett J's comments were only *dicta*: even if Maxwell lacked actual authority, he certainly had apparent authority to sign the share transfer forms. *Hambro* too might be explained on a different basis: it could be argued that the court considered that as a member of Lloyd's, Burnand had all the actual and apparent authority to do acts a member of Lloyd's ordinarily would. It was an express finding by the trial judge that underwriting guarantee policies was part of the ordinary business of a Lloyd's underwriter.[228] As apparent authority reasoning was less developed then and its estoppel basis was only incipient,[229] perhaps less weight should be given to the finding that there was no holding out by the

[221] Worthington (n 213) 133–39.
[222] Worthington (n 213) 135–39.
[223] Watts (n 213). Now see *Bowstead & Reynolds* (n 5) paras 3-011–3-012.
[224] Watts (n 213) 273–74.
[225] Watts (n 213) 279–80.
[226] Watts (n 213) 272–74.
[227] Smith, 'Fiduciary Relationships: Ensuring the Loyal Exercise' (n 52) 613.
[228] *Hambro* (n 216) 19.
[229] I Brown, 'The Significance of General and Special Authority in the Development of the Agent's External Authority in English Law' [2004] *Journal of Business Law* 391.

principals to the claimant.[230] Alternative solutions for addressing *Hambro* might also exist.[231]

ii. Breaches of Other Duties

Does any breach of a subordinate agent's duties mean that he lacks actual authority, ie has no power to act for the principal?[232] Sometimes this suggestion is made, typically relying on the House of Lords' decision in *Criterion Properties plc v Stratford UK Properties*.[233] But *Criterion* provides little support for that view.

In that case Criterion and Stratford formed a limited partnership. Fearing a takeover of Criterion, Criterion's directors signed a 'poison pill' agreement with Oaktree, giving it the right to have its interest in the partnership bought out on favourable terms if Criterion was taken over. After the takeover did not occur, Criterion sought to rescind the agreement. An application for summary judgment was appealed to the House of Lords. The lower courts applied principles of knowing receipt,[234] seeing the central issue as whether it would be unconscionable for Oaktree to hold Criterion to the agreement.[235] The House of Lords unanimously held that this was the wrong approach.[236] Whether Oaktree could hold Criterion to the agreement turned on whether Criterion's directors had actual or apparent authority to enter into the agreement.[237] If either were present, then the agreement was valid, and benefits transferred under it could not be recovered, subject to rescission of the contract. But if the directors had neither actual nor apparent authority, then the benefits transferred under the agreement could be recovered.[238] But it was concluded that the authority issue could not be resolved by the House of Lords, as the issue was not addressed before the lower courts, and so it was left to be resolved at trial or further interlocutory applications.[239] *Criterion* thus does not support the view that an agent lacks authority where acting in breach of any duty.

Instead, the cases paint a unified picture: mere breaches of duties by an agent do not affect the agent's power to act for the principal. Cases which might suggest the contrary are ones where the agent was not acting in good faith and for proper

[230] *Hambro v Burnand* [1903] 2 KB 399 (KB) 413–14.

[231] See eg P Watts, 'Deeds and the Principals of Authority in Agency Law' (2002) 2 *OUCLJ* 93, 96–98. See also Watts (n 213) 278–79 ('much to be said for simply cauterising *Hambro* from our law').

[232] Eg J Payne, 'Company Contracts and Directors' Authority' [2010] *LMCLQ* 187, 190; but see also J Payne and D Prentice, 'Company Contracts and Vitiating Factors: Developments in the Law on Directors' Authority' [2005] *LMCLQ* 447, 447–55.

[233] (n 150).

[234] Relying on *Bank of Credit and Commerce International (Overseas) Ltd v Akindele* [2001] Ch 437 (CA).

[235] *Criterion Properties plc v Stratford UK Properties* [2002] EWHC 496 (Ch), [2002] 2 BCLC 151; [2002] EWCA Civ 1783, [2003] 1 WLR 2108.

[236] *Criterion* (n 150) [3]–[4] (Lord Nicholls); [21]–[27] (Lord Scott).

[237] *Criterion* (n 150) [3]–[4] (Lord Nicholls); [21]–[27] (Lord Scott).

[238] *Criterion* (n 150) [4] (Lord Nicholls).

[239] *Criterion* (n 150) [32] (Lord Scott).

purposes, for instance where the agent misappropriates the company's property for his own benefit.[240] If the agent enters self-dealing contracts, thus acting in breach of a duty to avoid conflicts of interest, the contract is voidable: valid, but can be set aside subject to bars to rescission.[241] Similarly, if the agent receives bribes from a third party to enter into a contract, again the contract is at most only voidable.[242] It has been successfully entered into but may be rescinded. An agent's breach of the duty of care or fiduciary duties may give the principal a claim for compensation for losses.[243] Likewise, agents may be made to account for profits acquired in breach of fiduciary duty.[244]

IV. Group Agency

The allocation and delegation of the company's powers to contract provides a better analysis of corporate contracting than agency analysis does, one more accurate and less productive of misunderstanding. As argued in Chapter 2, this view of attribution reflects important ideas of group agency. Groups, including companies, can generate collective intentions, beliefs, and goals *qua* group, which are not reducible to the intentions, beliefs, and goals of individual members. Such collective intentions, beliefs, and goals generally require the existence of decision-making procedures which incorporate beliefs and preferences of individual actors, enabling them to be processed into a corporate decision.

The company's constitution is the backbone of these decision-making processes. As shown in this chapter, it provides a rudimentary allocation of the company's powers to different groups and procedures for how decisions can be validly made by that group. This process enables individual inputs, such as beliefs and preferences of individual directors or shareholders to be incorporated and used to produce a group decision of the board or general meeting. As Chapter 2 shows,[245] the group decision is not just an aggregate of existing inputs. A group might reach a decision with which a large minority of members disagreed.

[240] Eg *Heinl* (n 212); *Clark v Cutland* [2003] EWCA Civ 810, [2004] 1 WLR 783.

[241] *Hely-Hutchinson* (n 11) 585–86 (Lord Denning MR), 589–91 (Lord Wilberforce), 594 (Lord Pearson); *Guinness* (n 92) 692–93 (Lord Templeman).

[242] *Parker v McKenna* (1874–75) LR 10 Ch App 96 (CA) 118 (Lord Cairns LC), 124–45 (James LJ); *Panama and South Pacific Telegraph Co v India Rubber, Gutta Percha, and Telegraph Works Co* (1874–75) LR 10 Ch App 515 (CA) 528–29; *Armagas* (n 11) 742–43 and 744–45 (Goff LJ); *Logicrose Ltd v Southend United Football Club Ltd (No 2)* [1988] 1 WLR 1256 (Ch) 1260–62 (Millett J); *Hurstanger Ltd v Wilson* [2007] EWCA Civ 299, [2017] 1 WLR 2351 [39]; *Tigris International NV v China Southern Airlines Co Ltd* [2014] EWCA Civ 1649; *UBS AG v Kommunale Wasserwerke Leipzig GMBH* [2017] EWCA Civ 1567, [2017] 2 CLC 584; *Wood v Commercial First Business Ltd* [2021] EWCA Civ 471.

[243] *Swindle* (n 185); *Gwembe Valley* (n 185).

[244] *Cook* (n 171); *CMS Dolphin Ltd v Simonet* [2001] EWHC 415, [2002] BCC 600 (Ch); *Gwembe Valley* (n 185); *Ultraframe (UK) Ltd v Fielding* [2005] EWHC 1638 (Ch); *Murad* (n 184); *Warman v Dwyer* [1995] HCA 18, 182 CLR 544.

[245] See Ch 2 above.

Yet even the minority would be able to accept the decision as being the group's decision, even if they personally disagreed with it.

Once a decision to contract is reached, the board or general meeting can implement the decision by entering the contract itself, or more commonly, by authorising one of its number or another person to so act. Exceptionally, the board could itself contract as the company[246] by affixing its common seal.[247] Companies can still contract in this way,[248] but need not do so, since there is no longer any requirement for the company to have a seal.[249] Now, the company can execute contracts by signature,[250] or it can authorise another person to reach the agreement. In *John Shaw and Sons (Salford) Ltd v Shaw*, the board passed a resolution to instruct the company's solicitors to commence proceedings against one of its directors, which they duly did,[251] and in *Runciman v Walker Runciman plc*, the board informally agreed to amend its directors' employment contracts to increase the notice period, which was then implemented by one of the executive directors.[252] Regardless of which method is used, in both cases the decision-making processes of the board or general meeting generates distinctly corporate intentions, beliefs, and desires, which are then acted on by the board itself by empowering another to take the necessary actions.

Decisions to contract taken and implemented by the board or general meeting generally reflect the company's group agency, with exceptions in cases of one-man companies. The same analysis is true of decisions taken and implemented by subordinate agents, who typically derive their powers from the board to whom the company's powers have been allocated. When the board decides to delegate powers to a chief executive officer, the board's decision to delegate and the grant of delegation are themselves exercises of the company's group agency. It results in the subordinate agent having the ability to make decisions for the company and do acts to further those decisions. The subordinate agent's intentions and beliefs are thus incorporated into the decision-making process. Like the board or general meeting, the subordinate agent has the power to make decisions, incorporating those intentions, beliefs, and goals, and act to implement those decisions. Although done by a single individual, there is no real difference from the decisions made and acts done by the board or general meeting. Both reflect acts done by the company as a group agent.

[246] Eg *Church v Imperial Gas Light & Coke Co* (1838) 6 Ad & E 846, 112 ER 324; *Northside Developments Pty Ltd v Registrar-General* [1990] HCA 32, 170 CLR 146.

[247] CA 2006, s 43(1). For other types of corporations, see Corporate Bodies' Contracts Act 1960.

[248] CA 2006, s 44.

[249] CA 2006, s 45. Problems with misuse of the seal were not uncommon, see eg *D'Arcy v Tamar Kit Hill and Callington Railway Co* (1866–67) LR 2 Ex 158 (Ct of Exch).

[250] Eg CA 2006, s 44(2)(b).

[251] (n 85) 129.

[252] (n 103) 225–26, 230.

V. Attribution and Other Routes to Liability

The discussion above might appear all-encompassing. But it is important to recognise that there are legal routes other than attribution which lead to companies owing contractual duties and possibly even acquiring contractual rights. Three such routes are discussed here: the 'indoor management rule', statutory deeming provisions, and apparent authority. None of these routes involve the attribution of acts to the company based on group agency. Rather, they involve different forms of deemed liability, justified on a different value entirely: the protection of third parties dealing with companies in good faith.[253]

A. Indoor Management

What if the board or general meeting acts outside their powers? One significant common law doctrine was the 'indoor management' rule.

A standard, albeit somewhat unsatisfactory, account of the indoor management rule's history is as follows. It was thought that whether the company was bound where the board or general meeting acted outside their powers turned on whether the third party knew, or ought to have known, that the board or general meeting was acting outside their powers.[254] The precise mechanism by which the company would be bound, or its effects, were often not well-explained. This approach appeared to provide some protection for third parties dealing with the board or general meeting in good faith, but this protection was substantially eroded by a doctrine of 'constructive notice'. Under that doctrine, third parties dealing with companies were deemed to have constructive notice of the company's memorandum and articles and thus of any limitations inside, plausibly because the company's memorandum and articles were public documents and available for inspection. The indoor management rule was developed to temper the effect of constructive notice.

Though named after *Turquand's Case*,[255] the rule was most clearly stated in *Morris v Kanssen*: 'persons contracting with a company and dealing in good faith may assume that acts within its constitution and powers have been properly and duly performed and are not bound to inquire whether acts of internal management have been regular'.[256] As examples, the indoor management rule was used to validate acts done where apparent officers of the company had not been properly

[253] See generally A Griffiths, *Contracting with Companies* (Oxford, Hart Publishing, 2005).
[254] *Gower's* (n 12) para 7-6.
[255] *Royal British Bank v Turquand* (1856) 6 E&B 327 (Ct of Exch).
[256] (n 2) 474 (Lord Simonds).

appointed in accordance with the constitution[257] and where documents were apparently executed but requisite authority had not been obtained.[258]

Modern cases clarify both indoor management's role and its doctrinal basis. As to the former, *East Asia Co Ltd v PT Satria Tirtatama Energindo* emphasised that '[t]he indoor management rule is a rule that a person dealing with a company in good faith may assume that acts within its constitution and powers have been properly and duly performed'.[259] Classic cases involve non-compliance with formalities for appointing company officers or executing documents. Some early cases suggested that if the articles provided that powers could be granted under certain conditions, third parties who knew of the relevant article could rely on the indoor management rule to assume that power had been duly granted.[260] But this view has since been rejected.[261] '[T]he indoor management rule cannot be used to create authority where none otherwise exists … [it] only has scope for operation if it can be established independently that the person purporting to represent the company had actual or ostensible authority to enter into the transaction'.[262]

As to the rule's doctrinal basis, *Freeman* suggested that the indoor management rule is best seen as a species of estoppel, akin to apparent authority.[263] The company – through some duly empowered group or individual, most commonly the board – makes representations as to the authority of a group or individual by permitting them to act in the management and conduct of part of the business.[264] The indoor management rule does not involve the attribution of acts. It only estops the company from relying on non-compliance with internal procedures, contrary to representations it has made. Its justification: to enable 'the wheels of business' to 'go smoothly round'.[265] By enabling third parties to assume that what appears to be in order is in order, third parties are given greater protection, and transaction costs are reduced, since the need for costly monitoring and inquiries is reduced.

The indoor management rule is thus importantly distinct, both in doctrinal basis and normative justification, from the attribution of acts based on the company's allocated and/or delegated powers. The former relies on estoppel, justified by the protection of third parties and reduction of transaction costs; the latter turns

[257] Eg *In re County Life Assurance Co* (1869-70) LR 5 Ch App 288 (CA); *Mahony v East Holyford* (1874–75) LR 7 HL 869 (HL); *Duck v Tower Galvanizing Co Ltd* [1901] 2 KB 314 (KB).

[258] *Turquand* (n 255) (no authority from general meeting); *County of Gloucester Bank v Rudry Merthyr Steam and House Coal Colliery Co* [1895] 1 Ch 629 (CA).

[259] (n 11) [102].

[260] Eg *Biggerstaff v Rowatt's Wharf* (n 49); *British Thomson-Houston Co v Federated European Bank* [1932] 2 KB 176 (CA).

[261] See eg *Houghton & Co v Nothard, Lowe & Wills* [1927] 1 KB 246 (CA); *Kreditbank Cassel GmbH v Schenkers Ltd* [1927] 1 KB 826 (CA) 840–41 (Scrutton LJ); *Akai Holdings* (n 11) [59]; *East Asia* (n 11) [62]–[65].

[262] *Akai Holdings* (n 11) [59], approving of *Northside* (n 249).

[263] *Freeman* (n 3) 506–507. Compare Watts, 'Deeds and the Principles of Authority in Agency Law' (n 231) suggesting that *Turquand* also sets out a separate rule applicable only to deeds.

[264] *Freeman* (n 3) 506–507.

[265] *Morris* (n 2) 475 (Lord Simonds).

on the allocation and delegation of the company's own powers, reflecting acts done by the company as group agent.

B. Deeming Provisions

The indoor management rule was soon to be overtaken by another alternative where the board acts without powers. For some purposes, statute *deemed* certain acts within the board's powers, even though they were not. Deeming provisions were first introduced in the UK in 1972 after the UK joined the European Communities (later the European Union) and became bound to implement the First Company Law Directive.[266] Their first appearance was in section 9(1) of the European Communities Act, which provided that:

> In favour of a person dealing with a company in good faith, any transaction decided on by the directors shall be deemed to be one which it is within the capacity of the company to enter into, and the power of the directors to bind the company shall be deemed to be free of any limitation under the memorandum or articles of association ….

In *TCB Ltd v Gray*, it was accepted that 'the manifest purpose of both the directive and the section is to enable people to deal with a company in good faith without being adversely affected by any limits on the company's capacity or its rules for internal management'.[267] But the wording of section 9(1) caused some concern[268] and successive rounds of statutory changes followed in 1985, 1989, and then the 2006 Act. The current position is set out in section 40(1) of the 2006 Act, which provides that:

> In favour of a person dealing with a company in good faith, the power of the directors to bind the company, or authorise others to do so, shall be deemed to be free of any limitations under the company's constitution.

The fundamental point of these provisions is to protect third parties dealing with the company in good faith from limitations on the board's power in the company's constitution. Lack of good faith will be difficult to establish: a person dealing with a company 'is not bound to enquire into any limitation on the power of the directors to bind the company or authorise others to do so',[269] 'is presumed to have acted in good faith unless the contrary is proved',[270] and, most exceptionally, 'is not to be regarded as acting in bad faith by reason only of his knowing that an act is beyond

[266] (n 68).
[267] *TCB Ltd v Gray* [1986] Ch 621 (Ch) 635. See also *International Sales and Agencies Ltd v Marcus* [1982] 2 CMLR 46 (QB).
[268] Eg the argument there had been no 'transaction decided on by the company' when the board failed to comply with the articles in sealing debentures, see eg *TCB*, ibid 636.
[269] CA 2006, s 40(2)(b)(i).
[270] CA 2006, s 40(2)(b)(ii).

the powers of the directors under the company's constitution'.[271] The company's constitution here includes resolutions and agreements between the shareholders or any class of them.[272]

Section 40 thus goes quite far in providing protection for third parties dealing with the company, but some of its limitations must be stressed. First, it only applies where there is some transaction between the company and some other person,[273] which does not include corporate insiders such as directors.[274] Second, section 40 only protects those dealing with the 'directors' but not those dealing with the general meeting.[275] For our purposes, the crucial point is that these deeming provisions created by statute are distinct from the attribution of acts based on the allocation and delegation of powers. The two also have different justifications. The aim of deeming provisions is again to protect innocent third parties from limitations in the directors' powers, thus reducing the need for third parties to engage in costly investigations and monitoring of the directors.

C. Apparent Authority

The above two alternative routes to attributing acts at common law concerned the board and the general meeting. When subordinate agents act outside the scope of their powers, their principals may nonetheless be bound by their acts to the extent that the agent had 'apparent authority', a doctrine of considerable practical significance.

Unlike actual authority, apparent authority is a relationship between the principal and third party. The orthodox view today is that apparent authority operates as an estoppel by representation.[276] Like other estoppels by representation, it must thus be shown that the principal made representations to the third party, these representations were reasonably relied upon, and that the third party suffered detriment as a result.[277] Representations may take the form of words or conduct, or even appointing the agent to a specific position.[278] They must be from the

[271] CA 2006, s 40(2)(b)(iii).

[272] CA 2006, s 40(3).

[273] *EIC Services Ltd v Phipps* [2004] EWCA Civ 1069, [2004] 2 BCLC 160 (shareholders receiving bonus issue, under s 35A CA 1985); *Re Hampton Capital Ltd* [2015] EWHC 1905 (Ch), [2016] 1 BCLC 374 (money misappropriated from company) and see also *International Sales* (n 267) (on European Communities Act 1972, s 9(1)).

[274] *Smith v Henniker-Major & Co* [2002] EWCA Civ 762, [2002] 2 BCLC 655 (directors); *EIC Services* ibid (shareholders in bonus issue).

[275] *Gower's* (n 12) para 7-13.

[276] *Freeman* (n 3) 503; *Armagas* (n 11) 731 (Goff LJ), affirmed 777 (Lord Keith); *Akai Holdings* (n 11) [52]; *East Asia* (n 11) [42]. For difficulties, see *Bowstead & Reynolds* (n 5) paras 8-027–8-028.

[277] *East Asia* (n 11) [41]–[43], [75].

[278] *Bowstead & Reynolds* (n 5) paras 8-013–8-014.

principal: an agent cannot 'self-authorise'.[279] In the case of companies, the representations must be traceable ultimately to persons who had the power to make such representations on behalf of the company.[280] The third party's reliance on these representations must be reasonable,[281] which it will not be if he knows that the agent lacks actual authority to do the act[282] or has reason to believe that the agent lacks actual authority and fails to make the inquiries a reasonable person would have.[283] As an estoppel by representation, it operates as a rule of evidence precluding the representor from averring facts contrary to his own representation.[284]

Some commentators in England and the United States have argued that apparent authority is simply an application of the objective theory of contract formation.[285] But prevailing English authority does not support this view. Two further defects can be pointed out. First, it suggests that apparent authority ought only to apply in contractual situations, when it is clear that apparent authority has wider application.[286] Second, under the objective theory of contract formation, the principal ought to obtain rights against the third party, not merely owe it duties, without needing to satisfy ratification requirements.[287] But under English law, the dominant view, consistent with estoppel, is that when a transaction is entered into with only apparent authority, the principal owes only duties to, but obtains no rights against, the third party.[288]

Apparent authority thus presents a third route towards establishing that a company owed contractual duties. When an individual acts with apparent authority, his acts are not attributed to the company. The company is simply estopped from denying the agent's authority. This separate doctrinal mechanism has a different justification from that of the attribution of acts. The former protects the reasonable reliance on representations emanating from the principal, the latter reflects acts done by the company as group agent.

[279] *British Bank v Sun Life* (n 205); *Armagas* (n 11) 733–34 (Goff LJ).

[280] *Freeman* (n 3) 505.

[281] *The Raffaella* (n 11) 41.

[282] *Russo-Chinese Bank v Li Yau Sam* [1910] AC 174 (PC) 184–85; *Armagas* (n 11) 777 (Lord Keith); *East Asia* (n 11) [61].

[283] *East Asia* (n 11) [75]–[93], *cf Akai Holdings* (n 11) [49]–[71] (Lord Neuberger NPJ).

[284] Eg *Ogilvie v West Australian Mortgage and Agency Corpn Ltd* [1896] AC 257 (PC) 270; *Greenwood v Martins Bank Ltd* [1932] 1 KB 371 (CA); *Avon CC v Howlett* [1983] 1 WLR 605 (CA), citing G Spencer Bower and A Turner, *Estoppel by Representation*, 3rd edn (Butterworths, 1977).

[285] Eg WW Cook, 'Agency by Estoppel' (1905) 5 *Columbia LR* 36; WW Cook, 'Agency by Estoppel – A Reply' (1906) 6 *Columbia LR* 34; M Conant, 'The Objective Theory of Agency: Apparent Authority and the Estoppel of Apparent Ownership' (1968) 47 *Nebraska LR* 678; T Krebs, 'Agency Law for Muggles: Why There is No Magic in Agency' in A Burrows and E Peel (eds), *Contract Formation and Parties* (Oxford, Oxford University Press, 2010).

[286] Most clearly *Armagas* (n 11) 738–39 (Goff LJ), affirmed on appeal at 782 (Lord Keith). See most recently *Ciban Management Corpn v Citco (BVI) Ltd* [2020] UKPC 21, [2021] AC 122 [28].

[287] *Bowstead & Reynolds* (n 5) paras 8-028–8-029.

[288] *Bowstead & Reynolds* (n 5) para 8-012; *cf Eastern Distributors Ltd v Goldring* [1957] 2 QB 600 (CA) 611, interpreting the Sale of Goods Act 1979, s 21(1).

VI. Conclusion

This chapter has argued that despite the dominance of agency analysis in corporate contracting, it is preferable to focus on the company's allocation and delegation of its powers. It does not require resolving contentious debates about agency definitions, is more consistent with the incorporation process, and avoids inappropriate features of agency law from being applied to the board and general meeting.

This chapter has shown that whether contracting is effected by the board or general meeting, or by delegates, the same four questions are in play. These are: (i) does the company have powers to enter this contract? (ii) have these powers been properly allocated and/or delegated to the person purporting to exercise it? (iii) was the person exercising it within its scope? (iv) was the exercise of the power proper? The most difficult of these questions was the last, where it was necessary to distinguish between different flaws in corporate contracting. While some amount only to a breach of duty but not a lack of power, other flaws meant that conditions precedent to the successful exercise of the power had not been met. This analysis of attribution reflects ideas of group agency: these acts are the company's acts because they are produced through a decision-making structure to effect the company's own intentions, beliefs, and goals.

But it is important to note that attribution is not the only route by which companies may owe duties under contracts. Several different routes have been developed to achieve other policy goals, such as the protection of third parties acting in good faith and the reduction of transaction costs. Three are discussed here: deeming provisions via statute, the 'indoor management rule', and apparent authority. But they do not attribute acts. Instead, they use different doctrinal mechanisms to the attribution of acts, justified by different bases. While important, they are also importantly distinct from the attribution of acts.

4

Attributing Acts in Tort

This chapter turns next to the attribution of acts in tort law. Tort law is the law of civil wrongs;[1] wrongs are breaches of duties.[2] Perhaps surprisingly, it is unclear whether attribution rules exist at all in large swathes of tort law, and if they do, what they are. In torts involving statement-making, agency reasoning is sometimes used.[3] For other torts, most assume that the doctrine of 'vicarious liability' provides the attribution rules.[4] But here, a problem exists. Orthodoxy holds that vicarious liability is a form of strict liability imposed on one person for the wrong of another, even though the former had not committed a tort.[5] What is being attributed to the employer is not the individual's *acts*, but his 'liability'.[6] On this view, it remains unclear whether tort law has rules attributing acts. Their content likewise remains mysterious.

This chapter argues that, contrary to this view, tort law has – and has always had – rules attributing acts. Prior to 1956, those rules could be found in the body of law known as 'vicarious liability'. 'Vicarious liability' then attributed the acts of one person (for convenience, 'the employee') to another (similarly, 'the employer'). This doctrine applied to both corporate and non-corporate employers. Acts were attributed to companies if they were performed by those who had powers to perform those acts allocated or delegated to them. But after 1956, the law changed, and the label 'vicarious liability' became used to describe a doctrine

[1] P Birks, 'The Concept of a Civil Wrong' in DG Owen (ed), *The Philosophical Foundations of Tort Law* (Oxford, Oxford University Press, 1996).

[2] ibid 33.

[3] P Watts and F Reynolds (eds), *Bowstead & Reynolds on Agency*, 22nd edn (London, Sweet & Maxwell, 2020) paras 8-176–8-177, 8-180–8-182. See also P Watts, 'Principals' Tortious Liability for Agents' Negligent Statements – Is "Authority" Necessary?' (2012) 128 *LQR* 260.

[4] PL Davies and S Worthington, *Gower: Principles of Modern Company Law*, 10th edn (London, Sweet & Maxwell, 2016) paras 7-2, 7-31; B Hannigan, *Company Law*, 5th edn (Oxford, Oxford University Press, 2018) para 4-2.

[5] Terminology first coined by G Williams, 'Vicarious Liability: Tort of the Master or of the Servant?' (1956) 72 *LQR* 522.

[6] This is a difficult word, generating much scholarly literature about what it means. Nonetheless, the language is well-established in the vicarious liability context and so it is retained here. For further discussion on 'liabilities' post-wrong, see eg T Liau, 'Standing in Private Law' (DPhil thesis, University of Oxford, 2020) Ch 2, and see also S Steel and R Stevens, 'The Secondary Legal Duty to Pay Damages' (2020) 136 *LQR* 291, *cf* B Zipursky, 'Civil Recourse, not Corrective Justice' (2003) 91 *Georgetown LR* 695; S Smith, 'Duties, Liabilities and Damages' (2011) 125 *Harvard LR* 1727; SA Smith, 'A Duty to Make Restitution' (2013) 26 *Canadian Journal of Law and Jurisprudence* 157; SA Smith, *Rights, Wrongs, and Injustices: The Structure of Remedial Law* (Oxford, Oxford University Press, 2019) 191–99.

attributing the employee's liability, not his acts. This change did not mean that post-1956, the attribution of acts disappeared. Instead, it is argued that the best interpretation is that acts could still be attributed on the same basis as before – a suggestion consistent with the case law.

I. 'Vicarious Liability' and Other Doctrines

Before moving on, it may be helpful to provide a brief introduction to 'vicarious liability', a doctrine which has generated much case law[7] and scholarly literature.[8] Two other adjacent doctrines will also be discussed: non-delegable duties, and apparent authority.

A. Vicarious Liability

Cox v Ministry of Justice describes vicarious liability as follows: 'Vicarious liability in tort is imposed upon a person in respect of the act or omission of another individual, because of his relationship with that individual, and the connection between that relationship and the act or omission in question.'[9] Although most common in respect of torts, a person can also be held vicariously liable for another's statutory[10] or equitable wrong.[11]

This description usefully captures vicarious liability's two main requirements. First, there must be a qualifying relationship between the person who had committed the wrongful act and the person sought to be held liable. Employment is a key example. Second, there must be a qualifying connection between the wrongful

[7] Eg *Lister v Hesley Hall Ltd* [2001] UKHL 22, [2002] 1 AC 215; *Dubai Aluminium Co Ltd v Salaam and others* [2002] UKHL 48, [2003] 2 AC 366; *Majrowski v Guy's and St Thomas's NHS Trust* [2006] UKHL 34, [2007] 1 AC 224; *Various Claimants v Catholic Child Welfare Society and others* [2012] UKSC 56, [2013] 2 AC 1 (the *Christian Brothers* case); *Cox v Ministry of Justice* [2016] UKSC 10, [2016] AC 660; *Mohamud v WM Morrison Supermarkets plc* [2016] UKSC 11, [2016] 2 WLR 821 (*Mohamud*); *Armes v Nottinghamshire CC* [2017] UKSC 60, [2017] 3 WLR 1000; *Barclays Bank plc v Various Claimants* [2020] UKSC 13, [2020] AC 97; *WM Morrison Supermarkets plc v Various Claimants* [2020] UKSC 12, [2020] AC 989 (*Morrisons*).

[8] Eg T Baty, *Vicarious Liability: A Short History of the Liability of Employers, Principals, Partners, Associations and Trade-Union Members with a Chapter on the Law of Scotland and Foreign States* (Oxford, Clarendon Press, 1916); Williams (n 5); PS Atiyah, *Vicarious Liability in the Law of Torts* (London, Butterworths, 1967); JW Neyers, 'A Theory of Vicarious Liability' (2004) 43 *Alberta LR* 287; R Stevens, *Torts and Rights* (Oxford, Oxford University Press, 2007) Ch 11; P Giliker, *Vicarious Liability in Tort* (Cambridge, Cambridge University Press, 2010); A Gray, *Vicarious Liability: Critique and Reform* (Oxford, Hart Publishing, 2018); C Beuermann, *Reconceptualising Strict Liability for the Tort of Another* (Oxford, Hart Publishing, 2019).

[9] *Cox* (n 7) [15].

[10] Eg *Majrowski* (n 7); *Morrisons* (n 7).

[11] Eg *Dubai Aluminium* (n 7).

acts done and the doer's relationship with the person sought to be held liable. The acts done must be within the individual's 'course of employment'. Before *Lister v Hesley Hall Ltd*,[12] this requirement would have been satisfied where the acts were expressly authorised acts, or unauthorised acts which could have been regarded as wrongful modes of performing authorised acts – the 'Salmond test', named after the textbook-writer who formulated it.[13]

Both requirements raised difficulties, especially the latter. While negligent acts could be described as wrongful modes of performing authorised acts, intentionally wrongful acts often could not. Vicarious liability for intentional wrongs was therefore rare under the Salmond test.[14] But starting from the 1990s, courts across the Commonwealth were confronted with cases involving children who had been sexually abused at care facilities or boarding schools by those employed to care for them.[15] To accommodate them, English courts expanded the two requirements of vicarious liability to hold the abusers' employers vicariously liable.[16]

In England the first change occurred in *Lister v Hesley Hall Ltd*, where the House of Lords departed from the Salmond test, laying down the 'close connection' test: an act would be within the course of employment if it was so closely connected to acts which were authorised so as to make it fair, just, and reasonable that the defendant be held liable for it.[17] The close connection test has been repeatedly affirmed by all levels of English courts.[18] Later, the other requirement of a qualifying relationship was expanded in the *Christian Brothers* case to include relationships 'akin to employment'.[19] Qualifying relationships are now ones where 'harm is wrongfully done by an individual who carries on activities as an integral part of business activities carried on by a defendant and for its benefit and where the commission of the wrongful act is a risk created by the defendant by assigning those activities to the individual in question'.[20] This change addressed cases where the sexual abuser was not in an employment relationship with the party to be held liable, such as that between Catholic brothers and their Order.[21] It now

[12] (n 7).
[13] RFV Heuston and RA Buckley, *Salmond and Heuston on Torts*, 21st edn (Canada, Thomson Professional Pub Canada, 1996) 443.
[14] Eg sexual abuse: *Trotman v North Yorkshire County Council* [1999] LGR 584 (CA).
[15] In Canada, see eg *Bazley v Curry* [1999] 2 SCR 534 (SCC); *Jacobi v Griffiths* [1999] 2 SCR 570 (SCC); *John Doe v Bennett* [2004] 1 SCR 436 (SCC); *EB v Order of the Oblates of Mary Immaculate in the Province of British Columbia* [2005] 3 SCR 45 (SCC). In Australia, see *New South Wales v Lepore* [2003] HCA 4, (2003) 212 CLR 511, and now see *Prince Alfred College v ADC* [2016] HCA 37, (2016) 258 CLR 134. In the UK, see *Lister* (n 7); *E v English Province of Our Lady of Charity* [2012] EWCA Civ 938, [2013] QB 722; the *Catholic Brothers* case (n 7).
[16] For background and alternatives, see P Giliker, 'Analysing Institutional Liability for Child Sexual Abuse in England and Wales and Australia: Vicarious Liability, Non-Delegable Duties and Statutory Intervention' (2018) 77 *CLJ* 506.
[17] *Lister* (n 7) [28] (Lord Steyn).
[18] Eg *Dubai Aluminium* (n 7); *Mohamud* (n 7); *Morrisons* (n 7).
[19] The *Catholic Brothers* case (n 7) [60].
[20] *Cox* (n 7) [24], applied in *Armes* (n 7) [54]–[60].
[21] The *Catholic Brothers* case (n 7).

includes the relationship between prisoners and the prison authorities in whose kitchens they worked[22] and between foster parents and public authorities who put children in their care,[23] but does not include relationships historically designated as those with 'independent contractors'.[24] As will be discussed later, these changes are connected to the orthodox basis of vicarious liability today.

B. Non-Delegable Duties

'Vicarious liability' is often regarded as closely related to 'non-delegable duties',[25] with one commentator going as far as to describe them as two routes around the employer-employee-victim triangle.[26] Different jurisdictions have different conceptions of 'non-delegable duties'; here we focus only on that doctrine under English law. What is unique about 'non-delegable duties' there is the content of the duty. As *Woodland v Swimming Teachers Association* explained,

> a common law duty of care 'does not usually demand compliance with a specific obligation. It is only when an act is undertaken by a party that a general duty arises to perform the act with reasonable care.' The expression 'non-delegable duty' has become the conventional way of describing those cases in which the ordinary principle is displaced and the duty extends beyond being careful, to producing the careful performance of work delegated to others.[27]

Thus, a non-delegable duty is not just a duty imposed on the duty-bearer to take reasonable care in delegating performance but, typically, a duty to ensure that care is taken if delegated.[28] It is best understood as a duty to ensure a certain outcome, or a duty to succeed, not merely to try.[29] As the duty-bearer commits a wrong when the duty is breached, his liability for the wrong is clearly personal.[30]

Perhaps the most difficult question concerns when non-delegable duties are owed. It appears to be a rag-bag category which includes the duties of employers to provide safe systems of work,[31] duties when dealing with extra-hazardous materials,[32] and on some accounts, duties under bailments.[33] Attempting to

[22] *Cox* (n 7) [32]–[44].
[23] *Armes* (n 7) [59]–[73].
[24] *Barclays* (n 7). See also *Kafagi v JBW Group Ltd* [2018] EWCA Civ 1157.
[25] See generally R Stevens, 'Non-Delegable Duties and Vicarious Liability' in J Neyers et al (eds), *Emerging Issues in Tort Law* (Oxford, Hart Publishing, 2007); Stevens, *Torts and Rights* (n 8) 114–23.
[26] T Weir, *A Casebook on Tort*, 10th edn (London, Sweet & Maxwell, 2004) 292.
[27] *Woodland v Swimming Teachers Association* [2013] UKSC 66, [2014] AC 537 [5] (Lord Sumption).
[28] *Bulk Oil Steamship Co Ltd v Cardiff Channel Dry Docks & Pontoon Co Ltd* (*The Pass of Ballater*) [1942] P 112, 117 (Probate, Divorce & Admiralty Division); *Woodland* (n 27) [7], [11].
[29] SA Smith, 'Duties to Try and Duties to Succeed' in A Dyson et al (eds), *Defences in Tort* (Oxford, Hart Publishing, 2015).
[30] *Woodland* (n 27) [3]–[4].
[31] Eg *Wilson & Clyde Coal Ltd v English* [1938] AC 57 (HL).
[32] Eg *Honeywill and Stein Ltd v Larkin Brothers* [1934] 1 KB 191 (CA); *Biffa Waste Services Ltd v Maschinenfabrik Ernst Hese GmbH and others* [2008] EWCA Civ 1257.
[33] Eg *Morris v CW Martin & Sons Ltd* [1966] 1 QB 716 (CA).

give the doctrine some coherence, *Woodland* identified two situations where non-delegable duties would be owed. First is where the defendant employs an independent contractor to perform some function which is inherently hazardous or liable to become so in the course of his work.[34] Second is where the duty that arises has three characteristics. It must arise from an antecedent relationship between claimant and defendant, it must be a positive or affirmative duty to protect a particular class of persons against a particular class of risks, and it must be personal to the defendant.[35] But questions remain. For instance, should sexual abuse cases like *Lister* be analysed as non-delegable duties cases? This is a contentious matter, turning at least partly on when non-delegable duties are owed;[36] space precludes further consideration of the issue.

C. Apparent Authority

A third doctrine worth briefly mentioning at this juncture is apparent authority. A full description of apparent authority appears in Chapter 3. As explained, whether in contract formation or in torts, 'apparent authority' does not involve the exercise of the principal's powers by the person whose acts are sought to be attributed. Instead, it operates as an estoppel by representation, precluding a representor who has made representations as to its agent's authority from subsequently denying that authority as against a representee who has reasonably relied on the representations.

Apparent authority's scope for operation in tort law is limited, simply because torts are often such that there will be no opportunity for representations to be made to a victim, nor will the victim reasonably rely on any representations. Examples of victims of negligent driving or physical or sexual assaults provide good illustrations.[37] But apparent authority might apply to torts of misstatement, where it might be argued, for example, that an agent committing deceit or negligent misrepresentations did so with apparent authority from his principal.[38] Where the

[34] *Woodland* (n 27) [6]. Eg *Wilson & Clyde* (n 31) (duty to provide safe system of work); *McDermid v Nash Dredging and Reclamation Co Ltd* [1987] AC 906 (HL) (duty to operate safe system of work).

[35] *Woodland* (n 27) [7]. Eg *Gold v Essex County Council* [1942] 2 KB 293 (CA); *Cassidy v Ministry of Health* [1951] 2 KB 343 (CA); *Roe v Minister of Health* [1954] 2 QB 66 (CA); *X (Minors) v Bedfordshire CC* [1995] 2 AC 633 (HL), and *Woodland* itself (education authority assuming duty to ensure that pupil's swimming lessons are carefully conducted and supervised).

[36] Eg Stevens, *Torts and Rights* (n 8); Stevens, 'Non-Delegable Duties and Vicarious Liability' (n 25); *Lister* (n 7) [55]–[56] (Lord Hobhouse).

[37] At least, under the conventional definition of apparent authority, *cf* different definitions used in C Beuermann, 'Vicarious Liability and Conferred Authority Strict Liability' (2013) 20 *Torts Law Journal* 265; C Beuermann, 'Tort Law in the Employment Relationship: A Response to the Potential Abuse of an Employer's Authority' (2014) 21 *Torts Law Journal* 169; C Beuermann, 'Vicarious Liability: A Case Study in the Failure of General Principles?' [2017] *Professional Negligence* 179, 191–92. See now Beuermann, *Reconceptualising Strict Liability for the Tort of Another* (n 8). See also the use of 'authority' in *Prince Alfred College v ADC* [2016] HCA 37, especially [81].

[38] *Bowstead & Reynolds* (n 3) paras 8-176–8-177, 8-180–8-182.

agent does so, the principal may be estopped from denying his authority, resulting in the principal being personally liable to the victim. We return to this topic near the end of this chapter.

II. The Conceptual Basis of Vicarious Liability

Armed with the basics of vicarious liability and adjacent doctrines, we can now turn to a difficult question: what is vicarious liability's conceptual basis? Orthodoxy today adopts the 'servant's tort' theory of vicarious liability, rather than the 'master's tort' theory. Different variants of the servant's tort theory exist, but the version adopted by English courts today attributes the employee's 'liability' for committing a wrong to the employer, not the employee's acts.

A. Servant's Tort Theory

As the name – the 'servant's tort' theory – suggests, it is the employee who must have committed a wrong, not the employer. An employer can be held vicariously liable even if he committed no wrong. He is being held strictly liable for the wrong of another. On this theory, vicarious liability is a true exception to the general rules of tort law which generally impose liability only upon those who have committed wrongs against the victim.[39]

As an exception to general rules of tort law, the doctrine requires special justification. Leading justifications are explicitly policy-based. Such policy justifications include enterprise liability: since the employer has put in place an enterprise which creates risks, it is fair or just that he bears the losses that result when those risks materialise;[40] the employer's deep pockets;[41] his superior ability for loss-spreading;[42] deterrence of the employer;[43] and the employer's control over the employee.[44]

Although not often clearly distinguished in the literature, there are two possibilities for the precise legal mechanism involved in the servant's tort theory. One possibility is that it is the employee's wrong – the breach of duty – which is attributed to the employer. Another is that what is attributed to the employer

[39] *Woodland* (n 27) [3] (Lord Sumption); *Armes* (n 7) [30] (Lord Reed). See also Birks, 'The Concept of a Civil Wrong' (n 1).

[40] *Bazley v Curry* (n 15) [30]–[31]; *Dubai Aluminium* (n 7) [21]; *Majrowski* (n 7) [9]; the *Catholic Brothers* case (n 7) [86]–[87]; *Cox* (n 7) [22] and [29]; *Armes* (n 7) [67]. See generally D Brodie, 'Enterprise Liability: Justifying Vicarious Liability' (2007) 27 *OJLS* 493; D Brodie, *Enterprise Liability and the Common Law* (Cambridge, Cambridge University Press, 2010).

[41] *Cox* (n 7) [20].

[42] *Cox* (n 7) [20].

[43] Eg *Bazley v Curry* (n 15) [30]–[35].

[44] *Cox* (n 7) [21]; *Armes* (n 7) [56].

are the consequences of breach, commonly described as the employee's liability[45] to pay damages to the victim.

On either of these two versions, the servant's tort theory can easily be distinguished from non-delegable duties and apparent authority. While the latter two establish the defendant employer's personal liability for his own wrong, the first involves holding him liable for a wrong he did not commit.

B. Master's Tort Theory

A competing view of vicarious liability, the 'master's tort' theory, was first identified by Glanville Williams over 60 years ago.[46] It largely[47] faded from sight until 2006, when it was revived by Robert Stevens.[48] Since then it has been endorsed by others.[49]

Under the master's tort theory, it is the employer who must commit the wrong, not the employee. An employer can be vicariously liable even if the employee commits no tort. Like other torts, the employer is held liable to the victim because he commits a wrong against the victim. Vicarious liability is special only because the tort is being established through the acts of the employee, which are treated as the employer's. On this theory, what is attributed are the employee's *acts*, not the employee's wrong, nor the employee's liability to the victim. One advantage of this account is that it requires no exception to the general rules of tort law which impose liability on a defendant only for wrongs he has committed. It therefore requires no special justification for departing from ordinary tort law rules.

Despite modern scepticism, it is possible to find language that supported the master's tort theory dating back to the Middle Ages, though the system of civil litigation and reliance on the forms of action means that it is difficult to find a single coherent explanation of vicarious liability during that period.[50] In *Middleton v Fowler*, Holt CJ explained that '[n]o master is chargeable with the acts of his servant, but when he acts in execution of the authority given by his master … then the act of the servant is the act of the master'.[51] Other case law statements appeared over the next two centuries. Lord Mansfield's statement that 'for all civil purposes the act of the sheriff's bailiff is the act of the sheriff'[52] was approved of by Ashurst J

[45] See earlier n 6 on the difficulties with this word.

[46] G Williams, 'Vicarious Liability: Tort of the Master or of the Servant?' (1956) 72 *LQR* 522.

[47] But see eg E Weinrib, *The Idea of Private Law*, 1st edn (Oxford, Oxford University Press, 1995) 185–87. See now E Weinrib, *The Idea of Private Law*, 2nd edn (Oxford, Oxford University Press, 2012) 185–87.

[48] R Stevens, 'Vicarious Liability or Vicarious Action?' (2006) 123 *LQR* 30; Stevens, *Torts and Rights* (n 8) Ch 11.

[49] For a very similar view see Gray, *Vicarious Liability* (n 8) Ch 8.

[50] W Swain, 'A Historical Examination of Vicarious Liability: A "Veritable Upas Tree"?' (2019) 78 *CLJ* 640.

[51] *Middleton v Fowler* (1698) 1 Salk 282, 91 ER 247.

[52] *Ackworth v Kempe* (1778) 1 Dougl 40, 42.

in *Woodgate v Knatchbull*, where Ashurst J said '[t]his holds indeed in most instances with regard to servants in general'.[53] Littledale J held in *Laugher v Pointer* that '[s]ervants represent the master himself, and their acts stand upon the same footing as his own'.[54] In *Hutchinson v York, Newcastle & Berwick Railway*, Alderson B said that '[t]he principle upon which a master is in general liable … is that the act of his servant is in truth [sic] his own act'.[55]

How might the master's tort theory be distinguished from adjacent doctrines? Both the master's tort theory of vicarious liability and non-delegable duties involve the defendant's personal liability for his own breach of duty. The difference between the two lies in the content of the duty owed. For vicarious liability, the content of the duty is unremarkable: for negligence, the ordinary standard of reasonable care; for trespass to the person, a duty not to infringe another's bodily integrity, and so on. But as discussed above, the content of non-delegable duties typically differs, usually involving an outcome-based duty.

Similarly, both the master's tort theory and apparent authority also involve the defendant's personal liability, albeit established in different ways. Under the former, the defendant breaches a duty by attributing the employee's acts to it. In the latter, the defendant's breach of duty is established through an estoppel. His representation to the victim that an employee has a certain authority to act, coupled with the victim's reasonable reliance on the representation, estops the defendant from denying the individual's authority. As we will see later, the attribution of acts under the master's tort theory is based on the exercise of allocated and delegated powers by individuals, while apparent authority is an estoppel aimed at protecting innocent third parties.

III. Pre-1956 Law

In most cases, whether the servant's tort or master's tort theory is adopted does not change the outcome of cases. But sometimes it does. This section examines four categories of cases where the view adopted made a difference to the outcome. It shows that until 1956 in England, vicarious liability adopted the master's tort theory: it attributed the employee's acts to the employer, not his wrong or liability flowing from it.[56]

A. Employee Owes a Duty to Victim; Employer Does Not

In the first category, the employee owes a duty to the victim, but the employer does not. The classic case is where the employee is the driver of a vehicle who

[53] *Woodgate v Knatchbull* (1787) 2 TR 154.
[54] *Laugher v Pointer* (1826) 5 B & C 547, 553.
[55] *Hutchinson v York, Newcastle & Berwick Railway* (1850) 5 Exch 343, 350.
[56] See generally *Pioneer Mortgage Services Pty Ltd v Columbus Capital Pty Ltd* [2016] FCAFC 78 [48]–[50] (Edelman J).

allows a passenger to travel with him, contrary to his employer's instructions. The view once was that the employer owed no duty of care to trespassers, so only the employee would owe a duty of care to the victim.

It matters which theory was adopted. Under either version of the servant's tort theory, an employer would be liable: the employee's wrong or liability could be attributed to the employer, rendering him similarly liable. But under the master's tort theory, it would not be. Even if the employee's acts were attributed, the employer would breach no duty through the employee's acts, and thus commit no wrong, incurring no liability.

What is attributed?	**Liability**	**Wrong**	**Acts**
Employee owes a duty, employer does not. Is employer liable?	Yes	Yes	No

In the leading case, *Twine v Bean's Express Ltd*,[57] the employer was held not liable. This supports the master's tort theory. The employer supplied a commercial van and driver to a bank. The van driver was instructed not to allow unauthorised persons to travel in company vehicles. Nonetheless, the driver gave lifts to Twine, a mailman of the bank. The driver drove carelessly, got into an accident, and Twine was killed. Twine's widow, as his executrix, sued the driver's employer. Uthwatt J accepted that the driver owed a duty of care to the passenger, which he had breached. However, the driver's employer did not owe a duty of care to the passenger because the then-prevailing view was that no duty of care was owed to trespassers.[58] Owing no duty, the employer could not have breached it. Thus, the employer was not liable. This outcome is explicable only by the master's tort theory.

The reasoning of Uthwatt J at first instance also clearly supports the master's tort theory:

> The law attributes to the employer the acts of a servant done in the course of his employment and fastens upon him responsibility for those acts. In determining the duty of the employer and the duty of the servant on any occasion, all the circumstances have to be considered. In the general run of cases, the duty of both is the same; but this is a coincidence, not a rule of law. The general question in an action against the employer, such as the present, is technically: 'Did the employer in the circumstances which affected him owe a duty?' – for the law does not attribute to the employer the liability which attaches to the servant.[59]

Twine was followed in *Conway v George Wimpey Ltd*.[60] The defendant company employed workers at Heathrow Airport to carry materials via lorry. Lorry drivers

[57] *Twine v Bean's Express Ltd* [1946] 1 All ER 202 (CA).
[58] Now see *Rose v Plenty* [1976] 1 WLR 141 (CA).
[59] *Twine* (n 57) 204.
[60] *Conway v George Wimpey Ltd* [1951] 2 KB 266 (CA).

were given strict instructions to carry only the company's employees as passengers. In violation of the prohibition, drivers sometimes gave lifts to others working on the site. The victim was one such passenger. He was injured when he alighted from the lorry, requiring his leg to be amputated below the knee. Asquith LJ, delivering the Court of Appeal's main reasoned judgment, accepted that the case was materially similar to *Twine*, with the only issue being whether the victim was a trespasser.[61] Concluding that he was,[62] Asquith LJ followed *Twine*. Though the employee committed a breach of duty, the employer did not since it owed no duty to the victim. The victim's claim against the employer failed, supporting the master's tort theory.

An interesting contrasting example with similar facts is the High Court of Australia's decision in *Darling Island Stevedoring & Lighterage v Long*.[63] When *Darling Island* was decided in 1957, the House of Lords in England had already started moving away from the master's tort theory. But Kitto and Webb JJ's reasoning suggests that there was still some support for the master's tort theory in Australia then. In *Darling Island*, statutory regulations imposed a duty to securely fasten hatch beams only on the 'person in charge' of loading and unloading a ship but not his employer. The defendant's foreman failed to do so before loading and unloading. The beam was displaced, and the claimant wharf labourer was injured by the beam. He sought to establish the defendant's vicarious liability. The High Court of Australia concluded that the defendant employer was not liable.

Some members of the court clearly supported the master's tort theory. Kitto J considered the reasoning of cases like *Twine*, concluding that 'the true principle makes the master responsible for the servant's acts and not for his liabilities'.[64] Similarly, Taylor J, after discussing the old authorities, concluded that '[t]he early learning on this branch of the law does not suggest to my mind any reason for forming the opinion a master is, or ever was, answerable for the torts, as distinct from the acts of his servants'.[65] As Webb J explained, since the regulations only imposed a duty on the employee and not the employer, even if the employee's acts were attributed to the employer, the employer breached no duty, committing no wrong for which he could be held liable to the claimant. These members clearly adopted the master's tort theory, seeing vicarious liability as attributing acts. But not all did. Fullagar J thought it was neither necessary nor profitable to discuss the theoretical justification of vicarious liability but, if necessary, he favoured the servant's tort theory. He viewed vicarious liability as a 'true vicarious liability', arguing that 'the master is liable not for a breach of duty resting on him and broken by him but for a breach of duty resting on another and broken by another'.[66]

[61] ibid 273–74 (Asquith LJ).
[62] ibid.
[63] *Darling Island Stevedoring & Lighterage v Long* [1957] HCA 26, (1957) 97 CLR 36.
[64] ibid 66.
[65] ibid 70.
[66] ibid 57.

B. Employee Has a Personal Defence; Employer Does Not

In the second category, both the employee and employer owe duties to the victim, but only the employee has a personal defence to actions brought by the victim. One such example involves the spousal defence under section 12 of the Married Women's Property Act 1882, which provided that 'no husband or wife shall be entitled to sue the other for a tort'.[67] It was based on a common law rule which prevented spouses from successfully suing each other. The rule was often attributed to the fiction that the wife and husband were one person.[68] That fiction and most of its applications were statutorily abolished, with section 12 preserving a defence for personal torts. Although not universal,[69] the common view now is that section 12 blocks the liability of one spouse against another,[70] though the former still commits a wrong.[71] It might be justified by the 'public policy' goal of not encouraging litigation between spouses.[72]

Consider situations where one spouse injured another, where both worked for the same employer. The victim could not succeed in an action against the other spouse because of the defence, but could the victim successfully sue the spouse's employer for damages?

Under the master's tort theory, the answer was simple. If the employee's acts were attributed to the employer, the employer would be liable. Through the employee's acts, the employer would breach its duty to the victim, committing a wrong for which it had no defence.

But if the servant's tort theory attributes the employee's *liability* to the employer, then the employer should not be liable. As the employee-spouse bears no liability because of section 12, there is nothing that can be attributed to the employer. If, however, the servant's tort theory attributes the employee's *wrong* to the employer, the outcome depends on whether section 12 applies to prevent the employer from incurring liability for the wrong. The cases suggest that it does not: the justification for giving the spouse a defence does not extend to the employer.[73] Others should not 'hide behind the skirts of [the husband's] immunity'.[74]

[67] Emphasising the policy-motivated angle to such cases, see J Dietrich and I Field, 'Statute and Theories of Vicarious Liability' (2019) 43 *Melbourne University LR* 515, 531–34.

[68] See eg *Philips v Barnet* (1876) 1 QBD 436, 438; *Broom v Morgan* [1953] 1 QB 597 (CA) 607 (Singleton LJ); J Story, *Commentaries on Equity Jurisprudence: As Administered in England and America*, vol 2, 7th edn (Boston, Little, Brown and Co, 1853) §1367.

[69] *cf* the view that s 12 only made the tort unenforceable, eg *Broom v Morgan* (n 68) 609–10 (Denning LJ), but *cf* 611–12 (Hodson LJ); *Tooth & Co v Tillyer* [1956] HCA 49, (1956) 95 CLR 605, 615 (Dixon CJ, Williams, Webb and Fullagar JJ).

[70] J Goudkamp, *Tort Law Defences* (Oxford, Hart Publishing, 2013) 128. See also Goudkamp, 2, 6–7 ('releases' from liability).

[71] *Broom v Morgan* (n 68) 612 (Hodson LJ); *Waugh v Waugh* [1950] NSW St Rp 20, (1950) 50 SR (NSW) 210, 215, following *Schubert v Schubert Wagon Co* (1928) 249 NY Reports 253; *Tooth & Co v Tillyer* (n 69) 618 (Dixon CJ, Williams, Webb and Fullagar JJ), 619 (McTiernan J).

[72] *Broom v Morgan* (n 68) 607 (Singleton LJ); Goudkamp, *Tort Law Defences* (n 70) 128.

[73] *Waugh v Waugh* [1950] NSW St Rp 20, (1950) 50 SR (NSW) 210, 215 (NSWCA), following *Schubert v Schubert Wagon Co* (1928) 249 NY Reports 253.

[74] ibid.

What is attributed?	Liability	Wrong	Acts
Employee has a defence, employer does not. Is employer liable?	No	Yes	Yes

In such cases involving section 12, the employer was held liable. This outcome suggests that vicarious liability attributes either the employee's acts or his wrong. More importantly, the reasoning used by courts supports the master's tort theory – that vicarious liability attributes acts.

In *Smith v Moss*,[75] a wife was a passenger in a car owned by her mother-in-law and driven by her husband. The car collided with another due to the husband's negligence. The wife was injured. She succeeded in an action against her mother-in-law despite the presence of section 12. Charles J held that the husband had two capacities: that of husband, and that of agent for the mother-in-law. As the husband had been acting in his capacity as the mother-in-law's agent when driving, the mother-in-law could be held liable.

The reasoning in the Australian case of *Waugh v Waugh*[76] is even clearer. A wife was a passenger in a car driven by her husband but owned by her son. The husband drove negligently, causing the wife to suffer injuries. In a suit by the wife against the son, the son relied on section 12's equivalent.[77] This argument was firmly rejected by the New South Wales Court of Appeal. Maxwell J held:

> If the present action involved the position that she was suing her husband for negligence resulting in personal injuries, it must, of course, fail. But that is precisely what she is not seeking to do; on the contrary, she is suing not him, but his principal. If the principal is liable, it is because the act of the agent is in law the act of the principal. It is but one illustration of the maxim 'Qui facit per alium facit per se'; in some instances it is more properly the application of the maxim 'respondeat superior.' But in either case the act of the agent is in law the act of the principal – and for that reason the liability of the principal arises.[78]

All members of the court in *Waugh* regarded the judgment of Chief Justice Cardozo in the American case of *Schubert v Schubert Wagon Co* as highly influential.[79] In *Schubert*, a wife was hit by her husband's car on the highway, the husband then acting in service of his employer. In a judgment where by six other Justices of the court concurred, Cardozo CJ held that the employer was liable:

> An employer commits a trespass by the hand of his servant upon the person of another. The act, let it be assumed, is within the scope either of an express mandate or of an implied one … The employer must answer for the damage whether there is a trespass by

[75] *Smith v Moss* [1940] 1 KB 424 (KB).
[76] (n 73).
[77] Married Women's Property Act 1901 (New South Wales), s 16.
[78] *Waugh* (n 73) 213.
[79] *Schubert v Schubert Wagon Co* (1928) 249 NY Reports 253.

> direct command or trespass incidental to the business committed to the servant's keeping. In each case the maxim governs that he who acts through another, acts by himself.[80]

This reasoning strongly supports the master's tort theory.

The leading English case today is *Broom v Morgan*.[81] The employer owed a pub, the 'Bird in Hand', where the victim and her husband were both employed. The husband was employed as a manager and the victim as a helper serving drinks and preparing refreshments. The husband carelessly left a trapdoor open into which the victim fell, resulting in her injury. She brought a claim against the employer in respect of the husband's careless acts. Section 12 of the 1882 Act provided the husband with a defence, but not the employer. All three members of the Court of Appeal held that the employer was liable for the husband's negligence, relying on the idea that the husband's acts could be attributed to the employer.

Singleton LJ followed *Waugh* and *Schubert*, applying the maxim that 'he who acts through another acts by himself', and concluded that while section 12 provided the husband a defence, there was no reason why that defence should be extended to the employer.[82] Similarly, Hodson LJ accepted that the employer was liable 'for the act of her servant', describing this as '"vicarious liability", or, perhaps more accurately, vicarious act'.[83] The third member of the court was Denning LJ. The main ground of his decision was that the employer's liability was not a 'substituted liability whereby a person who is not morally answerable is made responsible for the liability of another',[84] but a personal one which remained on him notwithstanding the husband's defence. However, he seems to have regarded the personal liability as arising from what would be known today as a non-delegable duty: a duty to see that the employee's work was properly and carefully done.[85] Since it was not, the duty was breached. The alternative ground was that section 12 only prevented enforceability of the wrong,[86] a view now rejected.[87] In total, the outcomes of these cases and their reasoning supports the view that the employee's acts, not his wrong or liability, were attributed.

C. Employer Has a Defence; Employee Does Not

A third example from mid-twentieth century Australia suggests the same approach in cases where the employer has a defence, but the employee does not, the reverse of the last category.

[80] ibid 256–57.
[81] (n 68).
[82] ibid 606–607.
[83] ibid 612.
[84] ibid 607.
[85] ibid 608–609.
[86] ibid 609.
[87] See n 69 above.

One example of this type concerns the Crown's vicarious liability for wrongs committed by its public officers. In the United Kingdom, the Crown had a defence or 'immunity' from liability for torts until 1947, subject to certain exceptions.[88] That defence was based on the idea that the King (or Queen) could do no wrong.[89]

Again, the outcome depends on which theory is adopted. Under the master's tort theory, the employer ought not be liable. Even though the employee's act can be attributed to the employer, the latter has a defence to liability for breach of duty through that act.

What if vicarious liability attributes the employee's wrong or liability? This is more difficult since the outcome turns partly on the nature of the defence. If the defence prevents the Crown from incurring all forms of liability arising from wrongs, then even if liability or the wrong is attributed to the employer, he would be protected by the defence. The result: no liability. But if the defence was based only on the idea that the King could do no wrong, then, arguably, it would not apply to cases where liability is merely attributed to the employer. The Crown is merely being foisted with the liability of another. Less clearly, the same might also be true if the wrong was attributed if the maxim that 'the King can do no wrong' did not apply to attributed wrongs.

What is attributed?	**Liability**	**Wrong**	**Acts**
Employer has a defence, employee does not. Is employer liable?	Depends, maybe yes	Depends, maybe yes	No

In Australia, state immunity was generally abolished in 1902[90] but was preserved in cases where public officers who are 'charge[d] with a discretion and responsibility in the execution of an independent legal duty' commit torts in the course of their office.[91] *Little v Commonwealth* was one such case.[92] Mr Little lived in

[88] Crown Proceedings Act 1947 (10 & 11 Geo 6, c 44), s 2(3). Amendments to the Act further reduced the scope of some of these exceptions, eg Crown Proceedings (Armed Forces) Act 1987.

[89] Eg W Blackstone, *Commentaries on the Laws of England*, vol 1 (Oxford, Clarendon Press, 1765) 239; W Blackstone, *Commentaries on the Laws of England*, vol 4 (Oxford, Clarendon Press, 1769) 32–33; *Matthews v Ministry of Defence* [2003] UKHL 4, [2003] 1 AC 1163, [4] (Lord Bingham), [54] (Lord Hope), [81] (Lord Millett), [116] (Lord Walker).

[90] Claims against the Commonwealth Act 1902 (Cth), s 2.

[91] *Little v Commonwealth* [1947] HCA 24, (1947) 75 CLR 94 (Dixon J), following *Tobin v The Queen* [1864] EngR 21, 143 ER 1148; *Raleigh v Goschen* (1898) 1 Ch 73; *Baume v The Commonwealth* [1906] HCA 92, (1906) 4 CLR 97; *Fowles v Eastern and Australian Steamship Co Ltd* [1913] HCA 31, (1913) 17 CLR 149; *Zachariassen v The Commonwealth* [1917] HCA 77, (1917) 24 CLR 166; *Commonwealth v Zachariassen* (1920) 27 CLR 552; *Fisher v Oldham Corpn* (1930) 2 KB 364; *Field v Nott* [1939] HCA 41, (1939) 62 CLR 660.

[92] *Little v Commonwealth* [1947] HCA 24, (1947) 75 CLR 94 (Dixon J). After the 1960s, a different approach appeared to be taken: *Parker v The Commonwealth* [1965] HCA 12, 112 CLR 295; *De Bruyn v South Australia* (1990) 54 SASR 231 (SASC); *Bell v Western Australia* [2004] WASCA 205, 28 WAR 555; *Kable v State of New South Wales* [2012] NSWCA 243, perhaps due to a

Rockhampton but owned an island near it where he kept sheep and cattle. A police officer, following instructions transmitted from intelligence authorities, served on Little an order restricting his place of residence. Little returned to his island in preparation for the move. When he did not return, the police officer and two constables returned to bring him back to Rockhampton, where he was locked up under a detention order. Little alleged that the police officer had falsely imprisoned him. The action failed on other grounds, but if the public officer had made the arrests and detention during his office, the High Court of Australia concluded that the Crown would not have been vicariously liable. This outcome is consistent with the master's tort theory. It thus can be seen as providing some support for the master's tort theory, albeit less strong than the previous examples.

D. Contributory Negligence and Contribution

Further evidence in favour of the master's tort theory during this period can be found in the law on contributory negligence[93] and contribution. Only the master's tort theory can explain their operation.

In *Daniels v Anderson*, an employer company sued its auditors for losses incurred from unsupervised transactions.[94] The auditors sought to rely on the carelessness of the company's employees, attributing them to the company for contributory negligence. This argument succeeded. The 'both ways' test was used: the employee's acts will be attributed to the employer for contributory negligence if and only if the employer would otherwise be vicariously liable for those same acts.[95]

On the servant's tort theory, the use of this test is difficult to explain. Why should there be symmetry between cases where the employer is suing or defending a claim?[96] Policy reasons which might be used to justify holding the employer liable, such as the employer's deep pockets or superior loss-spreading ability, do not readily justify reducing the quantum of recovery when the employer is suing. But the 'both ways' test is easily explicable on the master's tort theory. In both cases, what we are concerned with is when the employee's acts can be attributed to the employer; this should be not change regardless of whether the employer is claimant or defendant.[97]

The master's tort theory also explains another feature of contributory negligence. In general, apportionment for contributory negligence can only be made in respect of the negligence of parties before the court. But this principle

different justification for the immunity, see eg *Mewett v Commonwealth* (1997) HCA 29, 191 CLR 471, reinterpreting the maxim that 'the King can do no wrong'.

[93] Once an 'all or nothing' defence. Now see the Law Reform (Contributory Negligence) Act 1945.

[94] *Daniels v Anderson* (1995) 16 ACSR 607 (NSWCA).

[95] ibid 725–26. See also G Williams, *Joint Torts and Contributory Negligence* (London, Stevens & Sons Limited, 1951) 432–36; A Bartlett, 'Attribution of Contributory Negligence: Agents, Company Directors and Fraudsters' (1998) 114 *LQR* 460.

[96] Stevens, *Torts and Rights* (n 8) 262.

[97] See Ch 7 below.

does not seem to apply where the employer is being held contributorily negligent for the employee's acts.[98] It is because the employee's acts are attributed to the employer, so his acts *are* the employer's. The parties involved are the victim and the employer, and both are before the court.

The master's tort theory also explains the operation of contribution. The victim may successfully sue the employer, who is held vicariously liable for his employee's wrong. The employer may then seek contribution[99] against another person who is 'liable for the same damage' suffered by the victim. As regards that person, the employer is treated as a blameworthy party rather than a wholly innocent party merely liable for his employee's wrongdoing.[100] This is difficult to explain on the servant's tort theory. But the master's tort theory easily explains this: acts are attributed to the employer not just for purposes of establishing that the employer committed a wrong against the victim, but also for contribution claims as against another joint tortfeasor.

IV. 1956 and after: Development of Servant's Tort Theory

1956 marked the start of a decline in support for the master's tort theory.[101] Proponents of the servant's tort theory over the master's tort theory typically point to two decisions of the House of Lords, *Staveley Iron & Chemical Co Ltd v Jones*[102] and *Imperial Chemical Industries v Shatwell*,[103] in support. After *Staveley* and *ICI*, the label 'vicarious liability' became used to describe a doctrine attributing liability, following the servant's tort theory.

A. *Staveley* and *ICI*

Staveley is widely regarded as the leading case rejecting the master's tort theory. A crane driver negligently injured a fellow employee while moving iron cores by crane; the victim sued his employers in negligence. Before the House of Lords, the issue was not whether the employer was liable, but whether the crane driver had been negligent and whether the victim had been contributorily negligent. The House of Lords held that the crane driver had been negligent, but the claimant

[98] Atiyah (n 8) 410.

[99] Law Reform (Married Women and Tortfeasors) Act 1935, s 6, now repealed and replaced by the Civil Liability (Contribution) Act 1978, s 2(1).

[100] Williams, *Joint Torts and Contributory Negligence* (n 95) 166–67. This was later confirmed, confusingly, after vicarious liability had become a doctrine attributing liability: *Dubai Aluminium Co Ltd v Salaam* [2002] UKHL 48, [2003] 2 AC 366, [43]–[49] (Lord Nicholls).

[101] See broadly *Pioneer Mortgage* (n 56) [51].

[102] *Staveley Iron & Chemical Co Ltd v Jones* [1956] AC 627 (HL).

[103] *Imperial Chemical Industries v Shatwell* [1965] AC 656 (HL).

was not contributorily negligent. But *Staveley* was not a case where the outcome depended on which theory of vicarious liability was adopted. Both employee and employer owed duties to the victim, and neither had defences personal to them. Regardless whether the act, wrong, or liability was attributed, the employer would still have been liable.

However, in *dicta*, Lord Reid considered the situation if the employee had not been negligent. As he explained:

> [I]f this means that the appellants could be held liable even if it were held that the crane driver was not himself guilty of negligence, then I cannot accept that view … It is a rule of law that an employer, though guilty of no fault himself, is liable for damage done by the fault or negligence of his servant acting in the course of his employment. The maxims respondeat superior and qui facit per alium facit per se are often used, but I do not think that they add anything or that they lead to any different results.[104]

This reasoning supports the servant's tort theory, not the master's tort theory. It saw the wrong of the employee as the necessary condition for liability, a departure from the pre-1956 cases.

Subsequently, *ICI v Shatwell* also provided further support for the servant's tort theory.[105] Two brothers, James and George Shatwell, were employed by the same employer to place explosives for blast operations in quarries. The previous practice was to test the explosives in the open, but safety concerns were raised, so the employer instructed its employees to conduct testing from a shelter. Defying these orders, the brothers conducted testing in the open. Both were injured. George sought to hold the employer vicariously liable for James' negligence and breach of statutory duty. Before the House of Lords, the main issues were whether James' negligence had caused the claimant's injury and, if so, whether James had voluntarily accepted the risk of injury. The answer to both questions was yes, so the employer was not liable.

Several members of the House of Lords focused again on whether the employee had committed a tort against the victim, a key requirement under the servant's tort theory. Viscount Radcliffe said that '[s]ince in this case the employer, if liable at all, is liable only by virtue of vicarious responsibility, I agree that the primary issue, if the respondent, George Shatwell, is to succeed here, is whether he could maintain an action for damages against his brother James'.[106] Similarly, Lord Hodson thought the case 'should be looked at first as if it were an action by George Shatwell against James Shatwell before the doctrine of respondeat superior is applied'.[107] Lord Pearce also approved of *Staveley*, holding that 'unless the servant is liable the master is not liable for his acts'.[108] He also accepted policy-based justifications for vicarious liability,[109] which fit more comfortably with the servant's tort theory.

[104] (n 102) 643.
[105] (n 103).
[106] (n 103) 676.
[107] ibid 681.
[108] ibid 686.
[109] ibid 685.

The tide was turning. Growing support for the servant's tort theory could be seen, likely influenced by the dominant view of tort law in the twentieth century. Tort law then was not heavily associated with the idea of a civil wrong, but was viewed only as a loss-compensation device, a tool for ensuring the efficient allocation of losses in society through compensation.[110] The servant's tort theory generally[111] seemed to fit well within this paradigm: it could shift loss from an impecunious wrongdoing employee onto his employer, who typically had deeper pockets, greater ability to spread risk via insurance and was better placed to avoid the losses from arising.[112] But definitive adoption of the servant's tort theory was only to come later.

B. Evidence for the Servant's Tort Theory

Fast-forward several decades. By *Lister*, the label 'vicarious liability' was widely accepted as referring to the attribution of liability. The servant's tort theory had triumphed. Three sources of evidence suggest this: the courts' language and reasoning; cases where the employer owed the victim a duty but the employee did not; and cases where the employee owed the victim a duty but the employer did not.

i. *Reasoning of Courts after* Lister

Perhaps the strongest evidence providing support for the servant's tort theory is the reasoning and language used by the courts to describe vicarious liability. While some evidence pre-dated *Lister*,[113] the strongest evidence can be found in and after *Lister*.[114] In *Lister*, the claimants had been sexually abused as children by a warden at a boarding house at which they resided. Many years later,[115] the claimants sought to hold the boarding house owners and managers vicariously liable for the warden's sexual abuse. Following an earlier Court of Appeal decision,[116] the lower courts concluded that sexual abuse was not within the warden's course of

[110] G Williams, 'Vicarious Liability and the Master's Indemnity' (1957) 20 *MLR* 220, 232.

[111] *cf Lister v Romford Ice and Cold Storage Co Ltd* [1957] AC 555 (HL), providing the employer with an indemnity against the employee under an implied contractual term, noted by T Weir, 'Subrogation and Indemnity' (2012) 71 *CLJ* 1.

[112] See eg S Deakin et al, *Markesinis and Deakin's Tort Law*, 7th edn (Oxford, Oxford University Press, 2013) 567–68; Giliker (n 8) Ch 8.

[113] See eg *X (Minors) v Bedfordshire County Council* [1995] 2 AC 633 (HL) 712.

[114] Most recently, see eg *Bilta (UK) Ltd (in liquidation) v NatWest Markets plc* [2020] EWHC 546 (Ch) [217]–[218], remitted for retrial on different grounds: *NatWest Markets plc v Bilta (UK) Ltd (in liquidation)* [2021] EWCA Civ 680.

[115] Raising difficult issues of limitation under *Stubbings v Webb* [1993] AC 498 (HL); later addressed in *A v Hoare* [2008] UKHL 6, [2008] 1 AC 844.

[116] *Trotman v North Yorkshire County Council* [1999] LGR 584 (CA).

employment, and the defendants were not liable.[117] However, the House of Lords unanimously reversed the Court of Appeal's decision and found the defendants vicariously liable.

Three points can be made. First, the descriptions of vicarious liability relied upon in *Lister* and post-*Lister* support the servant's tort theory. In *Lister*, both the leading speeches of Lord Steyn and Lord Millett reflect the servant's tort theory. Lord Steyn described vicarious liability as 'legal responsibility imposed on an employer, although he is himself free from blame, for a tort committed by his employee in the course of his employment'.[118] Similarly, Lord Millett firmly declared that:

> Vicarious liability is a species of strict liability. It is not premised on any culpable act or omission on the part of the employer; an employer who is not personally at fault is made legally answerable for the fault of his employee. It is best understood as a loss-distribution device.[119]

Post-*Lister* cases continue to repeatedly describe vicarious liability as involving liability for another's wrong, not his own wrong. In *Dubai Aluminium v Salaam*, Lord Millett described vicarious liability as a 'loss distribution device based on grounds of social and economic policy'.[120] Lord Hobhouse said that 'the vicariously liable employer has in law the same responsibility as his employee: the law attributes the responsibility of the employee to the employer'.[121] In *Woodland v Swimming Teachers Association*, Lord Sumption said that:

> In principle, liability in tort depends on proof of a personal breach of duty. To that principle, there is at common law only one true exception, namely vicarious liability. Where a defendant is vicariously liable for the tort of another, he commits no tort himself and may not even owe the relevant duty, but is held liable as a matter of public policy for the tort of the other.[122]

Similarly, in *Armes v Nottinghamshire CC*, it was again said that under vicarious liability, 'the law holds a defendant liable for a tort committed by another person'.[123]

Second, the servant's tort theory is also reflected in changes in the requirements for vicarious liability, especially the course of employment test. In *Lister*, Lord Steyn accepted that the Salmond test did not 'cope ideally' with intentional wrongdoing.[124] He therefore formulated a new 'close connection' test. The key question 'is whether the warden's torts were so closely connected with his employment

[117] *Lister* (n 7) [7]–[9] (Lord Steyn).
[118] ibid [14].
[119] ibid [65].
[120] *Dubai Aluminium* (n 7) [107].
[121] *Dubai Aluminium* (n 7) [74]. See also, describing liability as being 'imposed by a policy of the law on the employer': *Viasystems (Tyneside) Ltd v Thermal Transfer (Northern) Ltd* [2005] EWCA Civ 1151, [2006] QB 510 [55].
[122] *Woodland* (n 27) [3].
[123] *Armes* (n 7) [54].
[124] *Lister* (n 7) [20].

that it would be fair and just to hold the employers vicariously liable'.[125] This was so in *Lister*. The torts were committed on the premises of the defendants and in the time when the warden was caring for the children.[126] The sexual abuse was 'inextricably interwoven' with the warden's performance of his duties at the boarding house.[127] Similarly, for Lord Millett, vicarious liability is 'based on the general idea that a person who employs another for his own ends inevitably creates a risk that the employee will commit a legal wrong'.[128] Thus, the defendant school ought to be held vicariously liable for the warden's abuse. The school had entrusted its responsibility to care for the children to the warden, who 'abused the special position in which the school had placed him'.[129] This reasoning is premised on the search for reasons to hold one person liable for the wrong of another, not reasons to attribute acts.

Third, the servant's tort theory also explains the use of policy reasoning post-*Lister*. If vicarious liability is an exception to the general rule that tort liability requires the commission of wrongs, it requires special justification. The cases attempt to supply it by relying on policy. As *Armes* explains, '[f]or reasons of policy the defendant is held liable for the breach of a duty owed to the claimant by a third party'.[130] Policy factors were also explicitly relied on in the *Christian Brothers* case, including the employer's deeper pockets, creation of risk, and control over the employee.[131] Further reference was made to them in *Cox v Ministry of Justice*,[132] and they were again relied on and balanced against each other in *Armes*.[133] These reasons are thought to make it just for the employer to be held liable. Reliance on these policy factors fits most naturally if what was attributed was liability, not acts.

ii. Cases where Employee Owes a Duty, Employer Does Not

Cases where the employee owed a duty but the employer does not also suggest that vicarious liability post-1956 attributes liability, not acts. In *Majrowski v Guy's and St Thomas's NHS Trust*,[134] the victim, a gay man, had allegedly been harassed at his workplace by his departmental manager due to homophobia. This, he argued, was a breach of the Protection from Harassment Act 1997.[135] Both were employed by the defendant trust. The victim brought no claim against the department manager but instead sued the trust, seeking to hold it vicariously liable for the department

[125] ibid [28].
[126] ibid [20].
[127] ibid [28].
[128] ibid 244.
[129] ibid 250.
[130] *Armes* (n 7) [30].
[131] The *Christian Brothers* case (n 7) [35].
[132] *Cox* (n 7) [18]–[23].
[133] *Armes* (n 7) [59]–[71].
[134] (n 7).
[135] Protection from Harassment Act 1997, s 1.

manager's breach of statutory duty under section 3 of the Act. The House of Lords refused to strike out the victim's claim. Lord Nicholls framed the issue by asking:

> Does employers' vicarious liability arise unless the statutory provision expressly or impliedly excludes such liability? Or does employers' liability arise only if the statutory provision expressly or impliedly envisages such liability may arise?[136]

This reasoning only makes sense if the department manager's liability for breach of statutory duty was being attributed.[137] If the manager's acts were attributed, then the trust's liability turned on whether it owed the victim a duty under the Act. But if the manager's liability was attributed, that inquiry was unnecessary; what was necessary was that the Act did not exclude the attribution of liability.

A similar, more recent example is *WM Morrison Supermarkets plc v Claimants*.[138] Skelton was a senior auditor in Morrisons' internal audit team. He had been given the data to transmit to external auditors. After being subject to disciplinary proceedings for having slimming drugs shipped from Morrisons' post-room,[139] Skelton harboured a grudge against his employer. He copied the personal data of nearly 100,000 of Morrisons' employees, uploaded it onto a public file-sharing website, and sent CDs containing the file to three newspapers. Morrisons' current and former employees whose data had been disclosed sought to hold Morrisons vicariously liable for Skelton's breach of statutory duty under the Data Protection Act 1998,[140] amongst others.

The Supreme Court again approached the issue by asking whether the Data Protection Act 1998 impliedly excluded vicarious liability,[141] concluding that it does not. On the facts, Skelton's acts were not sufficiently closely connected to the acts he was employed to do, so Morrisons was not vicariously liable for Skelton's conduct. But had the requirements of vicarious liability been met, Morrisons would have been liable. This liability must have been truly vicarious, not personal, as it was found at first instance that Morrisons was not a 'data controller' within relevant provisions of the Data Protection Act 1998 and thus owed no duty under it to the victims. The 'vicarious liability' contemplated in *Morrison* could only have involved the attribution of liability, not acts.

iii. Cases where Employer Owes a Duty, Employee Does Not

The reverse situation, where the employer owes the victim a duty but the employee does not, also supports the attribution of liability. An example is provided by *Axon v Ministry of Defence*.[142] Commander Axon, the commanding officer of

136 *Majrowski* (n 7) [17].
137 Stevens, 'Vicarious Liability or Vicarious Action?' (n 48) 32; Stevens, *Torts and Rights* (n 8) 264–65.
138 (n 7).
139 In which Skelton carried out a side business: [2017] EWHC 3113 (QB) [17]–[21].
140 Data Protection Act 1998, s 4(4).
141 (n 7) [15].
142 *Axon v Ministry of Defence* [2016] EWHC 787 (QB).

the HMS Somerset in the Royal Navy, bullied junior officers aboard the ship and was dismissed from his position. A newspaper, *The Sun*, published stories about Axon's misconduct and subsequent removal, using information obtained from an employee at the Ministry of Defence, Ms Jordan-Barber. Axon sought to hold the Ministry of Defence vicariously liable for Jordan-Barber's breaches of confidence and misuse of private information. The claims failed because Jordan-Barber owed no duty of confidentiality to Axon and thus committed no tort against him. As Nicol J explained:

> [T]he Claimant cannot maintain a distinct claim for breach of confidence because he cannot show that Ms Jordan-Barber owed him any duty to keep any material confidential … I have no doubt that she owed a duty to preserve the confidentiality of information which she received in the course of her work and which she was not authorised to disclose to outsiders. However, that was a duty which she owed to either the Crown or the Ministry of Defence. It was not a duty which she owed to the Claimant.[143]

Later, Nicol J emphasised that '[i]t is only if [Ms Jordan-Barber] committed a tort against [the claimant] that any issue of vicarious liability could arise',[144] again providing further support for the servant's tort theory.

V. The Attribution of Acts after 1956

Pre-1956, vicarious liability attributed acts. After 1956, it attributed liability. But this does not mean that acts were no longer attributed after 1956. Although obscured from view, the attribution of acts still exists. Some cases, particularly misrepresentation ones, can only be explained as involving personal liability, established by attributing acts. For convenience, the person to whom acts are attributed will be referred to as 'the employer', and the person whose acts are attributed, 'the employee'. They show that even after 1956, acts could still be attributed.

A. Employer Owes Duty but Employee Does Not

First, consider cases where the employer owes a duty, but the employee does not. This situation is the reverse of that in *Twine* and *Darling Island*. The most prominent examples concern negligent misrepresentations.

A classic example is *Williams v Natural Life Health Foods Ltd.*[145] The defendant company provided brochures and financial predictions to prospective franchisees which had been prepared by Mistlin, its managing director and principal

[143] ibid [68].
[144] ibid [94].
[145] *Williams v Natural Life Health Foods Ltd* [1998] 1 WLR 830 (HL).

shareholder. Relying on them, the claimants entered a franchise agreement. The predictions were highly inaccurate and the claimants suffered losses. They sued both Mistlin and the company for negligent misrepresentation, but the company was dissolved, and the actions later proceeded against Mistlin alone.[146]

At first instance, Langley J concluded that the company had assumed responsibility over the representations[147] and thus owed a duty of care to Williams. It breached this duty when it supplied the inaccurate projections, committing the tort of negligent misrepresentation.[148] Both Langley J and the Court of Appeal[149] likewise concluded that Mistlin had committed the tort of negligent misrepresentation, but that conclusion was subsequently overturned by the House of Lords. As Lord Steyn explained, Mistlin had no personal dealings with Williams. Nothing that Mistlin said or did suggested that he had assumed responsibility for the statements in the projections.[150] There was not even evidence that the claimants believed that Mistlin was assuming responsibility.[151] He thus owed no duty of care to Williams and breached no duty by preparing the statements shown to the claimants. As Mistlin was not personally liable, he had no liability that could be attributed to the company. The company's liability could only be personal, established by attributing acts to it.

Similarly, in *Kooragang Investments Pty Ltd v Richardson & Wrench*,[152] the claimant lenders had relied on negligently made valuations provided by the defendant's valuer, Rathborne, in making loans to the GB Group. The claimants suffered loss and sued the defendants to recover their losses. The defendant firm had instructed its valuers not to provide further valuations to that Group, but Rathborne had acted against these instructions. Relevantly, Rathborne was also a director in one of the Group's companies.

The primary issue before the Privy Council was, as Lord Wilberforce put it, whether the defendants were 'vicariously responsible' for the valuer's negligence.[153] Concluding that they were not, the second issue – whether the defendants owed the claimants a duty of care for the valuations – did not need to be considered. Despite the language of 'vicarious responsibility', the Privy Council must have been dealing here with the defendant firm's personal liability. Otherwise, it would not have been necessary, as the Privy Council thought it was, to consider whether the defendants owed the claimants a duty of care.[154] That personal liability was to be established by attributing the acts of the firm's valuer to it.

[146] *Williams v Natural Life Health Foods Ltd* [1996] BCC 376 (QB) 377 (Langley J).
[147] See *Hedley Bryne & Co Ltd v Heller & Partners* [1964] AC 465 (HL).
[148] *Williams* (HC) (n 146) 381–82 (Langley J).
[149] ibid 385–87; *Williams v Natural Life Health Foods Ltd* [1997] BCC 605 (CA) 622–23 (Hirst LJ), 623 (Waite LJ), *cf* 624–25 (Sir Patrick Russell).
[150] *Williams* (HL) (n 145) 836–38 (HL) (Lord Steyn).
[151] ibid 838 (Lord Steyn).
[152] *Kooragang Investments Pty Ltd v Richardson & Wrench* [1982] AC 462 (PC).
[153] ibid 469.
[154] ibid 475. See also 469, identifying it as the second key issue.

B. Employer Breaches Duty but Employee Does Not

A second category is where an act done by an employee results in no breach of duty by the employee, but where attributed to the employer, constitutes a breach of duty by the employer.

Again, negligent misrepresentations provide a good example. *WB Anderson & Sons v Rhodes (Liverpool) Ltd* is one such example.[155] Rhodes supplied potatoes to Taylors on credit. Taylors was very tardy with payment and a substantial sum was outstanding at all material times. This was not picked up by anyone in Rhodes due to poor accounting practices by Rhodes' bookkeeper and manager. Later, Rhodes started acting as Taylors' commission agent. When potential sellers to Taylors asked one of Rhodes' agents about Taylors' reliability, the agent said that Taylors was 'all right'.[156] The claimants advanced potatoes to Taylors on credit. When Taylors failed to pay, they successfully sued Rhodes for making negligent misrepresentations.

It was found that Rhodes owed a duty of care to the claimants in respect of its representations, which it had breached through the negligence of its bookkeeper and manager. This could only be analysed as a personal liability case. As Cairns J explained, the agent was not negligent though he made the representations, and the bookkeeper and manager were negligent though they made no representations.[157] Individually, neither committed the tort of negligent misrepresentations,[158] and so they had no liability which could be attributed to Rhodes. The employer's liability must have been personal, established by attributing acts to it.

C. Employer Has No Defence, but Employee Does

A third category involves cases where the employer has no defence, but the employee does. Here, defamation provides an example. The publication of otherwise defamatory statements may be subject to defences, including qualified privilege. In *Egger v Viscount Chelmsford*,[159] a third party asked an unincorporated club if the claimant, Mrs Egger could be appointed to judge Alsatians at a dog show. The assistant secretary of the club, instructed by the club's sub-committee, published a letter defaming Mrs Egger. The occasion of the communication was privileged, but qualified privilege required that the words be published bona fide and without malice. The assistant secretary was not motivated by malice, but five out of eight of the committee members were.[160] Lord Denning MR emphasised that

[155] *WB Anderson & Sons v Rhodes (Liverpool) Ltd* [1967] 2 All ER 850 (Liverpool Assizes).
[156] ibid 854–55.
[157] ibid 856.
[158] ibid 856.
[159] *Egger v Viscount Chelmsford and others* [1965] 1 QB 248 (CA).
[160] ibid 258.

the assistant secretary was not liable: although she published the defamatory statement, she was innocent of malice and was entitled to the defence, notwithstanding the malice of the committee members.[161] However, the committee members who were motivated by malice could not rely on qualified privilege, and thus were liable for defamation. This required that the acts of the secretary be attributed to the committee members.

These three categories show that even after 1956, some cases can only be explained by an employer's personal liability, committed through acts attributed to him. What changed was that the rules attributing acts were no longer collected under the single banner of 'vicarious liability'. Examples of the attribution of acts were instead scattered across different parts of tort law. Their presence could thus easily go unnoticed.

VI. When are Acts Attributed?

This then leads to the final question: when are acts attributed? Pre-1956, this question was largely addressed within 'vicarious liability', which attributed acts then. Many of the rules attributing acts could be found within that doctrine.

Under pre-1956 vicarious liability, two requirements were necessary for acts to be attributed: the employer and employee had to be in a qualifying relationship, and the wrongful acts had to be in the 'course of employment', then determined by the Salmond test. These requirements implicitly adopt the same analysis as the attribution of acts in other areas of law. Both before and after 1956, attribution turned on four questions: (i) did the company have powers to do the act? (ii) were the company's powers allocated or delegated to the person acting? (iii) was the person acting within the scope of the power? (iv) was the power properly exercised?

A. *Ultra Vires*: The Company's Powers

Vicarious liability applies equally to corporate and non-corporate employers, explaining why vicarious liability contains no explicit requirements about the company's powers. But this requirement is implicitly assumed for corporate employers.

Controversy about a company's capacity and powers to do acts which constitute wrongs predate modern vicarious liability by centuries. It was once thought that the commission of wrongs would automatically be outside the company's capacity and powers.[162] As Joshua Getzler explains, as far back as 1562, in the

[161] ibid 264.

[162] See generally J Getzler, 'Disciplining Corporation through Tort Liability and Disability' (Law and Finance Workshop paper, University of Oxford, 2010) (unpublished).

Case of Norwich Corporation, Catesby J held that '[i]t cannot be denied that the Mayor, Sheriffs and commonalty are one entire body, which cannot be severed, and which cannot do any corporal wrong'.[163] But in *Yarborough v Governors of Bank of England*, Lord Ellenborough accepted that corporations could commit wrongs if they did or ordered acts to be done on their behalf, and those acts were 'of a tortious nature'.[164] The view that companies had no capacity or powers to commit wrongs was finally put to rest when Kelly CB concluded in *Mill v Hawker* that 'the law is now well settled that upon any tortious act committed by a corporation, or under its authority, or by its direction, trover or trespass is maintainable'.[165]

Just like a company's other powers, its powers to act may be expressly listed in the company's constitution. Thus, a company's powers to load or unload ships,[166] make representations to prospective business partners,[167] give lifts to passengers,[168] and so on, may be expressly provided for. If not, they would be implied, if necessary, to pursue their authorised objects. A company operating an omnibus-driving business would have implied powers to drive omnibuses and to hire drivers to do the driving.[169] Similarly, a company set up to run health food shops would at least have implied powers to make representations to prospective franchisees about projected returns from franchises of those shops.[170] These are generally ordinary powers. Where the company exercises these powers in a way constituting a wrong, there is no difficulty in saying it has committed a wrong.

B. Qualifying Relationships: Allocation and Delegation

A company's board of directors may sometimes authorise the doing of wrongful acts. In these cases, there is no difficulty in concluding that the company has committed a wrong. The analogous case of *Mill v Hawker* illustrates.[171] Members of a highway board passed a resolution directing their surveyor to remove an obstruction placed by the claimant on the claimant's field. The surveyor duly removed the obstruction. The claimant sued for trespass with the majority of the Court of Exchequer concluding that the action was maintainable. These cases show that where individuals or groups allocated the company's powers exercise them in a way which constitutes a wrong, there is no difficulty in attributing those acts to the company.

[163] ibid 14, citing *Case of Norwich Corporation* Mich 21 Eliz 4, fol 12 pl 4.
[164] *Yarborough v Governors of Bank of England* (1812) 16 East 6, 104 ER 991 (KB).
[165] *Mill v Hawker* (1873–74) LR 9 Ex 309 (Ct of Exch).
[166] *Darling Island* (n 63).
[167] *Williams v Natural Life* (n 145).
[168] *Twine* (n 57).
[169] Eg *Limpus v London General Omnibus Company* (1862) 1 H&N 526 (Ct of Exch).
[170] Eg *Williams v Natural Life* (n 145).
[171] (n 165).

But such situations will likely be rare: wrongful acts will often be done by lower-level individuals. When will their acts be attributed? The answer is found in the requirements of pre-1956 vicarious liability: those individuals must be delegated the company's powers to act.

The first of vicarious liability's two requirements, the qualifying relationship, implicitly reflects the delegation of the company's powers to act. Observing this requires abstracting away from detail. It is hardly an overstatement to say that the most common qualifying relationship pre-1956 was employment.[172] Employment once turned on the employer's effective control over how the employee did the work,[173] but now turns on multiple other factors as well, including ownership of tools used for performance, chance of profit, and who bears the risk of loss.[174] But other qualifying relationships existed, including agency[175] and partnership.[176] 'Casual delegation' cases, where the owner lends his car to another to drive, were also analysed as agency ones.[177]

These relationships all involve delegated powers. Perhaps this is clearest with agency and, relatedly, partnership. Agency involves the principal's delegation of powers to the agent, giving the agent a 'proxy power': a power to exercise the principal's own powers.[178] Partnership operates similarly. Partners act as agents of the firm and other partners, able to bind the firm and other partners when doing acts 'for carrying on in the usual way business of the kind carried on by the firm'.[179] Employment, too, appears to reflect delegation. The company's powers will typically be allocated to the board or general meeting and then delegated down the corporate hierarchy to managers, bookkeepers, drivers, bartenders, or petrol station attendants alike.[180] These employees exercise the company's powers to act when they make representations, verify accounts, serve drinks, receive payment for services, and more.

[172] P Morgan, 'Recasting Vicarious Liability' (2012) 71 *CLJ* 615, 625–28.

[173] M Jones (ed), *Clerk & Lindsell on Torts*, 23rd edn (London, Sweet & Maxwell, 2020) para 6-08, see especially *Short v J & W Henderson Ltd* (1946) 62 TLR 427 (HL) 429; *Mersey Docks and Harbour Board v Coggins and Griffith (Liverpool) Ltd* [1947] AC 1 (HL) 17.

[174] Eg *Montreal v Montreal Locomotive Works Ltd* [1947] DLR 161, 169 (PC); *Ready Mixed Concrete (South East) Ltd v Minister of Pensions and National Insurance* [1968] 2 QB 497 (QB).

[175] *Barwick v English Joint Stock Bank* (1867) LR 2 Ex 259 (Exch Chamber); *Hamlyn v John Houston & Co* [1903] 1 KB 81 (CA); *Lloyd v Grace, Smith & Co* [1912] AC 716 (HL); *Colonial Mutual Life Assurance Society Ltd v Producers and Citizens Co-Operative Assurance Co* [1931] HCA 53, (1931) 46 CLR 41; *'Thelma' (Owners) v University College School* [1953] 2 Lloyd's Rep 613, 618 (Mayor's and City of London Ct).

[176] See eg Partnership Act 1890, s 10.

[177] *Hewitt v Bonvin* [1940] 1 KB 188 (CA) 191; *Launchbury v Morgans* [1973] AC 127 (HL) 135 (Lord Wilberforce), 140 (Lord Pearson), 144 (Lord Cross), 148 (Lord Salmon). In Australia, see also *Soblusky v Egan* [1960] HCA 9, (1960) 103 CLR 215. On extension to other vehicles: *Scott v Davis* [2000] HCA 52, (2000) 204 CLR 333 [8]–[9] (Gleeson CJ).

[178] R Leow, 'Understanding Agency: A Proxy Power Definition' (2019) 78 *CLJ* 99. See Ch 3 above.

[179] Partnership Act 1890, s 5, and see before *Lindley & Banks on Partnership*, 20th edn (London, Sweet & Maxwell, 2020) para 12-01.

[180] Eg *Warren v Henlys Ltd* [1948] 2 All ER 935 (KB).

While agency and partnership do evoke ideas of delegation, two reasons may be ventured for why employment does not explicitly reference delegation. First, employers may not always be companies, so defining employment using corporate-only features may be inappropriate. Second, a single definition of employment was once used across multiple areas of law, whether for tax, social security, labour law, or torts,[181] though this is no longer the case. Since an employee for one purpose would be an employee for another, a definition of employment had to accommodate different concerns in multiple areas of law. It might be that, though important for vicarious liability (and attribution), ideas of delegation were unsuitable for other contexts where the definition would be used.

The requirement of delegation is evident in both pre-1956 vicarious liability law and in post-1956 cases involving the employer's personal liability. The same relationships, agency and employment, are emphasised. In *WB Anderson*, Cairns J concluded that the representation of Rhodes' agent could be attributed as 'he acted as their servant or agent in making the representation'.[182] In *Egger v Viscount Chelmsford*, involving an unincorporated body, the secretary publishing the defamatory statements must have been delegated the powers of the club's sub-committee to do so.[183] The sub-committee must have derived its own powers from the club's committee, who were likely allocated powers under the club's constitution.

C. The Course of Employment: Scope

Vicarious liability's other requirement, that the wrongful acts must be done in the 'course of employment', reflects the idea that only acts within a certain scope can be attributed.

Prior to 1956, the course of employment was governed by the 'Salmond test'. Only authorised acts, or unauthorised acts which could be regarded as wrongful modes of performing authorised acts, were within the course of employment.[184] The test had two limbs. The first limb, covering 'authorised acts', contemplates *expressly* authorised acts. Its lineage is traceable to old authorities focusing on the employer's express commands to act.[185] Cases like *Mill v Hawker* fall in this category.[186] But in practice, cases in this category were rare. Most cases fell within

[181] But now see *Barclays* (n 7) [29].

[182] *WB Anderson* (n 155) 856–57.

[183] (n 159).

[184] RFV Heuston and RA Buckley, *Salmond and Heuston on Torts*, 21st edn (London, Sweet & Maxwell, 1996) 443.

[185] *Caunt's Case* (1430) YB Mich 9 Hen VI pl 37, fo 53, reproduced in JH Baker, *Baker and Milsom Sources of English Legal History*, 2nd edn (Oxford, Oxford University Press, 2010) 561–62; *Morley v Gaisford* (1795) 2 H Bl 441, 443, 126 ER 639, 641 (Ct of Common Pleas); *Chandler v Broughton* (1832) 1 C & M 29, 149 ER 301 (Ct of Exch); *Gregory v Piper* (1829) 9 B & C 591, 109 ER 220 (KB); *Doolan v Hill* (1879) 5 VLR(L) 290 (VSC); *Sharrod v The London and North Western Railway Company* (1849) 4 Ex 580, 585–86, 154 ER 1345, 1347–48 (Ct of Exch).

[186] *Mill v Hawker* (n 165).

the second limb of the Salmond test: acts which were not expressly authorised but could be regarded as 'wrongful modes' of performing expressly authorised acts. Classic examples involve negligence, for example where a lorry driver negligently reversed the lorry, injuring a fellow worker.[187] But the second limb generally would not cover intentional torts. Sexually assaulting minors is not merely a wrongful mode of performing the authorised acts of caring for minors[188] and stealing mink fur coats is not a wrongful mode of cleaning them.[189] They are the very opposite of what was authorised.[190]

Once employment and other qualifying relationships are understood as involving delegations of power, this enquiry resolves itself into the familiar one of ascertaining the scope of the power delegated. This is a question of fact. This was not always difficult: barmaids[191] and petrol station attendants[192] are not authorised to apply physical force to customers, though a bouncer might be. Employees authorised to make statements to one client may not be authorised to make them to another. Most difficult are cases where employers had expressly prohibited employees from doing certain acts. It is a matter of construction whether the prohibition limits the scope of employment (ie the power delegated) or only certain modes of performance. Cases both during this period[193] and after[194] often preferred the latter.

The scope requirement is also observable post-1956. In *Kooragang Investments Pty Ltd v Richardson & Wrench*, attribution of the valuer Rathborne's acts seemed to turn on the same Salmond test.[195] His acts could not be attributed as they were outside the scope of what he had power to do for the company, as Lord Wilberforce explained:

> If one then inquires, as their Lordships think it correct to do, whether Rathborne had any authority to make the valuations in question, the answer is clear: it is given in clear and convincing terms by the trial judge. Rathborne was not authorised to make them: he made them during a period when the G.B. group were not in a client relationship with the defendants, when valuers were ordered not to do business with them …. A clearer case of departure from the course or scope of Rathborne's employment cannot be imagined: it was total.[196]

[187] *Lister v Romford* (n 111).
[188] Eg *Trotman* (n 14).
[189] *Morris v CW Martin* (n 33).
[190] See *Lister* (n 7) [57] (Lord Hobhouse).
[191] *Deatons Pty Ltd v Flew* [1949] HCA 60, (1949) 79 CLR 370, contrast *Petterson v Royal Oak Hotel Ltd* [1948] NZLR 136 (NZCA).
[192] *Warren* (n 180).
[193] Eg *Limpus v London General Omnibus Co* (1862) 1 H&N 526, *Ricketts v Thomas Tilling* Ltd [1915] 1 KB 644 (CA); *Canadian Pacific Railway v Lockhart* [1942] AC 591 (PC).
[194] Eg *Ilkiw v Samuels* [1963] 1 WLR 991 (CA); *Rose v Plenty* [1976] 1 WLR 141 (CA).
[195] *Kooragang* (n 152) 471, sometimes using 'course of employment' synonymously with 'actual authority' to distinguish it from ostensible or apparent authority.
[196] ibid 475.

In *Williams v Natural Life*, the acts of the managing director in preparing projections, and the acts of the agent in sending them to a prospective franchisee[197] were both attributed to the company. Both were, on the face of the judgments, acting within the powers delegated to them. Similarly, in *WB Anderson*, the manager, bookkeeper, and agent making the representation were all performing acts that they were hired to do: managing the books, and making representations as commission agent respectively. A requirement of scope is thus uncontroversial; it is implicit within the 'course of employment' test.

D. The Course of Employment: Proper Exercise?

Finally, is there a requirement that the powers allocated or delegated to the employee must be properly exercised? Such a view was once widespread. But today it has fallen out of favour, having been apparently rejected by the House of Lords in *Lloyd v Grace, Smith & Co.*[198] But this fails to account for apparent authority's role. Once apparent authority is accounted for, the cases support a general rule that acts are only attributable where not intentionally done adversely to what the employee believed to be the principal's interests.

Prior to *Lloyd v Grace*, the leading case on the point was *Barwick v English Joint Stock Bank*.[199] Willes J stated that '[t]he general rule is, that the master is answerable for every such wrong of the servant or agent as is committed in the course of the service and for the master's benefit, though no express command or privity of the master be proved'.[200] This apparently required that acts must be done for the master's benefit.

Five decades later, in *Lloyd v Grace*, the managing clerk of a solicitors' firm made false representations to a customer of the firm, inducing her to give him title deeds of two cottages and convey them to him. He then disposed of the property for his own benefit, so that the customer suffered loss. She sought to hold the firm vicariously liable. The House of Lords concluded that the firm was liable, and that Willes J 'cannot have meant that the principal is absolved whenever his agent intended to appropriate for himself the proceeds of the fraud'.[201] *Barwick* then fell out of favour.

But careful attention must be paid to *Lloyd v Grace*'s facts and reasoning. It involved deceit. As a misrepresentation tort, apparent authority becomes relevant. In other torts, such as where sexual assaults are committed, apparent authority has no relevance. The warden of a boys' home has no apparent authority to sexually abuse children under his care: his employer does not represent that

[197] *Williams* (n 145) 379.
[198] (n 175).
[199] (n 175).
[200] ibid 265.
[201] (n 175) 725 (Earl Loreburn).

he has such authority, nor could the victims reasonably rely on such representations. But apparent authority might apply in deceit: the employer, by putting the employee in a particular position, represents that the employee has authority to do acts which a person in that position ordinarily would. Customers who reasonably rely on those representations to their detriment can thus estop the company from denying the employee's apparent authority. The firm was liable in *Lloyd v Grace* because of apparent authority, as illustrated by Earl Loreburn LC's description of the applicable rule: '[i]f the agent commits the fraud purporting to act in the course of business such as he was authorized, *or held out as authorized*, to transact on account of his principal, then the latter may be held liable for it' (emphasis added).[202] The use of holding-out reasoning clearly references apparent authority. *Lloyd v Grace* is thus only weak authority for its dismissal of *Barwick*; it was decided on estoppel, not the attribution of acts.

The point thus remains open. Perhaps the best formulation of the rule is that powers must be properly exercised, but the test for proper exercise is that the employee must not intentionally act against the principal's interests in exercising the power. This fits much of the case law, which encompasses cases where the employer was found to have committed no tort where the employee performed acts intentionally adverse to the principal's interests. Examples would include misappropriating property from the employer's clients,[203] or violence towards customers where the customers sought to complain.[204] Conversely, it also accommodates cases where the employee simply did not consider the principal's interests or committed torts advertently or inadvertently while intending to act in the principal's interests. It thus accommodates ordinary negligence, an example of the last mentioned, where employers clearly can be liable.

The proper exercise requirement is more limited in tort law compared to contract law because the powers exercised are usually ordinary powers. As explained in Chapter 2, the difference might be explicable by the difference between legal and ordinary powers. No manifestation of intention to change legal relations is necessary to exercise ordinary powers. Many acts exercising ordinary powers may thus be done without any specific intention, especially those done carelessly. Taking this into account, the requirement of proper exercise is less demanding, permitting attribution of acts exercising ordinary powers unless they are intentionally done against the company's interests.

The requirement of proper exercise seems to persist post-1956. Consider *Kooragang*, where the employee, Rathborne, was by all accounts intending to act against the firm's interests and instead for his own interests when he issued valuations in defiance of his employer's instructions. He was a director in a member company of the group requesting the valuations, and thus stood to benefit from

[202] (n 198) 725.
[203] Eg *Lloyd v Grace* (n 175).
[204] Eg *Deatons* (n 191); *Petterson v Royal Oak Hotel Ltd* (n 191); *Warren v Henlys Ltd* (n 180); *Keppel Bus Co Ltd v Ahmad* [1974] 1 WLR 1082 (PC).

doing so. The Privy Council described Rathborne's valuations as done 'without any authority from the defendants, not on behalf of the defendants but in his own interest, without any connection with the defendants' business'; the firm could not be liable for those valuations.[205] Conversely, there seems no difficulty with attributing negligent acts. Thus, the negligent book-keeping in *WB Anderson* and the production of faulty financial projections in *Williams v Natural Life* could both be attributed to the respective companies. Where acts are done negligently, the employee does not intend to act adversely to the principal's interests. The act can still be attributed.

Further illustrations of the improper exercise requirement are now increasingly difficult to locate. The wider close connection test means that claimants are likely to prefer the less difficult route of attributing liability rather than seeking to attribute acts and hold the defendant personally liable.[206] Proof of the requirement is therefore more challenging. But there is some evidence for it. The requirement is also in line with the idea that acts must be done consistently with corporate policy to be the company's intentional acts.[207]

VII. Conclusion

Rules attributing acts in tort law remain unknown, even shrouded in mystery. This chapter has aimed to show that tort law did and does still have rules attributing acts. Before 1956, those rules were found under the doctrine of 'vicarious liability', then a doctrine attributing acts. After 1956, the label 'vicarious liability' became used to refer to a doctrine attributing liability, not acts. But this did not mean the demise of the attribution of acts. Some cases are still only explicable by attributing acts. It is argued that the best interpretation of the law post-1956 is that acts could still be attributed on the same basis as before. What changed was that the rules attributing acts were no longer collected under the single banner of 'vicarious liability', nor were they affected by changes in the post-1956 'vicarious liability' doctrine, including the adoption of the close connection test.

When acts would be attributed was thus found in the pre-1956 requirements for vicarious liability, namely a qualifying relationship and the Salmond test. These requirements reflect the same four questions for the attribution of acts: (i) did the company have powers to do the act? (ii) was the person doing the act allocated or delegated the company's powers to act? (iii) was the act within the scope of the power, and (iv) was the power properly exercised?

[205] (n 152) 475.

[206] Eg *Armagas Ltd v Mundogas SA* [1986] AC 717 (HL); *Quinn v CC Automotive Group Ltd t/a Carcraft* [2010] EWCA Civ 1412; *Winter v Hockley Mint* [2018] EWCA Civ 2480; *Frederick v Positive Solutions (Financial Services) Ltd* [2018] EWCA Civ 431.

[207] Eg P French, *Collective and Corporate Responsibility* (New York, Columbia University Press, 1984) 43–44.

5

Attributing Acts in Unjust Enrichment

Identifying unjust enrichment's attribution rules is no easy task. In contract and tort, attribution rules are generally associated with agency law and vicarious liability respectively. But very little is known about unjust enrichment's attribution rules. As an editor of *Goff & Jones on Unjust Enrichment*,[1] the leading practitioner text on the subject, remarked relatively recently, '[in] over 50 years since the publication of the first edition of *Goff & Jones*, there is virtually no learning on the attribution rules applicable within the law of unjust enrichment'.[2] This situation might be partly explained by unjust enrichment's youth.[3] Only recognised in England as an independent body of law by the House of Lords in 1991,[4] its scope and justification remain controversial,[5] rendering identification of its attribution rules even more perilous.

Against this backdrop, two important recent contributions have been made by Peter Watts[6] and Stephen Watterson.[7] Both seek to identify attribution rules used in some 'unjust enrichment' or 'restitution' claims,[8] with Watts focusing on principals

[1] The latest edition is C Mitchell et al, *Goff & Jones on the Law of Unjust Enrichment*, 9th edn (London, Sweet & Maxwell, 2016).

[2] S Watterson, 'Agents and Organisations: Attribution Rules in Unjust Enrichment Claim' [2017] *Restitution Law Review* 255.

[3] For some rare exceptions, see P Watts, 'Imputed Knowledge in Restitutionary Claims – Rationales and Rationes' in S Degeling and J Edelman (eds), *Unjust Enrichment in Commercial Law* (Sydney, Thomson Reuters, 2008); B Tompkins, 'Restitutionary Liability for Third Party Negligent Statements' [2014] *Restitution Law Review* 61; P Watts and F Reynolds (eds), *Bowstead & Reynolds on Agency*, 22nd edn (London, Sweet & Maxwell, 2020) paras 8-159–8-175 (*Bowstead & Reynolds*). For some related issues, see also R Stevens, 'Why Do Agents "Drop Out"?' [2005] *LMCLQ* 101.

[4] *Lipkin Gorman v Karpnale Ltd* [1991] 2 AC 548 (HL).

[5] See especially R Stevens, 'The Unjust Enrichment Disaster' (2018) 134 *LQR* 574; L Smith, 'Restitution: A New Start?' in R Havelock and P Devonshire (eds), *The Impact of Equity and Restitution in Commerce* (Oxford, Hart Publishing, 2019); A Burrows, 'In Defence of Unjust Enrichment' (2019) 78 *CLJ* 521; A Burrows, '"At the Expense of the Claimant": A Fresh Look' [2017] *Restitution Law Review* 167. Other recent contributions include P Watts, '"Unjust Enrichment" – the Potion that Induces Well-meaning Sloppiness of Thought' [2016] *Current Legal Problems* 289; C Webb, *Reason and Restitution: A Theory of Unjust Enrichment* (Oxford, Oxford University Press 2016); F Wilmot-Smith, 'Should the Payee Pay?' (2017) 37 *OJLS* 844; T Cutts, 'Materially Identical to Mistaken Payment' (2020) *Canadian Journal of Law & Jurisprudence* 31; T Cutts, 'Unjust Enrichment: What We Owe to Each Other' (2021) 41 *OJLS* 114.

[6] P Watts, 'The Acts and State of Knowledge of Agents as Factors in Principals' Restitutionary Liability' [2017] *LMCLQ* 386.

[7] Watterson (n 2). See also *Goff & Jones* paras 9-66–9.91 (mistake), Ch 8 (want of authority).

[8] Referred to as unjust enrichment claims for ease of reference. The relationship between the two is difficult and cannot be satisfactorily explored within the confines of this chapter.

receiving money or property rights, and Watterson focusing on mistaken payments by organisations. Examining different cases, both conclude that the attribution rules in unjust enrichment appear wider than in contract or tort.[9]

The central aim of this chapter is to show that the attribution rules in unjust enrichment are the same as those in contract and tort. Just as in those areas, attribution in unjust enrichment turns on the allocation and delegation of the company's powers to human individuals. This argument is developed by focusing on mistaken payments, widely regarded as the core case of unjust enrichment. To further minimise potential controversy, this chapter concentrates, where possible, on cases where there is no putative justifying ground for the payment.

This chapter first provides a basic introduction to the law on restitution for mistaken payments. It then examines different possible approaches to attribution, before turning to examine three cases, where the company: (i) makes a mistaken payment; (ii) induces a mistaken payment to be made; or (iii) receives a mistaken payment. These examples show that, contrary to recent arguments, unjust enrichment's attribution rules are just the same as they are in contract and tort, no wider and no narrower. This is a merit, not a fault. It avoids inconsistencies in attribution within a single mistaken payment claim, between different types of mistaken payment claims, and between claims in unjust enrichment and those in other branches of private law.

I. Mistaken Payments

A pays B, thinking he owes B a debt. He does not. A paid under a mistake. Can A recover the payment? In England, and in many other jurisdictions,[10] he can. *Kelly v Solari* is a key example.[11] Mr Solari took out a life insurance policy with an insurance company. When he died, the insurance company paid out on the policy to Mr Solari's estate, mistakenly thinking that the policy was valid. But the policy had lapsed due to non-payment of premiums. The company had paid under a mistake. In the Court of Exchequer, Parke B held that:

> I think that where money is paid to another under the influence of a mistake, that is, upon the supposition that a specific fact is true, which would entitle the other to the money, but which fact is untrue, and the money would not have been paid if it had been known to the payer that the fact was untrue, an action will lie to recover it back, and it is against conscience to retain it.[12]

[9] Watts (n 6) 410; Watterson (n 2).

[10] *David Securities Pty Ltd v Commonwealth Bank of Australia* [1992] HCA 48, (1992) 175 CLR 353 (Australia); *BMP Global Distribution Inc v Bank of Nova Scotia* (2009) 1 SCR 504 (SCC) (Canada); American Law Institute, *Restatement Third: Restitution and Unjust Enrichment* (American Law Institute Publishers 2011) §5 (the United States); *Seagate Technology Pte Ltd v Goh Han Kim* [1994] SGCA 126, [1994] 3 SLR(R) 836 (Singapore).

[11] *Kelly v Solari* (1841) 9 M&W 54, 152 ER 24.

[12] ibid 58.

A new trial was thus ordered to ascertain the company's knowledge.[13]

The mistaken payment of a non-existent debt was regarded by Peter Birks, perhaps the most influential figure in the modern law of unjust enrichment,[14] as unjust enrichment's 'core case'.[15] Recovery of the payment could not be explained by a wrong committed by the payee, nor by the payee's consent to repay.[16] Birks thus concluded that recovery could only be explained by 'unjust enrichment', an 'event' generating the 'response' of restitution.[17]

Unjust enrichment claims are conventionally analysed by a series of questions, asking (1) was the defendant enriched? (2) was his enrichment at the claimant's expense? (3) was it unjust? (4) were there any defences? Sometimes a fifth question is asked: (5) does the claimant have a personal or proprietary right to restitution?[18] A positive answer to the first three questions would give rise to a right to restitution. This approach, developed by Birks, was endorsed by Lord Steyn in *Banque Financière de la Cité v Parc (Battersea) Ltd*[19] and applied as recently as in 2013 in *Benedetti v Sawiris*.[20]

Applied to the mistaken payment, the payee B would be enriched at the payor A's expense by the payment, and A's mistake would be the 'unjust factor', the ground for restitution. More recent cases have since downplayed the importance of the questions, emphasising that the questions themselves are not 'legal tests' but only 'signposts towards areas of inquiry'.[21] With that caveat in mind, it is still clear that the mistaken payment by A to B in the scenario above generates a right to restitution, subject to defences.

A few points on mistake as an 'unjust factor' may be helpful before proceeding. First, what is a mistake? A mistake here is an erroneous belief about some present fact or law.[22] It must be distinguished from 'mispredictions', which concern future events.[23] In *Pitt v Holt*, Lord Walker also distinguished mistakes from ignorance. He observed that ignorance 'is not, as such, a mistake', though 'it can lead to a false belief or assumption which the law will recognise as a mistake'.[24] A payor will also

[13] ibid 57 (Lord Abinger CB).

[14] For a comparative account of Birks' influence in England and Singapore, see R Leow and T Liau, 'Birksian Themes and Their Impact in England and Singapore: Three Points of Divergence' [2021] *LMCLQ* 350.

[15] P Birks, *Unjust Enrichment*, 2nd edn (Oxford, Clarendon Press, 2005) 3 (mistaken payment of a non-existent debt).

[16] ibid 8–9.

[17] ibid 9.

[18] P Birks, *An Introduction to the Law of Restitution* (Oxford, Clarendon Press 1985, rev ed 1989) 20–21; Birks, *Unjust Enrichment* (n 15) 39.

[19] *Banque Financière de la Cité v Parc (Battersea) Ltd* [1999] 1 AC 221 (HL).

[20] *Benedetti v Sawiris* [2013] UKSC 50, [2014] AC 938 [10] (Lord Clarke).

[21] *Investment Trust Companies v RCC* [2017] UKSC 29, [2017] 2 WLR 1200 [41]. See similarly *Skandinaviska Enskilda Banken AB (Publ) v Conway* [2019] UKPC 36, [2020] AC 1111 [80].

[22] *Pitt v Holt* [2013] UKSC 26, [2013] 2 AC 108 [104], citing *Hookway v Racing Victoria Ltd* (2005) 13 VR 444, 451, and see also *Pitt* [108]–[109].

[23] *Dextra Bank and Trust Co Ltd v Bank of Jamaica* [2002] 1 All ER (Comm) 193 (PC); *Pitt* (n 22) [104], [109] (Lord Walker).

[24] (n 22) [105].

not be mistaken if he knows the true facts[25] or thought it was more likely than not that the true facts existed.[26]

Second, which mistakes count? Qualifying mistakes were historically limited. Older cases required that mistakes had to be of fact, not law,[27] and sufficiently serious[28] to generate rights to restitution. But even then, 'spontaneous' mistakes uninduced by the recipient could generate rights to restitution, as *Kelly v Solari* illustrates. Recovery gradually became available for a wider range of mistakes, until Goff J's influential decision in *Barclays Bank Ltd v WJ Simms Son & Cooke (Southern) Ltd*[29] expanded the range of qualifying mistakes to all causative mistakes of fact.[30] Recovery was then still unavailable for mistakes of law, until *Kleinwort Benson v Lincoln City Council* abolished the mistake of law bar in 1998.[31] Thereafter, payments made under causative mistakes, whether of fact or law, could generate rights to restitution.[32] The causal test is typically the but-for test, but where the mistake was induced by the recipient, a looser test of causation applies.[33]

Third, a right to restitution of a mistaken payment only arises where there is no 'justifying ground' (or 'legal basis') for the payment.[34] Classic examples of justifying grounds include valid contractual obligations[35] or court orders,[36] where the valid legal obligation to pay provides a good reason why the recipient is entitled to receive and retain the payment. Rights to restitution of the payment only arise if the justifying ground is first nullified. Admittedly, nullifying contracts for uninduced unilateral mistakes by the payor may be difficult.[37] As these fact scenarios add unnecessary additional complexity, this chapter focuses on the simple mistaken payment with no putative justifying ground for the payment where possible.

[25] *Kelly v Solari* (n 11) 58 (Lord Abinger CB).

[26] *Marine Trade SA v Pioneer Freight Futures* [2009] EWHC 2656 (Comm), [2009] 2 CLC 657 [76]–[77].

[27] Eg *Bilbie v Lumley* (1802) 2 East 469, 102 ER 448.

[28] Compare *Kelly v Solari* (n 11); *Aiken v Short* (1856) 1 H&N 210, 156 ER 1180; *Morgan v Ashcroft* [1938] 1 KB 49 (CA).

[29] *Barclays Bank Ltd v WJ Simms Son & Cooke (Southern) Ltd* [1980] QB 677 (QB).

[30] *Lloyds Bank plc v Independent Insurance Co Ltd* [1999] 2 WLR 986 (CA); *Deutsche Morgan Grenfell Group plc v IRC* [2006] UKHL 49, [2006] 3 WLR 781 (*DMG*).

[31] *Kleinwort Benson v Lincoln City Council* [1999] 2 AC 349 (HL).

[32] ibid 373, 385 (Lord Goff); *DMG* (n 30) [41], [59]–[60] (Lord Hope).

[33] See A Burrows, *The Law of Restitution* (Oxford, Oxford University Press, 2011) 92–93; *Goff & Jones* (n 1) para 9–62. Compare E Bant, 'Causation and Scope of Liability in Unjust Enrichment' [2009] *Restitution Law Review* 60.

[34] See generally *Goff & Jones* (n 1) Chs 2–3.

[35] Eg *Fairfield Sentry Ltd (in liquidation) v Migani* [2014] UKPC 9, [2014] 1 CLC 611.

[36] Eg *Marriot v Hampton* (1797) 7 TR 269, 101 ER 969; *Wilson v Ray* (1839) 10 Ad & El 82, 113 ER 32; *Clydesdale Bank Ltd v Schröder & Co* [1913] 2 KB 1 (KB); *Minshall v HMRC* [2015] EWCA Civ 741, [2015] Lloyd's Rep FC 515.

[37] *Goff & Jones* (n 1) para 9–97.

II. Attribution Rules in Unjust Enrichment Claims

Armed with an overview of restitution of mistaken payments, we can now turn to attribution. Claims for restitution of mistaken payments are well-established, tracing their lineage as far back as the thirteenth century.[38] It may therefore be surprising that the applicable attribution rules remain largely shrouded in mystery. We briefly consider four possible options for attributing acts: the directing mind and will; special rules of attribution in *Meridian Global Funds Management v Securities Commission*;[39] agency rules; and rules wider than agency. Some potential difficulties with these options are also pointed out.

A. Directing Mind and Will

First, attribution might turn on the 'directing mind and will' approach. Problems with this approach have already been canvassed elsewhere.[40] Under this approach, only the acts of a (typically) senior person who embodied the company could be attributed to the company. But there is scant evidence of the directing mind and will approach being used here, since even mistaken payments made by a junior employee on behalf of a company are recoverable. In the classic case of *Barclays Bank v Simms*,[41] a junior bank employee paid out on a cheque, mistakenly overlooking a stop instruction from the customer. Goff J held that the bank was entitled to restitution of the payment. As Goff J emphasised, 'it is clear that the mistake of the bank, in overlooking the drawer's instruction to stop payment of the cheque, caused the bank to pay the cheque'.[42] The employee's payment acts were straightforwardly attributed to the bank; the bank made the payment through the employee. But the employee could not have been the company's directing mind and will, at least not without diluting the test so far that its core meaning is lost.

B. *Meridian*'s Special Rules

A second possibility is that *Meridian*'s 'special rules' might be used. This would require that courts consider the purpose and policy of the substantive rule requiring attribution in formulating a special rule of attribution. But there is little evidence of this approach in recovering mistaken payments. Far from explicitly

[38] D Ibbetson, 'Development at Common Law' in E Bant et al (eds), *Research Handbook in Unjust Enrichment and Restitution* (Cheltenham, Edward Elgar, 2020) 29.
[39] *Meridian Global Funds Management v Securities Commission* [1995] UKPC 5, [1995] 2 AC 500.
[40] See Ch 2 above.
[41] (n 29).
[42] ibid 703.

formulating attribution rules, courts often attribute acts with scant discussion of attribution. Even in Goff J's magisterial judgment in *Barclays Bank v Simms*, he simply concluded that it was 'clear' that the bank had made the payment.[43] Payment by the company may not even be disputed, as in *Chase Manhattan Bank NA v Israel-British Bank (London) Ltd*, where the claimant bank's servant gave erroneous instructions to make a payment that were later carried out by other employees of the claimant.[44] The payment was straightforwardly regarded by all as being made by the bank.[45]

C. Agency Rules

Third, agency rules might be used. For example, the leading English agency text, *Bowstead & Reynolds on Agency*, adopts agency analysis in attributing acts of receipt. Considering the situation when the agent receives mistaken payments for his principal, Article 89(4) states:

> A disclosed principal can be subject to restitutionary claims brought in respect of money paid (and sometimes other property transferred) to an agent in connection with transactions effected within the agent's actual or apparent authority, even though the principal has not personally received it.[46]

Thus, for *Bowstead & Reynolds*, an agent's acts of receipt can be attributed to the principal where the agent acts with actual or apparent authority, whether the principal is a company or not.[47] It must be noted that even *Bowstead & Reynolds* does not argue that agency principles are used to attribute all acts in mistaken payment claims; it suggests a different, looser test when attributing acts of payment to the principal.[48]

But objections might be made to the straightforward application of agency rules. These have already been canvassed in earlier chapters, necessitating only a brief restatement. First, while an agency analysis may be apt for subordinate agents, it does not straightforwardly accommodate acts done by those allocated the company's powers directly under the company's constitution.[49] Agency involves delegation. But the allocation of the company's powers cannot be understood as a product of delegation since both the company and its constitutional allocation of powers come into being at the same moment: the time of incorporation. There is no prior moment where the company exists prior to its powers being allocated; there is thus no room for delegation. Agency analysis thus seems inapt to capture all instances of attribution.

[43] ibid 703.
[44] *Chase Manhattan Bank NA v Israel-British Bank (London) Ltd* [1981] Ch 105 (Ch) 114.
[45] ibid.
[46] *Bowstead & Reynolds* (n 3) para 8–168, discussed at para 8–174.
[47] See also *Bowstead & Reynolds* (n 3) para 1-028 on agency's applicability to attribution.
[48] *Bowstead & Reynolds* (n 3) para 8–166, citing Watterson (n 2), discussed below.
[49] See Ch 3 above.

Second, there is a conceptual problem with regarding attribution as turning on 'agency rules', here including both actual and apparent authority. As seen earlier, the two have different doctrinal and normative bases.[50] Actual authority is a legal power, but apparent authority is an estoppel by representation. While actual authority involves a delegation of the principal's powers, apparent authority does not.[51] Treating apparent authority as a rule of attribution acts is thus erroneous. While an important part of the picture in how companies may be held liable, it says nothing about the attribution of acts.

D. Rules Wider than Agency?

The previous three approaches are familiar, but the same cannot be said of the fourth. Proposed by leading commentators including Stephen Watterson and Peter Watts, this new approach adopts rules wider than the agency doctrines of actual and apparent authority.[52] Three variants can be identified.

i. Payment Made in Good Faith on Principal's Behalf

The first variant has been identified in attributing payment acts. In several pages of an important and wide-ranging article on attribution rules in unjust enrichment claims, Watterson examined cases where the company, as payor, seeks to recover its mistaken payments.[53] But which payments are its own? Watterson cautiously identifies two approaches to answering this question: agency rules, and a second, broader approach.[54] Watterson explains that under this 'broader approach', 'an organisation might rely on an agent's mistake merely by showing that the agent was purporting to discharge his duties/responsibilities as agent in good faith'.[55] The organisation might thus rely on the mistake even if the agent acted without authority.[56] The tentative conclusion is that the 'few cases that confront this problem seem more consistent with this broader approach', with the sole authority discussed being *Agip (Africa) Ltd v Jackson*.[57]

Whether this account is in fact more consistent with the law will be addressed later in this chapter. But it is fair to point out a more fundamental problem. This broader approach seems to blur the dividing line between mistaken payments and payments made with a 'want of authority', 'lack of consent', 'ignorance', or some

[50] See Ch 3 above.
[51] *cf* American Law Institute, *US Restatement of the Law Third, Agency* (American Law Institute Publishers 2006) § 2.03.
[52] Watterson (n 2); Watts (n 6).
[53] Watterson (n 2).
[54] ibid 267.
[55] ibid.
[56] ibid.
[57] *Agip (Africa) Ltd v Jackson* [1990] Ch 265 (Ch), appealed: [1991] Ch 547.

other equivalent.[58] It must be admitted that the existence, scope of, and explanation for the latter category of claims remain contested,[59] but there is some evidence in the cases that restitution of payments of company funds made by someone lacking authority is available on grounds of the lack of authority or consent.[60] *Goff & Jones*, of which Watterson is an editor, similarly accepts the existence of such claims, which it regards as unjust enrichment ones.[61]

The two types of cases seem importantly different. In a mistake claim, the company asserts that it made a mistaken payment. It relies on the mistaken payment being its own. Mistake cases thus involve the successful, albeit impaired, exercise of powers. But want of authority-type situations are very different. Where the company brings a 'want of authority' claim, the company relies on the agent's lack of authority to do the act. It relies on the act done not being its own. These are cases where there is no attempt by the company to exercise its powers at all.[62] As *Re Hampton Capital* recognised, these situations are more akin to theft.[63] They are doings *to*, not by the company.

But the broader approach to attribution blurs the distinction between the two, as Watterson recognises. As he accepts, one implication of the broader approach is that where an agent who has general authority 'honestly oversteps its boundaries in a particular case', his acts of payment and mistaken belief can still be attributed to the principal, so the principal can bring a mistake claim,[64] in addition to an alternative 'want of authority' claim.[65] With respect, accepting that both claims could lie on the same facts is contradictory. The principal would be accepting both that the payment was its own and that it was not. The line between the two may sometimes be thin, but it is fundamental.

ii. Close Connection

A second variant has been suggested in cases where mistaken payments are induced by misrepresentations. Here Benedict Tompkins has argued that the

[58] For discussion of this category of unjust factors, see Birks, *Introduction* (n 18) 140–41; Birks, *Unjust Enrichment* (n 15) 154–56; R Chambers and J Penner, 'Ignorance' in S Degeling and J Edelman (eds), *Unjust Enrichment in Commercial Law* (Sydney, Thomson Reuters, 2008); Burrows (n 33) Ch 16; G Virgo, *Principles of the Law of Restitution*, 3rd edn (Oxford, Oxford University Press, 2015); J Edelman and E Bant, *Unjust Enrichment* (Oxford, Hart Publishing, 2016) Ch 12; *Goff & Jones* (n 1) Ch 8; M Bryan, 'No Intention to Benefit' in E Bant et al (eds), *Research Handbook on Unjust Enrichment and Restitution* (Cheltenham, Edward Elgar, 2020) 363.

[59] See references ibid.

[60] Eg *Great Investments Ltd v Warner* [2016] FCAFC 85, (2016) 243 FCR 516 [56]–[69] (without authority); *Compañia De Navegación Palomar SA v Koutsos, Isabel Brenda* [2020] SGHC 59 [123]–[130] (lack of consent).

[61] *Goff & Jones* (n 1) Ch 8.

[62] Chambers and Penner (n 58).

[63] *Re Hampton Capital* [2015] EWHC 1905 (Ch).

[64] Watterson (n 2) 267.

[65] ibid.

representations of 'non-agent employees' can be attributed even if the statement-maker lacks actual or apparent authority.[66] 'Non-agent employees' are defined as individuals 'who [have] not been vested with any authority to make statements (or contracts) on behalf of the employer' but where 'making such statements is something "closely connected" with her course of employment or the class of actions that she is employed to do'.[67]

Again, whether the current law reflects this approach will be dealt with later in this chapter. For now it suffices to say that this approach clearly draws from the post-*Lister v Hesley Hall*[68] law on vicarious liability which adopts a similar 'close connection' test. But it is not so clear why borrowing from vicarious liability is desirable. Borrowing from vicarious liability also inherits its difficulties. By any measure, application of the close connection test has been problematic, necessitating multiple visits to the House of Lords, Supreme Court, and Privy Council over the last two decades.[69] It must be doubted whether much would be gained from introducing these problems into attribution. Perhaps more importantly, post-*Lister* vicarious liability and the attribution of acts are fundamentally different. As seen in Chapter 4, post-*Lister* vicarious liability attributes the liability of employees for wrongdoing to their employers. The close connection test is thus aimed at identifying the necessary connection in that situation. But there is no reason why it ought to apply where *acts* are being attributed.

iii. Some Legitimate Role in Transaction

The third variant of attribution rules also concerns cases where mistakes are induced by misrepresentations. Here, Peter Watts argues that there might be a 'cascade of rules'.[70] At the top, where the misrepresentation was made by an agent with actual or apparent authority, the principal (whether corporate or not) might 'find himself subject to liability in contract and tort, and not just in restitution'.[71] As Watts explains, 'below that level come statements made by agents who are employees'.[72] Here, in tort, though not in contract, it appears that principals may be liable for misrepresentations made by employees in the course of employment or with a sufficiently close connection to the employment for the principal to be justly liable.[73] The correctness of this proposition is left open by Watts, who notes

[66] Tompkins (n 3).
[67] Tompkins (n 3) 86.
[68] [2001] UKHL 22, [2002] 1 AC 215.
[69] See eg *Lister* ibid; *Bernard v Attorney General of Jamaica* [2004] UKPC 47; *Mohamud v WM Morrison Supermarkets plc* [2016] UKSC 11, [2016] 2 WLR 821; *WM Morrison Supermarkets plc v Various Claimants* [2020] UKSC 12, [2020] AC 989.
[70] Watts (n 6) 405.
[71] ibid.
[72] ibid.
[73] ibid.

that contradictory lines of authority exist.[74] Like Tompkins, Watts accepts that if this is true in tort, it should also be true in restitutionary claims.[75]

But Watts then suggests that there is yet another tier of rules, confined to the law of restitution. Relying on *Armagas Ltd v Mundogas SA*,[76] Watts suggests two possible propositions:

> The relevant passage in the judgment suggests two propositions, one more radical than the other. First, where the only remedy being sought by a claimant is the setting aside of a contract (and the consequential recovery of any property transferred), it is not necessary to show that the statement was made within the agent's actual or apparent authority. Secondly, and more tentatively, where the statement was fraudulent (or involved the bribing of an agent of the counterparty), it may not matter if the person acting was not an agent at all.[77]

Watts accepts that the second proposition 'has not got off the ground', but he does affirm the first proposition.[78] In his words, the 'case law suggests that a right of rescission arises from an agent's misrepresentation even if the agent had no authority, actual or apparent, to be making the relevant statement'.[79] For Watts, this proposition would clearly be engaged where an agent purports to make a contract without actual or apparent authority and the contract is adopted by the principal. The principal would then 'be ratifying the contract, and is almost certain to be hoist thereby with that agent's misstatements'.[80] He accepts that the proposition would go further; just how far is not clear.

In short, it appears that the agent's misrepresentations can be attributed to the principal so that the latter can rescind a contract where two conditions are met: 'the agent will have to have had some legitimate role in the transaction',[81] and 'the principal must in some way have approved of, or "approbated", some part of the events relevant to the claim. In cases where the principal wants, and is able, to disown all participation in those events, liability will not usually arise in the law of restitution'.[82]

It is fair to say that the scope of this approach remains relatively uncertain. What counts as a legitimate role in the transaction remains open, as does when the principal has sufficiently approbated relevant events. Furthermore, as Watts accepts, this analysis suggests that attribution in restitutionary claims is wider than in contract and tort. One explanation offered for this is that 'a restitutionary

[74] Eg *Armagas Ltd v Mundogas SA* [1986] AC 717; *So v HSBC Bank plc* [2009] EWCA Civ 296, [2009] 1 CLC 503. See generally P Watts, 'Principals' Tortious Liability for Agents' Negligent Statements – Is "Authority" Necessary?' (2012) 128 *LQR* 260.

[75] Watts (n 6) 405.

[76] (n 74).

[77] Watts (n 6) 406.

[78] ibid.

[79] ibid.

[80] ibid 408.

[81] ibid.

[82] ibid 411.

defendant has only to effect restitution, and is not exposed to the relatively open-ended duty that arises in contract and tort to compensate a claimant for losses'.[83] But this is a right-sided justification for attribution, focusing on the remedies available for the right being enforced. Like other right-sided reasons, this reason fails to fit the form of attribution, the thing to be justified: the connection between act, individual, and company.

III. Payments

Watterson, Tompkins, and Watts's accounts all suggest that attribution rules in restitutionary claims are wider than those in contract or tort. Some problems in principle with adopting their views have already been canvassed. But does English law support their conclusions? In this section and the next two, it is argued that there is little evidence that attribution rules in unjust enrichment claims differ from those in other branches of private law. Attribution rules here conform to the same general structure already seen: the allocation and delegation of the company's own powers to act. The same four questions are asked: (i) does the company have power to do the act? (ii) was that power allocated or delegated to the person doing the act? (iii) is the power being exercised within its scope? (iv) is the power properly exercised?

This section examines the first area where attribution of acts is relevant: the attribution of acts of payment to the company. The next, in Section IV, deals with attribution of representations, and the third, in Section V, with acts of receipt.

A. Whose Acts of Payment?

Before examining whose acts of payment can be attributed to the company, it is first necessary to say something about what 'acts of payment' are. What constitutes an act of payment depends on the payment method used. Payments may take many different forms: physical delivery of the coins and banknotes, cheques, or funds transfers. For the first, physical delivery of the thing constitutes the relevant act of payment.[84] If payment is made by cheque, acts of payment may include the drawing of a cheque in favour of the payee, as in *Kelly v Solari*,[85] or the bank's acceptance of a cheque presented to the bank and crediting of the amount in the cheque to the recipient's bank account, as in *Barclays Bank v Simms*.[86] If payment is made by funds transfer, then the relevant acts of payment may include completing

[83] ibid.
[84] M Bridge et al, *The Law of Personal Property*, 3rd edn (London, Sweet & Maxwell, 2017) para 27-003.
[85] (n 11).
[86] (n 29).

the transfer form,[87] or delivering instructions to the payor's bank, whether by transfer form or payment orders.[88] A single payment may thus involve multiple payment acts.

As has been suggested above, payment acts of senior individuals within the corporate hierarchy will typically be attributable. The classic case of *Kelly v Solari* illustrates.[89] An insurance company mistakenly paid Mrs Solari, Mr Solari's executrix, on a policy over Mr Solari's life, although the policy had lapsed due to non-payment of premiums. The relevant acts of payment were performed by three directors of the insurance company, who drew a cheque in favour of Mrs Solari[90] and physically handed the cheque to Mrs Solari's agent.[91] It was assumed that the directors' acts of payment could be attributed to the company.

But attribution is not only limited to acts done by directors or other senior individuals. Recall *Barclays Bank v Simms*,[92] where an ordinary employee of the bank mistakenly overlooked the stop instruction, paying out on the cheque and crediting the payee's account. Similarly, in *Chase Manhattan v Israel-British Bank*, it was again employees of the claimant New York firm who paid the recipient English bank twice, the second time by mistake caused by a clerical error.[93] In *BP Oil International v Target Shipping*, the relevant acts of payment were authorised by junior employees in the Demurrage department.[94] Again, it was assumed that the relevant acts of payment could be attributed to the company.

So far, there is no sign of wider attribution rules. The cases are consistent with the first two requirements for attribution: (i) that the company has the powers to do those acts; and (ii) that the acts must have been performed by someone allocated or delegated the company's powers to do those acts.

The first is likely uncontroversial. It is hard to imagine cases where companies' constitutions will not expressly provide for the company's powers to make payments. But even if they do not, it is even harder to imagine cases where such powers will not be implied; they are necessary for the company to do business and pursue its objects.

Nor is the second difficult. The board of directors, for instance, will typically be allocated the company's powers of management under the constitution, including powers to make payments. They may then delegate them down the corporate hierarchy to individual employees, even rank-and-file employees.[95] Just as in other areas, identifying whether acts have been allocated or delegated is a question of

[87] Eg *Jones v Churcher* [2009] EWHC 722 (QB).
[88] Eg *Agip* (n 57).
[89] (n 11).
[90] ibid 25.
[91] ibid 26.
[92] (n 29).
[93] (n 44) 114.
[94] *BP Oil International v Target Shipping* [2012] EWHC 1590 (Comm), [2012] 2 CLC 336.
[95] For why allocations of power under the constitution are best not analysed as straightforward examples of agency, see Ch 3 above.

fact, requiring careful examination of the company's practices, not merely the formal documents. Powers may thus be allocated or delegated informally, consistently with other areas of law. Thus, in *Re Hampton Capital*, although the acts of payment had been made directly by a duly appointed director of the company, the evidence was that another person, Mr Mayweather, the 'driving force behind the Company', had directed them to be made.[96] The function of the appointed director was 'to give effect to Mr Mayweather's instructions'.[97] Although not formally appointed, the latter must have possessed very substantial powers to act for the company. Had he exercised them properly, his acts would have been attributable to the company.

B. Scope: Which Acts of Payment?

Which acts of payment will be attributed? Here, recall Watterson's tentative conclusion that the cases 'seem more consistent' with the approach that 'an organisation might rely on an agent's mistake merely by showing that the agent was purporting to discharge his duties/responsibilities as agent in good faith'.[98] The key case cited is *Agip (Africa) Ltd v Jackson*.[99] However, when examined more closely, *Agip* does not stand for this proposition.

Agip was an oil company which carried on business in Tunisia. Over many years it was defrauded by its chief accountant, who fraudulently altered payee names on payment orders and delivered those payment orders to Agip's bank, the Banque du Sud. The bank acted on the payment orders, debiting Agip's account and crediting the named payees. When Agip discovered the frauds, it sought restitution of the payments from the recipients for mistake. The recipients argued that the bank had no authority to make the transfer since the payment orders were forged and thus could not be said to have acted as Agip's authorised agent, so Agip could not recover.[100]

At first instance, Millett J rejected this argument, accepting that the bank was the 'lawfully authorised agent of the plaintiffs with a general authority to debit their account and transfer the money in accordance with their instructions'.[101] Millett J's reasoning was substantially accepted by the Court of Appeal. Fox LJ, delivering the court's sole reasoned speech, stressed that the Banque du Sud 'plainly intended to pay as agent of Agip',[102] so its mistake and payment could be attributed to Agip. These statements might appear to support the conclusion that acts can be attributed even if the agent lacks authority to pay.

[96] (n 63) [9].
[97] ibid [10].
[98] Watterson (n 2) 267.
[99] (n 57).
[100] See *Agip* (HC) (n 57) 284; *Agip* (CA) (n 57) 561–62.
[101] *Agip* (HC) (n 57) 285.
[102] *Agip* (CA) (n 57) 562.

But in *Agip*, the agent – the Banque du Sud – did have actual authority (a power)[103] to pay on behalf of Agip. One way of testing whether it had authority to make the transfer was to ask whether the bank was entitled to debit Agip's account, which turned on whether it had done so with authority. It did. Agip sued the Banque du Sud to have its account re-credited, but it failed.[104] This is clear evidence that the agent had the authority to pay. As Fox LJ accepted:

> it was said that there were no instructions because the order was bad. I do not feel able to accept that … The Tunisian court refused to order Banque du Sud to re-credit Agip's account. For practical purposes, therefore, the order was given effect to according to its tenor as if it were a proper order. Everything that was done (i.e. the payments and the debit) stands good so far as the banking transaction is concerned …. It seems to me, therefore, that the order must be regarded as having been paid by Banque du Sud as agent for Agip. That, however, does not alter the circumstance that it was money paid under a mistake of fact. The defendants accepted that a principal could recover where there was either (i) mistaken payment by an authorised agent within his instructions or (ii) mistaken payment in breach of instructions by using money entrusted to the agent by the principal. The present case can be brought within, at any rate, the first of these.[105]

This result is due to the interposition of two different persons who might be described as Agip's 'agents': the chief accountant and the bank. As seen in the diagram below, the payment by Agip was effected partly through the acts of its chief accountant, who handed the completed payment orders to the bank. The bank then acted on the payment orders by debiting Agip's account and crediting the payee's account.

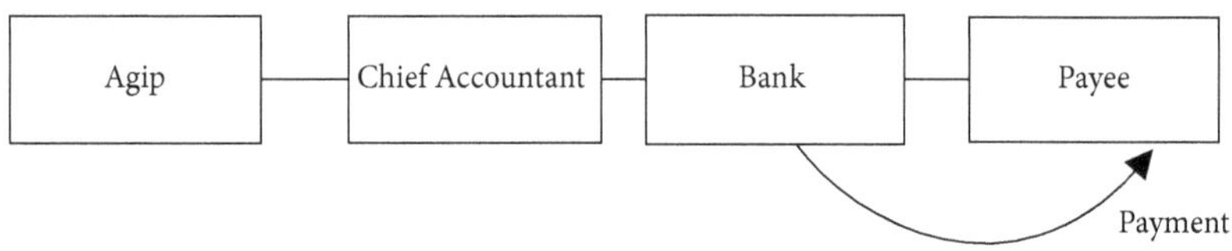

Although the chief accountant was acting outside the scope of the powers delegated to him by Agip in delivering forged payment orders to the bank, forgeries are not automatically nullities.[106] The company may be estopped from disputing their validity if the forged documents were put forward by someone with apparent authority to warrant their validity.[107] The chief accountant was such a person. He was delegated the company's powers to place completed orders and corresponding invoices before authorised signatories and deliver the signed orders to the bank, though no power to sign or amend payment orders. Although lacking power to amend payment orders, he was held out by Agip as the person who had

[103] *Bowstead & Reynolds* (n 3) para 1-001.
[104] *Agip* (CA) (n 57) 561.
[105] ibid 562–63.
[106] *cf Ruben v Great Fingall Consolidated* [1906] AC 439 (HL) 443 (Lord Loreburn LC).
[107] *Lovett v Carson Country Homes Ltd* [2009] EWHC 1143 (Ch), [2009] 2 BCLC 196 [90]–[94].

the power to deliver signed orders to the bank and to represent that they were legitimate instructions emanating from the company. He did so, and the bank reasonably relied on that holding out. As Fox LJ stressed, there was nothing in the circumstances to put the bank on notice about any impropriety. The order presented to it 'appeared perfectly regular',[108] and the bank had 'no reason at all to doubt its authenticity'.[109] The chief accountant had apparent authority to deliver payment orders and warrant their validity which the bank relied upon in making the transfer. When the bank made the transfer, it acted within its powers to act for Agip.

Agip is thus not good authority for the proposition that payment acts can be attributed where the agent was purporting to discharge his duties as an agent in good faith even if he lacked actual or apparent authority. Rather, it was a case where one agent, the chief accountant, was acting with apparent authority in giving apparently legitimate instructions to another agent, the bank. The bank, relying on the instructions which it was entitled to rely on under apparent authority, acted within its powers. This explains why Agip could not get an order to have the bank re-credit its account: as far as the bank was concerned, it had acted properly and within the scope of its powers.

A similar analysis might be offered in respect of *Niru Battery Manufacturing Co v Milestone Trading Ltd (No 1)*.[110] Niru contracted with Milestone to purchase lead from the latter. Payment was to be by letter of credit from Bank Sepah upon the presentation of documents including a bill of lading. Mahdavi, who effectively controlled Milestone,[111] procured a third party, Maritime, to issue and present a false bill of lading to Bank Sepah. Bank Sepah relied on it and paid under the letter of credit. It was common ground that Bank Sepah had paid under a mistake, with the live issue concerning the availability of a change of position defence. It was thus assumed that Bank Sepah's acts of payment under the letter of credit could be attributed to Niru.

The same reasoning as in *Agip* applies: Bank Sepah had powers to act for Niru when it paid. It reasonably relied on Maritime's apparent authority to issue and present genuine bills of lading to it, having no reason to doubt the authenticity of the documentation received. This explains why Niru did not challenge Bank Sepah debiting its account with the amount paid out under the letter of credit. Like in *Agip*, this claim would rightly have failed.

Matters would be different if, in *Niru* or *Agip*, the bank could not reasonably rely on the representations of the bill of lading issuer or the chief accountant, for instance because the documents were objectively suspicious on their face. In that case, there having been no instructions which the bank was entitled to rely on, the

[108] *Agip* (CA) (n 57) 562.
[109] ibid 562.
[110] *Niru Battery Manufacturing Co v Milestone Trading Ltd (No 1)* [2002] EWHC 1425, appealed: [2003] EWCA Civ 1446, [2004] QB 986.
[111] *Niru* (HC) (n 110) [41]–[43].

bank would be acting outside the scope of its powers in paying, and *Agip* and *Niru* would not have been able to recover the payment for mistake.

Far from showing that a different approach is taken, *Agip* and *Niru* are consistent with the general approach that the scope of attributable acts turns on the scope of the actor's power to act for the company. In those cases, the interposition of not one but two parties meant that the parties' relationships needed careful working out. But the applicable principles are no different.

As in attributing acts in other areas, the actor must act within the scope of the powers allocated or delegated to him. The scope of the actor's powers is a question of fact. In ascertaining the facts, a helpful question is to ask what the individual's job was, as *BP Oil International Ltd v Target Shipping Ltd* put it.[112] This explains why directors' acts are typically attributable. They will ordinarily have extensive powers which are either formally[113] or informally[114] delegated to them. Managers, employees, and secretaries[115] alike may also be allocated or delegated the powers to perform payment acts. Both acts exercising legal and ordinary powers alike may be attributed, with physical transfers, signing cheques, and filling in transfer forms to banks falling in the first category, and physical delivery of bank transfer forms or cheques to banks falling in the second.

C. Proper Exercise

More difficult are cases where the individual whose acts are sought to be attributed is acting improperly. For example, he may act in his own interests rather than the company's. These cases are difficult because the mere fact that recovery is available is inconclusive about whether there is a proper exercise requirement. Restitution of the payment might be available for mistake, but even if not, it may be for ignorance, powerlessness, lack of consent, or want of authority. Though the recognition of these unjust factors remains controversial in England,[116] it appears less so outside it.[117]

Nonetheless, it appears that the cases here are consistent with the view that, like in contract and tort, that powers must be exercised in good faith and for proper purposes. For legal powers, the person exercising the power must do so in what he

[112] (n 94) [229].
[113] Eg *Kelly v Solari* (n 11).
[114] *Re Hampton Capital* (n 63).
[115] Eg *Jones v Churcher* (n 87), concerning attribution to a unincorporated sole proprietorship, but on a secretary's powers to act for a registered company, see *Panorama Developments (Guildford) Ltd v Fidelis Furnishing Fabrics Ltd* [1971] 2 QB 711 (CA).
[116] See references at n 58.
[117] See references at n 60, and see also *Criterion Properties plc v Stratford UK Properties LLC* [2004] UKHL 28, [2004] 1 WLR 1846 [4] (Lord Nicholls); *AAHG, LLC v Hong Hin Kay Albert* [2016] SGHC 274, [2017] 3 SLR 636.

believes to be the company's interests; for ordinary powers, the person exercising it must not intend to act contrary to what he believes to be the company's interests.[118]

The former is perhaps more common. An illustration is found in *Re Hampton Capital*, where the company's sole director exercised legal powers to give instructions to the company's bank to make payments to persons identified by the company's 'driving force' where these payments were not for the company's business or otherwise for the benefit of the company.[119] The money was described by George Bompas QC, sitting as a High Court judge, as 'stolen money'.[120] The payment could not be attributed to the company, but the company could recover via a 'want of authority'-type claim. Similarly, in *Clark v Cutland*, a director and shareholder of the company procured large payments to be made into his pension funds for his own benefit.[121] This was again treated as equivalent to a stolen payment: a theft.[122] It is important to note that even if the individual had no power to make payment for the company, his purported attempts to do so may have some legal effects.[123] They are not complete nullities.[124] The most obvious effect that the act may have is to confer a legal title on the recipient; the details may turn on the mode of payment.[125]

Conversely, mere negligence does not constitute acting against what the individual believes to be the principal's interests, explaining why careless acts of payment may still be attributed to the company. Thus, in *Chase Manhattan*, an employee's careless acts in making a clerical error in ordering a second payment, were discovered by another employee, but only partially implemented by other employees. Goulding J regarded them as all being attributable to the company.

IV. Induced Mistakes: Representations

The second concerns mistakes induced by misrepresentations. If the payor is induced to make payments by misrepresentations, when will the representations be attributed to the payee? As explained earlier, finding that the payee induced the payment may bring the payor some practical advantages, such as a less onerous causal requirement between mistake and payment.[126] Watts and Tompkins have

[118] See similarly Ch 4 above.
[119] *Re Hampton Capital* (n 63) [22]–[24].
[120] ibid [24].
[121] *Clark v Cutland* [2003] EWCA Civ 810, [2004] 1 WLR 783.
[122] ibid [21]–[23].
[123] See similarly *Agip* (n 57) 283–84.
[124] *Re Hampton Capital* (n 63) [23].
[125] Eg for physical delivery of chattels, the recipient obtains a possessory title to the chattel, albeit one inferior to the company's: *Costello v Chief Constable of Derbyshire* [2001] EWCA Civ 381, [2001] 1 WLR 1437.
[126] See text to n 33.

suggested that rules of attribution may be wider than in contract and tort here. They rely on *Refuge Assurance Co Ltd v Kettlewell*, a recisssion case.[127] But this reading of *Refuge* does not withstand scrutiny. *Refuge* is entirely consistent with the view that only acts done by someone allocated or delegated the power to do that act can be attributed.

A. Watts and Tompkins' Arguments

In *Refuge*, the claimant, Sarah Kettlewell, had a life insurance policy with the defendant insurance company. She was unable to keep up with the premiums and wanted to allow the policy to lapse. The company's district superintendent and another of the company's agents made misrepresentations to her that if she continued paying premiums on the existing policy for another four years, she would get a 'free policy', ie the policy would continue to be on foot but she would not need to pay further premiums thereafter. She duly paid the premiums for another four years. When no free policy materialised, she successfully sought to rescind the policy and recover the premiums paid for those four years.

For Watts, this was a case where 'the agent making the statement had no actual or apparent authority to be making it'.[128] He therefore concludes that *Refuge*,[129] as well as dicta in older cases,[130] suggests that 'a right of rescission arises from an agent's misrepresentation even if the agent had no authority, actual or apparent, to be making the relevant statement'.[131] For Watts, while 'it is also unclear just what status or minimum of authority an agent would have to have possessed in order to trigger [the principle]', the agent must have had 'some legitimate role in the transaction'.[132]

Refuge is also the key authority in Tompkins' argument, which is based on the idea that the payee cannot 'approbate and reprobate'.[133] If the representations made induced the payor to enter into the contract, then the payee cannot both rely on the contract to justify retention of the benefit and disown the representations.[134] But this principle does not indicate which representations ought to be attributed to the payee. For this, Tompkins relies on *Refuge*,[135] arguing that the necessary connection for attribution is that the making of the statement is 'closely connected' to acts the statement-maker was employed to do.[136] Although *Refuge* is a rescission

[127] *Refuge Assurance Co Ltd v Kettlewell* [1907] 2 KB 242, affirmed on appeal [1908] 1 KB 545 (CA); [1909] AC 243 (HL) (dismissed without reasons).
[128] Watts (n 6) 407.
[129] ibid 406.
[130] Eg *New Brunswick Railway v Conybeare* (1862) 9 HL Cas 711, 725–26.
[131] Watts (n 6) 406.
[132] ibid 408.
[133] Tompkins (n 3) 92.
[134] ibid 92–93.
[135] ibid 93.
[136] ibid 94–95.

case, Tompkins regards the 'close connection' test as applicable even in cases of simple mistaken payments where no contract is present.

In support of this wider rule of attribution, both Watts and Tompkins rely on Phillimore J's statement that:

> If a principal appoints a person as his agent to obtain bargains, any representation which the agent makes with the object of obtaining a bargain, and which results in a bargain being obtained, is one the principal must make good.[137]

B. Analysing *Refuge*

Taken out of context, the latter part of Phillimore J's statement might initially appear to suggest a wider approach to attribution than in other branches of private law. But when read against the county court's findings of facts and the Court of Appeal decision, it does not suggest a broader approach to attributing representations.

At first instance, the county court judge found that the company's agents were employed to procure proposals for insurance policies, though they had no authority to enter any contracts for the company.[138] This would carry with it the implied power to make representations, an integral part of procuring prospective insureds to take up policies. Analogies may be usefully drawn to the tort case of *Colonial Mutual Life Assurance Society Ltd v Producers and Citizens Co-operative Assurance Co of Australia Ltd*.[139] There, an insurance company's agent made defamatory statements about the solvency of the company's rivals. The agent lacked power to enter contracts for the company, but it was within his scope of employment to solicit and obtain proposals.[140] As Dixon CJ explained, this 'authorized him on its behalf to address to prospective proponents such observations as appeared to him appropriate'.[141] In other words, he had implied powers to make representations for the company. The same could be said of *Refuge*. The company's agents also had implied powers to make representations for the company when they were employed to procure proposals for policies.

Against this background, recall Phillimore J's statement:

> If a principal appoints a person as his agent to obtain bargains, any representation which the agent makes with the object of obtaining a bargain, and which results in a bargain being obtained, is one the principal must make good.[142]

[137] *Refuge* (Div Ct) (n 127) 246–47.
[138] ibid 243.
[139] *Colonial Mutual Life Assurance Society Ltd v Producers and Citizens Co-operative Assurance Co of Australia Ltd* [1931] HCA 53, (1931) 46 CLR 41.
[140] ibid 49 (Dixon CJ).
[141] ibid 50 (Dixon CJ).
[142] *Refuge* (Div Ct) (n 127) 246–47.

This statement is readily explicable when read against the facts. Phillimore J was stressing that if the principal appoints someone to obtain bargains, then it is not just the very act of obtaining the bargain that is attributable to the company. The agent may have implied powers to do other acts which are incidentally necessary to obtaining that bargain, including making representations. They too are attributable. The agents were acting as the company, not as 'strangers to the [company]'.[143]

The Court of Appeal provides further support for this analysis. Lord Alverstone CJ held that the company would also have been liable in damages for deceit had a claim in tort been brought.[144] He rejected the argument that the agent acted without authority, reasoning that 'there are a number of cases which shew that, if the agent is there to do business for the benefit of the principal, the principal is responsible for representations made by the agent in the course of the business'.[145] Barnes P shared Lord Alverstone CJ's conclusions on authority on which he had 'nothing further to add'.[146] Even the third judge, Buckley LJ, who disagreed on other aspects, agreed that Sarah Kettlewell could recover the premiums as damages which the company had received 'by the fraud of [their] agent';[147] 'they cannot afterwards repudiate the agency, and say that the act which has been done by the agent is not an act for which they are liable'.[148] This analysis too suggests that the company's agents did have powers to make representations. As they acted within the scope of their powers and in the interests of the company, those representations could be attributed to the company, even for a tort claim.

Although *Refuge* was appealed to the House of Lords, the appeal was dismissed, and the decision of the lower courts affirmed without reasons being given. The Court of Appeal is thus the most senior appellate body to give a reasoned decision in *Refuge*. Both their reasoning and Phillimore J's, properly contextualised against the facts, suggest that the insurance company's agents did have powers to make representations for the company. Those representations could be attributed. They could be attributed both to establish the company's deceit, as Lord Alverstone CJ and Barnes P accepted, and to enable Sarah Kettlewell to rescind the policy and recover the excess premiums paid.

Refuge itself thus provides little support for a wider attribution rule in attributing representations to payees. Far from showing that different rules of attribution exist in unjust enrichment, *Refuge* indicates that the same rule is adopted for the same question ('can A's representation be attributed to the company?') regardless of whether the question is asked for the claimant to obtain damages for the company's fraudulent misrepresentation, or for the claimant to rescind a contract induced by that misrepresentation.

[143] ibid 246.
[144] *Refuge* (CA) (n 127) 550.
[145] ibid.
[146] ibid.
[147] *Refuge* (CA) (n 127) 552.
[148] ibid 552–53.

V. Receipt

The last case concerns receipt of a mistaken payment by a company. Here there are no arguments that attribution is wider than elsewhere in private law.

Receipt may sometimes be straightforward: where a funds transfer is made to a recipient, the recipient's credit balances with its bank will increase, while the payor's credit balances with his own bank will be correspondingly reduced.[149] The recipient can be seen as receiving a new right to the increased credit balance, losing the right to the original balance.[150]

It is in cases involving physical delivery of cash, cheques, or other property, that receipt tends to be most difficult. When will physical receipt by an individual constitute receipt by the company? This is not an easy question. As *Bowstead & Reynolds* says, 'the precise bounds of a principal's liability in such circumstances are still being settled'.[151] It is argued that the cases here are consistent with the general argument of this chapter that acts are attributed where done in the exercise of the company's own powers, which have been allocated or delegated to the individual or group doing the act.

Two caveats must be mentioned. First, although the focus here is on receipt, no position is taken on whether a more active form of participation by the recipient is necessary for rights to restitution to arise.[152] It suffices to note that receipt is probably the minimum level of participation necessary by a payee. Second, the difficult issue of when the person obtaining physical receipt can similarly be required to make restitution is not considered here.[153] In other words, this chapter does not aim to provide an account of the defence(s) of ministerial receipt or payment over to an agent.[154]

[149] See generally M Brindle and R Cox, *Law of Bank Payments*, 5th edn (London, Sweet & Maxwell, 2017) Ch 3, especially paras 3-002–3-003.

[150] T Cutts, 'Modern Money Had and Received' (2018) 38 *OJLS* 1, 21.

[151] *Bowstead & Reynolds* (n 3) para 8–174.

[152] Eg Stevens, 'The Unjust Enrichment Disaster' (n 5) (acceptance), and contrast Burrows, 'In Defence' (n 5); H Scott, 'Change and Continuity in the Law of Unjust Enrichment' [2019] *Acta Juridica* 469, 481–83.

[153] On some accounts, the agent only has a defence if he pays over or accounts irreversibly for the payment to the principal: *Holland v Russell* (1861) 1 B&S 424, 121 ER 773; *Agip* (HC) (n 57) 288; *Portman BS v Hamlyn Taylor Neck (A Firm)* [1998] PNLR 664 (CA) 669; *Jones v Churcher* (n 87); *High Commissioner for Pakistan v the 8th Nizam of Hyderabad* [2016] EWHC 1465 (Ch) [140]–[150]; *High Commissioner for Pakistan in the United Kingdom v Prince Muffakham Jah* [2019] EWHC 2551 (Ch), [2020] Ch 421 [286]–[290]. On others, the agent need not make restitution where he receives as agent, even if he still retains the monies, see eg *Jeremy D Stone Consultants Ltd v National Westminster Bank plc* [2013] EWHC 208 (Ch) [240]–[243]; *Sixteenth Ocean GmbH & Co KG v Société Générale* [2018] EWHC 1731 (Comm), [2018] 2 Lloyd's Rep 465 [109]; *Skandinaviska Enskilda Banken AB (Publ) v Conway* [2019] UKPC 36 [87].

[154] See eg Burrows (n 33) Ch 21; Virgo (n 58) Ch 25; Edelman and Bant (n 58) Ch 15; *Goff & Jones* (n 1) Ch 28.

A. Whose Receipt?

Perhaps the most prominent situation where acts of receipt will be attributed is where mistaken payments are received. A long line of authority indicates that mistaken payments received by agents for the principal can be attributed to the principal. As Erle CJ put in *Edgell v Day*, 'The general principle of law is, that a payment of money to an agent is payment to the principal.'[155] More recently, in *Portman BS v Hamlyn Taylor Neck*, Millett LJ said that 'The true rule is that where the plaintiff has paid money under (for example) a mistake to the agent of a third party, he may sue the principal whether or not the agent has accounted to him, for in contemplation of the law the payment is made to the principal and not to his agent.'[156]

Here 'agent' is used broadly: this principle has been applied across different agency relationships, from receiver-principal[157] to solicitor-client,[158] but it also seems to apply to human individuals receiving for a company. As will be seen later, in cases like *Russo-Chinese Bank v Li Yau Sam*[159] and *Thompson v Bell*,[160] there seemed no difficulty in principle with attributing receipt by employees to the company, though attribution there failed for other reasons.

Two additional points must be emphasised. First, the mistaken payor must have intended to pay the company and not the agent. As Alderson B asked in *Thompson v Bell*, 'was the money paid to the bank, or to the manager individually?'[161] This requirement is necessary to establish that the company was enriched at the payor's expense.[162] Where the payor intended to pay the company, 'the agent is the proxy of his principal'.[163] The 'series of transactions between claimant and the agent, and between the agent and the defendant [company], is therefore legally equivalent to a transaction directly between the claimant and the defendant'.[164]

Second, and conversely, the agent must receive the money for the company. Thus, in *Portman Building Society*, the receipt by the solicitors' firm could be attributed to the claimant building society, as the firm 'acknowledged that it was the Society's money, held to the order of the Society and it was applied in accordance with the Society's instructions'.[165]

Taken collectively, these points are consistent with the position that acts will be attributed where done by someone who is either allocated the company's powers to

[155] *Edgell v Day* (1865) Law Rep 1 CP 80, 84.
[156] (n 153) 207.
[157] *Sadler v Evans* (1766) 4 Burr 1984, 98 ER 34.
[158] *Edgell v Day* (n 155); *Portman BS* (n 153).
[159] *Russo-Chinese Bank v Li Yau Sam* [1910] AC 174 (PC).
[160] *Thompson v Bell* (1854) 10 Exch 10, 156 ER 334.
[161] ibid.
[162] *Investment Trust Companies* (n 21).
[163] ibid [48].
[164] ibid [48].
[165] (n 153) 668.

act under its constitution (most commonly, the board of directors or general meeting), or who is delegated the company's powers to act. The emphasis on 'agency', though also including other relationships, captures the latter idea, identifying situations of delegated powers. Receipt ought to be similarly attributable if performed by someone allocated, rather than delegated, the company's powers to act. In either case, the company's own powers to receive are being exercised, albeit through the physical body of another.

B. Scope: When Will Receipt be Attributed?

Receipt will be attributed where the individual is acting within the scope of the powers allocated or delegated to him. As seen earlier, *Bowstead & Reynolds* uses straightforward agency reasoning here, so that receipt can be attributed if the agent has actual or apparent authority to do so,[166] even if the agent receives the money for the principal and later misapplies it.[167]

It is suggested that *Bowstead & Reynolds*'s statement is partially correct. It correctly identifies acts can be attributed where the agent has 'actual authority'. The concept of actual authority here reflects cases where powers are delegated to the agent. But this is not the only scenario where acts can be attributed; they can also be where the individual exercises powers to act which are allocated to him under the company's constitution. As explained in Chapter 3, it is preferable not to see the allocation of powers as straightforward examples of agency. The statement is also problematic in another way. While 'actual authority' enables acts to be attributed, apparent authority does not, operating instead as an estoppel. The two doctrines thus have different doctrinal bases and justifications.

The scope inquiry here operates similarly to that seen elsewhere in this chapter, and indeed in earlier chapters on the attribution of acts. If an illustration is needed, *Russo-Chinese Bank v Li Yau Sam* provides one.[168] Its facts are quite unusual today. The defendant Hong Kong bank set up a department which arranged telegraphic funds transfers for Chinese customers, managed by a Chinese official called a 'compradore'.[169] The compradore had no authority to enter contracts with Chinese customers unless they had been expressly agreed to by the bank's manager; his role was solely to arrange the details and submit them to the manager for consideration.[170] The claimant wanted to make a transfer to a nominee in Shanghai and so visited the department.[171] The compradore took down the details, went into the next room, and apparently consulted with the manager, before taking

[166] *Bowstead & Reynolds* (n 3) para 8–174.
[167] *Bowstead & Reynolds* (n 3) para 8–199.
[168] (n 159)
[169] ibid 178–79.
[170] ibid 185.
[171] ibid 182.

the claimant's money, apparently to effect the transfer.[172] The apparent visit to the manager had been a pretence. The funds were never received in Shanghai; the compradore had spent them for his own purposes.[173] The claimant then sued the bank to recover the money paid to the compradore. The claim failed.

Much of the Privy Council's advice focused on apparent authority[174] because it was clear that the compradore's acts could not be attributed to the bank. Short shrift was given to the claimant's argument that the compradore was the manager's 'alter ego' so that the compradore's receipt could be attributed to the manager and thus to the bank.[175] Lord Atkinson emphasised that attribution would fail, as:

> [the compradore] was authorized to arrange the details of the negotiations for the 'telegraphic transfers' of money to be submitted to the manager for approval, but he had no authority to receive money for the purpose of such transfers until those details had been so submitted and approved of, that is, until a binding contract had been entered into by the manager on behalf of the bank to transmit the money on the terms approved of when received.[176]

Thus, the compradore was acting outside the scope of his powers to act for the bank.

C. Proper Exercise

If unjust enrichment's attribution rules are the same as those elsewhere in private law, then powers to receive must also be properly exercised, ie in good faith and for proper purposes. But this proposition is not easy to prove. The point is often not discussed explicitly, but it is at least consistent with some important cases like *Swire v Francis*[177] and *Thompson v Bell*.[178]

In *Swire*, general agents hired a firm, R Francis & Co, to advance payment on goods received, for which it would later be reimbursed. The firm in turn hired Shaw as agent. Shaw credited the firm's accounts with advances and drew on the general agents for the balances shown on the accounts, which they paid out on. But the credited advances were fictitious. Shaw then misappropriated the money.[179] The Privy Council concluded that Shaw's acts in crediting the firm's accounts and drawing bills to cover the balance were 'in the ordinary course of business',[180] relying on other apparent authority cases like *Barwick v English Joint Stock Bank*.[181]

[172] ibid 182.
[173] ibid 183.
[174] Which failed since the bank had only held the compradore out as having limited powers, which the claimant knew of.
[175] ibid 185.
[176] ibid 185.
[177] *Swire v Francis* (1877) 3 App Cas 106.
[178] (n 160).
[179] (n 177) 113–14.
[180] ibid 113.
[181] *Barwick v English Joint Stock Bank* (1866–67) LR 2 Ex 259 (Exch Chamber).

This case can be variously interpreted, but on either interpretation, it appears consistent with a proper exercise requirement for attribution. One possible interpretation is that Shaw had credited and drawn the bills in good faith and in the firm's interests, and so properly exercised powers of receipt, but then later misappropriated the funds in a separate set of events. On this interpretation, the decision is perfectly consistent with a proper exercise requirement. A second possible interpretation is that Shaw had not received in good faith and in the firm's interests, so his acts could not be attributed to the firm. But the firm was still estopped from denying Shaw's authority. It is not obvious from the case report which interpretation is preferable, especially as Shaw had absconded and no evidence was available as to his intentions. But on either interpretation the outcome is consistent with a proper exercise requirement.

Thompson can be analysed similarly. A bank manager made misrepresentations to a customer, inducing her to hand money over to him to purchase houses.[182] He did not purchase the houses and absconded with the money instead. The claimant successfully sued the bank to recover the payment. Again, this result might indicate that powers must be properly exercised, a requirement which the bank manager had not met, but that the bank was estopped from denying the manager's authority through apparent authority. There is some evidence for this interpretation in the case. The jury found that the manager was 'appointed to conduct the entire business irrespective of the partners' and that the payor believed that he was acting as the bank's agent.[183] Both of these findings would now go towards establishing apparent authority. The former would establish a representation by the partners to the manager that the manager had authority, while the latter finding would go towards reasonable reliance.[184] Alternatively, though perhaps less likely on the facts, it might also be seen as a case where there was a proper purpose requirement which was met when the money was received in good faith and in the company's interests, so receipt could be attributed to the bank, even though the funds in the hands of the manager were later misapplied.

The cases here are at least consistent with the view that same attribution rules apply in unjust enrichment as elsewhere.

VI. Reasons in Favour of Consistency

Little evidence appears for wider attribution rules in unjust enrichment. Conversely, unjust enrichment's attribution rules seem to conform to the approach elsewhere in private law, where attribution turns on the allocation and delegation of the company's powers.

[182] (n 160).
[183] (n 160) 335 (Pollock CB).
[184] On both requirements, see eg *Freeman & Lockyer v Buckhurst Park Properties (Mangal) Ltd* [1964] 2 QB 480 (CA).

It is submitted that, in principle, there are also good reasons to reject suggestions that attribution in unjust enrichment claims should be different from those elsewhere in private law. It would lead to inconsistency within a single unjust enrichment claim, and inconsistency between unjust enrichment and other private law claims. These undesirable consequences would detract from the coherence of the law.

A. Inconsistency within a Single Unjust Enrichment Claim

First, even those who accept that unjust enrichment's attribution rules are wider than those elsewhere may accept that wider rules only apply to specific types of claims, or specific acts. Recall, for example, that, for Watts, the attribution of representations turns on principles wider than agency, but the attribution of acts of receipt are based on agency principles. This suggests that attribution for one act within a single claim may differ from another. Attribution of receipt, payment, and statement-making may thus all differ. Within a single unjust enrichment claim, a multiplicity of attribution rules might be used. The same question is being asked, but different answers are given. This creates inconsistencies, which appear difficult to justify.

B. Inconsistency between Claims where There is a Contract and Those Without

Second, different attribution rules in unjust enrichment from those in contract create additional inconsistencies because some unjust enrichment claims rely on contractual attribution rules. As explained earlier, where benefits are transferred pursuant to a valid contractual obligation to do so, restitution of that benefit will not follow unless the obligation is first invalidated. The valid obligation provides a 'justifying ground', or basis, for the payment and its retention. But determining whether there is a valid contractual obligation to transfer the benefit itself turns on contract's attribution rules.

Criterion Properties plc v Stratford UK Properties LLC[185] displays this reasoning. Criterion and Oaktree formed a limited partnership. Fearing a takeover of Criterion, Criterion and Oaktree later entered into a 'poison pill' agreement which gave Oaktree power to buy shares in Criterion. The takeover did not occur, and Criterion then sought to extricate itself from the agreement, which it argued did not bind it. Before the lower courts Criterion's argument was that Oaktree had acted unconscionably in holding Criterion to the agreement, relying on knowing receipt.[186] But the House of Lords rejected this approach. Both Lord Nicholls and

[185] *Criterion Properties* (n 117).
[186] *Bank of Credit and Commerce International (Overseas) Ltd v Akindele* [2001] Ch 437 (CA).

Lord Scott, who gave the only reasoned speeches, emphasised that whether the contract was valid and binding on the parties turned not on unconscionability but on whether Criterion's directors had properly exercised their powers to enter into the contract or whether Criterion was estopped from denying their authority by apparent authority.[187] As Lord Nicholls explained:

> If, applying these principles, the agreement is found to be valid and is therefore not set aside, questions of "knowing receipt" by B do not arise. So far as B is concerned, there can be no question of A's assets having been misapplied … If, however, the agreement is set aside … and irrespective of whether B still has the assets in question, A will have a personal claim against B for unjust enrichment.[188]

Whether Criterion's unjust enrichment claim succeeded thus depended on contractual attribution rules.

Another example is *Guinness plc v Saunders*.[189] Three directors of Guinness, acting as a committee of the board of directors, agreed to award the defendant special remuneration for services in a takeover bid.[190] Subsequently Guinness tried to recover the monies paid out to the defendant. It turned out that the committee did not have the authority to award the defendant special remuneration.[191] The contract was therefore void, and the House of Lords allowed the claimant company to recover the monies paid to the defendant in unjust enrichment.

Were different attribution rules used in unjust enrichment and contract, another inconsistency would arise. One or more sets of attribution rules would be used in attributing acts of payment or receipt, but a separate set used in determining if there was a valid contractual obligation which justified the payee's receipt and retention of the payment. Within a single claim, the law would be giving different answers to the same question. This is a result hardly conducive to the coherence of the law.

C. Inconsistency between Unjust Enrichment Claims and Other Private Law Claims

Apart from inconsistency within a single unjust enrichment claim, there would also be inconsistency between unjust enrichment claims and other private law claims. A set of facts may give rise to alternative claims in unjust enrichment or in tort; the claimant can elect between them.[192] It would be inconsistent were different rules adopted to attribute representations to companies depending on whether

[187] (n 117) [4] (Lord Nicholls), [21]–[31] (Lord Scott).
[188] ibid [4].
[189] *Guinness plc v Saunders* [1990] 2 AC 663 (HL).
[190] ibid.
[191] ibid 686–89 (Lord Templeman).
[192] *United Australia Ltd v Barclays Bank Ltd* [1941] AC 1 (HL) 28.

the claim was one in contract, tort, or unjust enrichment. For instance, individuals acting for a company may make fraudulent misrepresentations to a victim to induce her to hand over property rights, as in *Lloyd v Grace, Smith & Co*,[193] so this could have been analysed as a deceit case. But recovery might also be analysed in unjust enrichment terms.

An example is *Thompson v Bell*.[194] As discussed earlier, the defendant's bank manager represented to the claimant that a certain property was available and advised her to purchase it as an investment. She agreed, handing over the purchase price to the manager, who absconded with it. She sued the bank for money had and received, succeeding before the Court of Exchequer. Though the form of action of money had and received is inconclusive as to the reason for recovery,[195] Pollock CB and Alderson B's reasoning appears more consistent with restitutionary thinking. In separate speeches, both emphasised that the jury found that the manager had been acting as the defendant bank's agent in the transaction. When the claimant paid the manager, she paid the bank, so that the money was 'still in the hands of the bank' and thus could be recovered.[196] The focus was not on the manager's wrong, but rather on the bank's receipt of a payment caused by the claimant's mistake.

The value of coherence seems particularly strong in unjust enrichment because of its close interplay and overlap with other areas of law. It would be odd, to say the least, if different rules of attribution were used in attributing representations to a company depending on whether the victim was suing in deceit or in unjust enrichment. Similarly, it seems difficult to justify using one set of attribution rules to invalidate contractual obligations under which benefits are conferred, and another set to recover those benefits. And it would certainly be inconsistent if, within a single unjust enrichment claim, one attribution rule is used for one act, and another for a different act. In principle, there are thus good reasons to resist a move towards wider, different attribution rules in unjust enrichment than elsewhere in private law. Fortunately, this does not seem to be the law's current position.

VII. Conclusion

Unjust enrichment's attribution rules have been under-explored. Focusing on the core case of restitution of a mistaken payment, this chapter has explored important recent arguments that unjust enrichment's attribution rules are wider than those in other branches of private law. Various difficulties in principle exist. Furthermore, the case law reveals very little evidence that wider rules of attribution are adopted in restitutionary claims to recover mistaken payments.

[193] *Lloyd v Grace, Smith & Co* [1912] AC 916 (HL).
[194] (n 160).
[195] J Edelman, 'Money Had and Received: Modern Pleading of an Old Count' [2000] *Restitution Law Review* 547, especially 557–67.
[196] (n 160) 13 (Pollock CB), 14 (Alderson B).

In the attribution of payment acts, misrepresentations inducing mistakes, and receipt, attribution is consistent with the analysis suggested in earlier chapters. Just as in contract and tort, attribution of acts turns on whether the person doing the act was allocated or delegated the company's power to act, acted within the scope of the power, and acted in good faith and for proper purposes. This view suggests that law of attribution is more coherent, both within restitutionary claims and across private law, than it is commonly thought to be.

6

Attributing Knowledge

This chapter moves away from attributing acts to consider the attribution of one state of mind: knowledge. Many different mental states might be attributed: intention; beliefs; knowledge; and dishonesty, amongst others. Investigations into each might be warranted. But such investigations would be unmanageable within the constraints of this book, necessitating a narrower focus in this chapter.

Three reasons might be given for focusing on knowledge. First, many cases concern the attribution of knowledge, including *Meridian*. Yet it is often unclear when and why knowledge is attributed. Answering these questions brings immediate practical payoffs, providing a way for courts, counsel, and academics to approach attribution problems.

Second, since the attribution of knowledge is an issue regularly faced by the courts, the large number of reported cases provides a wide range of material on which to draw. By contrast, investigating other mental states which are relied on only in specific contexts is likely to be more challenging.

Third, the attribution of knowledge alone already provides answers to attributing a number of other so-called 'mental states' in private law. Many so-called 'mental states' in private law are in fact standards of conduct, where the actor's conduct is assessed objectively in light of what he knows. Dishonesty is an example: it asks whether the actor's conduct, judged against his knowledge of the circumstances, would be regarded by ordinary honest people as dishonest.[1] Other plausible examples might include unconscionability[2] or good faith.[3] An investigation into knowledge thus already addresses some other 'mental states' in private law. Even if attributing knowledge does not provide the answers, analogies may be appropriately drawn between the rules attributing knowledge and those attributing

[1] *Royal Brunei Airlines Sdn Bhd v Tan* [1996] 2 AC 378 (HL); *Barlow Clowes International Ltd v Eurotrust International Ltd* [2005] UKPC 37, [2006] 1 WLR 1476; *Ivey v Genting Casino UK Ltd (t/a Crockfords Club)* [2017] UKSC 67, [2018] AC 391; *Group Seven Ltd v Notable Services LLP* [2019] EWCA Civ 614, [2020] Ch 129; *cf Twinsectra Ltd v Yardley* [2002] UKHL 12, [2002] 2 AC 164.

[2] Generally referring to unconscionable conduct, see eg *Bank of Credit and Commerce International (Overseas) Ltd v Akindele* [2001] Ch 437 (CA) (knowing receipt).

[3] Which may have different meanings in different contexts, see eg *Imperial Group Pension Trust Ltd v Imperial Tobacco Ltd* [1991] 1 WLR 589 (Ch); *Yam Seng Pte Ltd v International Trade Corpn Ltd* [2013] EWHC 111 (QB) [119]-[154]; *Hayes v Willoughby* [2013] UKSC 17, [2013] 1 WLR 935 [14]; *UC Rusal Alumina Jamaica Ltd v Miller* [2014] UKPC 39, [2015] Pens LR 15 [51]; *IBM United Kingdom Holdings Ltd v Dalgleish* [2017] EWCA Civ 1212, [2018] PLR 1.

other mental states, such as intentions and beliefs.[4] Knowledge thus provides a good starting point, laying the groundwork for further inquiry.

In this chapter, it is argued that knowledge will be attributed where the knowledge is: (i) possessed by an individual allocated or delegated the company's powers; and (ii) material to the individual's exercise of those powers. Despite apparent disunity, English law adopts a surprisingly consistent approach to when knowledge will be attributed. Nor is such a rule unknown; a similar rule is adopted by the US *Restatement (Third) of the Law of Agency*.

I. The Current Law

Although knowledge was attributed to companies routinely across the nineteenth and twentieth centuries, a definitive statement of the relevant principles in private law claims is lacking. Two early approaches were the 'directing mind and will' test, and agency rules, later followed by the highly context-specific approach in *Meridian Global Funds Management v Securities Commission*.[5] Although *Meridian* has since been used in some atypical scenarios, it is not used routinely in private law claims where attribution of knowledge is necessary.

A. Directing Mind and Will

The first possibility is that knowledge can only be attributed if possessed by the company's 'directing mind and will', a familiar approach by now. This approach can be seen in the influential case of *El Ajou v Dollar Land Holdings plc*.[6] Mr El Ajou, a wealthy Arab businessman, paid away large sums in a fraud. The sums passed through multiple countries before being received by Dollar Land Holdings plc. El Ajou sued Dollar Land for knowing receipt, which required him to show that Dollar Land had received the assets with sufficient knowledge that it would be unconscionable for it to retain the benefit of the assets.[7] Dollar Land's director, Ferdman, knew that the funds were proceeds of fraud. Could his knowledge be attributed to Dollar Land? The Court of Appeal concluded that it could; the company was a knowing recipient.

Hoffmann LJ identified two approaches to attribution. One was the directing mind and will test. At first instance, Millett J also applied this test, but concluded that Ferdman was not the directing mind and will.[8] He exercised no independent

[4] See eg *JSC Medzhdunarodniy Promyshlenniy Bank v Pugachev* [2017] EWHC 2426 (Ch).
[5] *Meridian Global Funds Management v Securities Commission* [1995] UKPC 5, [1995] 2 AC 500.
[6] *El Ajou v Dollar Land Holdings plc* [1994] BCC 143 (CA).
[7] *Akindele* (n 2).
[8] *El Ajou v Dollar Land Holdings* [1993] BCC 698 (Ch) 719.

judgement, and acted entirely upon the directions of the company's beneficial owners and their consultant who made the decisions. Ferdman only signed the documents and ensured that the paperwork was in order.[9] On appeal, Hoffmann LJ applied the test more loosely. He concluded that 'different persons may for different purposes satisfy the requirements of being the company's directing mind and will'.[10] The crucial question was 'whether in relation to the Yulara transaction [under which the company acquired the assets], Mr Ferdman as an individual exercised powers on behalf of the company which so identified him'.[11] Hoffmann LJ held that he did. '[A]s far as the constitution of [the company] was concerned, he committed the company to the transaction as an autonomous act which the company adopted by performing the agreement',[12] even though he signed the agreement under the directions of the company's beneficial owners.

B. Agency Principles

A second approach to attributing knowledge also discussed in *El Ajou* was agency law. Much case law on the imputation of an agent's knowledge to his principal exists. But the cases 'can vary a great deal and care is needed in analysing [them]',[13] as Hoffmann LJ recognised. Whether there is a general test for attributing or imputing knowledge in agency law is doubtful. Even *Bowstead & Reynolds*, the leading agency text, accepts that 'The law on this topic is constituted by a plethora of cases in different contexts, which are extremely difficult to reduce to any order'.[14] Agents may be of many kinds: stockbrokers, estate agents, solicitors, and others. Their diversity makes it difficult to draw up general rules. Nor is justifying such rules easy. One suggested justification is that the identities of the principal and agent merge, so that the agent's knowledge is the principal's knowledge.[15] This does not explain why the identities of the principal and agent merge; it merely describes the outcome of imputation floridly. Another is that the principal should not be able to use an agent to put himself in a better position than if he had dealt personally,[16] but no reason is given as to why. Nor is it evident from this justification when attribution should be available. Relying on 'agency rules' is fraught where the existence of such rules is disputed.

[9] ibid.

[10] *El Ajou* (CA) (n 6) 159.

[11] ibid.

[12] ibid 160.

[13] *El Ajou* (CA) (n 6) 156.

[14] P Watts and F Reynolds (eds), *Bowstead & Reynolds on Agency*, 22nd edn (London, Sweet & Maxwell, 2020) para 8-209.

[15] D Demott, 'When is a Principal Charged with an Agent's Knowledge?' (2003) 13 *Duke Journal of Comparative and International Law* 291, 312.

[16] *Bowstead & Reynolds* (n 14) para 8-209.

El Ajou takes a similar line. Illustrating the disparate nature of the cases, Hoffmann LJ identified three sub-categories of imputation under 'agency rules':[17] (i) where the agent's knowledge affects the performance or terms of an authorised contract;[18] (ii) where the principal has a duty to investigate or make disclosure;[19] and (iii) where the agent is authorised to receive communications.[20] The first includes attribution of an insurance agent's knowledge of material facts to the insurer,[21] the second includes dog-owners' duties to investigate their dogs' vicious tendencies,[22] and the third includes agents authorised to receive notices to quit from tenants.[23] The facts fell within none of these categories. Hoffmann LJ was especially concerned that cases in one category ought not be inappropriately applied to another.[24] Implicitly, the existence of a general test in agency law for imputing knowledge was doubted.

Thus, while it may be possible to attribute knowledge of agents to their principals within the three specific scenarios identified by Hoffmann LJ, it is doubtful whether it is possible to formulate a general test applying across all agents. In turn this casts doubt on whether agency law can provide general rules and justifications for corporate attribution.

C. *Meridian*: Purpose of the Substantive Rule

Just a few years after *El Ajou* came Lord Hoffmann's magisterial speech in *Meridian*. *Meridian* has already been discussed in detail,[25] necessitating only a quick review of its key points. Meridian's chief investment officer and senior portfolio manager had used the company to acquire shares in a public company. The key question was whether their knowledge could be attributed to Meridian under a New Zealand statute[26] so that Meridian owed duties to disclose its shareholding. Lord Hoffmann, delivering the advice of the Privy Council, held that the chief investment officer's knowledge could be attributed.[27] Meridian thus owed duties of disclosure, which it breached when it failed to disclose.

As discussed earlier, Lord Hoffmann identified three categories of attribution rules: the primary rules, general rules, and the special rules of attribution. The primary rules look to specific provisions in the company's constitution or

[17] *El Ajou* (CA) (n 6) 156.
[18] ibid.
[19] ibid.
[20] ibid 156–57.
[21] ibid 156, citing *Blackburn Low & Co v Vigors* (1887) 12 App Cas 531 (HL).
[22] ibid 156, citing *Baldwin v Casella* (1872) LR 7 Ex 325 (Ct of Exch).
[23] ibid 157, citing *Tanham v Nicholson* (1872) LR 5 HL 561 (HL).
[24] ibid 156.
[25] See Ch 2 above.
[26] New Zealand Securities Amendment Act 1988, s 20.
[27] *Meridian* (n 5) 511.

judge-made company law providing for attribution; the general rules are agency rules. Where neither provide the answer, the court may fashion special rules of attribution, considering the purpose and policy of the substantive rule to decide whose knowledge ought to be attributed.

But both the primary and the general rules appeared inapplicable. The company's constitution and general company law typically do not state what knowledge can be attributed to the company. This was likely also the case in *Meridian*. As to the general rules, Lord Hoffmann appears to have implicitly accepted that they could not apply because the statute required a state of mind of the person 'himself', as opposed to his servants or agents.[28] His earlier judgment in *El Ajou* plausibly also suggests another, arguably better, reason for the general rules' inapplicability: agency rules imputing an agent's knowledge to his principal were too diverse to provide answers to the specific question of *corporate* attribution. Thus, a special rule of attribution was fashioned.[29] The purpose and policy of the relevant statute was to compel the immediate disclosure of substantial shareholdings by companies in fast-moving markets.[30] Thus, it was 'the person who, with the authority of the company, acquired the relevant interest' whose knowledge could be attributed.[31]

Post-*Meridian*, special rules were formulated in some other cases. In *Bank of India v Morris*, a special rule of attribution was formulated to attribute a bank officer's knowledge of suspicious transactions to the bank. The bank thus committed fraudulent trading under section 213 of the Insolvency Act 1986.[32] In *Lebon v Aqua Salt Co Ltd*, another Privy Council decision where the Board's advice was delivered by Lord Hoffmann, a special rule of attribution was also formulated.[33] There, Mauritian law provided that a purchaser of land who knew of a prior sale would not take free of the rights of the first purchaser. The second purchaser, a company, had the knowledge of its controller attributed to it, so that it knew of the first purchaser's rights.[34] The company was thus acting 'a faute', and could not take free of the first purchaser's rights.[35]

While courts occasionally formulate 'special rules', they rarely do so in routine private law claims such as dishonest assistance, knowing receipt, or deceit. Courts do attribute knowledge in such claims, but when and why knowledge is attributed remains somewhat enigmatic. A convincing explanation of when and why knowledge is attributed in private law is still wanting.

[28] ibid 507.
[29] ibid.
[30] ibid 511.
[31] ibid.
[32] *Bank of India v Morris* [2005] EWCA Civ 693, [2005] BCC 739.
[33] [2009] UKPC 2, [2009] BCC 425.
[34] ibid [26].
[35] ibid [26]–[27].

II. Attributing Knowledge

As Chapter 2 explained, the reasons given for attribution must fit its form. Attributing acts treats *this* act of *this* individual as *this* company's. The reason for attribution must fit this shape, connecting act, individual, and company in a single normative sequence. Likewise, attributing knowledge requires a reason why *this* knowledge of *this* individual is that of *this* company. Again, knowledge, individual, and company must be linked together in a normative sequence.

It is argued that this connection exists where two requirements are met. First, the knowledge must be possessed by an individual allocated or delegated the company's powers to act. Second, that knowledge must be material to the exercise of the powers allocated or delegated to the individual. Collectively, these two requirements form the 'materiality' test.

A. Knowledge's Function

It may first be helpful to explain knowledge's function in private law: it changes the character of acts done or yet to be done. This may occur in multiple ways.

First, knowledge may be a condition for the creation of new primary duties. Possessing knowledge thus changes the character of subsequent acts yet to be done. *Meridian* is an example: Meridian's knowledge that it became a substantial shareholder in a public company generated new statutory duties to make disclosure of the substantial shareholdings. If Meridian then failed to comply with this duty, it would be acting wrongfully. The existence of knowledge thus changes the character of subsequent acts done, or not done, by Meridian. Other examples plausibly falling within this category include the duty to restore misapplied trust property when the actor knows that he has received the property in breach of trust (knowing receipt),[36] the duty of a landowner to inform a party relying on a representation that the latter is acting on a mistake when the landowner knows of the mistake (proprietary estoppel),[37] and duties under constructive trusts to re-convey mistaken payments to the payor once the payee knows of the mistake (constructive trusts over mistaken payments of money).[38]

Alternatively, knowledge might be constitutive of a wrong – a breach of duty.[39] Acts done without knowledge may not be wrongful but may be where done with knowledge. There is no general duty imposed on people not to make false representations to others. Innocent misrepresentations are not wrongs. But making a

[36] C Mitchell and S Watterson, 'Remedies for Knowing Receipt' in C Mitchell (ed), *Constructive and Resulting Trusts* (Oxford, Hart Publishing, 2010) 132.

[37] I Samet, 'Proprietary Estoppel and Responsibility for Omissions' (2015) 78 *MLR* 85.

[38] *Westdeutsche Landesbank Girozentrale v Islington LBC* [1996] AC 669 (HL) 705, 715 (Lord Browne-Wilkinson).

[39] P Cane, 'Mens Rea in Tort Law' (2002) 20 *OJLS* 533 (describing it as the 'independent' function); W Chan and AP Simester, 'Four Functions of Mens Rea' (2011) 70 *CLJ* 381 (discussing moral wrongs).

false representation knowing the true facts or being reckless as to whether the facts are true is a wrong;[40] the same is now true of making a false representation negligently.[41] Similarly, there is no general duty against assisting others. Assisting another to transfer funds from one bank account to another is not inherently problematic. It may even be virtuous, worthy of praise. But matters are different if the assister knows that he was participating in a breach of trust or fiduciary duty. He then commits the wrong of dishonest assistance.[42] Or, on the view that knowing receipt is wrongs-based, knowledge is constitutive of the wrong of receiving assets known to have been dissipated in breach of trust or fiduciary duty,[43] or of subsequently dealing with them inconsistently with the trust.[44] Without that knowledge, no wrong is committed.[45] In this category, knowledge changes the character of the actor's acts from neutral or even virtuous to wrongful.

Third, knowledge might qualify or defeat the actor's rights. This is most common with defences: a bona fide purchaser of legal rights can take free of prior equitable rights encumbering legal title if she gives value and takes bona fide without notice of the prior equitable rights.[46] But if she knows of the prior rights, then she will take subject to those rights. Likewise, a person who has changed his position has a defence to some unjust enrichment claims[47] unless he acted in bad faith[48] or was a wrongdoer.[49] Actual knowledge of the facts generating the claim would constitute bad faith. Here too an actor's acts are coloured by his knowledge. His lack of knowledge might justify giving him a defence to protect his security of receipt or autonomy in dealing with assets, but protection is no longer warranted where he has the relevant knowledge. Thus, the actor cannot ignore prior equitable rights, nor can he avail himself of the change of position defence.

In all three cases, the character of the acts done, or to be done by the actor, is changed by his knowledge.

[40] *Derry v Peek* (1889) LR 14 App Cas 337 (HL).

[41] Since *Hedley Byrne & Co Ltd v Heller & Partners Ltd* [1964] AC 465 (HL).

[42] *Royal Brunei* (n 1); *Twinsectra* (n 1); *Barlow Clowes* (n 1); *Group Seven* (n 1).

[43] L Smith, 'Unjust Enrichment, Property and the Structure of Trusts' (2000) 116 *LQR* 412.

[44] W Swadling, 'The Nature of "Knowing Receipt"' in PS Davies and J Penner (eds), *Equity, Trusts and Commerce* (Oxford, Hart Publishing, 2017).

[45] *In re Montagu's Settlement Trusts* [1987] Ch 264 (Ch); *Agip (Africa) Ltd v Jackson* [1991] Ch 547 (CA).

[46] Eg *Macmillan Inc v Bishopsgate Investment Trust and others (No 3)* [1995] 1 WLR 978, 1000 (Ch).

[47] *Lipkin Gorman v Karpnale Ltd* [1991] 2 AC 548 (HL) 579–80 (Lord Goff), applying eg to mistake claims: *Kleinwort Benson v Lincoln City Council* [1999] 2 AC 349 (HL) 381 (Lord Goff); *Deutsche Morgan Grenfell v IRC* [2007] 1 AC 558 (HL) [38] (Lord Hope); *Test Claimants in the FII Group Litigation v RCC* [2012] UKSC 19, [2012] 2 AC 337 [48] (Lord Walker), but not to *ultra vires* taxes levied by public authorities: *Test Claimants in the FII Group Litigation v Revenue and Customs Commissioners* [2014] EWHC 4302 (Ch) [309]–[315], upheld [2016] EWCA Civ 1180, [284]–[285], [312], [336], nor in claims to recover voidable preferences under insolvency legislation: *Skandinaviska Enskilda Banken AB (Publ) v Conway* [2019] UKPC 36, [2019] 3 WLR 493 [100]–[117].

[48] *Lipkin Gorman*, ibid 580 (Lord Goff); *Niru Battery Manufacturing Co v Milestone Trading Ltd* [2004] EWCA Civ 487, [2004] QB 985; *Jones v Churcher* [2009] EWHC 722 (QB).

[49] *Lipkin Gorman* (n 47) 580 (Lord Goff); *Barros Mattos Jnr v MacDaniels Ltd* [2004] EWHC 1188 (Ch), [2005] 1 WLR 247; *Abou-Rahmah v Abacha* [2006] EWCA Civ 1492, [2007] 1 All ER (Comm) 827.

B. The Materiality Test

Attributing knowledge concerns the connection between knowledge, individual, and company. If knowledge changes the character of the acts done or to be done, this suggests that knowledge is only relevant where it can change the character of acts done *by the company*. This then breaks down into two requirements. First, the knowledge must be possessed by someone whose acts can be attributed to the company – someone allocated or delegated the company's powers to act. Second, such knowledge must be material to the exercise of those powers. Together, these requirements identify when knowledge can be connected to the company.

This requirement happily excludes two extremes, neither of which has been adopted by the case law. At one extreme, even the knowledge of someone wholly unconnected to the company might be attributed to it. If so, in *Meridian*, the knowledge of the Securities Commission, of the company whose shares were acquired, or of other parties in the market, might be attributed to Meridian. Similarly, in the *Bank of India* case, the knowledge of passersby outside the bank premises might be attributed. At the other extreme, only the knowledge of extremely senior individuals in the company, such as its chairman or managing director, might be attributed. In the *Bank of India* case, the Court of Appeal firmly rejected the bank's argument that only the board's knowledge could be attributed. But courts have adopted neither approach. A middle ground is taken. Only knowledge possessed by an individual allocated or delegated the company's powers to act can be attributed to the company.

But this requirement alone is over-inclusive. Not all knowledge possessed by an individual allocated or delegated the company's powers ought to be attributed. Some knowledge is purely personal: the individual's knowledge of his tooth-brushing habits, his children's favourite foods, or bitter family feuds. Knowledge of these facts is wholly unconnected to the company. Courts have shown no enthusiasm for this extreme, rejecting it outright. In *Re Marseilles Extension Railway Co*, James LJ remarked rhetorically: 'Is it to be imputed to the banking company that they have knowledge of everything the director knows about his own private affairs? Such a proposition seems most unreasonable'.[50] At another extreme, it might be suggested, as it was in *Re Hampshire Land*, that knowledge will only be attributed if the individual has a duty to receive it and to communicate it to the company.[51] This approach, conversely, is too narrow. Employees may frequently possess knowledge relevant to the acts that they perform, but rarely will they owe specific duties to receive and communicate the information. Furthermore, as *El Ajou* recognised, merely owing duties to communicate information does not justify treating that duty as if it had been performed when it has not.[52]

[50] *Re Marseilles Extension Railway Co* (1871–1872) LR 7 Ch App 161 (CA) 170.

[51] *Re Hampshire Land* [1896] 2 Ch 743 (Ch), citing *Re Marseilles*, ibid 169; *Gale v Lewis* (1847) 9 QB 730, 115 ER 1455.

[52] *El Ajou* (CA) (n 6) 157–58.

It is suggested that the most appropriate approach is to attribute only knowledge *material* to the acts which the individual is empowered to do for the company. The materiality requirement thus enables knowledge of the individual's family or social affairs to be excluded, unless related to the individual's powers to act for the company. Under this requirement, one's knowledge of her child's best friends, her mother's illness, or an old friend's character would normally not be attributable. But the knowledge of advisors to a transaction, corporate compliance employees who detect potential wrongdoing, and in-house accountants who know of suspicious circumstances, would all be attributable if they were material to the exercise of these individuals' powers.

This position is not unknown. A similar approach is suggested by the US *Restatement (Third) of the Law of Agency*:

> § 5.03 Imputation Of Notice Of Fact To Principal
>
> For purposes of determining a principal's legal relations with a third party, notice of a fact that an agent knows or has reason to know is imputed to the principal if knowledge of the fact is material to the agent's duties to the principal, unless the agent
>
> (a) acts adversely to the principal as stated in § 5.04, or
>
> (b) is subject to a duty to another not to disclose the fact to the principal.[53]

This section is intended to apply to all agents, not just those through whom companies act. It was not adopted in English law because of concerns specific to particular agents, such as solicitors and property agents. These agents might know of prior interests in property in earlier transactions. To attribute that knowledge to principals they subsequently acted for was thought inappropriate.[54] But a materiality test is apt in attributing knowledge to companies, neatly delineating an individual's personal knowledge from that related to his corporate role.

While the *Third Restatement* focuses on the materiality of knowledge to the agent's *duties* to the principal, it is more appropriate here to focus on the materiality of knowledge to the *powers* which have been allocated or delegated to the individual in corporate attribution. As knowledge operates to change the character of the individual's acts, the company's powers to act ought to be the focus.

At this point two potential objections might be briefly addressed. Both are dealt with elsewhere in this book. First, it might be suggested that even material knowledge ought not be attributed where the knowledge-holder is acting fraudulently or in breach of duty to the company. This fraud or breach of duty exception was first suggested in *Re Hampshire Land*[55] but has since been the subject of recent decisions

[53] American Law Institute, *Restatement (Third) of the Law of Agency* (American Law Institute Publishers, 2007) §5.03.

[54] See eg *Warrick v Warrick* (1745) 3 Atk 291, 26 ER 970; *Worsley v Earl of Scarborough* (1746) 3 Atk 392, 26 ER 1025.

[55] (n 51).

by ultimate appellate courts.[56] Its scope and justification are controversial.[57] For present purposes it suffices to note that no such exception applies in establishing the company's duties or liabilities for breach.[58] In deceit, knowledge has been attributed even where the individual is defrauding the company[59] and in *El Ajou* and *Meridian*, it appeared irrelevant that the knowledge-holders were breaching duties owed to the company. As Lord Hoffmann said in *Meridian*, '[t]he fact that [A] did the deal for a corrupt purpose and did not give such notice because he did not want his employers to find out cannot in their Lordships' view affect the attribution of knowledge and the consequent duty to notify'.[60] Even proponents of the exception only think it applies where the company is enforcing its rights. These cases are dealt with in Chapter 7, where it is argued that no fraud exception applies even there.

Second, it might be objected that the materiality test might be too wide, leading to the attribution of 'too much' knowledge. A plausible concern is that a junior employee's knowledge might be attributed under the materiality test, even if his senior colleagues knew nothing when acting. The real problem here is not with the attribution of knowledge, but with aggregation. The concern is that companies might too easily breach duties or incur liability if acts and knowledge in two different persons could be readily aggregated together. This is examined in Chapter 8, which shows that English law has taken a very restrictive approach to aggregation. The problem of attributing 'too much' knowledge is thus not a live one.

III. Illustrations

Before proceeding to the case law, it may be helpful to briefly set out how the materiality test might apply to different groups of individuals.

A. The Company's Controller or Chief Moving Force

It is easily observable that the knowledge of the company's 'controlling mind', 'moving force',[61] or 'guvnor'[62] is generally attributed to the company.[63] This result

[56] *JC Houghton & Co v Nothard, Lowe and Wills, Ltd* [1928] AC 1 (HL); *Belmont Finance Corpn v Williams Furniture Ltd* [1979] Ch 250 (CA); *Stone & Rolls Ltd (in liquidation) v Moore Stephens* [2009] UKHL 39; [2009] 1 AC 1391; *Bilta (UK) Ltd (in liquidation) v Nazir* [2015] UKSC 23, [2015] 2 WLR 1168; *Singularis Holdings Ltd v Daiwa Capital Markets Europe Ltd* [2019] UKSC 50, [2019] 3 WLR 997.

[57] See *Bowstead & Reynolds* (n 14) para 8-214.

[58] *cf* in Australia, *Beach Petroleum NL v Johnson* (1993) 43 FCR 1 but see now *Grimaldi v Chameleon Mining NL (No 2)* [2012] FCAFC 6 [282]–[286].

[59] *Lloyd v Grace, Smith & Co* [1912] AC 716 (HL).

[60] *Meridian* (n 5) 511.

[61] *Grimaldi* (n 58).

[62] *Gilford Motor Co Ltd v Horne* [1933] Ch 935 (CA).

[63] See eg *Crown Dilmun v Sutton* [2005] EWHC 52 (Ch) [190]–[196].

holds in knowing receipt and dishonest assistance cases where corporate opportunities are diverted from one company by its controller to the controller's newly created company in breach of fiduciary duty.[64] The controller's knowledge that the diverted contracts properly belonged to the former is attributed to the new company for both knowing receipt and dishonest assistance. In deceit, a similar result obtains. In *Komercni Banka AS v Stone & Rolls Ltd*, banks were defrauded by Stone & Rolls into advancing letters of credit pursuant to fake documents.[65] Stone & Rolls's controller, Stojevic, knew that the documents were fake. When the banks sued Stone & Rolls for deceit, Stojevic's knowledge was attributed to it.

The reason is simple. Such an individual will have extensive powers allocated or delegated to him, at least informally. The wider an individual's powers to act for the company, the more information will be material to the exercise of those powers. Hence, the wider the range of knowledge attributable. In the knowing receipt cases, the controller's knowledge that the diverted contracts ought to have gone to the first company was material to the exercise of his powers for the new company in contracting for it. His knowledge made those acts improper, generating knowing receipt liability. Likewise, Stojevic's knowledge that the documents leading the banks to advance letters of credit were false was also material to the acts he was empowered to do for the company, which must have included advancing the documents to the bank and receiving the letters of credit. It too could be attributed.

B. Directors

Like knowledge held by controllers, knowledge of company directors is also often readily attributed. As Viscount Dunedin said in *JC Houghton v Nothard, Lowe and Wills Ltd*, 'It may be assumed that the knowledge of directors is in ordinary circumstances the knowledge of the company.'[66] More recently, the same sentiments were repeated by Moore-Bick LJ in *Mohammad Jafari-Fini v Skillglass Ltd*:[67] 'In general … I think that information relevant to the company's affairs that comes into the possession of one director, however that may occur, can properly be regarded as information in the possession of the company itself.'[68]

While often true, this is not an invariable rule. It is usually true of executive directors in larger companies and directors of smaller companies, who are typically allocated or delegated extensive powers. A wider range of knowledge would be material to their delegated powers, and thus attributable. But some directors have more limited powers, such as non-executive directors of large companies. The point is clearer from the older cases. In *Powles v Page*,[69] bank directors'

[64] See Section IV.B below.
[65] *Komercni Banka AS v Stone & Rolls Ltd* [2002] EWHC 2263 (Comm), appealed on different grounds [2003] EWCA Civ 311, [2003] 1 Lloyds Rep 383.
[66] (n 56) 14.
[67] *Mohammad Jafari-Fini v Skillglass Ltd* [2007] EWCA Civ 261.
[68] ibid [98].
[69] *Powles v Page* (1846) 3 CB 16, 136 ER 7.

knowledge about a customer's accounts was not attributable to the bank where the directors had no share in managing the accounts; a similar point was made in *Re Carew's Estate Act*.[70] That knowledge was not material to their powers to act for the company.

C. Secretary

A secretary once had very limited powers to act for the company. In *Barnett, Hoares & Co v South London Tramways Co*, a secretary was referred to as 'a mere servant' whose 'position is that he is to do what he is told, and no person can assume that he has any authority to represent anything at all'.[71] Correspondingly, cases then took a very limited view of when a secretary's knowledge could be attributed. In *Société Générale de Paris v Tramways Union*, a company's secretary learnt information about an equitable assignment relevant to the company's business while attending a family funeral. It was held that the company had not obtained notice of the assignment through the secretary.[72] This result is explicable by the limited powers the company secretary then had.[73] However, the position changed over time. By 1928, it was accepted that knowledge of the company's secretary could be attributed 'if the thing of which knowledge is predicated was a thing within the ordinary domain of the secretary's duties'.[74] The secretary continued to grow in importance,[75] eventually being described as 'the chief administrative officer of the company'[76] with his powers enlarging correspondingly. *Tramways Union* should have been decided differently today.

D. Shareholders

Can the knowledge of shareholders be attributed? This was the issue in *Julien v Evolving TecKnologies and Enterprise Development Co Ltd*,[77] which will be discussed in full below. While it was unnecessary to decide the issue on the facts, the Privy Council was hesitant to attribute the knowledge of the company's sole shareholder to the company under a limitation statute. Instances where shareholders' knowledge has been attributed appear rare. Generally, cases where a shareholder's knowledge has been attributed are ones where the shareholder is

[70] *Re Carew's Estate Act* (1862) 31 Beav 39, 54 ER 1051.
[71] *Barnett, Hoares & Co v South London Tramways Co* (1887) 18 QBD 815 (CA) 817.
[72] *Société Générale de Paris v Tramways Union* (1884) 14 QBD 424 (CA) 438.
[73] See eg *Barnett* (n 71); *George Whitechurch Ltd v Cavanagh* [1902] AC 117 (HL); *Ruben v Great Fingall Consolidated* [1906] AC 439 (HL). Things have now changed: *Panorama Developments (Guildford) Ltd v Fidelis Furnishing Fabrics Ltd* [1971] 2 QB 711 (CA).
[74] *Houghton* (n 56) 14.
[75] *Panorama* (n 73) 716 (Denning LJ).
[76] ibid 717 (Salmon LJ).
[77] *Julien v Evolving TecKnologies and Enterprise Development Co Ltd* [2018] UKPC 2, [2018] BCC 376.

also a director or controller of the company;[78] attribution is thus explicable by his status as director or controller. The individual's status as a shareholder alone seems to rarely, if ever, trigger attribution.

The materiality test might help explain why. The company's constitution ordinarily allocates powers to the shareholders in general meeting as a whole, but not to individual shareholders. The role of individual shareholders is to constitute the general meeting and contribute to the decision reached at meetings. Nor will it be common for the company's powers to be delegated to a single shareholder. As individual shareholders will generally not be allocated or delegated the company's powers to act, their knowledge will not be material to the exercise of those powers; it therefore is not attributable.

E. Clerical Staff

There is no general rule that the knowledge of persons in clerical or administrative positions cannot be attributed. In *BP Oil International Ltd v Target Shipping Ltd*, the payee advanced a similar argument that 'the state of mind of persons in clerical functions who merely execute the decisions of those responsible is irrelevant'.[79] The argument was rejected by Andrew Smith J, who concluded that there was no such general rule.[80] What is important is whether the knowledge is material to the powers allocated or delegated to the knowledge-holder. The wider the scope of such powers, the more likely that knowledge will be attributable. This question is at best only tangentially dependent on whether the knowledge-holder is in a clerical position or not.

IV. The Case Law

This section considers four categories of cases: statutory liability; knowing receipt; dishonest assistance; and deceit. The materiality test can explain the outcomes in these cases. It also better addresses other possible scenarios.

A. Statutory Liability

First, consider the well-known cases of statutory liability where the statute does not specify any attribution rules.[81] No better starting point can be found than

[78] See eg the knowing receipt cases in Section IV.B below.

[79] *BP Oil International Ltd v Target Shipping Ltd* [2012] EWHC 1590 (Comm), [2012] 2 CLC 336 [228].

[80] ibid [228].

[81] An example of clearly specified statutory attribution rules is found in the Insurance Act 2015, ss 3–6. See pre-Act insurance cases generating difficult attribution questions, eg *PCW*

Meridian. The Privy Council formulated a rule of attribution that it was the person who acquired the relevant interest with the company's authority whose knowledge could be attributed to it.[82] As Koo, the company's chief investment officer, had acquired the shares with Meridian's authority, his knowledge could be attributed to Meridian.

The materiality test can explain this result. By being appointed to the position of chief investment officer, he would have been delegated powers to buy shares for Meridian and report relevant information about share trading to the legal or compliance departments. His knowledge that Meridian had acquired shares in the target company was clearly material to the powers delegated to him to report relevant information arising from share trading. That knowledge thus qualified his acts in not making disclosure of the substantial shareholdings to other relevant departments within Meridian. The language of the rule formulated by the Privy Council, centred around 'authority', reflects the focus on the powers allocated or delegated to the individual. 'Authority' in agency law, in its central sense of actual authority, is a power.[83]

The materiality test not only explains the outcome here but is better able to address other possible scenarios. What if shares were transferred to Meridian due to the stock exchange's mistake, so that Meridian became a substantial shareholder without its employees or agents having acquired the shares for it? Alternatively, what if an employee in Meridian's corporate compliance team, empowered to monitor the company's compliance with securities laws, then became aware of the share transfer? Could the stock exchange or the compliance officer's knowledge be attributed to the company? The rule formulated in *Meridian* provides no answer. At worst it might suggest that the employee's knowledge ought not be attributed. But the materiality test provides a superior analysis. The employee's knowledge should be attributed: it was material to the acts he was empowered to do for the company, such as to monitor the company's compliance with securities laws, even if he had nothing to do with the share acquisition. But the stock exchange's knowledge should not, as the exchange was not allocated or delegated powers to act for the company.

A second case is *Bank of India v Morris*. A bank manager entered transactions which he knew were suspicious on behalf of the bank. As in *Meridian*, the Court of Appeal attributed his knowledge to the bank under section 213 of the Insolvency Act 1986 because he had authority to deal with the customer for those transactions.[84] The materiality test also explains this result. The manager was delegated powers to contract for the bank, and the suspiciousness of potential

Syndicates v PCW Reinsurers [1996] 1 WLR 1136 (CA); *Re Group Josi v Walbrook Insurance Co Ltd* [1996] 1 WLR 1152 (CA); *Re Odyssey (London) Ltd v OIC Run-Off Ltd* [2001] Lloyd's Rep IR 1 (QB).

[82] *Meridian* (n 5) 511.

[83] Eg *Bowstead & Reynolds* (n 14) para 1-001 (actual authority).

[84] *Bank of India* (n 32) 763. See also, at first instance, *Morris v Bank of India* [2004] EWHC 528 (Ch), [2004] BCC 404 [120].

transactions would be material to those powers. The manager should have taken further steps before proceeding with the suspicious transactions, such as consulting his line manager or the legal department.

One advantage of the materiality test is that it more readily captures scenarios where the knowledge-holder did not have authority to enter the transaction, but where his knowledge should still be attributed. Key examples include knowledge possessed by back-end staff such as accountants or in-house counsel officers. They would not be delegated powers to transact with customers, but knowledge they possessed about the suspiciousness of ongoing transactions could only be highly material to the acts they were empowered to do, including conducting investigations, reporting to the authorities, or consulting senior management.

A third example is the Privy Council case of *Julien v Evolving Tecknologies and Enterprise Development Co Ltd*,[85] concerning attribution of a shareholder's knowledge. The claimant Eteck made investments in an IT business. The investments failed spectacularly and Eteck suffered loss. When Eteck sued its directors in negligence for causing it to make the investments without due diligence, the directors argued that Eteck's claim was time-barred. The relevant limitation statute was materially similar to section 32 of the English Limitation Act 1980.[86] It provided that in cases of fraud, concealment, or mistake, time starts running from the date where the claimant had discovered the fraud, concealment or mistake or could with reasonable diligence have discovered it. The directors sought to attribute the knowledge of Eteck's sole shareholder, the Minister of Finance in Trinidad and Tobago, to Eteck so that the relevant facts were known to or discoverable by Eteck. The Court of Appeal of Trinidad and Tobago decided that the knowledge was not attributable, nor was it discoverable.

Since the Privy Council concluded that Eteck's claim failed for the breach's lack of discoverability,[87] it was unnecessary to resolve the attribution issue. But had it been necessary, Lord Briggs admitted that '[t]he Board would have found it difficult to reach a clear determination of this important question'. Rival arguments were 'evenly balanced'.[88] He concluded that 'the Board would on balance have been reluctant to disturb the decision of the Court of Appeal' that the sole shareholder's knowledge was not attributable.[89]

The Privy Council clearly did not find the question easy. Lord Briggs considered several bases for attribution, including the rule that under certain conditions[90] shareholders could act unanimously to make informal decisions for

[85] (n 77). Noted by P Watts, 'Attribution and Limitation' (2018) 134 *LQR* 350; R Leow, 'Attributing Shareholders' Knowledge: Corporate Attribution One Step Further?' [2018] *LMCLQ* 316.

[86] Trinidad and Tobago Limitation of Certain Actions Act 1987, s 14.

[87] ibid [73].

[88] ibid [62].

[89] ibid [62].

[90] Eg the company's solvency: *Re Duomatic* [1969] 2 Ch 365 (Ch). For others see *Ciban Management Corpn v Citco (BVI) Ltd* [2020] UKPC 21, [2021] AC 122 [31]–[47].

the company;[91] the duty to report relevant knowledge to the company about its affairs,[92] and the fashioning of a special rule of attribution.[93] But each had its own problems. Unanimous shareholder action was 'not a concept easily applicable to a body of shareholders, who have no reason to be unanimous about matters concerning the company otherwise than when making some relevant decision'.[94] There was no duty here on shareholders to report knowledge about the company's affairs.[95] And there were difficulties with delineating the scope of a special rule of attribution. Was it to apply to sole shareholders only? A majority of shareholders? Or even a minority capable of bringing a derivative action? Even if some of these might be excluded, the difficulties with 'defining such a special rule of attribution in terms which would not be exorbitant, or unfair in different factual contexts, [would] remain',[96] in Lord Briggs's words.

The materiality test provides a superior analysis. First, one must ask what powers were allocated or delegated to the shareholder under the constitution. As the sole shareholder, it could also act as the general meeting. No detailed exposition of Eteck's constitution can be found in the case report, but neither individual shareholders nor the general meeting typically has management powers such as powers to bring claims on behalf of the company against its directors for breach of duty.[97] These powers are typically allocated to the board instead.[98] If so, the general meeting can only control the exercise of the board's powers by altering their articles or refusing to re-elect directors of whose acts they disapprove.[99] So, the shareholder was not allocated or delegated powers to bring claims for the company. The second question under the materiality test is whether the knowledge possessed by the sole shareholder was material to the exercise of those powers. Knowledge of the directors' breach of duty would be material to their powers to remove the directors. But the shareholder lacked power to bring claims on behalf of the company. Knowledge material to such powers could not be attributed since that knowledge did not qualify acts attributed to the company. A shareholder's knowledge should only be attributable for limitation where he has power to bring claims for the company. But the Minister of Finance, by all accounts, lacked such powers. The Court of Appeal of Trinidad and Tobago and the Privy Council reached the right result, and this explains why.

[91] An extension of the *Re Duomatic* rule, ibid. See also *Multinational Gas and Petrochemical Co v Multinational Gas and Petrochemical Services Ltd* [1983] Ch 258 (CA); *Ciban*, ibid [31]–[47], discussed by *Julien* (n 77) [44]–[56].

[92] ibid [54]–[56].

[93] ibid [57]–[58].

[94] ibid [53].

[95] ibid [55]–[56].

[96] ibid [58].

[97] Eg *John Shaw and Sons (Salford) Ltd v Shaw* [1935] 2 KB 113 (CA).

[98] *Model Articles for Public Companies*, Model Art 3; *Model Articles for Private Companies Limited by Shares*, Model Art 3.

[99] *John Shaw* (n 97) 134 (Greer LJ). See also *Automatic Self-Cleansing Filter Syndicate v Cunninghame* [1906] 2 Ch 34 (CA).

B. Knowing Receipt[100]

A second set of cases where knowledge is a necessary element of a cause of action is knowing receipt. Classically concerning the receipt of trust property or their traceable proceeds in breach of trust, it now extends to receipt of assets dissipated in breach of fiduciary duty.[101] Knowing receipt liability requires showing that rights have been dissipated in breach of trust or fiduciary duty, the recipient had beneficially received[102] those rights or their traceable substitutes, and that he had such knowledge that would make it unconscionable for him to retain the benefit of such rights.[103]

Perhaps surprisingly, it is not easy to find cases of corporate knowing recipients. The reason for this is hard to discern. Within the few existing cases, two alternative approaches are adopted in holding corporate recipients to be knowing recipients.[104] The first, older approach, treats the company as a human person's 'creature' or 'alter ego', piercing the corporate veil.[105] The company and its human controller are seen as one and the same.[106] The second approach, conversely, fully respects the company's separate legal personality. No corporate veil-piercing occurs. The company commits knowing receipt as an independent actor, with the acts and knowledge of human persons attributed to it. There is now good reason to be sceptical about the continued existence of the first model.[107] Few cases supported it, and the veil-piercing analysis used there was re-explained by the Supreme Court in *Prest v Petrodel Resources Ltd*.[108] Veil-piercing continues to be fraught, with the Supreme Court recently casting further doubt on aspects of *Prest*.[109] Recent cases support the second attribution-based model,[110] on which we will focus. Three cases are considered as exemplars: *El Ajou*,[111] *Grimaldi v Chameleon Mining NL (No 2)*,[112] and *Aerostar Maintenance International Ltd v Wilson*.[113]

[100] This discussion here borrows from R Leow, 'Equity's Attribution Rules' (2021) 15 *Journal of Equity* 35.

[101] Objecting to these cases being put under the same banner as dissipations in breach of trust, see eg Swadling, 'The Nature of "Knowing Receipt"' (n 44) 305–306.

[102] *Agip (Africa) Ltd v Jackson* [1990] Ch 265.

[103] *Akindele* (n 2), see previously *Re Montagu's* (n 45).

[104] See generally J Glister, 'Equitable Liability of Corporate Accessories' in Davies and Penner (n 44).

[105] *Gencor ACP Ltd v Dalby* [2000] EWHC 1560 (Ch), [2000] 2 BCLC 734; *Trustor AB v Smallbone (No 2)* [2001] EWHC 703 (Ch), [2001] 1 WLR 1177.

[106] Glister, 'Equitable Liability' (n 105) 277–82. Examples include *Gencor* ibid; *Trustor* ibid; *CMS Dolphin Ltd v Simonet* [2001] EWHC 415 (Ch), [2002] BCC 600; possibly also *Cook v Deeks* [1916] 1 AC 554 (PC).

[107] Glister, 'Equitable Liability' (n 104) 276.

[108] *Prest v Petrodel Resources Ltd* [2013] UKSC 34, [2013] 2 AC 415, especially [31]–[33] and [68], discussed by Glister, 'Equitable Liability' (n 104) 280.

[109] *Hurstwood Properties (A) Ltd v Rosendale Borough Council* [2021] UKSC 16, especially [65], [68]–[71].

[110] See in addition to the authorities discussed below, *Alesco Risk Management Services Ltd v Bishopsgate Insurance Brokers Ltd* [2019] EWHC 2839 (QB), especially [383]–[388], though the knowing receipt claim failed as there was no breach of fiduciary duties.

[111] (n 6).

[112] (n 58).

[113] *Aerostar Maintenance International Ltd v Wilson* [2010] EWHC 2032 (Ch).

The first is *El Ajou*. Dollar Land received sums as investments in a property development project. Ferdman, Dollar Land's director, knew that the sums were proceeds of a fraud perpetuated on El Ajou. The Court of Appeal unanimously held that Ferdman's knowledge could be attributed to Dollar Land, so the latter was liable in knowing receipt. Although Hoffmann LJ used a weak form of the 'directing mind and will' approach to reach this conclusion, the outcome can be easily explained by the materiality test. Indeed, it reflects some of the reasoning of the judges. For Hoffmann LJ, it was key that 'Ferdman as an individual exercised powers on behalf of the company', most significantly in signing the relevant agreements on behalf of the company.[114] As he explained, '[As] far as the constitution of DLH [the company] was concerned, he committed the company to the transaction as an autonomous act which the company adopted by performing the agreement'.[115] This reasoning emphasises the first requirement for attribution under the materiality test: the knowledge must be possessed by someone allocated or delegated the company's powers to act. The second requirement would also be met. Ferdman's knowledge about the source of funds was material to the powers he had to act for Dollar Land, including to contract to receive the funds as investments by the fraudsters. It could thus be attributed.

Second, in the Australian case of *Grimaldi v Chameleon Mining NL*, Murchison, a company, wanted to purchase rights in iron tenements in the Jack Hills region of Western Australia but lacked the necessary finances. Grimaldi, a de facto director of Chameleon,[116] and the director and moving force in Murchison,[117] procured cheques to be drawn by another director, Barnes, on Chameleon's account. The cheques were to enable Murchison to purchase the rights and were made payable to the vendors. These transactions were for Murchison's benefit; Chameleon gained no benefit from them.[118] Chameleon later sued Murchison for knowing receipt. The Full Court concluded that Murchison was a knowing recipient.[119] Grimaldi knew that the advances were suspicious: the money advanced was a large part of Chameleon's funds, Chameleon received no benefit from making the advances, Grimaldi and Barnes were in a position of conflict but were the effective decision-makers, and the decisions were made 'precipitately', when Chameleon was short of funds.[120] This knowledge was attributed to Murchison.

Although it was 'common ground'[121] that Grimaldi's knowledge could be attributed to Murchison,[122] the Full Federal Court gave little explanation for this conclusion. At first instance the court relied on Grimaldi being 'the controlling

[114] *El Ajou* (CA) (n 6) 159.
[115] ibid 160.
[116] *Grimaldi* (n 58) [323]–[328].
[117] ibid [8].
[118] ibid [333].
[119] For discussion of the attribution of acts, see Leow, 'Equity's Attribution Rules' (n 100).
[120] *Grimaldi* (n 58) [333].
[121] ibid [285].
[122] ibid [345].

mind' of Murchison;[123] a similar description was used on appeal.[124] The materiality test might provide a better explanation of this result. Grimaldi wielded very substantial powers over the management of Murchison's affairs, not least to receive payments on behalf of Murchison. He knew that the payments were suspect. As in *El Ajou*, his knowledge was material to the acts he was empowered to do for Murchison. It was rightly attributed.

The third and final example is *Aerostar Maintenance International Ltd v Wilson*.[125] Business opportunities were diverted by Wilson from one company, Aerostar, to another, Avman, in breach of his fiduciary duties to the former. Wilson was Aerostar's managing director, and Avman's director, promoter, and key moving force. Claims for knowing receipt, amongst others, were brought against Avman in respect of the contracts it had 'received'.[126] Wilson knew there had been a breach of fiduciary duty in diverting the contracts to Avman. This knowledge, Morgan J held, could be attributed to Avman. Again, no reasons were given for attribution. The materiality test supplies one. As Avman's chief moving force and director, Wilson had substantial powers to act for Avman. His knowledge that the contracts rightly belonged to Aerostar was material to those powers, changing the character of acts that he could and did take on behalf of Avman, including entering those contracts. They could be attributed.

Other examples of this type include *Odyssey Entertainment Ltd v Kamp*,[127] where sales agencies for movies including 'Manchester United', 'Space Chimps 2', 'Chalet Girl', and 'Postman Pat' were diverted from Odyssey to a new company, Timeless.[128] The diversions had been effected by Kamp, Odyssey's controller. The judge attributed Kamp's knowledge to Timeless, so that Timeless was a knowing recipient. Like *Aerostar*, this case was not complex. Kamp knew that these sales agency contracts would have been Odyssey's but for their diversion. He had very substantial powers to act for Timeless, and that knowledge was material to the acts which he had power to do.

Another, of slightly older vintage, is *CMS Dolphin v Simonet*.[129] Its facts are similar: in breach of fiduciary duties, Simonet, CMS Dolphin's managing director, set up a rival business, resigned from CMS Dolphin, and caused its staff and clients to move to the new company. CMS Dolphin sought an account of profits against the new company. Lawrence Collins J decided that an account of profits could be made because both company and Simonet had 'jointly participated in the breach of trust'.[130] This reasoning has now been criticised. The cases cited for

[123] *Chameleon Mining NL v Murchison Metals Ltd* [2010] FCA 1129 [699]. On the fraud exception's inapplicability, see also [2010] FCA 1129 [700]–[704], and on appeal, ibid [282]–[286], [345].
[124] *Grimaldi* (n 58) [8].
[125] (n 113).
[126] Relying on *Ultraframe Ltd v Fielding* [2005] EWHC 1638 (Ch) [1487]–[1491].
[127] *Odyssey Entertainment Ltd v Kamp* [2012] EWHC 2316 (Ch).
[128] ibid [205].
[129] (n 106).
[130] ibid [103].

it do not support it, and 'joint participation' in a breach of trust is not a cause of action in English law.[131] A better basis for the decision is the alternative one identified by Lawrence Collins J, that the company was liable to account for its profits because it had committed knowing receipt.[132] It had received assets dissipated in breach of Simonet's fiduciary duty to CMS Dolphin, and Simonet had actual knowledge of the facts constituting the breach and thus, knew that the assets had been so diverted. That knowledge was attributable to the new company. As the new company's chief moving force, he had substantial powers to act for it, which had been at least informally delegated to him, and his knowledge was material to the exercise of those powers.[133]

C. Dishonest Assistance[134]

Like knowing receipt, dishonest assistance by a company in a breach of trust or fiduciary duty might be analysed in two ways: the company may be treated as its human controller's alter ego, or the company may commit dishonest assistance as a distinct actor in its own right.[135] In the first instance decision of *Novoship (UK) Ltd v Mikhaylyuk*, it was suggested that the former would be limited to the relatively few cases where the controller is the sole owner, where no one else has a beneficial interest, and where the company's only function is to make and receive payment.[136] In cases where the company has recognisable business of its own,[137] the latter approach appears more apt, and seems to be the approach more widely adopted today.[138]

Understanding knowledge's role in dishonest assistance requires some background. Liability for dishonest assistance turns on three requirements: there must be a breach of trust or fiduciary duty;[139] and assistance of the breach by the alleged assister; which was dishonest.[140] Of these, the most difficult has been the

[131] *Ultraframe* (n 126) [1574]–[1576]; *National Grid Electricity Transmission plc v McKenzie* [2009] EWHC 1817 (Ch) [114]; *Aerostar* (n 113) [202]–[205].

[132] *CMS Dolphin* (n 129) [104]. With accounts of profits now clearly available for knowing receipt: *Akita Holdings Ltd v Attorney General of the Turks and Caicos Islands* [2017] UKPC 7, [2017] AC 590.

[133] Details of the rival company's structure and that of its predecessors is not entirely clear from the report, possibly because it had gone into liquidation and claims against it were no longer being pursued: ibid [3].

[134] The discussion here borrows from Leow, 'Equity's Attribution Rules' (n 100).

[135] Glister, 'Equitable Liability' (n 104). A third possibility exists: the company may be held vicariously liable for the dishonest assistance of its employees or other individuals, eg *Dubai Aluminium Co Ltd v Salaam* [2002] UKHL 48, [2003] 2 AC 366; *Group Seven* (n 1); *Bilta (UK) Ltd (in liquidation) v Natwest Markets plc* [2020] EWHC 546 (Ch) [215]–[216].

[136] *Novoship (UK) Ltd v Mikhaylyuk* [2012] EWHC 3586 (Comm) [413].

[137] Eg *CMS Dolphin* (n 129) [103].

[138] See *Bilta (UK) Ltd (in liquidation) v Natwest Markets plc* [2020] EWHC 546 (Ch) [215]–[216], but the case was remitted for retrial due to lengthy delay between trial and handing down of judgment: [2021] EWCA Civ 680; *Group Seven* (n 1) [112]–[154].

[139] It is unnecessary for this breach to be dishonest: *Royal Brunei* (n 1) 384–85.

[140] *Barnes v Addy* (1874) 9 Ch App 244, 251–52; *Royal Brunei* (n 1) 389.

requirement of 'dishonesty'. The position now is that an objective test of dishonesty applies in assessing the assister's conduct.[141] The actual state of the actor's knowledge or beliefs as to the facts must first be assessed.[142] Then the actor's conduct must be assessed, considering his knowledge and beliefs. The question is: taking into account the knowledge which he possessed, would ordinary honest people have regarded the actor's conduct as dishonest?[143] Although appearing to connote a state of mind, dishonesty in dishonest assistance is in fact a standard of conduct,[144] assessed in light of the actor's knowledge. There is no requirement that the actor must have realised that his conduct would transgress the standards of ordinary honest people.[145]

Three cases are again used as exemplars: *Royal Brunei Airlines v Tan*,[146] *Aerostar Maintenance v Wilson*,[147] and *Bilta (UK) Ltd v Natwest Markets plc*.[148]

In the classic case of *Royal Brunei*, the claimant airline appointed a company, BLT, as its travel agent for the sale of tickets. Ticket sales proceeds were to be held on trust by the company for the airline until accounting was effected. In breach of trust, BLT paid the money into its current account and dissipated it for its own purposes. Tan was the company's managing director and principal shareholder; he acted for the company in making payments into and from the company's own account. The Privy Council concluded that he was liable for dishonest assistance. He caused, or permitted, the company to apply the money in a way which he knew was unauthorised by the trust; this was dishonest.[149] The Privy Council also said:

> By the same token, and for good measure, BLT also acted dishonestly. The defendant was the company, and his state of mind is to be imputed to the company.[150]

This conclusion implicitly draws on the now-discredited directing mind and will test: Tan, the primary individual through whom the company acted, was the company, and so his state of mind was the company's as well. But the materiality test provides a better explanation. As the managing director who was 'effectively in charge and control of' BLT,[151] Tan was allocated or delegated expansive powers to act for BLT. His knowledge that the ticket sale proceeds were held on trust for the airline was material to the exercise of those powers, particularly to pay the money into BLT's account and dissipate it for BLT's purposes. It could thus be attributed to BLT for dishonest assistance.

[141] *Royal Brunei* (n 1); *Barlow Clowes* (n 1); *Ivey* (n 1); *Group Seven* (n 1); *cf Twinsectra* (n 1).
[142] *Ivey* (n 1) [74].
[143] See references at n 1.
[144] *Twinsectra* (n 1) [115] (Lord Millett).
[145] See references at n 1.
[146] (n 1).
[147] (n 113).
[148] (n 135).
[149] *Royal Brunei* (n 1) 393.
[150] ibid 393.
[151] ibid 383.

The second case is *Aerostar Maintenance v Wilson*, seen above in knowing receipt. A dishonest assistance claim was also brought. As in knowing receipt, the knowledge of Wilson, the director who had diverted contracts away from Aerostar to a new company, could be attributed to the new company. As its founder and director, Wilson had extensive powers to act for Avman. He knew that he was 'doing the dirty' on Aerostar and admitted 'that his conduct was "not correct"'.[152] This knowledge was material to the exercise of his powers and could be attributed to Avman, so that it was liable for dishonestly assisting Wilson's breach of fiduciary duty.[153] A similar conclusion was also reached in *Odyssey Entertainment Ltd v Kamp*, involving materially similar facts.[154]

A final, interesting example is *Bilta (UK) Ltd v Natwest Markets plc*,[155] a further installment of the Bilta litigation.[156] Bilta's former directors used Bilta to perpetuate a 'carousel' VAT fraud on EU carbon credits. Such frauds generated obligations by Bilta to account for output VAT to the revenue authorities, which would pay input VAT to another company.[157] It was inherent in the fraud that Bilta would always be insolvent and unable to pay. Over time, Bilta owed very substantial sums to the revenue authorities, eventually entering liquidation. In this case, Bilta, through its liquidators, sued the employers of traders who had bought large quantities of EU carbon credits in transactions forming part of the fraudulent scheme, seeking to hold them either directly or vicariously liable for dishonest assistance. They were the Royal Bank of Scotland and a subsidiary of a joint venture, RBS SEEL.

At first instance, Snowden J held that the traders' knowledge could be attributed to RBS for dishonest assistance; they 'were the persons who were given the authority to conduct the relevant trades on behalf of [the employers]'.[158] Similarly, the knowledge of the head of the trading desk, who was the line manager of one of the traders, could also be attributed to RBS, not just in respect of his own trading, but also in respect of his traders' trading.[159] Snowden J found that the traders knew that their trading was part of a VAT fraud. As RBS's conduct, assessed against that knowledge, would be regarded by ordinary honest people as dishonest, it was held liable for dishonest assistance.[160]

On appeal, the finding that the traders knew of the fraud was doubted.[161] There had been a lengthy delay of nineteenth months between the trial and judgment hand-down. The delay meant that the Court of Appeal could not be satisfied that

[152] *Aerostar* (n 113) [197].
[153] ibid [198]–[199].
[154] (n 127).
[155] (n 135).
[156] An earlier part of the saga being the important attribution decision in *Bilta (UK) Ltd v Nazir* (n 56).
[157] ibid [4] (Lord Neuberger, with whom Lords Clarke and Carnwath agreed). For further detail of these frauds, see *Red 12 Trading Ltd v HMRC* [2010] STC 589.
[158] (n 135) [222]. RBS SEEL had performed no relevant corporate acts of assistance: [218].
[159] ibid [223].
[160] ibid [434]–[443].
[161] *Bilta* (CA) (n 138) [93]–[97], [108], [118]–[119], [121]–[122].

the trial judge's findings and conclusions were correct;[162] a re-trial by a different judge was thus ordered.[163] But there was no criticism of the rest of Snowden J's reasoning on attribution, which is materially similar to that adopted in other cases, and therefore still valuable.

Once again, the materiality test fits with and can explain attribution's operation. The traders had powers to conduct trades for RBS.[164] If they knew that the trades were suspicious, that knowledge would be material to the exercise of those powers. It would suggest, for example, that further investigations ought to have been made before proceeding with the trades. Their failure to do so tainted their acts, rendering them dishonest by the standards of ordinary honest people. The head of the trading desk had powers to conduct trading but also to supervise the trades of subordinates.[165] As Snowden J pointed out at first instance, he could have instructed the trading to cease.[166] His knowledge of suspicious circumstances was likewise material to the exercise of those powers and could thus be attributed.[167]

Of note is the analysis concerning RBS's compliance officer, Mr Savage. He had imperfect knowledge of the circumstances and had sought to confirm the propriety of the transactions with more senior colleagues. His concerns allayed, he then gave instructions to continue 'business as usual' trading. RBS argued that after the instruction, it was Mr Savage's knowledge which ought to be attributed, not the traders or their line manager. Rejecting this argument, Snowden J emphasised that it was still the traders and not the compliance officer who had authority to make the trades; the former's knowledge ought not be 'displaced' by that of someone who 'had no authority from RBS to enter into any transaction, who did not know the full facts surrounding the trading, and who essentially followed a procedure designed to ensure that any wrongdoers would not be tipped off whilst an investigation took place'.[168] It must be stressed that this conclusion does not mean that the knowledge of back-end staff can never be attributed. Rather, it was impermissible to use Mr Savage's innocent lack of knowledge to replace the guilty knowledge of the traders and desk head. We turn to similar problems in Chapter 8.

D. Deceit

The last set of examples concerning deceit requires the least analysis, not least because some of its elements have already been examined in Chapter 4. A company

[162] ibid.
[163] ibid [122].
[164] *Bilta* (HC) (n 135) [222].
[165] ibid [223].
[166] ibid [223].
[167] ibid [223].
[168] ibid [433].

might be held vicariously liable for another's deceit,[169] or the acts and states of mind of human persons might be attributed to the company, so the latter personally commits the tort.[170] Our focus is on the latter.

Deceit requires that false statements be made by a statement-maker who knows or is reckless as to the statements' truth.[171] Knowledge of the statements' falsity must thus be attributed for the company to have committed deceit. Here too, the materiality test accurately captures when knowledge will be attributed.

Consider first the well-known House of Lords decision of *Lloyd v Grace, Smith & Co*,[172] which has been variously interpreted.[173] A managing clerk of a firm of solicitors made fraudulent misrepresentations to a customer of the firm, inducing her to part with title deeds to property and to sign other documents, which he then sold for his own benefit. He represented that he would sell the property for her and reinvest the proceeds in investments which would bring better returns. The firm was held liable for deceit. As explained above in Chapter 4, *Lloyd v Grace* is not best seen as an example of vicarious liability, but personal liability for deceit. The managing clerk's knowledge of the statements' falsity must have been attributable to the firm. The materiality test can explain this too. The clerk had powers delegated to him to conduct the business of the firm, including making representations and receiving property. His knowledge of his statements' falsity was material to his exercise of powers to make representations, if not others as well, and thus were rightly attributable.

S Pearson & So Ltd v Lord Mayor of Dublin, a case analysed in greater detail in Chapter 8 below, might provide a further illustration.[174] The claimants were contractors which had contracted with the Dublin Corporation to construct sewage works. Through their engineers, the Dublin Corporation had made false representations that a wall existed. Though the question was left to the jury, there was evidence that the representations were made to get a 'cheap job',[175] ie reduce the amount that the claimants were willing to tender for the project. If so, the engineers knew that the statements were false.[176] It would not have been difficult to attribute that knowledge to the Dublin Corporation. The engineers had power

[169] Eg *Armagas Ltd v Mundogas SA* [1986] AC 717 (HL); *Barings plc (in liquidation) v Coopers & Lybrand* [2003] EWHC 1319 (Ch), [2003] PNLR 34. See generally MA Jones (ed), *Clerk & Lindsell on Torts*, 23rd edn (London, Sweet & Maxwell, 2020) para 17-26.

[170] Eg *Komercni Banka AS v Stone & Rolls Ltd* [2002] EWHC 2263 (Comm), appealed on different grounds [2003] EWCA Civ 311.

[171] *Derry v Peek* (1889) 14 App Cas 337; *Standard Chartered Bank v Pakistan National Shipping Corpn* [1998] 1 Lloyd's Rep 684; *AIC Ltd v ITS Testing Services (UK) Ltd* [2006] EWCA Civ 1601, [2007] 1 Lloyd's Rep 555, [251].

[172] *Lloyd v Grace, Smith & Co* [1912] AC 716 (HL).

[173] Including as an example of vicarious liability, not personal liability: see eg *Lister v Hesley Hall* [2001] UKHL 22, [2002] 1 AC 215, [17] (Lord Steyn), [71]–[73] (Lord Millett), see also [36] (Lord Clyde); *Mohamud v WM Morrison Supermarkets plc* [2016] UKSC 11, [2016] 2 WLR 821 [20]; *Clerk & Lindsell on Torts* (n 169) para 17-26.

[174] *S Pearson & So Ltd v Lord Mayor of Dublin* [1907] AC 351 (HL).

[175] ibid 357 (Earl of Halsbury).

[176] ibid 353 (Lord Loreburn LC), 357 (Earl of Halsbury) 359 (Lord Ashbourne), 361 (Lord James).

to make statements to prospective tenderers; the falsity of their statements was material to their exercise of that power.

Over in the Antipodes, a final example is the High Court of Australia's decision in *Krakowski v Eurolynx Properties Ltd.*[177] The claimants purchased shop premises from the defendants on the basis that there was a tenant who was paying rent at a price which would give them a 10 per cent return. Unknown to them, the tenant had been given a side-deal including a three-month rent-free period and an initial lump sum payment. The defendant later represented that the lease agreement contained the entire agreement between them and the tenant. An agent and a director of the company knew of the side-deal and were responsible for the initial negotiations for the sale.[178] They also knew that the purchasers were willing to buy on the basis that the rent stated in the lease agreement was what the tenant was willing to pay for a lease of the property.[179] This knowledge was attributed to the defendant company.[180] As the lead judgment of Brennan, Deane, Gaudron and McHugh JJ explained, 'their knowledge was the knowledge of [the defendants] for they were the persons who were responsible for the initial negotiations and who had set the scene in which the representation had been made by the … proffered offer of sale'.[181]

The materiality test explains this outcome: the director and agent were delegated powers to introduce the purchasers to the defendants, though not to contract for the defendants. Their knowledge that the purchasers were only interested in properties which would yield a 10 per cent return was material to whether to make those introductions. It was thus rightly attributable. This result would not have been reached had the focus been solely on who had the power to enter the agreements on behalf of the company, as it was in *Meridian*, *Bank of India*, and *El Ajou*. Courts attribute knowledge more widely, and that wider set of situations is best captured by the materiality test.

V. Conclusion

This chapter has examined when knowledge can be attributed to companies. Orthodoxy here provides no simple answer. The aim of this chapter is to provide one: the materiality test. The materiality test asks two questions: what powers of the company were allocated or delegated to the individual, and was the knowledge possessed by the person material to his exercise of those powers? Only where knowledge is material to the exercise of those powers will it be attributable, a conclusion consistent with the existing case law.

177 *Krakowski v Eurolynx Properties Ltd* [1995] HCA 68, (1995) 183 CLR 563.
178 ibid [2]–[3].
179 ibid [38].
180 ibid.
181 ibid.

PART III

Difficult Problems

7

Attribution in Enforcing Duties

In recent years, one attribution problem has caused especial difficulty.[1] If acts and knowledge of an individual can be attributed to the company to establish the company's duties, breach of those duties, and liability for breach, can they attributed to the company when the company is bringing claims to enforce duties owed to it? This question typically arises when the defendant duty-bearer argues that it has a defence available to it due to the company's conduct, such as illegality, contributory negligence, or consent.

In the last decade, this question has been considered by the ultimate appellate court in the United Kingdom not just once or even twice, but a grand total of three times in *Stone & Rolls Ltd (in liquidation) v Moore Stephens*,[2] *Bilta (UK) Ltd (in liquidation) v Nazir*,[3] and *Singularis Holdings Ltd v Daiwa Capital Markets Europe*.[4] In *Bilta* and *Singularis*, the Supreme Court accepted that even if acts and knowledge can be attributed to establish the company's duties and liabilities for breach of duty, they may not be attributed when the company is bringing a claim to enforce duties owed to it.[5] When and why attribution is unavailable in the latter situation still remains difficult.

An alternative and simpler approach is adopted in contributory negligence. Under the 'both ways' test, if an act can be attributed to the company to establish its duties, breaches, and liabilities for breaches of those duties, then it can also be attributed where the company is enforcing duties owed to it. This analysis obviates

[1] Eg E Ferran, 'Corporate Attribution and the Directing Mind and Will' (2011) 127 *LQR* 239; P Watts, 'Illegality and Agency Law: Authorising Illegal Action' [2011] *Journal of Business Law* 213; S Watson, 'Organs, Agents and Identity in the English Courts' (2011) 23 *Singapore Academy of Law Journal* 762; E Lim, 'Attribution in Company Law' (2014) 77 *MLR* 794; J Payne, 'Corporate Attribution and the Lessons of Meridian' in PS Davies and J Pila (eds), *The Jurisprudence of Lord Hoffmann: A Festschrift for Leonard H Hoffmann* (Oxford, Hart Publishing, 2015); S Worthington, 'Corporate Attribution and Agency: Back to Basics' (2017) 133 *LQR* 118; E Lim, 'Attribution' in W Day and S Worthington (eds), *Challenging Private Law: Lord Sumption on the Supreme Court* (Oxford, Hart Publishing, 2020).

[2] *Stone & Rolls Ltd (in liquidation) v Moore Stephens* [2009] UKHL 39, [2009] 1 AC 1391.

[3] *Bilta (UK) Ltd (in liquidation) v Nazir* [2015] UKSC 23, [2015] 2 WLR 1168.

[4] *Singularis Holdings Ltd v Daiwa Capital Markets Europe* [2019] UKSC 50, [2019] 3 WLR 997. For other decisions in the Commonwealth raising the same point, see eg *Deloitte & Touche v Licent Inc* [2017] SCC 63, [2017] 2 SCR 855; *Ho Kang Peng v Scintronix Corp Ltd* [2014] SGCA 22, [2014] 3 SLR 329; *Red Star Marine Consultants Pte Ltd v Personal Representatives of Satwant Kaur d/o Sardara Singh* [2019] SGCA 76, [2020] 1 SLR 115.

[5] *Bilta* (n 3) [7] (Lord Neuberger), [38], [42]–[43] (Lord Mance), [86]–[92] (Lord Sumption), [204]–[207] (Lords Hodge and Toulson); *Singularis* (n 4) [34].

the need to identify when and why attribution is, exceptionally, unavailable. It also brings welcome advantages, promoting consistency between contributory negligence and other cases. Perhaps most importantly, it minimises inconsistencies within attribution, avoiding the law saying that an act both is and is not the company's at the same time in private law. It is argued that this test should be adopted more generally. However, even if the act or knowledge is attributed, the company's claim will not necessarily fail; the effect of attribution depends on the substantive rule of law in question.

I. Three Major Decisions

A. *Stone & Rolls*

The modern starting point is the difficult and controversial decision of *Stone & Rolls*. The company, Stone & Rolls, was used by its sole owner and controller, Stojevic, as a vehicle to defraud banks. The fraud was later discovered; both Stone & Rolls and Stojevic were successfully sued for deceit by the banks.[6] Stone & Rolls was unable to pay damages and went into liquidation. Its liquidators sued Stone & Rolls's former auditors, the defendants, for breach of their duty of care and skill as auditors in failing to detect and prevent Stojevic's frauds. The auditors sought to strike out Stone & Rolls's claim, arguing that Stojevic's acts and knowledge could be attributed to Stone & Rolls, so the claim was founded on the company's fraud and should fail for illegality.

By a majority of 3–2, the House of Lords held that Stone & Rolls's claim should be struck out for illegality. However, they reached this outcome through different routes, taking diverse positions on contested issues in play. One was whether attribution turned on the company being a 'one-man' company. Another was about the scope of a 'fraud or breach of duty exception' to attribution, where attribution would be available except where the individual was acting fraudulently or in breach of duty.[7] The scope and purpose of the illegality doctrine was a third contested pressure point.[8] Yet another difficult question concerned whether the scope of the auditors' duty of care was relevant.

The majority comprised Lords Phillips, Walker, and Brown, with Lords Scott and Mance in the minority. Lord Phillips's decision turned primarily on two points. First, as Stone & Rolls was a one-man company where the only person managing

[6] *Komercni Banka AS v Stone & Rolls Ltd* [2002] EWHC 2263 (Comm), [2003] 1 Lloyd's Rep 383, partially reversed on appeal on different grounds but accepting that Stojevic was liable: *Komercni Banka AS v Stone & Rolls Ltd* [2003] EWCA Civ 311, [2003] CP Rep 58.

[7] Relying on *Re Hampshire Land* [1896] 2 Ch 743 (CA).

[8] Prior to *Patel v Mirza* [2016] UKSC 42, [2017] AC 467, compare eg *Tinsley v Milligan* [1994] 1 AC 340 (HL); *Gray v Thames Trains Ltd* [2009] UKHL 33, [2009] 1 AC 1339; *Hounga v Allen* [2014] UKSC 47, [2014] 1 WLR 2889; *Les Laboratoires Servier v Apotex Inc* [2014] UKSC 55, [2015] AC 430.

all aspects of the company's activities was acting fraudulently,[9] his fraudulent acts and states of mind ought to be attributed to the company. Second, the scope of the auditors' duty did not encompass protecting the interests of the creditors of the company.[10] All whose interests formed the subject of the auditors' duty of care had been party to illegal conduct.[11] Similarly, Lord Walker also concentrated on Stone & Rolls being a one-man company. He reasoned that there were no innocent parties in the company, so Stojevic's knowledge could be attributed under the illegality doctrine.[12] Lord Brown's decision too turned primarily on Stone & Rolls being a one-man company,[13] but again took a different path. For Lord Brown, Stojevic and the company were one and the same person for all purposes. Since Stojevic could not rely on his own illegality in bringing a claim, Lord Brown reasoned, the company should not be in a better position.[14]

By contrast, Lord Scott concluded that Stojevic's acts could not be attributed to the company because the company was a victim of the frauds,[15] and there were no public policy reasons why illegality should apply to relieve the auditors of liability.[16] The last member of the House of Lords, Lord Mance, took a starkly different route, focusing instead on the auditors' duties, and concluding that they ought to be held responsible to the company they were auditing. Amongst other features, the scope of the auditors' duty required them to report suspected or actual fraud to proper authorities,[17] especially since Stone & Rolls was insolvent at each audit date,[18] and its interests could not be limited solely to those of its shareholders.[19]

It is famously difficult to form a coherent ratio from the decisions in *Stone & Rolls*. The Law Commission regarded *Stone & Rolls* as having 'no majority reasoning' in its report on illegality.[20] Sitting in the Hong Kong Court of Final Appeal, Lord Walker subsequently recanted part of his speech in *Stone & Rolls*.[21] In *Bilta*, Lord Neuberger thought that, subject to two points, *Stone & Rolls* was 'best treated as a case which solely decided that the Court of Appeal was right to conclude that, on the facts of the particular case, the illegality defence succeeded and that the claim should be struck out'.[22] These two points that could be drawn from *Stone & Rolls* were, first, that illegality was unavailable where there were innocent

[9] *Stone & Rolls* (n 2) [49]–[56].
[10] ibid [84].
[11] ibid [86].
[12] ibid [168].
[13] ibid [201].
[14] ibid [195]–[196].
[15] ibid [117].
[16] ibid [120]–[122].
[17] ibid [269].
[18] ibid [265].
[19] ibid [270].
[20] Law Commission, *The Illegality Defence* (Law Com No 320, 2010) para 3.32.
[21] [2014] HKCFA 22, (2014) 17 HKCFAR 218 [101].
[22] *Bilta* (n 3) [24].

shareholders or directors and, more tentatively,[23] that the defence might be available where there are no innocent shareholders or directors.[24] Otherwise, Lord Neuberger thought that it would be best for *Stone & Rolls* to be '"put on one side" and marked "not to be looked at again"'.[25] But *Stone & Rolls* was not formally overruled; it continued to exert influence on lower courts as recently as in *Singularis*.[26]

B. *Bilta*

Academic commentary[27] and difficult cases boomed in *Stone & Rolls*' wake.[28] Unsurprisingly, the interaction between illegality and attribution soon returned to the Supreme Court in *Bilta*. Bilta was used by its directors to perpetuate VAT frauds, which left it obliged to account to the tax authorities for millions.[29] The fraud was discovered and Bilta went into liquidation. The liquidators sued Bilta's directors for breach of fiduciary duty. In response, the directors raised illegality, arguing that their wrongful acts or knowledge of those acts should be attributed to Bilta, so Bilta's claim would fail. All members of the Supreme Court unanimously dismissed the appeal, holding that the illegality defence failed. However, they took different routes in reaching this outcome. The speeches can be divided into two groups.

The first group, comprising Lords Neuberger (with whom Lords Clarke and Carnwath agreed), Mance, and Sumption, based their judgment primarily on attribution, not illegality. All three judges focused on the purpose of the relevant rule. Lord Mance's speech makes this particularly clear:

> As Lord Hoffmann made clear in *Meridian Global*, the key to any question of attribution is ultimately always to be found in considerations of context and purpose. The question is: whose act or knowledge or state of mind is for the purpose of the relevant rule to count as the act, knowledge or state of mind of the company?[30]

He concluded that attribution might thus be available for one purpose though not another. Where the company was enforcing duties owed by its officers to the company, it was 'self-evidently impossible'[31] for the directors' acts and states of

[23] ibid [28] (Lord Neuberger).
[24] ibid [80] (Lord Sumption); approved by [26]–[27] (Lord Neuberger, with whom Lords Clarke and Carnwath agreed); [50] (Lord Mance), *cf* [154] (Lords Hodge and Toulson).
[25] ibid [30].
[26] *Singularis* (n 4) [33].
[27] See n 1.
[28] Eg *Safeway Stores Ltd v Twigger* [2010] EWCA Civ 1472, [2011] 2 All ER 841; *Lexi Holdings plc v DTZ Debenham Tie Leung Ltd* [2010] EWHC 2290 (Ch); *Bilta (UK) Ltd (in liquidation) v Nazir (No 2)* [2013] EWCA Civ 968, [2014] Ch 52.
[29] For details of the type of fraud conducted, see *Bilta (UK) Ltd (in liquidation) v Natwest Markets plc* [2020] EWHC 546 (Ch), [1]–[30].
[30] *Bilta* (n 3) [41].
[31] ibid [42].

mind to be attributed. As Lord Mance explained, 'Any other conclusion would ignore the separate legal identity of the company, empty the concept of duty of content and enable the company's affairs to be conducted in fraud of creditors.'[32]

Lord Neuberger also agreed that attribution was unavailable in this context.[33] He said that:

> It is clear from 'the language of the rule ([as] it is in a statute) and its content and policy' that the 'act (or knowledge or state of mind) was *for this purpose* [not] intended to count as the act etc of the company', to quote and apply the test laid down by Lord Hoffmann in *Meridian Global*.[34]

Lord Sumption similarly concluded that the directors' acts and states of mind could not be attributed in claims by the company against the directors for breach of duty. For him, the breach of duty exception applied, since the duty being enforced existed to protect the company from the directors.[35] But later Lord Sumption also said that '[a]nother way of putting the same point is to treat it as illustrating the broader point made by Lord Hoffmann in *Meridian Global* that the attribution of legal responsibility for the act of an agent depends on the purpose for which attribution is relevant'.[36]

In the second group is the joint speech of Lords Toulson and Hodge, who based their decision primarily on illegality, not attribution. As they said, 'We do not consider the question of attribution to be the real issue in this case.'[37] For Lords Toulson and Hodge, illegality was developed on public policy grounds.[38] Allowing the directors here to rely on it would hamper, rather than promote, public policy. It would undermine the public interest underlying directors' duties that companies should be able to enforce directors' duties to protect the company's interests.[39] Thus, illegality should not apply to defeat the company's claim. But they thought that if illegality were insensitive to context and competing public policies, an attribution analysis would lead to the same result for similar reasons.[40] The reasoning on attribution thus mirrors that of the first group.

Bilta makes clear that where a company is enforcing duties owed by directors to it, those directors' unlawful acts and knowledge cannot be attributed to the company under illegality. But what if the company is enforcing duties owed to it by someone who did not do the unlawful acts, as in *Stone & Rolls*? Can those persons seek to attribute the acts of the wrongdoers? *Bilta* left this open, but *Singularis* soon returned to it.

[32] ibid.
[33] ibid [20].
[34] ibid.
[35] ibid [86]–[89].
[36] ibid [92].
[37] ibid [166].
[38] ibid [129].
[39] ibid.
[40] ibid [206], [209].

C. *Singularis*[41]

Singularis was a company set up to manage the personal assets of a Saudi Arabian businessman, Mr Al Sanea. Al Sanea was Singularis's chairman, director, and sole shareholder. Singularis held an account with Daiwa, a bank and brokerage firm. After stock financing arrangements between the two ended, Singularis's account was in credit of approximately US$204 million. Al Sanea instructed Daiwa to make payments from Singularis's account to members of a group controlled by Al Sanea. Daiwa did so. The money was lost. After Singularis went into liquidation, its liquidators sued Daiwa for dishonest assistance and breach of the *Quincecare* duty.[42] The latter obliges a bank to refrain from executing an order made by its customer where it has reasonable grounds to believe that the order is an attempt to misappropriate the customer's funds. In response, Daiwa argued that Al Sanea's acts and states of mind should be attributed to Singularis, so that Singularis's claims against Daiwa would fail, whether for illegality or other reasons.

At first instance, the dishonest assistance claims failed: Daiwa had not been dishonest.[43] However, Rose J held that Daiwa had breached the *Quincecare* duty.[44] Addressing Daiwa's counter-arguments, both the trial judge, Rose J, and the Court of Appeal held that Al Sanea's conduct and states of mind were not attributable to Singularis for Singularis's claims against Daiwa.[45] Even if they were attributable, Singularis's claim would not be defeated under illegality or any other grounds.[46] The Supreme Court affirmed both conclusions, with Lady Hale delivering the sole judgment.

Lady Hale affirmed the orthodox approach to attribution in *Bilta* that 'the key to any question of attribution was always to be found in considerations of the context and the purpose for which the attribution was relevant'.[47] Thus, 'where the purpose was to attribute responsibility between the company and its agents so as to determine their rights and liabilities to one another, the answer might not be the same as where the purpose was to apportion responsibility between the company and a third party'.[48] Lady Hale held that the trial judge was correct to say that 'there is no principle of law that in any proceedings where the company is suing a third party for breach of a duty owed to it by that third party, the fraudulent conduct of a

[41] This discussion draws on R Leow, 'Attribution and Illegality Again' (2020) 136 *LQR* 181.

[42] Named after *Barclays Bank plc v Quincecare Ltd* [1992] 4 All ER 363 (QB). See also *Lipkin Gorman v Karpnale Ltd* [1989] 1 WLR 1340 (CA). See further P Watts, 'The Quincecare Duty: Misconceived and Misdelivered' [2020] *Journal of Business Law* 403 for criticism of the duty.

[43] *Singularis Holdings Ltd v Daiwa Capital Markets Europe* [2017] EWHC 257 (Ch) [162].

[44] ibid [191]–[205].

[45] ibid [208]–[215]; *Singularis Holdings Ltd v Daiwa Capital Markets Europe* [2018] EWCA Civ 84 [50]–[60].

[46] *Singularis* HC (n 43) [216]–[220] (illegality), [221]–[228] (equal and opposite claim in deceit); *Singularis* CA (n 45) [61]–[67] (illegality), [68]–[72] (lack of causation); [73]–[80] (equal and opposite claim in deceit).

[47] *Singularis* (n 4) [30], [34].

[48] ibid [30].

director is to be attributed to the company if it is a one-man company'.[49] Contrary to what might be suggested by *Stone & Rolls*, there is no general rule that the acts and states of mind of the individual in a 'one-man company' would be attributed to the company for all purposes. It was therefore unnecessary to inquire into the test for a 'one-man company'.[50] However, even if that inquiry had been necessary, Singularis would not have been one, as the company had innocent directors and a substantial business.[51]

Applying the purposive approach, the 'context' of this case was Daiwa's breach of its *Quincecare* duty, whose purpose was to protect the company against the very kind of misappropriation of its funds that happened in this case.[52] Attribution was not possible because '[t]o attribute the fraud of that person to the company would be … to "denude the duty of any value in cases where it is most needed"'.[53] However, Lady Hale also held that 'even if attribution were established, none of [Daiwa's counter-arguments] is a very promising basis for denying liability'.[54] Three such arguments were considered: illegality; lack of causation between Daiwa's breach of duty and Singularis's loss; and Daiwa having an equal and countervailing claim in deceit against Singularis.

In short, *Bilta* and *Singularis* affirm the purposive, context-specific approach to attribution which is traceable to *Meridian*. In *Bilta*, Lords Neuberger, Mance, and Sumption all relied on *Meridian*'s fundamental contribution that 'the key to any question of attribution is ultimately always to be found in considerations of context and purpose'.[55] *Singularis* too accepted that the 'guiding principle' to any question of attribution was the context and purpose for which attribution is relevant.

II. When and Why is Attribution Unavailable?[56]

Bilta and *Singularis* establish that even if acts or knowledge are attributed for one purpose, they may not be attributed for another.[57] But the difficulty then lies in identifying when and why attribution is, exceptionally, *un*available. Three reasons seem to emerge: (i) the person seeking to attribute is involved in some relevant wrongdoing; (ii) whether the company has innocent shareholders or directors; and (iii) whether the duty owed would be 'denuded of value'. Of these, *Singularis* seems to prize the third most highly, but there is reason to doubt this approach.

[49] ibid [34].
[50] ibid [33].
[51] ibid.
[52] ibid [35].
[53] ibid.
[54] ibid [12].
[55] *Bilta* (n 3) [41].
[56] This discussion draws on Leow, 'Attribution and Illegality Again' (n 41).
[57] *Bilta* (n 3) [20] (Lord Neuberger), [41] (Lord Mance), [92] (Lord Sumption), [202] (Lords Toulson and Hodge); *Singularis* (n 4) [34].

A. Three Reasons

Bilta and *Singularis* suggest three reasons for attribution's unavailability when the company is suing to enforce duties owed to it.

First, it has been suggested that attribution will be unavailable where the defendant, who is seeking to attribute the wrongdoer's acts, is himself involved in the wrongdoing. Evidence for this can be found in *Bilta*, where Lords Toulson and Hodge thought that attribution would be unavailable where the defendant was an accessory to the individual's wrongdoing.[58] It too is consistent with *Bilta*'s conclusion that attribution would be unavailable in claims by the company against the wrongdoing individuals.

A second reason suggested is that the company had no innocent shareholders and directors. Support for this reason might be drawn from Lord Neuberger's speech in *Bilta*, where he suggested that attribution might be possible against third parties where the company itself had innocent shareholders and directors.[59] In a separate speech, Lord Mance also agreed with this,[60] and Lords Clarke and Carnwarth concurred with Lord Neuberger. This feature was seen as important at first instance and before the Court of Appeal in *Singularis*.[61] However, no real weight was placed on it by Lady Hale in the Supreme Court, though in any case the company in *Singularis* did have innocent directors.[62]

A third reason for attribution's unavailability is that attribution would 'denude the duty' being enforced of value. This was especially relied upon by Lords Neuberger, Mance, Toulson and Hodge in *Bilta* in explaining why unlawful acts of the company's directors would not be attributed to the company in claims against those very directors for breach of duty. Attribution would denude the directors' duties to the company of practical effect, rendering the protection that those duties gave to the creditors of an insolvent company 'empty'[63] or 'redundant'.[64] As directors' duties are now codified in the Companies Act 2006, allowing attribution would also be contrary to statutory policy.[65]

This reason was also relied on in the first instance and Supreme Court decisions of *Singularis*. At first instance, Rose J considered the effect of attribution on the duty being enforced by the company. In that case, the company's claim was against a third-party bank for breach of duty in following the instructions of an authorised signatory to pay out funds from the company's bank account when it knew or ought to have known that there was fraud.[66] To allow attribution

[58] ibid [207] (Lords Toulson and Hodge).
[59] ibid [26].
[60] ibid [50].
[61] *Singularis* HC (n 43) [212]; *Singularis* CA (n 45) [54].
[62] *Singularis* (n 4) [33].
[63] *Bilta* (n 3) [126] (Lords Toulson and Hodge).
[64] ibid [38] (Lord Mance).
[65] ibid [20] (Lord Neuberger), [126]–[130] and [208] (Lords Toulson and Hodge).
[66] ibid [184].

would 'denude the duty owed by [the bank] of any value in cases where it was most needed'.[67] Lady Hale, delivering the sole reasoned speech in the Supreme Court, affirmed this reasoning. She went on to add that '[i]f the appellant's argument were to be accepted in a case such as this, there would in reality be no *Quincecare* duty of care or its breach would cease to have consequences'.[68]

It must of course be noted that some judges rely on more than one reason. Lords Toulson and Hodge in *Bilta* seemed to rely on both the first and third: reliance on the first in at least some claims against third parties other than the wrongdoing directors or employees,[69] but reliance on the third in claims against the wrongdoing directors.[70] In the Court of Appeal in *Singularis*, Sir Geoffrey Vos's suggested that attribution turns on 'a detailed consideration of the factual context, the nature of the claim being made, and the purpose for which the attribution is sought'. This is wide enough to encompass endorsement of all three reasons.[71] But which reason is adopted matters. They do not always lead to the same answer.

B. 'Denuding the Duty of Value'

The reason which appears to have recently garnered the most support is the third, which appeared prominently in many of the speeches in *Bilta* and most recently in *Singularis*. But reasons for doubt exist. Although powerful at first sight, 'denuding the duty owed to the company of value' leaves open several problems.

First, why would the duty be denuded of value simply because the company's claim fails? Duties play valuable functions other than serving as grounds for their breach. They guide the conduct of the duty-bearer, providing reasons for action. Even if Singularis's claim against Daiwa failed for illegality because Al Sanea's acts and states of mind could be attributed to it, the conduct-guidance function of the *Quincecare* duty owed by Daiwa remains unchanged. Even if the duty itself could not be enforced against the duty-bearer, legal consequences may still follow. For instance, accessories to the breach of duty may be liable;[72] the duty itself may provide justification for benefits received, thus defeating claims to recover those benefits in restitution.[73] With great respect, it surely goes too far to say that if the

[67] ibid.

[68] *Singularis* (n 4) [35].

[69] *Bilta* (n 3) [207], discussing claims by the company for conspiracy, dishonest assistance, or knowing receipt.

[70] ibid [206].

[71] *Singularis* CA (n 45) [59].

[72] Eg dishonest assistance; procurement, authorisation, or combination in a tort; or inducement of breach of contract. See generally PS Davies, *Accessory Liability* (Oxford, Hart Publishing, 2015).

[73] Eg *Kleinwort Benson Ltd v Lincoln City Council* [1999] 2 AC 349 (HL) 408 (Lord Hope); *Fairfield Sentry Ltd v Mignani* [2014] UKPC 9, [2014] 1 CLC 611. See generally C Mitchell et al (eds), *Goff & Jones: The Law of Unjust Enrichment*, 9th edn (London, Sweet & Maxwell, 2016) Chs 2–3.

individual's acts and states of mind could be attributed, there would 'in reality be no *Quincecare* duty' or 'its breach would cease to have consequences'.[74]

Second, the test is not easy to apply across myriad scenarios. How does it work for doctrines other than illegality? Or in suits against persons other than the wrongdoing directors?

On the former, *Bilta* indicates that directors' duties will be 'denuded of value' if their wrongful acts and states of mind could be attributed to the company in the company's suit against them for illegality. But what about, say, contributory negligence? If the wrongdoing director's acts and states of mind could be attributed, it would only reduce the quantum of damages the company was entitled to obtain. Arguably, small reductions in the damages recoverable would not denude the duty of value. The duty is still present and being enforced; breach of the duty would still lead to damages being awarded, albeit with a reduction. But at first instance in *Singularis*, Rose J suggested that acts and states of mind could not be attributed even for contributory negligence.[75] Neither the Court of Appeal nor the Supreme Court returned to the point, so it remains open. But the point is not just limited to contributory negligence. What about consent? Or estoppel? Or clean hands? Questions remain open about how the test is to be applied where attribution is sought for other doctrines.

On the latter, *Bilta* indicates the answer where the company is enforcing directors' duties owed to it and illegality is raised. But what if the company's suit is against a third party other than the wrongdoing directors? This seems to depend on who the third party is and what duty exactly is at issue. *Singularis* indicates that the *Quincecare* duty would be denuded, while *Stone & Rolls*'s result suggests that duties of care owed by auditors of the company would not be. But it is not clear why. In *Singularis*, Lady Hale thought that the auditors' duty in *Stone & Rolls* was to report on the company's accounts to those with a proprietary interest or concerned with its management and control, but if the company already knows the true position, then the auditor's negligence does not cause loss.[76] With respect, this reasoning relies on causation, not attribution. It thus is unclear when and why claims against third parties will fail because the relevant duty is denuded of value.

Third, the 'denuding of value' test accepts that acts and knowledge may not be attributed in one context though attributed in another. This results in inconsistency within the law. The law may even contradict itself, saying that acts or knowledge both are and are not the company's at the same time. One area of inconsistency is with attribution in contributory negligence. As we will see shortly, a different, 'both ways' test applies there: an individual's acts will be attributed to the company to establish its contributory negligence if they would also be attributed to establish

[74] See n 68 above.
[75] *Singularis* HC (n 43) [249].
[76] *Singularis* (n 4) [36].

the company's liability for breach of duty. By contrast, *Singularis* suggests that even if attribution is possible in the latter, it will not be in the former.

In short, it remains difficult to identify precisely when and why attribution will be unavailable when the company is bringing claims to enforce duties owed to it, even if the 'denuding of value' reason is the sole one adopted. This creates obvious difficulties. Recall that in the immediate aftermath of *Bilta*, Jackson LJ accepted that 'The length and multiplicity of the different analyses in those passages [in *Bilta*] do not make life easy for practitioners and judges dealing with attribution issues on a day-to-day basis'.[77] It is doubtful if *Singularis* has resolved these difficulties.

III. The 'Both Ways' Test

The law of contributory negligence suggests that a simpler solution exists: the 'both ways' test. Adopting it more generally would bring welcome advantages.

A. The Test

Where a company brings an action against some third party for their breach of duty to the company, the third party may allege that the company was contributorily negligent, through the acts of its directors or employees.[78] In the leading New South Wales Court of Appeal decision of *Daniels v Anderson*,[79] the company sued its auditors for breaching its duty of care in contract and tort in failing to detect and report substantial deficiencies in the company's records and internal controls. In response, the auditors alleged that the company, through its directors, was contributorily negligent for the losses that resulted. The New South Wales Court of Appeal found that the company was contributorily negligent through the acts of its directors. Consequently, the damages awarded to the company were reduced by 33.33 per cent.[80] Clarke and Sheller JJA approved of and applied the 'both ways' test.[81]

Under the 'both ways' test, an individual's acts will be attributed to the company to establish the company's contributory negligence if and only if the company would be liable for that individual's actions to some other third party.[82] If an act

[77] *Howmet Ltd v Economy Devices Ltd & others* [2016] EWCA Civ 847 [71].

[78] Now under the Law Reform (Contributory Negligence) Act 1945.

[79] *Daniels v Anderson* (1995) 15 ACSR 607, [1995] PNLR 727 (NSWCA). In contrast, in *Duke Group v Pilmer* [1998] SASC 6529, the contributory negligence argument failed because the individuals whose conduct was sought to be attributed to the company were not acting as agents for the company.

[80] *Daniels* (n 79) 868, 878.

[81] ibid 868–69.

[82] ibid 868.

is attributed to establish the company's liability, it will also be to establish the company's contributory negligence.[83] While this is said to include vicarious liability or otherwise,[84] such statements must be understood against the relevant background: the test was formulated at times when 'vicarious liability' involved personal liability, with acts being attributed to the employer. The better view is that it does not include modern-day vicarious liability, which attributes liability and on much wider bases than before.[85]

Although rising to prominence in *Daniels*, the 'both ways' test had been applied long before then.[86] As long ago as in *The Bernina*, it was accepted that 'If the negligence of the driver is to attributed to the passenger for one purpose, it would be impossible to say he is not to be affected by it for others.'[87] This is key. If attribution is available in establishing the company's duties and liability for breach, it is also available when the company is enforcing duties owed to it.

B. Advantages

Perhaps the greatest merit of the 'both ways' test is that no special justification is needed for when and why attribution is unavailable. Attribution is available when the company is enforcing duties owed to it for the very same reasons that it is elsewhere: it has allocated and delegated its own powers to groups or individuals who have exercised it. Done in accordance with the company's internal allocation of powers, an act does not cease to be the company's simply because it is enforcing duties owed to it, rather than being sued. Adopting this approach thus avoids the difficulties with when a duty may be 'denuded of value' or otherwise inconsistent with attribution; it also avoids problems of inconsistency and contradiction.

Had we adopted this simple position in the recent illegality cases, unnecessary problems would have been avoided. It is still not too late. Moving forward, the best approach is to adopt the 'both ways' test in determining when acts can be attributed to the company. On this alternative solution, regardless of whether the company is suing or being sued, attribution turns on the familiar questions of whether the company had the power to act, proper allocation and delegation of those powers, their scope, and proper exercise.

But one major caveat remains. It has often been assumed that just because acts or knowledge can be attributed to the company, the company's claim will

[83] See generally A Bartlett, 'Attribution of Contributory Negligence: Agents, Company Directors and Fraudsters' (1998) 114 *LQR* 460.

[84] *Daniels* (n 79) 869.

[85] See also Bartlett (n 83) 469–70.

[86] The term was coined by Bartlett (n 83) but it was the approach long before then, see G Williams, *Joint Torts and Contributory Negligence* (London, Stevens & Sons Ltd, 1951) 115; PS Atiyah, *Vicarious Liability in the Law of Torts* (London, Butterworths, 1967) 409–14.

[87] (1887) 12 PD 58, 99 (Lopes LJ).

automatically fail. This is incorrect. Even if an act or state of mind can be attributed to the company, attribution alone tells us nothing about what the effect of that attribution will be on the company's claim. As we will see, the effect of attribution on the claim depends on the private law doctrine in question.

IV. The Effect of Attribution

This section and the next show that even if acts or knowledge are attributed to the company when the company is suing to enforce duties owed to it, the effect of attribution depends on the substantive rule of law to which it applies. This section deals with the effects of some less controversial doctrines before the next deals with illegality.

A. Effects of Attributing Acts

If the individual's acts can be attributed to the company when the company is bringing an act against the individual or third party, the effect of attribution depends on the substantive rule of law in question. Here, the most prominent examples are contributory negligence, contribution and indemnities, and clean hands.

i. Contributory Negligence

The first possibility is that the individual's acts are attributed to the company for contributory negligence. Contributory negligence was once a complete defence to a claim. On proof that the claimant was contributorily negligent, his claim would fail entirely, even if his fault was relatively minor compared to the defendant wrongdoer's fault.[88] After statutory reform by the Law Reform (Contributory Negligence) Act 1945, contributory negligence now apportions liability. Section 1(1) of the 1945 Act provides that where a person suffers damage partly as the result of his own fault and partly as the result of the fault of one or more other persons, the damages recoverable in respect thereof shall be reduced to such extent that the court thinks just and equitable having regard to the claimant's share in the responsibility for the damage.[89]

As we have seen, in *Daniels v Anderson*,[90] the acts of the wrongdoing directors were attributed to the company to establish the company's contributory

[88] Eg *Butterfield v Forrester* (1809) 11 East 60, 103 ER 926; *Cayzer, Irvine & Co v Carron Co* (1884) 9 App Cas 881 (HL). This rule was subject to exceptions, see eg *Davies v Mann* (1842) 10 M & W 546, 152 ER 588; *British Columbia Electric Railway Co Ltd v Loach* [1916] 1 AC 719 (PC).

[89] Law Reform (Contributory Negligence) Act 1945, s 1(1).

[90] *Daniels* (n 79).

negligence. However, this does not mean that the company's claim will necessarily fail completely. The extent to which it will do so depends on the ordinary application of principles of contributory negligence. In *Daniels*, the defendant auditors' liability was reduced by 33.33 per cent when the directors' acts were attributed to the claimant company.[91]

A similar English example is *Barings plc v Coopers & Lybrand*,[92] where Barings sued its auditors for failing to detect the fraud of one of Barings's rogue traders, Leeson. During the audit, Leeson made false representations to the auditors about certain transactions and the balances held in an account. Barings was liable for Leeson's fraudulent representations.[93] Later, it was held that Leeson's actions could be attributed to Barings in establishing Barings's contributory negligence.[94] This was consistent with the general rule that when assessing the fault of 'the claimant' under the 1945 Act,[95] the judge 'should look at [the claimant company] itself, and those to whom were delegated the functions which a company's directors and management would usually perform'.[96] As a result, Barings's claim was reduced by amounts varying from 50 to 80 per cent across different time periods, taking into account other management failures by Barings.

ii. Contribution and Indemnity

Second, the company might bring a claim against the wrongdoing individual to obtain either contribution or an indemnity. This typically requires the company to attribute the individual's (wrongful) acts to the company to show that it suffered loss due to the individual's acts, even if the acts were wrongful. But even if the wrongful acts were attributed, what proportion of liability is borne between the company and the individual depends on the rules of contribution or indemnities; it turns on the relative fault between company and the individual.

If, between the individual and the company, the fault lay solely with the individual, then the company can obtain a full indemnity from him, as *Lister v Romford Ice & Cold Storage Co*[97] shows. There, the House of Lords held that where the company was vicariously liable to a victim due entirely to its employee's wrongful acts, the company could obtain a full indemnity from the employee. Since the company was only liable to the victim through the individual, the company was

[91] ibid 868, 878.

[92] *Barings plc v Coopers & Lybrand* [2003] EWHC 1319 (Ch), [2003] PNLR 34.

[93] ibid [693]–[720].

[94] ibid [961]–[964].

[95] In *Barings*, contributory negligence was considered under provisions of the Singaporean Contributory Negligence and Personal Injuries Act (Cap 54, 2002 Rev Ed), which were identical to the equivalent provisions in the 1945 Act. No evidence was led to suggest that Singapore law differed from English law on this point and the parties agreed that it should be treated the same as English law: ibid [895].

[96] ibid [910].

[97] *Lister v Romford Ice & Cold Storage Co* [1957] AC 555 (HL).

able to recover from the individual a full indemnity for the damages it had to pay the victim.

However, if between the individual and the company, the fault did not lie solely with the individual, then liability might be apportioned differently.[98] A good example is provided by *Jones v Manchester Corpn*,[99] where a hospital doctor who had been qualified for five months accidentally administered an overdose of anaesthetic to a patient, causing the patient's death. As between the doctor and hospital, the doctor was not solely at fault for the resulting death,[100] because the hospital was also independently at fault for failing to provide a reasonably competent person to work with or supervise the junior doctor.[101] As between the junior doctor and the hospital, the hospital's contribution was assessed at 80 per cent while the doctor's was assessed at only 20 per cent.[102] Again this was assessed on the basis of the respective blameworthiness of the company and the individual.

In each case, though acts and knowledge were attributed, the company's claim did not automatically fail. The outcome instead turned on the effect of the doctrines in question.

iii. Clean Hands

Third, it might be argued that the wrongdoing individual's acts are to be attributed to the company so that the company's claim fails because it lacks 'clean hands'.[103] In *Marshall Futures Ltd v Marshall*,[104] the company was a futures broker which held client monies on trust. The company's liquidator sued the company's former directors and officers for breaching their fiduciary duties and duties of care to the company, dishonestly assisting the company in its breach of trust, and failing to keep proper accounts. The defendants argued that the company's claims should be struck out because it came with unclean hands, since it was relying on its own breaches of trust. Tipping J rejected this argument on the basis that the company was now in the liquidators' hands, and the liquidators had clean hands. In any event, it was accepted that dirty hands are not an absolute bar.[105] On the facts, the circumstances were such that the company's claim would not be defeated.[106]

[98] R Stevens, *Torts and Rights* (Oxford, Oxford University Press, 2007) 127–28.
[99] *Jones v Manchester Corpn* [1952] 2 QB 852 (CA).
[100] ibid 868.
[101] ibid 863.
[102] ibid 866 (Singleton LJ), 872 (Denning LJ), assessed under the contribution regime then: Law Reform (Married Women and Tortfeasors) Act 1935, s 6. See now Civil Liability (Contribution) Act 1978, s 2(1).
[103] See generally J McGhee and S Elliott (eds), *Snell's Equity*, 34th edn (London, Sweet & Maxwell, 2019) para 5-010.
[104] *Marshall Futures Ltd v Marshall* [1992] 1 NZLR 316 (NZHC).
[105] ibid 330–31.
[106] ibid.

This is in line with more recent elucidation of the 'clean hands' doctrine. In *UBS AG (London Branch) v Kommunale Wasserwerke Leipzig GmbH*, Lord Briggs and Hamblen LJJ accepted that clean hands applies only to conduct which has 'an immediate and necessary relation to the equity sued for', such that the wrongdoer is 'seeking to derive advantage from his dishonest conduct in so direct a manner that it is considered unjust to grant him relief'.[107] Furthermore, clean hands requires 'a multi-factorial [assessment] to be conducted by the trial judge, with which an appellate court will be slow to intervene'.[108] Even if the directors' acts were attributed to the company, the company, in suing the directors for their breach of duty, would not fall within this test. Its claim will not automatically fail for lack of 'clean hands' where acts are attributed to it.

B. Effects of Attributing Knowledge

Alternatively, it might also be argued that an individual's knowledge can be attributed to the company so that the company's claim fails. Three different doctrines are discussed below: conspiracy, consent, and estoppel by acquiescence. Again, they show that even if knowledge were attributed, the company's claim may not fail; this turns on other features specific to individual private law doctrines.

i. Conspiracy

The first example is conspiracy. This argument was raised in *Belmont Finance Corporation Ltd v Williams Furniture Ltd*.[109] Belmont's directors entered an elaborate transaction on behalf of Belmont so that its shares could be bought by other companies. This was a breach of section 54 of the Companies Act 1948, which carried criminal consequences. When Belmont's liquidator brought actions for breach of trust against the directors, the directors sought to attribute their knowledge to Belmont. Their aim: to show that Belmont was a party to a criminal conspiracy and thus could not recover against the directors. This argument was rejected by Buckley LJ, who held that the directors' knowledge could not be attributed to Belmont because the directors were acting in fraud of Belmont and that Belmont was a victim of the conspiracy.[110]

However, the much shorter and simpler answer to *Belmont* and other cases of conspiracy is that even if the individual's knowledge was attributed to the company, mere knowledge does not in itself establish a conspiracy. If two people

[107] *UBS AG (London Branch) v Kommunale Wasserwerke Leipzig GmbH* [2017] EWCA Civ 1567, [2017] 2 Lloyd's Rep 621 [171].

[108] ibid.

[109] *Belmont Finance Corpn Ltd v Williams Furniture Ltd* [1979] Ch 250. For further discussion, see C Witting, 'Intra-Corporate Conspiracy: An Intriguing Prospect' (2013) 72 *CLJ* 178, especially 195–99.

[110] *Belmont* (n 109) 261–62.

know a particular fact, does that mean that they have conspired with each other? The answer must be no. Something more than mere knowledge is required to establish a conspiracy. What this is depends on whether criminal conspiracy is in question or the civil doctrine of conspiracy to injure by unlawful means. At least some intention to conspire seems necessary. But merely attributing the individual's knowledge of entering into the unlawful agreement to the company itself is insufficient.

ii. Consent

Second, it might be argued that the company's claim against the individual or some third party fails because the individual's knowledge can be attributed to the company, so that the company has implicitly consented to it. In *Multinational Gas and Petrochemical Co v Multinational Gas and Petrochemical Services*,[111] the claimant company sued its directors and agent for negligently providing financial information and making decisions. One argument was that those responsible for the management and direction of the claimant's affairs knew or ought to have known that the agent acted negligently and had implicitly consented to it. The Court of Appeal firmly rejected this argument. Lawton LJ emphatically said that 'knowledge of negligence does not necessarily amount to consent to negligence'.[112] Similarly, May LJ held that '[t]he fact that all the members of the company knew of the acts constituting such breaches and knew that those acts were in breach of that duty does not prevent them from constituting the tort of negligence against the company nor by itself release the directors from liability for it'.[113] Knowledge alone is not enough.[114] Even if the individual's knowledge was attributed to the company, this alone is insufficient to constitute consent. As with conspiracy, something more is needed. Therefore, the company's claim will not automatically fail.

iii. Estoppel by Acquiescence

The third doctrine to consider is that of estoppel by acquiescence. The classic case involving this doctrine is *Houghton v Nothard, Lowe & Wills Ltd*.[115] The claimant Nothard was formed as a joint venture by two companies which were fruit importers, the Preserving Company and the George Wills Company. The founding companies each appointed two directors to the claimant Nothard; the Lowes were those appointed from the Preserving Company. Acting for the Preserving

[111] *Multinational Gas and Petrochemical Co v Multinational Gas and Petrochemical Services* [1983] Ch 258 (CA).
[112] ibid 269.
[113] ibid 280.
[114] ibid 282.
[115] *Houghton v Nothard, Lowe & Wills Ltd* [1928] AC 1 (HL).

Company, the Lowes agreed with Houghton that Houghton would advance the Preserving Company funds in exchange for retaining 70 per cent of the proceeds of the fruit it sold for Nothard. Nothard's other directors were unaware of the agreement. Later, a dispute between Houghton and Nothard arose, and Nothard brought a counterclaim for the proceeds of sale of fruit, which had been retained by Houghton. In response, Houghton argued that Nothard was estopped by acquiescence from asserting that the agreement was unauthorised because of its directors' knowledge of the transaction.

Nothard's counterclaim succeeded. Nothard was not party to the agreement, nor was it estopped from denying the existence of the arrangement because of the Lowes' knowledge. The main reason given was that the directors' knowledge could not be attributed to the company because they were acting in breach of duty to the company.[116] However, the 'fraud exception' or 'breach of duty' exception has been heavily criticised by academic commentators,[117] and in *Bilta*, a majority of the Supreme Court downplayed reliance on a breach of duty exception, viewing it merely as part of the general question of whether attribution is appropriate.[118]

A better analysis is that even if their knowledge could be attributed, the estoppel argument would have failed. For there to be estoppel by acquiescence, the acquiescing party must know the relevant facts and then refrain from intervening. Even if knowledge had been attributed, the Lowes' acts in standing by and not informing Houghton about the unauthorised agreement could not be attributed to the company. While the Lowes would have had the powers to keep relevant information from counterparties, their acts were not done in good faith in what they believed to be the company's interests. The proper exercise requirement was not met. In short, the problem here was attribution of the relevant acts, not the attribution of knowledge.

V. Illegality

These earlier examples show that even where the individual's acts and knowledge are attributed to the company, the company's claim will not automatically fail. This turns on the precise doctrine requiring attribution, its requirements, and the effect of attribution. The same is true for illegality. The difficulty was that until *Patel v Mirza*,[119] the latter two were unclear in illegality.

[116] ibid 14–15 (Viscount Dunedin), 19 (Viscount Sumner).

[117] See especially P Watts, 'Imputed Knowledge in Agency Law – Excising the Fraud Exception' (2001) 117 *LQR* 300.

[118] *Bilta* (n 3) [9] (Lord Neuberger), [37] (Lord Mance), [181] (Lords Toulson and Hodge), *cf* [86] but contrast also [92] (Lord Sumption).

[119] *Patel v Mirza* [2016] UKSC 42, [2017] AC 467.

A. *Patel v Mirza*

Prior to *Patel v Mirza*, the law on illegality had been embroiled in controversy. Different House of Lords and Supreme Court decisions in the last decade took different approaches to the purpose of the illegality doctrine, its underlying principles, and when a claim would be barred because of illegality.[120]

There were two main options in relation to how to approach the law of illegality. The first was the 'reliance rule' accepted by the House of Lords in *Tinsley v Milligan*.[121] On this approach, a claim would fail if the claimant had to rely on her own illegality to establish the claim. Critics argued that the reliance rule produced arbitrary results, led to uncertainty about when the rule and its exceptions applied, and that it caused injustice.[122]

The reliance rule's chief rival was the 'structured discretion' or 'range of factors' approach initially recommended by the Law Commission as early as in 1999.[123] This approach would give courts a broad statutory discretion to decide whether the claim should fail for illegality. Relevant factors include the seriousness of the illegality, whether the decision would deter individuals from illegality, and whether allowing the claim would further or hinder the illegal purpose in question. After further consultation,[124] the Law Commission proposed in its 2010 Report to introduce a statutory structured discretion to decide the effect of illegality only for a limited range of trusts, but to leave the development of illegality in other areas to the courts.[125] But these proposals for statutory reform were not adopted.

In *Patel v Mirza*, a majority of the Supreme Court favoured a limited 'range of factors' approach, while the minority, most notably Lord Sumption, preferred a modified reliance rule. On either approach, the claims will likely succeed despite the illegality even if the wrongdoing individual's acts or knowledge can be attributed to the company.

[120] See eg *Gray v Thames Trains Ltd* [2009] UKHL 33, [2009] 1 AC 1339; *Hounga v Allen* [2014] UKSC 47, [2014] 1 WLR 2889; *Les Laboratoires Servier v Apotex Inc* [2014] UKSC 55, [2015] AC 430.

[121] *Tinsley v Milligan* [1994] 1 AC 340 (HL).

[122] Law Commission, *The Illegality Defence* (Law Com No 320, 2010) paras 2.13–2.15. See also A Burrows, 'Illegality after Patel v Mirza' (2017) 70 *Current Legal Problems* 55.

[123] Law Commission, *Illegal Transactions: The Effect of Illegality on Contract and Trusts Law* (Law Com CP No 154, 1999); Law Commission, *The Illegality Defence in Tort* (Law Com CP No 160, 2001).

[124] Law Commission, *The Illegality Defence: A Consultative Report* (Law Com CP No 189, 2009).

[125] In the Law Commission's 2010 Report, the proposal was only to give courts a statutory discretion in relation to a limited range of trusts where the purpose of the creation of the trust is to conceal the beneficiary's interest in the trust property in connection with a criminal purpose: (n 122) paras 1.17, 1.29. In claims for breach of contract, unjust enrichment, tort, or legal property rights, the Law Commission thought that a statutory discretion was unnecessary as it was open to the courts to develop the law in ways which would render it clearer, more certain, and less arbitrary, and that this was in fact what the courts appeared to be doing: (n 122) para 1.11.

B. The Range of Factors Approach

In *Patel*, the majority was led by Lord Toulson, with whom Lady Hale, Lord Kerr, Lord Wilson and Lord Hodge agreed. Lord Toulson held that:

> one cannot judge whether allowing a claim which is in some way tainted by illegality would be contrary to the public interest, because it would be harmful to the integrity of the legal system, without a) considering the underlying purpose of the prohibition which has been transgressed, b) considering conversely any other relevant public policies which may be rendered ineffective or less effective by denial of the claim, and c) keeping in mind the possibility of overkill unless the law is applied with a due sense of proportionality.[126]

Lord Neuberger also appeared to favour this more discretionary approach more generally, although he thought that there should be a general rule allowing recovery for cases of restitution for unjust enrichment.[127]

More recent cases affirm Lord Toulson's approach and confirm its application outside restitution. It was applied in *Singularis* where Singularis brought claims for breach of Daiwa's *Quincecare* duty, which arises either as an implied term in the banker-customer contract or under the tort of negligence.[128] Similarly, in *Stoffel & Co v Grondona*,[129] Grondona was sued for non-repayment of mortgage loans which had been obtained as part of a mortgage fraud. Grondona then sued Stoffel, the solicitors acting for the other party involved in the mortgage fraud, seeking an indemnity, or contribution, or damages for breach of duty or contract. The majority approach in *Patel* was affirmed and applied,[130] as it was also in the tort case of *Henderson v Dorset Healthcare University NHS Foundation Trust*.[131] As a unanimous seven-member panel of the Supreme Court said in *Henderson*, 'Patel concerned a claim in unjust enrichment, but there can be little doubt that it was intended to provide guidance as to the proper approach to the common law illegality defence across civil law more generally'.[132]

For present purposes, the majority view's application in *Singularis* is most relevant. At first instance, Rose J held that even if the acts of the company's director and sole shareholder could be attributed to the company, the company's claim

[126] *Patel* (n 119) [101].

[127] Lord Neuberger concluded that 'When faced with a claim based on a contract which involves illegal activity … the court should, when deciding how to take into account the impact of the illegality on the claim, bear in mind the need for integrity and consistency in the justice system, and in particular (a) the policy behind the illegality, (b) any other public policy issues, and (c) the need for proportionality': ibid [174], see more generally [169]–[175].

[128] As explained in *Federal Republic of Nigeria v JP Morgan Chase Bank NA* [2019] EWHC 347 (Comm) [21] (Professor Andrew Burrows QC sitting as a Deputy Judge of the High Court), appealed on different grounds: [2019] EWCA Civ 1641.

[129] *Stoffel & Co v Grondona* [2020] UKSC 42, [2021] AC 540.

[130] ibid [21]–[47].

[131] *Henderson v Dorset Healthcare University NHS Foundation Trust* [2020] UKSC 43, [2021] AC 563.

[132] ibid [76] (Lord Hamblen JSC, with whom Lord Reed PSC, Lord Hodge DPSC, Lady Black, Lord Lloyd-Jones, Lady Arden, and Lord Kitchen JJSC agreed).

would not be barred because of illegality on the 'range of factors' approach.[133] The purpose of the prohibition on breach of fiduciary duty was to protect the company from becoming a victim of the wrongful exercise of power by the officers of the company,[134] while that against knowingly producing false documents was to protect third parties from being deceived and the company from having its funds misappropriated.[135] Applying Lord Toulson's test, first, neither purpose would be enhanced by preventing the company from recovering against the director. Second, it would not enhance the law's integrity to undermine the balance that had been struck when companies and third parties were both victims of a fraud. Denying the company's claim would also materially impact the role of banks and financial institutions in reducing financial crime and money laundering. Third, denying the claim would be disproportionate to the illegality. This analysis was upheld by the Court of Appeal[136] and the Supreme Court.[137]

This analysis suggests that claims by a company against the wrongdoing individual or third parties for breaches of duty will very rarely, if ever, fail for illegality. It will typically be contrary to the purpose of the duties for the company's claim to fail, and it would usually also be disproportionate to the illegality. One instance where it might not be contrary to the purpose of the duty is where the scope of the duty was such that there was no breach at all,[138] in which case the company's claim fails independently of illegality.

C. The Modified Reliance Test

On the reliance test, the company's claims against the wrongdoing individual or third parties for breaches of duty would likely fail, because the company would have to rely on the individual's wrongful act to establish that it had suffered loss caused by the breach of duty.

The minority in *Patel* accepted the reliance test but emphasised that there are exceptions to the rule. For Lord Sumption, the illegality doctrine's underlying principle was that 'for reasons of consistency the court will not give effect, at the suit of a person who committed an illegal act (or someone claiming through him), to a right derived from that act'.[139] Courts cannot coherently give effect to legal rights founded on acts which are contrary to other rules of law.[140] To do so would be to 'give with one hand what it takes away with another'.[141]

[133] *Singularis* HC (n 43) [220].
[134] ibid [218].
[135] ibid.
[136] *Singularis* CA (n 45) [50]–[60] (attribution), [66] (illegality).
[137] *Singularis* (n 4) [16]–[18].
[138] As was argued in *Stone & Rolls* (n 2) by Lord Phillips at [85]–[86]. See also Ferran (n 1) 251–57.
[139] *Patel* (n 119) [233].
[140] ibid [230]–[232].
[141] ibid [232], citing *Hounga* (n 120) [55] (Lord Hughes).

However, Lord Sumption accepted that there were exceptions to this principle, which are broadly reflected in the proposition that the illegality principle is available only where the parties were *in pari delicto* in relation to the illegal act.[142] Two main categories of cases can be identified from the case law. The first is where the claimant's participation in the illegal act is treated as involuntary, for example, because it has been induced by the defendant's fraud, undue influence or duress, or because the illegal act is one which the claimant is only responsible for under a statute imposing strict liability.[143] The second category comprises cases where the application of the illegality principle is inconsistent with the rule of law which makes the act illegal.[144] Examples include protective statutes which aim to protect persons in the claimant's position from exploitation by persons such as the defendant.[145]

On this modified reliance approach, claims by a company against either the wrongdoing individual himself or against third parties for their breaches of duty owed to the company will also rarely, if ever, fail for illegality. Even if the company needs to rely on its own illegal acts to establish that the company has suffered loss that was caused by the breach, application of the illegality principle will, in virtually all cases, be inconsistent with the rule making the act illegal.

Thus, whether the majority or minority approach to illegality is adopted, the same outcome will be reached: the company's claims against either the wrongdoing individual himself or third parties generally will not be denied on the basis of illegality solely because of the attribution of the wrongful acts of the individual or his knowledge of his own acts.

VI. Applying the Analysis to *Stone & Rolls*, *Bilta*, and *Singularis*

If the same rules of attribution used to establish the company's own duties and liabilities are also applied when the company is enforcing duties owed to it, attribution turns again on familiar questions concerning the company's allocation and delegation of its powers. This avoids difficulties with identifying when and why attribution is unavailable. Perhaps most importantly, it avoids inconsistencies in the law, promoting the rationality of the law. This section shows how the cases of *Stone & Rolls*, *Bilta*, and *Singularis* would be analysed under this approach.

[142] *Patel* (n 119) [241].
[143] ibid [242].
[144] ibid [243]–[244].
[145] ibid [233], eg *Kiriri Cotton Co Ltd v Dewani* [1960] AC 192 (PC).

A. *Stone & Rolls*

Applying this analysis to the facts of *Stone & Rolls*, it is submitted, with respect, that the House of Lords reached the wrong result in that case. Although some of Stojevic's acts could be attributed to Stone & Rolls, even if those acts were attributed, Stone & Rolls's claim against its auditors should not have been struck out for illegality after *Patel*. Furthermore, much of the reasoning on attribution in *Stone & Rolls* considered irrelevant features.

First, which acts or knowledge might be attributed to Stone & Rolls? One act was Stojevic's paying away monies received from the banks to third parties. As Stone & Rolls's controller and manager, Stojevic had substantial allocated or delegated powers to make payments. But these powers were improperly exercised: they were exercised in Stojevic's own interests, rather than the company's. Those acts thus could not be attributed to Stone & Rolls.

Another set of acts which might be attributable were the fraudulent misrepresentations made by Stojevic to banks, which induced them to make loans to the company. The reported facts suggest that Stojevic had ordinary powers to make those representations. However, these acts would likely fail the requirement of proper exercise, and so they should not be attributable to Stone & Rolls. A successful earlier action brought by the banks against Stone & Rolls for deceit is probably best justified either by apparent authority or the attribution of liability.[146]

However, even if those misrepresentations were attributed to Stone & Rolls in its claim against the auditors, the claim would not fail on either approach in *Patel*. Under the majority's approach,[147] it is necessary to consider, (a) the underlying purpose of the prohibition that was transgressed and public policies supporting denial of the claim;[148] (b) public policies against denial of the claim; and (c) whether denial would be proportional to the illegality. Under stage (a), the purpose of the prohibition transgressed (deceit) could be said to be the protection of the third-party banks.[149] This purpose would not be advanced by denying Stone & Rolls's claim against their auditors, a different party altogether. Nor do there seem to be other relevant public policies supporting denial. Instead, under stage (b), allowing the claim could arguably be said to promote the accountability of auditors in detecting financial crime.[150] And were it necessary to consider (c),[151] it

[146] *Komercni Banka AS v Stone & Rolls Ltd* [2002] EWHC 2263 (Comm), appealed on different grounds [2003] EWCA Civ 311, [2003] 1 Lloyds Rep 383.

[147] *Patel* (n 119) [101].

[148] As clarified in *Henderson* (n 131) [116]–[120].

[149] See eg J Neyers, 'Form and Substance in the Tort of Deceit' in A Robertson and J Goudkamp (eds), *Form and Substance in the Law of Obligations* (Oxford, Hart Publishing, 2019) for a more precise argument about the gist of the tort of deceit.

[150] Eg *Singularis* HC (n 43) [218]. See also Ferran, 'Corporate Attribution and the Directing Mind and Will' (n 1) 256–57.

[151] Proportionality may not always need to be considered, eg if the balancing of policy considerations is firmly against denying the claim: *Henderson* (n 131) [123].

would likely be disproportionate to deny Stone & Rolls's claim against its auditors simply because Stojevic's fraudulent misrepresentations could be attributed to Stone & Rolls.

Even if the minority's approach was adopted, it is unlikely that Stone & Rolls's claim would have been struck out for illegality. Although Stone & Rolls would need to rely on its own illegal acts to establish that it had suffered loss,[152] application of the illegality principle would be inconsistent with deceit – the rule of law making the act unlawful. Deceit is intended solely to protect the representee, here the defrauded banks. Applying the illegality principle to a claim by Stone & Rolls against its auditors would be inconsistent with the purpose of deceit.[153]

This analysis helps clarify another aspect of *Stone & Rolls*. The judgments repeatedly focused on the attribution of Stojevic's knowledge to the company and exceptions to attributing that knowledge. Despite this, none of them explained why the attribution of Stojevic's knowledge was relevant to the company's claim. This was probably because it was not. The most plausible reason for discussing knowledge is that Stone & Rolls, through Stojevic, might have consented to the auditor's breach. But as we have already seen, mere knowledge of a breach does not constitute consent to it.[154]

B. *Bilta*

Bilta can be dealt with even more quickly. Here, it is submitted that the Supreme Court's conclusions were correct in principle and ought to be affirmed.

First, the acts of Bilta's directors should not have been attributed to Bilta. Even though Bilta's directors would likely have the company's powers to enter transactions of the kind they did, these powers were not properly exercised; they were not exercised for Bilta's benefit. Thus their acts could not be attributed to the company.[155]

However, even if those acts could have been attributed, *Patel* indicates that Bilta's claims against its directors would not have failed. On *Patel*'s majority approach, under stage (a), the relevant prohibition was against directors acting in breach of their duties to the company. The purpose of this prohibition was to protect the company from its directors' unlawful acts. This purpose certainly would

[152] As recognised by *Bilta* (n 3) [43] (Lord Mance).

[153] Similarly see *Standard Chartered Bank v Pakistan National Shipping Corpn (Nos 2 and 4)* [2002] UKHL 43, [2003] 1 AC 959, [14]–[15] (Lord Hoffmann) (contributory negligence).

[154] See Section IV.B.ii above.

[155] Because of the directors' apparent authority, HMRC would possess rights against the company under the transactions, but the company would have obtained no rights against HMRC. This is often described as a rule that apparent authority creates 'liability only', following from the nature of apparent authority as based on estoppel by representation. See further Ch 3 above; P Watts and F Reynolds (eds), *Bowstead & Reynolds on Agency*, 22nd edn (London, Sweet & Maxwell, 2020) para 8-012.

not be advanced by denying the company's claims for the directors' breach of duty. Under stage (b), there are unlikely to be significant countervailing relevant public policies. If it were necessary to consider proportionality at all,[156] under stage (c), denying the company's claim would also be disproportionate.

The same result is reached on the minority view. Even though the company would need to rely on the directors' acts to show that those acts had caused it to suffer loss, the aim of the prohibition against the directors' breach of duty is to protect the company from its directors' unlawful acts. It thus falls into the exception for protective rules of law.[157]

C. *Singularis*

Finally, the discussion above also suggests that the Supreme Court's conclusions in *Singularis* were correct in principle. The acts potentially attributable to Singularis were the instructions given by Al Sanea to Daiwa to make payments out of the company's bank accounts. These instructions constituted a breach of Al Sanea's fiduciary duties to Singularis. Like *Stone & Rolls*, those acts were not attributable to Singularis since they were done for the benefit of Al Sanea's other companies, not for Singularis. They failed the requirement of proper exercise.

However, even if those acts were attributed, Singularis's claim would not have failed for illegality under the majority approach in *Patel*, for the reasons given by Rose J and accepted by Lady Hale, which were discussed earlier. The minority approach would yield the same answer. Even if Singularis needed to rely on those instructions, for example, to show that Al Sanea's acts had caused it to suffer loss, the aim of the prohibition against breaches of fiduciary duty is to protect the company, so it too falls within the exception for protective rules of law, and Singularis's claim would not be defeated by illegality.

VII. Conclusion

Despite the amount of academic and judicial ink spilt on the topic of attribution and illegality, a simpler route through the maze can be mapped. The same rules and outcome to attribution used to determine the company's duties, breach of those duties, and liabilities, should also apply where the company is enforcing duties owed to it. If acts and knowledge are attributed for the former, they should also be attributed for the latter. This is the 'both ways' test already used in contributory negligence.

[156] *Henderson* (n 131) [123].
[157] *Patel* (n 119) [244].

The error was in assuming that attributing that act or knowledge to the company means that its claim necessarily fails. Even if the act or knowledge can be attributed, its effect on the claim depends on the private law doctrine in question. Well-known rules of law such as contributory negligence, contribution, consent, and estoppel by acquiescence show this. Importantly, this is so even for illegality. Under either approach in *Patel*, the company's claim would rarely – if ever – fail. This analysis removes the difficulty in identifying when attribution ought not be available when the company is enforcing duties owed to it. It also promotes consistency, avoiding the law being required to say that the act or state of mind is both the company's and not the company's at the same time.

8

Aggregation

Aggregation problems operate at a level one step removed from basic problems of attribution. In the attribution of acts and knowledge, the key concern is what connects the act or knowledge, individual doing the act or possessing that knowledge, and the company. This analysis is likely to suffice for small organisations, where the company's activity is coordinated only through a few individuals. The same individuals will likely possess both the knowledge and do the acts relevant to a single claim.

But these days, companies are often large, complex organisations, with many different individuals simultaneously acting for them in different but overlapping capacities. They will be doing different acts, possessing different knowledge, each of which might be individually attributable to the company. This then raises a question: When, if ever, is it possible to add together the acts and knowledge of two or more individuals acting for the company, so that the company is liable for their combined effect? This problem is one of aggregation.[1] It is the central problem addressed by this chapter.

On one extreme view, the law might adopt a position that it is never possible to aggregate together the acts and knowledge of two individuals, A1 and A2. On another extreme, it might accept that it is always possible to so aggregate, even if A1 and A2 are wholly unaware of each other's act or knowledge and have no grounds for suspecting such act or knowledge. Or a middle ground could be adopted, allowing aggregation in some limited circumstances.

This chapter argues that English law adopts the middle ground, permitting aggregation of individually attributable acts and knowledge where there is a certain connection between them. Its core argument is that A1's knowledge and A2's act can be aggregated if A1, knowing the truth, (i) knows or suspects that A2 will perform the act, and (ii) intends that A2 does so.

Section I first introduces some classic fraudulent misrepresentation cases where aggregation issues have been raised. They show that for act and knowledge

[1] The term 'aggregation' is sometimes used indiscriminately to refer to several different problems. For example, it has been used to refer to adding together knowledge possessed by different agents of the company so that the company can be liable for the composite knowledge of those agents, eg *Commonwealth Bank of Austalia v Kojic* [2016] FCAFC 186. 'Aggregation' is sometimes also used to refer to adding together different negligent acts to make out a more serious fault element of gross negligence, see eg *R v HM Coroner for East Kent, ex p Spooner* (1989) 88 Cr App R 10 (QB). These other problems found under the label of aggregation are not considered by this chapter.

to be aggregated, there must be some connection between them. It is not enough that A1's knowledge and A2's act are each individually attributable to the company. Section II argues that the connection between A1's knowledge and A2's act is satisfied by the 'knowing and intending' test. The test is then applied to fraudulent misrepresentation cases and mistaken payments.

I. Connecting Act and Knowledge

A. *Cornfoot v Fowke*

A classic starting point is the decision of the Exchequer Chamber in *Cornfoot v Fowke*.[2] This involved a human, not corporate, principal but is typically regarded as the leading authority even for aggregation in companies.

The facts are simple. Sir FG Fowke was interested in renting a house to educate his children. He approached an agent, Clarke, who recommended one owned by Cornfoot. When Fowke went to view the house, he was met by Clarke's father. Fowke then asked if there was anything objectionable about the house. Clarke's father said, 'Nothing whatsoever', and Fowke agreed to rent the property. The day after signing the agreement, he learnt that the house was next to a 'brothel of the worst description', 'a house of ill fame'.[3] Fowke refused to take possession of the house. Cornfoot sued for breach of contract, and Fowke pleaded that he had been induced to enter the contract by Cornfoot's fraudulent misrepresentation. But there was a difficulty. Although the agent, Clarke's father, had made the misrepresentation to Fowke, he did not know that the house was next to a brothel. The principal, Cornfoot, knew the true facts but made no representation himself. Had Cornfoot made a fraudulent misrepresentation?

The majority held that Cornfoot had not. Barons Rolfe, Alderson, and Parke all decided that there was no fraud by Cornfoot or Clarke's father. Cornfoot made no representation though he knew the truth, and Clarke's father made the representation but did so innocently. Thus neither had committed fraud. As Rolfe B said, it was necessary 'to bring home fraud to the principal' but:

> that was certainly not done in this case, where all the facts are consistent with the hypothesis, that the plaintiff innocently gave no directions whatever on the subject, supposing that the intended tenant would make the necessary inquiries for himself, or even with the stronger supposition that he expressly desired Clarke not to make any representation at all on the subject.[4]

However, all three judges emphasised that it would not always be the case that the principal had not committed fraud simply because he personally made no

[2] *Cornfoot v Fowke* (1840) 6 M&W 358, 151 ER 450.
[3] ibid 360.
[4] ibid 370.

representation. As Rolfe B explained, two such situations where Cornfoot would have committed deceit were:

> if the plaintiff, knowing of the nuisance, expressly authorised Clarke to state that it did not exist, or to make any statement of similar import; or if he purposely employed an agent, ignorant of the truth, in order that such agent might innocently make a false statement believing it to be true, and might so deceive the party with whom he was dealing, in either of these cases he would be guilty of a fraud.[5]

Similarly, Parke B stressed that:

> if the [principal] not merely knew of the nuisance, but purposely employed an ignorant agent, suspecting that a question would be asked from him, and at the same time believing or suspecting that it would, by reason of such ignorance, be answered in the negative, the plaintiff would unquestionably be guilty of a fraud … for then the representation of the agent, which [the principal] intended to be made, would be the same as [the principal's] own; and his own representation, coupled with his knowledge of its falsehood, would doubtless be a fraud.[6]

Alderson B too expressed similar caveats.[7] Under *Cornfoot v Fowke*, it was not possible to aggregate the act of an innocent agent with the knowledge of his principal without more. Some connection between the two was necessary for aggregation.

B. Suggestions of a Wider Approach

But there soon came cases suggesting a wider approach. In the next important case, *S Pearson & Son v Lord Mayor of Dublin*,[8] members of the House of Lords made some comments that could be read as allowing aggregation in wider circumstances.

In that case, the Dublin Corporation sought contractors to construct certain sewage works. Its engineers drew up plans and drawings, which were sent by different agents to the potential contractors, Pearson & Son. The plans and drawings represented that a wall existed at a certain location and had certain dimensions. Pearson & Son then contracted to do the work. When they started work, they discovered that the wall was not as described in the plans. They performed the contract and then sued the Dublin Corporation for deceit, claiming damages for their losses in executing more costly works than would otherwise have been required. The contract contained provisions which stipulated that the contractor should satisfy himself as to the dimensions and other things connected to

[5] ibid.
[6] ibid 374 (Parke B).
[7] ibid 371–72 (Alderson B).
[8] *S Pearson & Son v Lord Mayor of Dublin* [1907] AC 351 (HL).

the contract works and that the corporation did not hold itself responsible for incorrect information or inaccuracies in the drawings or specifications.[9] The House of Lords concluded that the Dublin Corporation could not rely on this clause where there had been fraud; a new trial was thus ordered, leaving the question of deceit to the jury.[10]

But statements by some members of the House of Lords appeared to suggest that the act and knowledge of two individuals could be aggregated even if each were unaware of the other's act or knowledge. For example, Lord Loreburn LC said that 'The principal and the agent are one, and it does not signify which of them made the incriminated statement or which of them possessed the guilty knowledge'.[11] Similarly, the Earl of Halsbury said that:

> If it was supposed to decide that principals and agent could be so divided in responsibility that – like the schoolboy's game of 'I did not take it, I have not got it' – the united principal and agent might commit fraud with impunity, it would be quite new to our jurisprudence … I cannot conclude without saying that I desire to associate myself entirely with the observations which have been made by the Lord Chancellor, that it matters not in respect of principal and agent (who represent but one person) which of them possesses the guilty knowledge or which of them makes the incriminating statement. If between them the misrepresentation is made so as to induce the wrong, and thereby damages are caused, it matters not which is the person who makes the representation or which is the person who has the guilty knowledge.[12]

These statements seemed to point in a different direction from *Cornfoot*. They were then relied on by *London County Freehold and Leasehold Properties v Berkeley Property and Investment Co Ltd*,[13] which likewise suggested a wider approach to aggregation than *Cornfoot*.

There, the claimants were interested in purchasing blocks of flats from the defendant and wished to know about the state of rental revenues by tenants of the flats. Schedules containing those details were sent to the claimants. But the schedules did not state whether rents were paid punctually and without dispute. The claimant thus raised inquiries about those points, and answers were given which said that there were no disputes and rents were paid promptly with a few immaterial exceptions.[14] Those representations were untrue.[15]

Could the claimants obtain damages for fraudulent misrepresentations made by the defendant? Dixey was the solicitor and managing director of the defendant company.[16] Although the answers had been signed off in his name, they had been

[9] ibid 351.
[10] ibid 354–55 (Lord Loreburn LC), 356 (Earl of Halsbury).
[11] ibid 354.
[12] ibid 358–59.
[13] *London County Freehold and Leasehold Properties v Berkeley Property and Investment Co Ltd* [1936] 2 All ER 1030 (CA).
[14] ibid 1042 (Slesser LJ).
[15] ibid.
[16] ibid 1045 (Slesser LJ).

made by a subordinate solicitor who was Dixey's conveyancing clerk, De Rees.[17] De Rees himself had made the representations without knowledge that they were false; he had consulted the defendant's property manager, Addis.[18] There was some evidence which suggested that Addis knew that the representations were false and that they were being made.[19]

The Court of Appeal unanimously held that the claimant's deceit claim succeeded. Taking the widest approach was Romer LJ, who said that:

> It is quite plain that Mr De Rees made the representation in all innocence, but he made it as agent for and on behalf of his principals, the defendant company, and they knew that the representation was false … Captain Dixey and Mr Addis, for instance, must have known between them that the statement was untrue, and the fact, if fact it be, that they did not know that the representation as being made is, in my judgment, immaterial …
>
> There was at one time a difference of judicial opinion upon the question whether a representation made by an agent innocently on behalf of a principal can be treated as a fraudulent representation for which the principal is liable, when the principal, though having no knowledge that the representation is made, knows that it is untrue. But it has now been laid down by the House of Lords that in such a case the principal is as much liable as though he had himself made the representation knowing it to be untrue: *S Pearson & Son, Ltd. v. Dublin Corpn.*[20]

Applying Lord Loreburn's reasoning in *S Pearson*, Romer LJ thus concluded that 'the defendant company and Mr De Rees are one'. The conclusion: it was possible to aggregate Dixey and Addis's knowledge and De Rees's representation so that the defendant company had committed deceit.[21] Eve LJ's reasoning was similar. He held that: 'The company and its agents must be regarded as one, and the former deemed to have the knowledge of its agents in relation to the business'.[22]

At some points, the third member of the court, Slesser LJ, did appear to take a similar line. For instance, he said that:

> The agent and principal are in law one for the purpose of the acts which make up the fraudulent misrepresentation; and equally the same considerations apply if, as here, both De Rees and Addis were servants of the same corporation and the ingredients of the fraud are all to be found in the acts of one principal … it matters not that one element in that wrong is to be traced to Mr. Addis and another element to Mr De Rees.[23]

But it was also relatively clear that on the facts, Slesser LJ found that Addis had approved the statement that was being made and 'knew all about them'.[24] If this

[17] ibid.
[18] ibid 1046 (Slesser LJ).
[19] ibid 1046 (Slesser LJ), and contrast 1050 (Romer LJ). See also 1051 (Eve LJ).
[20] ibid 1050.
[21] ibid.
[22] ibid 1051.
[23] ibid 1047.
[24] ibid 1046.

finding was correct, *London County* was not a case where it was necessary to aggregate an innocent act and innocent knowledge. Any wider comments were thus only *dicta*.

Nonetheless, the strong statements, particularly by Romer LJ, appeared to allow aggregation of an act and knowledge where the knowledge-holder did not know the act was being done and the act-doer did not know of the other's knowledge.

C. The Return of a Connection between Act and Knowledge

Disquiet with *London County* was quickly felt. Sharp criticism soon followed; amongst others, Patrick Devlin (as he was then) disparaged the decision for allowing the creation of a guilty mind from two innocent minds.[25] *London County* was swiftly re-interpreted the very next year in *Anglo-Scottish Beet Sugar Corpn v Spalding UDC*.[26] There, the question was a different one. The claimant company's employees had made overpayments to the defendant, not knowing that the amounts due were lower. The company's managing director did know that the lower amount was due. Had the company had paid with full knowledge of the relevant facts? If so, it could not recover the payment.[27] The defendant relied on *London County*, arguing that the employees' payments could be combined with the managing director's knowledge so that the company had paid with full knowledge.

Atkinson J firmly rejected this conclusion. Even if these principles applied to mistake, he was 'not satisfied that a company can be saddled with fraud unless some agent has guilty knowledge with reference to the representation complained of'.[28] As Atkinson J explained, *London County* did not support the aggregation of acts and knowledge in different people without more. This was particularly clear from Slesser LJ's speech, which seemed to rely heavily on the evidence that Addis had known about and approved the statement that was made. As Atkinson J said:

> There is nothing whatever in that judgment to suggest the principle now contended for by [the defendant's counsel]. There is nothing there to suggest that Slesser LJ would have held the defendants liable if the fact had been that Mr Addis had not been communicated with in any way at all, and if he had not communicated any untrue information to Mr De Rees. On the contrary, it seems to me to indicate that the fraud of Addis was essential for a judgment against the defendants … he knew that the statement was going to be made; he knew it was untrue and he knew it was untrue because of the wrong information which he had himself supplied.[29]

[25] P Devlin, 'Fraudulent Misrepresentation: Division of Responsibility between Principal and Agent' (1937) 53 *LQR* 344, 363.

[26] *Anglo-Scottish Beet Sugar Corpn v Spalding UDC* [1937] 2 KB 607 (KB).

[27] Following *Kelly v Solari* (1841) 9 M&W 54, 152 ER 24.

[28] *Anglo-Scottish* (n 26) 627.

[29] ibid 623–24.

More difficult was Romer LJ's speech, which seemed to suggest that it did not matter that act and state of mind were done by different persons. Atkinson J examined Romer LJ's speech carefully, concluding that his decision was based on Addis or Dixey knowing that the misrepresentation was made or was being made. In short, 'all that was decided in the case was that a principal is liable for fraud where the fraudulent information supplied by one agent is handed on to a third party by an innocent agent'.[30] *Anglo-Scottish* seemed to favour *Cornfoot*, rejecting the broader approach suggested in *London County*.

The next case which followed, *Hill (Gordon) Trust Ltd v Segall*,[31] similarly followed *Cornfoot*. It reiterated that it was not possible to aggregate together the representations of an innocent agent and his principal's knowledge of the representations' falsity where the principal did not know the statement was being made. The defendant Segall had hired agents to sell a property which was used as a school. The agents had represented that Segall was the property's owner. While Segall had contracted to purchase the property, he had not received vacant possession under the unusual terms of the sale contract, which permitted the earlier seller to delay completion until alternative accommodation for the school's students could be found. The Court of Appeal decided that there had been no misrepresentation: Segall obtained equitable rights to the property under the sale agreement and could be described as the owner. But had the representation been false, it was held that Segall had not committed deceit. The agents made the representations innocently, and while Segall knew the facts, he did not know or authorise the agents to make the representations. Following *Cornfoot*, it was not possible to aggregate act and knowledge.

The leading modern case is *Armstrong v Strain*,[32] which reaffirmed *Cornfoot* and accepted *Anglo-Scottish*'s re-interpretation of *London County*. Like in the other cases, Strain had appointed an agent who innocently made false representations. Strain knew the facts which rendered the representation false, but he had not authorised Skinner to make the representation and did not know that the representation was being made. Had Strain committed deceit? The trial judge, Devlin J, who had previously criticised *London County*,[33] chose not to follow it, instead preferring *Hill (Gordon) Trust*. Strain had not committed deceit; it was not possible to aggregate Strain's knowledge and the agent's act. On appeal, the Court of Appeal agreed.

As Singleton LJ explained, *London County* had been misunderstood.[34] It was a case where Addis knew the purpose for which his answer was to be used, as

[30] ibid 627.
[31] *Hill (Gordon) Trust Ltd v Segall* [1941] 2 All ER 379 (CA).
[32] *Armstrong v Strain* [1952] 1 KB 232 (CA).
[33] See n 25.
[34] *Armstrong* (n 32) 242.

Slesser LJ had accepted.[35] There was sufficient material to find that Addis was fraudulent. *London County* thus stood for no broader proposition than 'that a principal was liable for fraud where the fraudulent information supplied by one agent is handed on to a third party by an innocent agent',[36] as Atkinson J had suggested in *Anglo-Scottish*.[37] Birkett LJ agreed. The third member of the court, Charles Romer LJ, the son of Mark Romer LJ who had decided *London County*, was at pains to stress that Mark Romer LJ had only followed what he had (mistakenly) thought was the principle emerging from *S Pearson* and was not intending to found a new principle.[38] Shorn of authority from *S Pearson*, *London County* had lost much of its force. In short, *Armstrong* thus returned to the original principle in *Cornfoot*: some connection between act and knowledge was necessary for aggregation.

Today *Armstrong* remains good law, with few cases having challenged it. Modern affirmations of *Armstrong* are not difficult to find. One example is found in *Greenridge Luton One Ltd v Kempton Investments Ltd*.[39] In *Stanford International Bank Ltd (in liquidation) v HSBC Bank plc*, it was described as a 'thoroughly well-established principle in English law' that neither principal nor agent had committed fraud where the agent innocently made misrepresentations and the principal knew the true facts but did not know that the statement was being made.[40] Several reasons might be mooted for Armstrong's continud endorsement. First, the decisive rejection of a broader approach may well have led litigants to think (probably rightly) that future challenges were unlikely to succeed. Second, the practical impetus for relying on aggregation in deceit also waned following the development of a tort of negligent misrepresentations;[41] victims no longer needed to bring fraud home to the principal to recover damages.

In other words, some connection is needed between act and knowledge for them to be aggregated. But what connection? This is the subject of the next section.

II. The 'Knowing and Intending' Test

In this section, it is argued that the applicable test appears to be the 'knowing and intending' test: the knowledge and acts of A1 and A2 will only be aggregated where two requirements are met. A1, knowing the truth, must: (i) know or suspect that A2 will perform the act, and (ii) intend that A2 does so.

[35] ibid.
[36] ibid 243.
[37] *Anglo-Scottish* (n 26) 623–24.
[38] *Armstrong* (n 32) 248–49.
[39] *Greenridge Luton One Ltd v Kempton Investments Ltd* [2016] EWHC 91 (Ch) [77]–[79].
[40] *Stanford International Bank Ltd (in liquidation) v HSBC Bank plc* [2020] EWHC 2232 (Ch) [48], affirmed on appeal: [2021] EWCA Civ 535.
[41] Eg *Hedley Byrne & Co Ltd v Heller & Partners Ltd* [1964] AC 465 (HL).

A. Fraudulent Misrepresentations

The clearest evidence of when aggregation will not be available is found in *Cornfoot*. Cornfoot identified three situations where the principal commits deceit even if he personally made no representation. One example is where the principal knows the true facts and expressly authorised the agent to make untrue statements, even if the agent does not know the true facts.[42] Another is where the principal knows the true facts and intentionally employs an agent who does not know the truth, in order that the agent might innocently make a false statement believing it to be true.[43] A third scenario is where the principal knows the true facts and intentionally employs an agent who does not know the truth, suspecting that a question would be asked of him and believing or suspecting that it would be answered falsely.[44]

These situations, though formulated for human principals, apply equally to companies. Reformulated to accommodate corporate principals acting through human individuals, they are as follows:

(i) an individual A1 knows the true facts and expressly authorised another individual A2 to make untrue statements;
(ii) an individual A1 knows the true facts and intentionally employs another individual A2 who does not know the truth, in order that A2 might innocently make a false statement believing it to be true;
(iii) an individual A1 knows the true facts and intentionally employs another individual A2 who does not know the truth, suspecting that a question would be asked of A2 and believing or suspecting that it would be answered falsely.

In these cases, it is assumed that A1's knowledge and A2's act would individually be attributable to the company. A1's acts of authorising or employing A2 must also be attributable to the company.

S Pearson and *London County* suggest another instance where the company would have committed deceit:

(iv) an individual A1 knows the true facts, and prepares written statements containing falsehoods (*S Pearson*) or tells falsehoods (*London County*) which A1 knows will be passed along to the victim by another individual A2, who does not know the truth.

In *S Pearson*, the Dublin Corporation's engineers prepared plans and drawings which contained misrepresentations as to the existence and dimensions of certain walls. The plans and drawings were then transmitted to the contractors by other agents of the Dublin Corporation, who did not know the representations were untrue. Although the key question in that case was whether the Dublin

[42] *Cornfoot* (n 2) 370 (Rolfe B). See also 371 (principal instructed agent to make untrue statements).
[43] ibid 371 (Rolfe B)
[44] ibid 374 (Parke B).

Corporation could rely on an exculpatory clause and whether the jury should decide the question of fraud, there is evidence in Lord Halsbury's speech that the engineers had deliberately made the representations to obtain a 'cheap job', ie induce the contractors to tender a lower price than they otherwise would have.[45] This evidence suggests that the company had committed deceit.[46]

In *London County*, Addis, the defendant company's property manager, knew the true facts but provided false answers to De Rees, the conveyancing clerk and subordinate solicitor of the company's managing director. De Rees did not know that the answers were untrue, but there was evidence from Slesser LJ's speech that Addis both knew that the representations were false and that they were being made.[47]

These scenarios are consistent with the 'knowing and intending' test. In all, A1 either knew or suspected that false statements would be made by an innocent A2. A1 also intended that they be made. Such intention is most often inferred from A1's actions. The test also explains why aggregation was not possible in *Hill (Gordon) Trust* and *Armstrong*. In both, the principal or A1 did not know or suspect that A2 was making the misrepresentation, nor did A1 intend that A2 make the representations.

The analysis in two recent cases provides further support for both requirements of this test. In the first, *UBS AG (London Branch) v Kommunale Wassserwerke Leipzig GmbH*,[48] A1's intention that A2 make the misrepresentation was emphasised. The defendant German municipal water company KWL sold credit protection to banks on complex derivative products. During the 2007–2008 global financial crisis, entities in the portfolio defaulted and KWL became liable to pay the banks very large sums. KWL had entered these transactions to obtain upfront payments, but it received relatively little of the amounts paid out by UBS. Instead, the money had been siphoned off by Value Partners, KWL's financial advisors, who used some of the amounts to pay bribes to one of KWL's managing directors, Heininger, who had clearly been dishonest.

The aggregation issue arose in a dispute concerning one set of transactions between KWL, an intermediary bank Depfa, and UBS. These had been structured as a series of two transactions, one between KWL and Depfa, and another between Depfa and UBS. Depfa claimed to have rescinded its derivatives contracts with UBS for UBS's misrepresentations.

Males J held that representations had been made to Depfa that UBS had no knowledge of Value Partners's or Heininger's dishonesty[49] and that the transaction was not known to be tainted.[50] The falsity of these representations was

[45] *S Pearson* (n 8) 356–57.

[46] See also *Anglo-Scottish* (n 26) 620.

[47] *London County* (n 13) 1046 (Slesser LJ), and contrast 1050 (Romer LJ). See also 1051 (Eve LJ).

[48] *UBS AG (London Branch) v Kommunale Wassserwerke Leipzig GmbH* [2014] EWHC 3615 (Comm), appealed on other grounds: [2017] EWCA Civ 1567.

[49] ibid [740]–[741].

[50] ibid [748].

known to two individuals acting for UBS, Bracy and Sanz-Paris.[51] Could Bracy and Sanz-Paris's knowledge of the true facts be aggregated together with UBS's misrepresentations?

Males J analysed the situation as follows:

> Accordingly there are four matters to be considered. The first is whether Mr Bracy's knowledge of the dishonesty of Value Partners and Mr Heininger is to be regarded as the knowledge of UBS. The second, on the hypothesis that only Mr Bracy had the relevant knowledge, is whether Mr Bracy intended that the representation should be made to Depfa (or a bank in the position of Depfa). The third, on the same hypothesis, is whether his intention is likewise to be regarded as the intention of UBS. The fourth is whether the hypothesis that only Mr Bracy had the relevant knowledge is correct.[52]

Most important for our purposes is the second question, which emphasises that Bracy (A1) must have intended that the misrepresentation be made. This provides support for the intention requirement in the 'knowing and intending' test.

On the facts, Males J concluded that Bracy did know the true facts, his knowledge could be attributed to UBS,[53] and he intended that the representations should be made to Depfa.[54] Had it been necessary, there was also sufficient evidence that Sanz-Paris similarly had the requisite knowledge and intention.[55] Thus either of their knowledge could be aggregated with the representations made by UBS to Depfa, *prima facie* entitling Depfa to rescind the contracts.

Some further support for the 'knowing and intending' test appears in the second case, *Marme Inversiones 2007 SL v NatWest Markets plc*.[56] Marme entered into interest rate swap agreements with the defendant banks, which were set by reference to the Euro Interbank Offered Rate (EURIBOR). Marme sought rescission of the swaps and damages for fraudulent misrepresentation, alleging that RBS had made representations about the integrity of the EURIBOR-setting process. The chief allegations focused on a Mr Moroyoussef, who was RBS's head of European Interest Rate Derivatives. He had previously manipulated EURIBOR in his role at a previous bank and was eventually convicted. Marme alleged that Moroyoussef had continued his fraudulent activities while at RBS.

Marme's claims for misrepresentation failed as Picken J concluded that the alleged representations had not been made. However, if they had been, Picken J considered how the problem would be addressed. He endorsed Males J's reasoning, this time emphasising the other requirement that A1 must know or suspect that the misrepresentation was being made. As Picken J said:

> The real question, in the circumstances, is … as to whether Mr Moryoussef knew that any representations (as it happens, the EURIBOR Representations) were being made

[51] ibid [751]–[753].
[52] ibid [760].
[53] ibid [761]–[766].
[54] ibid [767]–[771].
[55] ibid [771]–[772].
[56] *Marme Inversiones 2007 SL v NatWest Markets plc* [2019] EWHC 366 (Comm).

> by others at RBS or should be treated as knowing that such representations were being made even if he did not actually know this to be the case.[57]

Similarly, he later said that:

> if the EURIBOR Representations were false, then, necessarily, Mr Moryoussef knew the facts which made them false, but Marme must still prove that Mr Moryoussef intended Marme to rely on the representations and it is not enough merely … to infer that this was Mr Moryoussef's intention because 'the natural and probable result of Mr Moryoussef and others failing to share their knowledge with the world – and hence what they are taken to have intended – was that parties, such as Marme, would continue to rely on the EURIBOR Representations'. As Mr Quest QC explained, to make such an inference skips a stage in the reasoning in a case such as the present where the person said to have the requisite intention is not the person who made the representation … *That is whether Mr Moryoussef was aware that RBS had engaged in conduct towards Marme which was capable of giving rise to any implied representations at all.*[58] (emphasis removed and added)

This paragraph likewise stresses the importance of Moryoussef's knowledge or suspicion that representations were made by RBS to Marme. Support for the 'knowing and intending' test can thus be found in two recent, reasoned English decisions on the point.

Apparently pointing in a different direction is the High Court of Australia's decision in *Krakowski v Eurolynx Properties Ltd*,[59] which appears to suggest a broader approach. The Krakowskis wanted to purchase an investment property. Their nephew acted for them in the negotiations. In discussions between the nephew and Eurolynx's selling agent, Cini, the nephew made clear that they wanted a property whose rental income would provide a 10 per cent return per annum. Cini returned and said they had found such a property. The Krakowskis then contracted to purchase the property from Eurolynx, with the contract providing details of the lease agreement with the tenant. But, unknown to the Krakowskis, Eurolynx had also entered into a side-agreement with the tenant, giving the tenant a rent-free period as well as a substantial sum to fit out the premises. Later, the tenant failed to pay rent. The Krakowskis discovered the side-agreement and sought rescission of the contract of sale for Eurolynx's fraudulent misrepresentations, along with damages for deceit and other statutory claims. Victorian law then provided that contracts for the sale of land could only be avoided for fraudulent misrepresentations, not other misrepresentations. By a majority, the High Court of Australia held that Eurolynx had made a fraudulent misrepresentation and remitted the case back to the lower courts to determine whether rescission was available.

All the members of the court agreed that a material misrepresentation had been made by Eurolynx when the side agreement had not been disclosed in the

[57] ibid [263].
[58] ibid [263].
[59] *Krakowski v Eurolynx Properties Ltd* [1995] HCA 68, (1995) 183 CLR 563.

contract for sale. But was it fraudulent? The majority, Brennan, Deane, Gaudron and McHugh JJ, held that it was. Eurolynx's officer, Gilbert, had authorised the solicitors to provide the statements and contract of sale,[60] but there was no evidence that either Gilbert or the solicitor knew that the representation was material to the purchasers. However, the majority explained that Eurolynx's knowledge did not depend solely on Gilbert or the solicitors, but also on the knowledge of Eurolynx's other agents, Cini and Ryan:

> The mind of Eurolynx does not depend upon the acceptance of the evidence of Gilbert alone as to his appreciation of the significance of the separate agreement. Account must be taken of the evidence that Eurolynx' agent (Cini) and Eurolynx' officer (Ryan) who had first procured the agreement of [the nephew] to buy unit 12 knew that the purchasers were willing to buy on the footing that the rent reserved by the lease was what the tenant had been and was willing to pay for a lease of the property offered to them.[61]

The majority then continued to say that:

> A division of function among officers of a corporation responsible for different aspects of the one transaction does not relieve the corporation from responsibility determined by reference to the knowledge possessed by each of them.[62]

In other words, it was not just Gilbert or the solicitor's knowledge which was potentially attributable, but also Cini and Ryan's knowledge. Cini and Ryan had not been called to give evidence.[63] In the absence of their evidence, the majority drew inferences that Eurolynx intended or was willing that the representation be conveyed.[64] The solicitor had similarly not been called; her absence gave the majority greater confidence in drawing inferences against Eurolynx.[65] The majority thus concluded that Eurolynx had acted fraudulently in failing to disclose the side-agreement.

By contrast, Toohey J concluded that the misrepresentation was not fraudulent because Eurolynx and its agents did not think the side-agreement was relevant.[66] In doing so, Toohey J considered only Eurolynx's knowledge through Gilbert and the solicitor, but not the knowledge of other agents.

On its face, the majority's decision in *Krakowski* appears inconsistent with the 'knowing and intending' test. It aggregated the knowledge of Eurolynx's negotiating agents, Cini and Ryan, with the representations made by its solicitor and another employee Gilbert, despite there being no finding that Cini and Ryan knew, suspected, or intended that the representation was made. But *Krakowski* is arguably better rationalised in a different way. The majority's decision turned on

[60] ibid 585.
[61] ibid 582.
[62] ibid 583.
[63] ibid.
[64] ibid.
[65] ibid 584.
[66] ibid 590–92.

Eurolynx's significant omissions to call key witnesses, including Cini and Ryan. Their evidence as to what they knew and why they acted was crucially important to aggregation. Eurolynx's failure to call them caused the majority to draw negative inferences against Eurolynx that it had known, through Cini and Ryan, that the representations were material to the Krakowskis, and that it had known and intended that the false representations were made. *Krakowski* then is best understood as a case turning on the inferences that could be drawn in the absence of key witnesses, rather than adopting a wider approach to aggregation.

B. Dishonest Assistance

Aggregation issues might similarly arise in dishonest assistance. An individual A2 might assist in a breach of trust or fiduciary duty without knowing facts which would make his conduct dishonest by the standards of ordinary honest people. But another individual A1 might know such facts. The same question of aggregation then arises: can A1's knowledge be aggregated together with A2's act, making the company for whom A1 and A2 are acting a dishonest assister?

A recent decision considering this question is *Stanford International Bank Ltd (in liquidation) v HSBC Bank plc*.[67] The claimant SIB was a bank run by its ultimate beneficial owner, Stanford. It had allegedly been run as a Ponzi scheme from start to finish. Heavily indebted, SIB entered liquidation. Its liquidators sued the defendant bank, HSBC, which had acted as a correspondent bank to SIB and operated four accounts for SIB, for dishonest assistance. The issue was whether dishonesty had been sufficiently pleaded. SIB's counsel pleaded dishonesty against HSBC collectively but not against any particular individual. At first instance, Nugee J held that this was insufficient. He applied the general principle in *Armstrong*, explaining:

> I was shown a number of citations which make it entirely clear that current English law is that one cannot aggregate two innocent minds to make a dishonest whole. The classic case is drawn from a case of alleged fraudulent misrepresentation … a case called *Armstrong v Strain*… That, as I say, is a thoroughly well-established principle in English law. It is conveniently summarised by Newey J, as he then was, in a case called *Greenridge Luton One Ltd v Kempton Investments Ltd* [2016] EWHC 91 (Ch) at [77] to [79], which it is not necessary for me to read out, but under the heading, 'Aggregation of knowledge', he sets out the proposition that the law does not recognise any conception of composite fraud, referring to *Armstrong v Strain*, and it is there put forward as an entirely orthodox and uncontroversial statement of the law, as, to my mind, indeed it is.[68]

He concluded that:

> It seems to me, however, that the position on the authorities is very simple and very stark. In a case of dishonesty you cannot say of two people, A and B, or however many

[67] *Stanford International Bank Ltd (in liquidation) v HSBC Bank plc* [2020] EWHC 2232 (Ch), affirmed on appeal: [2021] EWCA Civ 535.

[68] ibid [47]–[48].

people it is, that although no single one of them is dishonest somehow the corporate entity for which they work is dishonest.[69]

The claimant had not alleged knowledge of any individual within HSBC that SIB was a Ponzi scheme,[70] nor had it pleaded that HSBC did not investigate SIB's affairs more carefully because it had a targeted suspicion that its affairs were fraudulent.[71] Thus there was insufficient pleading of dishonesty. Nugee J ordered the allegation of dishonest assistance to be struck out.

On appeal, the Court of Appeal of Sir Geoffrey Vos MR, Moylan LJ, and Arnold LJ fully endorsed Nugee J's reasoning. Sir Geoffrey Vos MR, delivering the sole reasoned judgment, confirmed that 'the judge correctly stated the applicable principles' on aggregation.[72] On the facts, he too agreed that SIB's pleadings of dishonest assistance ought to be struck out.[73]

Vos MR's affirmation of *Armstrong* in this context suggests that the same test for aggregation is used in both fraudulent misrepresentations and dishonest assistance. If the 'knowing and intending' test applies there, it should also apply to dishonest assistance.

C. Mistaken Payments

Aggregation problems may also arise where mistaken payments are made. An individual A2, acting for a company, may mistakenly pay another. But another individual A1 may know the true facts. Can A1's knowledge and A2's act be aggregated? If so, then the company would have paid knowing the true facts; it would not be able to recover the payment.[74]

Two earlier cases suggest that A1 must know that A2 is paying another. This approach would be stricter than the 'knowing and intending' test, which allows aggregation in cases where A1 only suspects that A2 is paying another, even if A1 does not know that A2 is doing so.

The first is the *Anglo-Scottish* case,[75] discussed above. The company's managing director in Glasgow, A1, entered into an agreement with the defendant district council to pay lower sums on water payments. But the company's commercial manager (A2) in Nottingham and factory manager at Spalding (A3) were not notified. The district council continued invoicing the company at the old rate. Invoices at the old rate were passed for payment by A3 to A2, who drew cheques which were signed by A1 without further checks. Payments at the old rate continued for

[69] ibid [51].
[70] ibid [64].
[71] ibid [65].
[72] *Stanford* (CA) (n 67) [42].
[73] ibid [44]–[47].
[74] *Kelly v Solari* (n 27) 58–59 (Lord Abinger CB), 59 (Rolfe B).
[75] *Anglo-Scottish* (n 26).

nearly ten years before the mistake was discovered. The defendant argued that A1's knowledge and A2's payment acts could be aggregated.

Atkinson J rejected this argument, concluding that the company could recover the mistaken payments, subject to limitation.[76] His sole explanation was that: 'In my opinion the mere fact that some agent of the company knew of the second agreement is immaterial so long as he had no idea that it was not being acted upon'.[77] This analysis suggests that it was necessary for aggregation that the managing director knew that payments that were not due were being made.

Similarly, in *Turvey v Dentons (1923) Ltd*,[78] Dentons held a 99-year lease of land which entitled them to deduct income tax from the rental payments. The lease had been obtained by Dentons' secretary, Littmann (A1). Administration of the company's daily business was conducted by Baker, the assistant secretary (A2). A1 told A2 about the lease but did not tell him that it was for 99 years. A2 mistakenly believed that it was for 10 years and told the company's accountant (A3) so. Dentons thus paid the landlord rent without deducting for income tax. It later discovered the error and withheld subsequent rental payments to compensate themselves for the earlier overpaid amount. When the landlord later sued for possession of the property and unpaid rent, Dentons argued that the unpaid rent should be set off against their earlier mistakenly overpaid rent. Pilcher J held that Dentons had mistakenly overpaid the earlier rent and could set it off against the unpaid rent.[79]

Pilcher J accepted that the overpayments were made by A2, Baker, the assistant secretary, and A3, the accountant, who mistakenly believed that the lease was one of 10 years.[80] But for the mistake, they would have deducted income tax from the rental payments.[81] A1 knew that the lease was one for which income tax could be deducted but did not know the basis upon which rent was being paid. Had he known, he would have intervened immediately. Although Pilcher J thought it was 'remarkable' that neither Baker nor the accountant had ever been told of the lease's term and that there was likely some degree of carelessness,[82] he held that:

> It is, however, clear upon authority that where … payments were made under a bona fide mistake of fact by an authorised agent of the company, the fact that some other agent may have had full knowledge of all the facts does not disentitle the company to recover the money so paid, *provided that the agent with the full knowledge does not know that the payments are being made on an erroneous basis*.[83] (emphasis added)

[76] ibid 627.
[77] ibid.
[78] *Turvey v Dentons (1923) Ltd* [1953] 1 QB 218 (QB).
[79] ibid 225, 228.
[80] ibid 223–24.
[81] ibid 224.
[82] ibid.
[83] ibid.

Here Pilcher J seems to have regarded it as necessary that A1 knew that A2 was paying another. This would suggest that aggregation was not available where A1 merely suspected that A2 was paying another.

Considering these cases, the editors of the eighth edition of *Goff & Jones* registered some doubt about this statement in *Turvey*. As they point out,

> The principle which Pilcher J derived from Atkinson J's very tentative statements is not obviously correct. Although it seems easy to accept that a claim based on an activating agent's mistake should not fail merely because another agent knows the true facts, it is less obvious why relief should be *automatically* denied where another agent knows the true facts, and that another agent will or may pay under a mistaken belief, but fails to take steps to ensure that that agent is informed of the truth before he acts. This would in effect penalise the principal for a failure of internal communication within his organisation – an outcome which sits uneasily alongside the long-established principle that a claimant's own negligent failure to discover the truth will not prevent recovery on the ground of mistake.[84]

Instead, they suggested that:

> It might instead be more consistent with the general law governing restitutionary claims for mistake to say that another agent's knowledge is only material if this knowledge, coupled with a failure to intervene to prevent the payment, enables it to be said that it was intended that the payment should be made in all events, regardless of the true facts. If it is not the principal who actually has this knowledge – and thus, an unvitiated intention to benefit the defendant – but another agent acting for the principal, then this finding would seem to depend on it being permissible to attribute that other agent's intention to the principal for this purpose. And that should probably depend on that agent having some superior responsibility for the decision-making process in question.[85]

These observations were considered in the current leading decision of *BP Oil International v Target Shipping*.[86] BP chartered a vessel from the defendant owners to transport cargo. A dispute over the charterparty terms arose and the owners demanded $1 million for overage freight, which BP paid. Later, it argued that the owners were not entitled to this amount and sought to recover the payments for mistake. At first instance, Andrew Smith J held that the defendant owners were only entitled to a reasonable fee for overage freight, not the full sum they had charged, and BP could recover the excess paid. The defendant argued that while two of BP's agents, Rickwood and Myers (collectively, A2), had mistakenly authorised the payments, another, Finlinson (A1), knew the true facts. If A1's knowledge could be aggregated with A2's, then BP's claim for restitution of the overpaid sums would fail.

[84] C Mitchell et al, *Goff & Jones: The Law of Unjust Enrichment*, 8th edn (London, Sweet & Maxwell, 2012) para 9–61.

[85] ibid.

[86] *BP Oil International Ltd v Target Shipping Ltd* [2012] EWHC 1590 (Comm), [2012] 2 CLC 336, overturned on appeal on other grounds: [2013] EWCA Civ 196, [2013] 1 Lloyd's Rep 561.

Andrew Smith J agreed with *Goff & Jones* that restitution should not automatically be denied where A1 knows that A2 is making a payment but disagreed that restitution should only be available if A1 intended to make payment in all events. As he continued:

> I think that *Goff & Jones* restrict rather too far the circumstances in which a principal's claim can be defeated by the state of mind of an employee who is not their paying agent, and *I accept Mr Berry's submission that in some circumstances Mr Finlinson's state of mind would have defeated BP's claim if he, knowing or suspecting that BP would or might pay more to the Owners than they were liable to pay, did not object to it and decided not to prevent it*. Mr Finlinson was, as Mr Berry said, 'responsible for the transaction', and more specifically responsible for deciding how much freight (including transatlantic overage freight) should be paid by BP. If he had accepted that the freight should include full transatlantic overage freight, it could not, to my mind, be said that *BP* made a mistake.[87] (emphasis added)

Applying this, Andrew Smith J concluded that A1's knowledge of the truth could not be aggregated with A2's payments, as A1 did not know or suspect that the excess would be paid.[88] BP could thus recover the overpayments.

The reasoning in *BP Oil* supports the 'knowing and intending' test, as it accepted that aggregation is possible if A1 either knows or suspects that A2 would pay another. Under that test, it would also be necessary to show that A1 intended that A2 paid. In the situation identified by Andrew Smith J, it would be easy to infer that A1 so intended if A1 did not object and decided not to prevent the payment. As the eighth edition of *Goff & Jones* suggested, that inference could be more readily drawn if A1 had superior responsibility for the relevant decision-making process.

These points were largely endorsed by the ninth edition of *Goff & Jones*, which regarded *BP* as a 'nuanced application of the principles suggested in the last edition of this book, rather than a significant extension or qualification of them'.[89] For them:

> The essential premise is that there may be another agent elsewhere in an organisation with material responsibility for the transaction, who had an unvitiated intention that what was done, should occur, and whose intention is properly attributed to his employer or principal, so as to bar the restitutionary claim.[90]

This comes very close to the 'knowing and intending' test.

While the cases have not so far explicitly formulated the 'knowing and intending' test, it is largely immanent in the existing case law and academic commentary. No change in substance is needed; all that is needed is to highlight what the law is already doing.

[87] ibid [239].
[88] ibid [241].
[89] C Mitchell et al, *Goff & Jones: The Law of Unjust Enrichment*, 9th edn (London, Sweet & Maxwell, 2016) para 9–84.
[90] ibid.

III. Aggregation's Importance

No account of corporate attribution would be complete without an account of aggregation. Even if acts and knowledge are individually attributable, the applicable approach to aggregation has a wide impact on when and why companies come under duties, breach them, and incur liability as a result. Without an account of aggregation, the attribution rules set out in the earlier chapters might give only a partial – perhaps even misleading – answer to these questions.

At one extreme, English law could have never allowed acts and knowledge of different individuals to be aggregated. Such an approach would mean that companies would be less likely to come under duties, breach them, or incur liability, than if aggregation were sometimes permitted. This approach seems to go too far. The concern is that complex organisations might be able to escape duties and the consequences of breach by dividing up acts and knowledge between many individuals. The concern, pithily expressed in *S Pearson*, is that 'the united principal and agent might commit fraud with impunity'.[91]

At another extreme, English law could also have adopted an expansive approach where any attributable acts could be aggregated with any attributable knowledge. Act and knowledge, though done by different persons with no connection to each other, could be combined. This approach would prejudice larger organisations. The more individuals acting for the company, the larger the pool of acts done by the company and the larger the pool of its combined knowledge. The likelihood that some act combined with some knowledge in that pool constitutes a breach of duty or triggers a duty increases correspondingly.

Neither of these approaches was adopted by English law. English law instead took a middle ground, requiring a connection between act and knowledge for aggregation. Earlier chapters stressed the importance of connecting act or knowledge, individual, and the company when attributing acts or knowledge to the company. Aggregation identifies a further requirement: act and knowledge must be connected to each other. As discussed in Chapter 6 above, knowledge in private law changes the character of acts from neutral to improper. An actor's knowledge may make otherwise lawful and unobjectionable acts wrongful, put the actor under new duties, or qualify the actor's rights. It is only if A2's act is sufficiently connected to A1's knowledge that the character of A2's acts is changed.

Perhaps the best justification for a wider approach is that act and knowledge can be aggregated even if done by different people because the company has failed to institute and operate effective systems to coordinate acts and communicate knowledge throughout the company. If so, the company's fault then lies in its failure to implement and maintain systems to ensure that material information held by individuals like A1 was communicated to other individuals like A2. But this

[91] *S Pearson* (n 8) 357.

argument indicates the problem. If the company's fault lies in its failure to maintain internal systems, then it can be criticised for this failing. But it should not be held dishonest, not mistaken, unconscionable, or guilty of other mental states. Fair labelling matters. Aggregation should not allow failures to maintain internal systems to be transformed into fraud or other flaws. The appropriate response is instead to institute a specific cause of action targeting that fault. Indeed, this is not without precedent, as 'failure to prevent' offences are increasingly being used in the criminal law to target persistent problems of bribery[92] and tax evasion,[93] amongst others being mooted.[94]

IV. Conclusion

Attributing A1's knowledge and A2's act turns on the allocation and delegation of the company's powers to A1 and A2. But this raises the difficult question tackled in this chapter: if A1's knowledge and A2's act are individually attributable to the company, when is it possible, if ever, to aggregate them together? In English law, the answer is found in the 'knowing and intending' test: Did A1 know or suspect, and intend that A2 do the act innocently? If so, A1's knowledge can be aggregated together with A2's act. Just as attribution requires a connection between act or knowledge, individual, and company, aggregation requires a connection between individually attributable acts and knowledge.

[92] Bribery Act 2010, s 7.
[93] Criminal Finances Act 2017, ss 45–46.
[94] Eg the proposed corporate offence of 'failing to prevent economic crime', see eg Ministry of Justice, *Corporate Liability for Economic Crime: Call for Evidence* (Cm 9370, 2017).

9

Conclusion

I. Central Claims

When and why are acts and knowledge of human individuals attributed to companies in private law? This is the central question addressed in this book. Widely regarded to be difficult, it apparently admits of no simple answer. On the orthodox view, attribution is a highly context-specific process. An act or state of mind attributed for one purpose may not be for another. If so, working out the applicable attribution rules across the vast array of claims spanning contract, tort, and unjust enrichment, across the common law and equity divide, would be a mammoth undertaking of enormous complexity.

This book shows that the answer to this question is not so complex after all. Its central contribution is to show that corporate attribution in private law turns on the allocation and delegation of the company's powers to act.

Key to this argument is its emphasis on attribution's shape and structure. Justifications must match the thing to be justified. The reasons given for attribution must therefore fit attribution's shape. Attribution treats *this* act or state of mind of *this* individual as that of *this* company. It concerns the connection between act or state of mind, individual, and company. This connection links the three in a single sequence. Reasons justifying when and why attribution is available must also fit this shape. Here, existing accounts of attribution run aground. Existing accounts are typically 'right-sided', justifying attribution by the nature and type of the right being enforced, the purpose and policy of the claim enforcing it, or all those factors and more. But these 'right-sided' features are of the wrong form. They do not fit the connection between act or state of mind, individual, and company. Instead, they are external to it.

This connection is found in the allocation and delegation of the company's own powers to act. The company, a legal person, is created with its own powers. These powers may be expressly or impliedly conferred on it. Through its constitution, those powers are allocated to groups such as the board of directors and shareholders in general meeting, and then further delegated. In this way, the company's powers are dispersed throughout the corporate hierarchy. Exactly how they are dispersed will vary from company to company. When those who are allocated or delegated the company's powers exercise the company's powers, they act as the company. No fiction is involved, only the application of ordinary legal concepts.

This account also suggests deeper normative significance for attribution. It suggests that attributed acts are largely intentional acts done by companies as agents, used here in a philosophical sense to refer to beings with capacity for action. This analysis tracks a growing literature on corporate group agency, which stresses that companies may be able to form group-level intentions and goals, and take action motivated by those intentions and goals. Those acts would be intentional acts; they would be acts that truly belong to the company as an actor, rather than events that merely happen to it. This is important: capacity to act as an agent is often regarded as a precondition to holding the actor responsible for the act, whether morally or otherwise. If attributed acts are intentional acts, objections that companies lack this capacity could be diffused. Similarly, some important accounts of private law regard the actor's agency as a precondition for it owing duties and having rights against others. The analysis in this book suggests how companies may be able to satisfy this requirement.

II. The Account, Illustrated

That attribution turns on the allocation and delegation of the company's powers was illustrated both with reference to the attribution of acts and the attribution of knowledge.

In the first part of the book, it was shown that attributing acts turns on four questions: (i) did the company have the power to do the act in question? (ii) was the company's power allocated or delegated to the individual doing the act? (iii) was the company's power exercised within its scope? (iv) was the power exercised properly? As Chapters 3–5 show, this analysis applies equally across contract, tort, and unjust enrichment. But different challenges are faced in each. In Chapters 3 and 4, the key challenge was an overabundance of existing analysis, in the form of agency law and vicarious liability respectively. In Chapter 5 the challenge was precisely the opposite; a dearth of learning on attribution existed.

In Chapter 3, the key contribution was to show that while agency analysis is apt for contracting by subordinate agents, it is less well-suited to analysing contracting by the board of directors or shareholders in general meeting. Potential stumbling blocks exist. Reliance on agency analysis embroils the law in controversy over contested definitions of agency, and risks importing inappropriate consequences. It was shown that the allocation and delegation of the company's powers provides a superior analysis. The analysis's utility is amply illustrated by an extensive range of cases spanning company law, agency law, and flaws in contracting both recognised at common law and equity, including lack of good faith, improper purposes, conflicts of interest, and lack of skill and care.

In Chapter 4, the chief difficulty centred around vicarious liability. The liability of companies for torts is typically dominated by vicarious liability. But that poses a puzzle. On the orthodoxy, vicarious liability attributes only liability, not acts. Does tort law then have no rules attributing acts? This puzzle is resolved when vicarious liability is carefully examined. It was shown that the doctrine underwent a dramatic change after 1956. Prior to 1956, 'vicarious liability' attributed acts. After 1956, it transformed into a doctrine attributing liability. But the attribution of acts did not disappear after 1956. Though no longer collected under the label of 'vicarious liability', acts were still attributed on the same basis as before. The rules attributing liability can thus be found largely in pre-1956 vicarious liability. They conform to the same analytical framework based on the allocation and delegation of the company's powers.

Unjust enrichment faced, and still faces, a different problem. While contract formation was dominated by agency analysis and tort law by vicarious liability, the attribution of acts in unjust enrichment was woefully under-examined until recently. This might fairly be attributed to unjust enrichment's relative youth and persistent controversies over its scope and shape. However, important recent contributions have argued that unjust enrichment's attribution rules are wider than those in contract or tort. Focusing on unjust enrichment's 'core case', the mistaken payment, Chapter 5 showed that this is not so. Attribution rules in unjust enrichment are just the same as in contract or tort, turning on the allocation and delegation of the company's powers. This is a merit, not a demerit. It promotes consistency in attribution both within a single unjust enrichment claim and between unjust enrichment and other branches of private law.

The second part of the book comprised a single chapter, Chapter 6, on the attribution of knowledge. Here scattered support exists for multiple approaches. Why knowledge is attributed is relatively un-explored. It was argued that, as with the attribution of acts, the reasons for attributing knowledge must fit attribution's form. Attributing knowledge thus requires us to connect knowledge, individual, and company. It was argued that this connection exists where the 'materiality test' is met. It comprises two requirements: the knowledge must be held by an individual allocated or delegated the company's powers to act, and the knowledge must be material to the exercise of those powers. Cases on statutory liability, knowing receipt, dishonest assistance, and deceit illustrate.

With the attribution rules for acts and knowledge identified, the third part of the book tackled two more difficult problems. The first has received enormous attention, the latter scarcely any.

The first of the two is generally viewed as the most pressing attribution problem today. Chapter 7 addressed the following question: even if acts or knowledge are attributed to establish a company's duties or liability for breach, will they be attributed when the company is enforcing duties owed to it? Mainstream thinking today indicates that there is no single answer. Sometimes it will, but sometimes not. It depends. This raises difficulties about when and why attribution will be exceptionally unavailable. Chapter 7 argued that a better approach is the 'both-ways' test used in contributory negligence. Under the 'both-ways' test, acts which are attributable to the company in determining its duties and liabilities are also attributable when the company is enforcing duties owed to it. The same is true of knowledge. However, the consequence of attribution is not that the company's claim inevitably fails; this turns on the private law doctrine in question. Illegality's effect, for example, may differ from that of contributory negligence, an indemnity, conspiracy, or consent.

Chapter 8 dealt with the difficult problem of aggregation. If the knowledge of A1 and acts of A2 can be individually attributed to the company, can they be aggregated together to establish the company's duties, breach, or liability? The approach taken here would have an important bearing on when and why companies owed duties, breached them, or incurred liabilities. English law accepts aggregation where a connection between act and knowledge is present. That connection is found where the 'knowing and intending' test is satisfied. The test has two requirements: the knowledge-holder, A1, must know or suspect that A2 was doing or would do the act innocently, and A1 must intend that A2 does the act innocently. Deceit, dishonest assistance, and mistaken payments provide illustrations.

III. Implications

The analysis offered in this book concerned attribution in private law to companies. But it might also suggest some further implications for corporate attribution in other areas of law. It may also have implications for attribution to other artificial legal persons. To illustrate, we focus here on corporate attribution in criminal law, and attribution to the Crown.

A. Corporate Attribution in Criminal Law

Corporate criminal liability has long been fraught with difficulty in England and elsewhere in the Commonwealth. Once described as 'an intractable subject', 'one of the blackest holes in criminal law',[1] its reform has occupied multiple Law Commissions,[2] with a consultation presently underway in England.[3] A recurrent complaint is that attribution in criminal law is overly restrictive, making corporate criminal liability unjustifiably rare.

It is often said that the criminal law adopts the directing mind and will (or 'identification') approach.[4] Although only relatively senior individuals can be the 'directing mind and will' of the company, it is not clear exactly who qualifies.[5]

[1] B Fisse, 'The Attribution of Criminal Liability to Corporations: A Statutory Model' (1991) 13(3) *Sydney Law Review* 277.

[2] Eg Law Commission, *Legislating the Criminal Code: Involuntary Manslaughter* (Law Com No 237, 1996); Law Commission, *Corporate Criminal Liability: A Discussion Paper* (9 June 2021); Australian Law Reform Commission, *Final Report: Corporate Criminal Responsibility* (ALRC Report 136, 2020).

[3] 'Law Commission seek views on corporate criminal liability' (*Law Commission*, 9 June 2021) www.lawcom.gov.uk/law-commission-seek-views-on-corporate-criminal-liability/.

[4] The key case being *Tesco Supermarkets Ltd v Nattrass* [1972] AC 153 (HL).

[5] 2021 Consultation Paper (n 2) paras 2.40–2.41.

This approach has been used to attribute both acts and states of mind to the company. But it has long been castigated.[6] It was thought to make corporate criminal liability for serious offences such as manslaughter too difficult to establish.[7] These failings, well-exhibited in collapses of prosecutions over the Southall train crash,[8] the capsizing of P&O's 'Herald of Free Enterprise',[9] and others,[10] led to the enactment of the Corporate Manslaughter and Corporate Homicide Act 2007.[11] But outside corporate manslaughter, it continues to be used.[12]

It may be that it is overly simplistic to say that the criminal law adopts the directing mind and will approach. A patchwork of other doctrines may also apply, particularly in regulatory offences.[13] First, a so-called doctrine of 'vicarious liability'[14] allows acts to be attributed even where performed by a low-level employee.[15] It has been applied in strict liability offences such as those involving selling[16] or possessing goods[17] or using vehicles,[18] and may also apply to some offences requiring *mens rea*, such as public nuisance.[19] Second, offences which impose a duty on a person, breach of which is a criminal offence,[20] may also attract the 'delegation' principle.[21] Under this principle, if the duty-bearer delegates performance of the duty to another, the *mens rea* of the delegate is attributable to the duty-bearer. Examples include cases where duties were imposed on persons not to knowingly permit prostitutes to visit a place where refreshments are sold or consumed,[22] not

[6] Eg C Wells, *Corporations and Criminal Responsibility*, 2nd edn (Oxford, Oxford University Press, 2001); J Gobert and M Punch, *Rethinking Corporate Crime* (Butterworths, 2003); A Pinto and M Evans, *Corporate Criminal Liability*, 2nd edn (London, Sweet & Maxwell, 2008) 55.

[7] Eg Wells (n 6) 100.

[8] *Attorney General's Reference (No 2 of 1999)* [2000] EWCA Crim 91, [2000] QB 796.

[9] *P&O Ferries (Dover) Ltd* (1990) 93 Cr App R 72 (Central Crim Ct).

[10] Home Office, *Corporate Manslaughter: The Government's Draft Bill for Reform* (Cm 6497, 2005).

[11] Law Commission, *Criminal Law – Involuntary Manslaughter* (CP 135, 25 Feb 1994); Law Commission, *Legislating the Criminal Code: Involuntary Manslaughter – Report* (Law Com No 237, 3 March 1996).

[12] *Attorney General's Reference (No 2 of 1999)* (n 8); *R v St Regis Paper Co Ltd* [2011] EWCA Crim 2527, [2012] 1 Cr App R 14; *R v A Ltd* [2016] EWCA Crim 1469, [2017] 1 Cr App R 1; *Serious Fraud Office v Barclays plc* [2018] EWHC 3055 (QB), [2020] 1 Cr App R 28.

[13] Wells (n 6) 101 regards there as being two different models of attribution, one based on the directing mind and will, and a broader approach exemplified by this patchwork of other doctrines.

[14] 2021 Consultation Paper (n 2) paras 2.11–2.18.

[15] *Director General of Fair Trading v Pioneer Concrete (UK) Ltd* [1995] 1 AC 456 (HL) 470 (Lord Nolan). It thus differs from modern day vicarious liability in tort, which attributes liability. Their similarity lies solely in allowing attribution even where the relevant acts are performed by low-level employees.

[16] *Coppen v Moore (No 2)* (1898) 2 QB 306 (QB).

[17] *Mullins v Collins* (1874) LR 9 QB 282 (QB); *Bond v Evans* (1888) 21 QBD 249; *Harrow London Borough Council v Shah and Shah* [2000] Crim LR 692 (QB).

[18] *James & Son v Smee* [1955] 1 QB 78 (QB); *Richardson v Baker* [1976] Crim LR 76 (Div Ct).

[19] *R v Stephens* (1866) LR 1 QB 702 (QB).

[20] Sometimes confusingly referred to as vicarious liability as well, because it allows attribution of mental states of low-level employees, see eg *Tesco Stores Ltd v Brent LBC* [1993] 1 WLR 1037 (Div Ct).

[21] Eg *Howker v Robinson* [1973] QB 178 (Div Ct), but *cf Vane v Yiannopoullos* [1965] AC 486 (HL).

[22] *Allen v Whitehead* [1930] 1 KB 211 (KB), under the Metropolitan Police Act 1839 (2 & 3 Vict c 47), s 44.

to knowingly permit disorderly conduct,[23] and not to supply '18' category videos to persons under that age knowingly or without reasonable grounds for believing that he/she had reached that age.[24] Third, like civil statutes,[25] criminal statutes may create bespoke attribution rules.[26] Fourth, the need for attribution may be reduced by creating new offences specific to companies, such as 'failure to prevent' offences, which criminalise failures to prevent bribery[27] and the facilitation of tax evasion.[28]

Against this background, the account of attribution advanced in this book may have much to offer. Its central claim is that attribution turns not on right-sided features, but on the connection between act or knowledge, individual, and company. But nothing limits this analysis to private law. It appears equally applicable to attribution to establish a company's criminal law rights and duties. If so, then there is good reason to think that attribution in criminal law ought to conform to the same pattern seen in private law.

One benefit of extending the account here to criminal law is that there is some evidence suggesting that the account is already implicitly adopted in criminal law. If so, the account could provide a more coherent and transparent account of when acts and knowledge are attributed.

As alluded to earlier, pockets of cases already exist where the acts of junior employees have been attributed. In the so-called 'vicarious liability' cases, employees' acts of throwing rubbish into a river,[29] selling liquor,[30] permitting gaming,[31] using vehicles,[32] and entering into agreements in breach of an injunction amounting to a contempt of court,[33] have all been attributed. Less clear is whether evidence of this wider approach to attributing acts can be seen in non-regulatory cases. But there is at least good reason to think that attribution in criminal law may be wider than commonly thought, and some evidence that it turns on whether the company's powers to act were allocated or delegated to the person doing the act.

Similarly, the account of attributing knowledge in private law also seems applicable at least in some cases in criminal law. Despite the apparent dominance of the directing mind and will test, the mental states of lower-level individuals may also be attributed under the delegation principle, where the *mens rea* required is typically knowledge. Thus in cases such as *Allen v Whitehead*,[34] and *Linnett v Commissioner of Metropolitan Police*,[35] knowledge of a pub's manager about activities within the

[23] *Linnett v Metropolitan Police Commissioner* [1946] KB 290 (KB), under the Metropolitan Police Act 1839 (2 & 3 Vict c 47), s 44.
[24] *Tesco Stores Ltd v Brent LBC* (n 20), under the Video Recordings Act 1984, s 11(1).
[25] Eg Insurance Act 2015, ss 3–6.
[26] Eg Specialist Printing Equipment and Materials (Offences) Act 2015.
[27] Bribery Act 2010, s 7.
[28] Criminal Finances Act 2017, ss 45–46.
[29] Eg *R v Stephens* (n 19).
[30] *Mullins v Collins* (n 17).
[31] *Bond v Evans* (n 17).
[32] *Richardson v Baker* (n 18).
[33] *Director General of Fair Trading* (n 15).
[34] *Allen v Whitehead* (n 22).
[35] *Linnett* (n 23).

pub was attributed to the licensee who had delegated management of the business to him. As *Linnett* explains, the manager's knowledge could be attributed as the licensee had 'delegated his duties, powers and authority' to him.[36] This reasoning tracks the materiality test used in private law: the managers were delegated powers to act, and their knowledge was material to their exercise of those powers.

Another benefit is that this account of attribution may be more consistent with an important group of accounts of criminal liability. These premise criminal liability on the actor being a moral agent,[37] which is typically understood as comprising several capacities, including having agency over their acts.[38] If attribution is understood only as a fictional deeming process, it seems difficult to justify corporate criminal liability on the same basis as the criminal liability of human individuals. But the account of attribution offered in this book may dispell this concern. It suggests that attributed acts are generally intentional ones, providing a way to accommodate attribution – and thus companies – within important accounts of criminal liability.

This account's applicability in criminal law thus deserves further exploration. It is noteworthy that a criminal law commentator has recently called for a wider approach to attribution, attributing the acts and states of mind of any employee with actual or apparent authority.[39] Private law rules were explicitly drawn on.[40] This account may be thus be attractive within criminal law circles. While this proposal shares some similarities with the account in this book, a key difference is that acts done with only apparent authority would not be attributable under the allocated powers analysis offered here. As explained earlier, apparent authority involves no allocation of power but only an estoppel and is justified on a different basis: the protection of innocent third parties. While this latter aim may be a legitimate justification for private law liability (though not acts or knowledge), whether it is a legitimate justification for criminal liability is rightly controversial.

To aid further work, two additional points may be worth mentioning. First, the account's general applicability may be limited by specific statutes as a matter of statutory construction.[41] But as seen in private law, this may be much rarer than some might envisage. A more helpful default position may be that attribution

[36] ibid 295.

[37] Eg RA Duff, *Intention, Agency & Criminal Liability* (Oxford, Basil Blackwell, 1990) 100–105; M Moore, 'Intention as a Marker of Moral Culpability and Legal Punishability' in RA Duff and S Green, *Philosophical Foundations of Criminal Law* (Oxford, Oxford University Press, 2013) 183; M Moore, *Placing Blame* (Oxford, Oxford University Press, 2010) 612–36; J Gardner, *Offences and Defences* (Oxford, Oxford University Press, 2007) 221–34. See most recently N Friedman, 'Corporations as Moral Agents: Trade-Offs in Criminal Liability and Human Rights for Corporations' (2020) 83 *MLR* 255.

[38] See AP Simester, *Fundamentals of Criminal Law: Responsibility, Culpability, and Wrongdoing* (Oxford, Oxford University Press, 2020) 77–78.

[39] M D'Souza, 'The Corporate Agent in Criminal Law – An Argument for Comprehensive Identification' (2020) 79 *CLJ* 91.

[40] ibid 107.

[41] Eg *R v St Regis Paper Co Ltd* [2011] EWCA Crim 2527, [2012] 1 Cr App R 14, where statutory construction was stressed.

generally conforms to allocated powers analysis unless the statute indicates otherwise, rather than to look afresh at each statutory offence to determine which attribution rules ought to apply. Second, while the account here has discussed the attribution of knowledge, there is much more work to be done on the attribution of other mental states. Compared to private law, criminal law makes greater use of subjective mental states. In private law, most so-called mental states (eg dishonesty or unconscionability) are really standards of conduct, assessed objectively in light of the actor's knowledge. The attribution of knowledge thus suffices to establish most private law mental states in a way which will likely not hold true for the criminal law.[42] While analogies may be plausibly drawn with the approach taken to knowledge, more work will be required here.

B. Implications for Attribution to Other Artificial Legal Persons

If attribution turns on the connection between act or state of mind, individual, and the person to whom the act or state of mind is to be attributed, there is again nothing that limits that analysis specifically to companies. It might conceivably apply equally to other artificial legal persons. Potential subjects of attribution may be wide-ranging, including limited partnerships, trade unions, and the Crown. We focus here on the last.

The Crown today may be understood in several different ways. At its narrowest, it refers solely to the Queen[43] or to an office which she currently occupies.[44] At its most expansive, it has been said to include all ministers and central government officials,[45] used essentially to mean the executive government of the country.[46] Whichever the case, the Crown is generally accepted to be a corporation sole,[47] an artificial legal person. Establishing the Crown's duties, breaches, or liabilities thus requires attribution of the acts and states of mind of the human persons who act for it. While attribution rules were less practically important when the Crown had substantial immunities, the erosion of those immunities[48] ought to rejuvenate interest in attribution to the Crown.

Focusing on the Crown's allocated and delegated powers in attributing acts or states of mind appears apt. Many pieces of the puzzle already exist, merely needing

[42] Though in dishonesty, see now *Ivey v Genting Casinos (UK) Ltd (t/a Crockfords Club)* [2017] UKSC 67, [2018] AC 391, followed in *R v Barton* [2020] EWCA Crim 575, [2020] 3 WLR 1333.

[43] Sir William Wade, 'The Crown, Ministers and Officials: Legal Status and Liability' in M Sunkin and S Payne (eds), *The Nature of the Crown: A Legal and Political Analysis* (Oxford, Oxford University Press, 1999) 24.

[44] JG Allen, 'The Office of the Crown' (2018) 77 *CLJ* 298.

[45] *Town Investments Ltd v Department of the Environment* [1978] AC 359 (HL) 381.

[46] *BBC v Johns* [1965] Ch 32 (CA) 79; ibid 381 (Lord Diplock).

[47] *Town Investments* (n 45) 384 (Lord Diplock), *cf* 400 (Lord Simon).

[48] After the Crown Proceedings Act 1947.

assembly. There is a long and storied history of analysis of the Crown's powers, variously categorised. Prerogative powers are powers unique to the Crown[49] and recognised by the common law,[50] statutory powers are those conferred under statute. A third category of 'administrative powers'[51] also exists, spanning powers to contract,[52] distribute written information,[53] consult with officials,[54] place wiretaps,[55] amongst others.[56] Some of these are legal powers, while some are ordinary powers.[57]

Again, it is well recognised that the Crown's powers are then either allocated or delegated (depending on one's conception of the Crown) to ministers, parliamentary secretaries, and other members of government. It is commonly said that the 'executive powers of government are, in general, exercised by or on behalf of the Crown'.[58] Ministers are described as servants of the Crown. Though civil servants work under the direction of ministers, they too are servants of the Crown and not the departmental minister.[59] Courts adopt an analysis familiar to those accustomed to private law: where these persons act for the Crown, their acts are attributed to the Crown. In *Town Investments Ltd v Department of the Environment*, when the Secretary of State for the Environment, a minister of the Crown, acquired a leasehold interest in certain premises 'for and on behalf of Her Majesty', those were acts done by the Crown. The tenant of the premises was the Crown, not the minister himself.[60] Similarly, assurances given by the War Office were attributed to and binding on the Crown, and thus other agents of the Crown.[61] Such powers must be properly exercised within their scope, though what constitutes proper exercise might conceivably differ from that in private law.

This analysis may thus go some way to fleshing out an account of attribution to the Crown. Its adoption may even have further knock-on implications, perhaps on cognate areas such as administrative law. In this vein, Farrah Ahmed has recently argued that those subject to judicial review are delegates of Parliament

[49] Wade (n 43) 30, citing Bl Comm 1.239.

[50] *R (Miller) v Prime Minister* [2019] UKSC 41, [2020] AC 373 [30].

[51] *R (on the application of New London College Ltd) v Secretary of State for the Home Department* [2013] UKSC 51, [2013] 1 WLR 2358. See further BV Harris, 'The "Third Source" of Authority for Government Action' (1992) 108 *LQR* 626; BV Harris, 'The "Third Source" of Authority for Government Action Revisited' (2007) 123 *LQR* 225; A Perry, 'The Crown's Administrative Powers' (2015) 131 *LQR* 652.

[52] *Rederiaktiebolaget Amphitrite v The King* [1921] 3 KB 500 (KB) 503; *Robertson v Minister of Pensions* [1949] 1 KB 227 (KB) 231; *Crown Lands Commissioner v Page* [1960] 2 QB 274, 287–88 (CA).

[53] *Royal College of Nursing v Dept of Health and Social Security* [1981] AC 800 (HL); *Gillick v West Norfolk and Wisbech Area Health Authority* [1986] AC 112 (HL).

[54] *Shrewsbury & Atcham BC v Secretary of State for Communities and Local Government* [2008] EWCA Civ 148, [2008] 3 All ER 548.

[55] *Malone v Metropolitan Police Commissioner* [1979] Ch 344 (Ch).

[56] See further Perry (n 51) 660–62.

[57] Perry (n 51) 659–64.

[58] A Young, *Turpin and Tompkins' British Government and the Constitution*, 8th edn (Cambridge, Cambridge University Press, 2021) para 6.3.1.

[59] *Bainbridge v Postmaster-General* [1906] 1 KB 178 (CA).

[60] *Town Investments* (n 45) 381 (Lord Diplock).

[61] *Robertson v Minister of Pensions* [1949] 1 KB 227 (KB).

or the Crown, with judicial review holding administrators to their moral duties as delegates.[62] This idea shares some foundations with the analysis offered here: it sees delegates as being able to exercise the legal powers of their delegators either directly or indirectly, such that the delegator is bound,[63] with the Crown as a delegator. Placing the spotlight more squarely on the allocation and delegation of powers may thus have other beneficial effects, perhaps even shedding further light on the relationship between constitutional and administrative law.[64]

IV. Tying the Threads Together

At first sight, investigating attribution appears a daunting task. Even limited to private law, the material covered is enormous, spanning the different branches of private law: contract, tort, and unjust enrichment, traversing the common law/equity jurisdictional divide, and with additional complexities added by agency law, company law, and statutory intervention. Orthodox views of attribution today reinforce this complexity. If an act or state of mind attributed for one purpose may not be for another, the difficulty in working out private law's attribution rules increases exponentially.

In this book, I have sought to show that attribution is not so complicated after all. Its central claim is that attribution turns not on 'right-sided' features, but on the connection between act and state of mind, individual, and the company. This connection is found in the allocation and delegation of the company's powers to act. Through this connection, company, individual, and act or knowledge are all linked in a single normative sequence. This explains exactly how context is relevant: the relevant context is the power to act which has been allocated or delegated to the actor doing the act or holding the knowledge.

While the facts may vary, the analysis does not. Regardless of whether the issue of attribution arises in contract, tort, unjust enrichment, or some aspect of equitable liability, the same question is being asked. The same answer should be given. Like should be treated alike. If this is so, then it may well be for corporate attribution in other areas of law, or even attribution to other artificial legal persons. Thus viewed, attribution forms a remarkably coherent and accessible whole. This might be viewed by some with surprise, even scepticism. But it is just so. This is no bad thing. It minimises inconsistencies and promotes coherence, ultimately enhancing the law's rationality.

[62] F Ahmed, 'The Delegation Theory of Judicial Review' (2021) 84 *MLR* 772.
[63] ibid 778–79.
[64] See eg J Gardner, 'Can There Be A Written Constitution?' in L Green and B Leiter, *Oxford Studies in Philosophy of Law: Volume 1* (Oxford, Oxford University Press, 2011) 170–74.

BIBLIOGRAPHY

Books

American Law Institute, *US Restatement (Third) of the Law of Agency* (American Law Institute Publishers 2006)

American Law Institute, *Restatement Third: Restitution and Unjust Enrichment* (American Law Institute Publishers 2011)

JH Baker, *Baker and Milsom Sources of English Legal History*, 2nd edn (Oxford, Oxford University Press, 2010)

William Blackstone, *Commentaries on the Laws of England*, vol 1 (Oxford, Clarendon Press, 1765)

—— *Commentaries on the Laws of England*, vol 4 (Oxford, Clarendon Press, 1769)

Michael Bridge et al, *The Law of Personal Property*, 3rd edn (London, Sweet & Maxwell, 2019)

Michael Brindle and Raymond Cox, *Law of Bank Payments*, 5th edn (London, Sweet & Maxwell, 2017)

George Spencer Bower and Alexander Turner, *Estoppel by Representation, 3rd* edn (Butterworths, 1977)

Andrew Burrows (ed), *English Private Law* (Oxford, Oxford University Press, 2013)

—— *The Law of Restitution* (Oxford, Oxford University Press, 2011)

Paul L Davies and Sarah Worthington, *Gower's Principles of Modern Company Law*, 10th edn (London, Sweet & Maxwell, 2016)

Simon Deakin, Angus Johnston and Basil Markesinis, *Markesinis and Deakin's Tort Law*, 7th edn (Oxford, Oxford University Press, 2013)

Derek French, *Mayson, French and Ryan on Company Law*, 36th edn (Oxford, Oxford University Press, 2019)

Brenda Hannigan, *Company Law*, 5th edn (Oxford, Oxford University Press, 2018)

RFV Heuston and RA Buckley, *Salmond and Heuston on Torts*, 21st edn (Canada, Thomson Professional Pub Canada, 1996)

Michael Jones (gen ed), *Clerk & Lindsell on Torts*, 23rd edn (London, Sweet & Maxwell, 2020)

Lindley & Banks on Partnership, 20th edn (London, Sweet & Maxwell, 2020)

John McGhee QC and Steven Elliott QC (eds), *Snell's Equity*, 34th edn (London, Sweet & Maxwell, 2019)

Charles Mitchell, Paul Mitchell, and Stephen Watterson, *Goff & Jones: The Law of Unjust Enrichment*, 8th edn (London, Sweet & Maxwell, 2012)

Charles Mitchell, Paul Mitchell and Stephen Watterson, *Goff & Jones on the Law of Unjust Enrichment*, 9th edn (London, Sweet and Maxwell, 2016)

Graham Virgo, *The Principles of the Law of Restitution*, 3rd edn (Oxford, Oxford University Press, 2015)

Peter Watts and Francis Reynolds (eds), *Bowstead & Reynolds on Agency*, 22nd edn (London, Sweet & Maxwell, 2020)

PH Winfield, *Principles of Contract*, 13th edn (London, Stevens & Sons, 1950)

Sarah Worthington, *Sealy & Worthington's Text, Cases, & Materials in Company Law*, 11th edn (Oxford, Oxford University Press, 2016)

Alison Young, *Turpin and Tompkins' British Government and the Constitution*, 8th edn (Cambridge, Cambridge University Press, 2021)

Monographs

PS Atiyah, *Vicarious Liability in the Law of Torts* (London, Butterworths, 1967)

Michael Ashdown, *Trustee Decision-Making: The Rule in Re Hastings Bass* (Oxford, Oxford University Press, 2015)

Thomas Baty, *Vicarious Liability: A Short History of the Liability of Employers, Principals, Partners, Associations and Trade-Union Members with a Chapter on the Law of Scotland and Foreign States* (Oxford, Clarendon Press, 1916)

Christine Beuermann, *Reconceptualising Strict Liability for the Tort of Another* (Oxford, Hart Publishing, 2019)

Peter Birks, *Introduction to the Law of Restitution*, rev edn (Oxford, Clarendon Press 1989)

—— *Unjust Enrichment*, 2nd edn (Oxford, Oxford University Press, 2005)

Michael Bratman, *Faces of Intention* (Cambridge, Cambridge University Press, 1999)

—— *Shared Agency: A Planning Theory of Acting Together* (Oxford, Oxford University Press, 2014)

Douglas Brodie, *Enterprise Liability and the Common Law* (Cambridge, Cambridge University Press, 2010)

Stephanie Collins, *Group Duties: Their Existence and their Implications for Individuals* (Oxford, Oxford University Press, 2019)

Matthew Conaglen, *Fiduciary Loyalty: Protecting the Due Performance of Non-Fiduciary Duties* (Oxford, Hart Publishing, 2010)

Paul S Davies, *Accessory Liability* (Oxford, Hart Publishing, 2015)

RA Duff, *Intention, Agency & Criminal Liability* (Oxford, Basil Blackwell, 1990)

Frank Easterbrook and Daniel Fischel, *The Economic Structure of Corporate Law* (Cambridge, Harvard University Press, 1991)

James Edelman and Elise Bant, *Unjust Enrichment*, 2nd edn (Oxford, Hart Publishing, 2012)

Vanessa Edwards, *EC Company Law* (Oxford, Oxford University Press, 1999)

Paul Finn, *Fiduciary Obligations* (Sydney, Law Book Co 1977)

Brent Fisse and John Braithwaite, *Corporations, Crime and Accountability* (Cambridge, Cambridge University Press, 1993)

Peter A French, *Collective and Corporate Responsibility* (Columbia, Columbia University Press, 1984)

John Gardner, *Offences and Defences* (Oxford, Oxford University Press, 2007)

Carsten Gerner-Beurle and Michael Schillig, *Comparative Company Law* (Oxford, Oxford University Press, 2019)

O Gierke, *Political Theories of the Middle Age*, transl FW Maitland (Cambridge, Cambridge University Press, 1900)

Margaret Gilbert, *On Social Facts* (London and New York, Routledge, 1989)

—— *Joint Commitment: How We Make the Social World* (Oxford, Oxford University Press, 2013)

Paula Giliker, *Vicarious Liability in Tort* (Cambridge, Cambridge University Press, 2010)

James Gobert and Maurice Punch, *Rethinking Corporate Crime* (Butterworths, 2003)

James Goudkamp, *Tort Law Defences* (Oxford, Hart Publishing, 2013)

Anthony Gray, *Vicarious Liability: Critique and Reform* (Oxford, Hart Publishing, 2018)

Andrew Griffiths, *Contracting with Companies* (Oxford, Hart Publishing, 2005)

F Hallis, *Corporate Personality* (London, Oxford University Press, 1930)

Reinier Kraakman and others, *The Anatomy of Corporate Law: A Comparative and Functional Approach*, 3rd edn (Oxford, Oxford University Press, 2017)

Visa Kurki, *A Theory of Legal Personhood* (Oxford, Oxford University Press, 2019)

Ernest Lim, *A Case for Shareholder Fiduciary Duties in Common Law Asia* (Cambridge, Cambridge University Press, 2019)

Christian List and Phillip Pettit, *Group Agency: The Possibility, Design, and Status of Corporate Agents* (Oxford, Oxford University Press, 2011)

FW Maitland, 'Moral Personality and Legal Personality' in David Runciman and Magnus Ryan (eds), *Maitland: State, Trust and Corporation* (Cambridge, Cambridge University Press, 2003)

Michael Moore, *Placing Blame* (Oxford, Oxford University Press, 2010)
Eric Orts, *Business Persons – A Legal Theory of the Firm* (Oxford, Oxford University Press, 2013)
Amanda Pinto and Martin Evans, *Corporate Criminal Liability*, 2nd edn (London, Sweet & Maxwell, 2008)
Joseph Raz, *The Authority of Law: Essays on Law and Morality* (Oxford, Oxford University Press, 1979)
Stephen A Smith, *Contract Theory* (Oxford, Clarendon Press, 2004)
—— *Rights, Wrongs, and Injustices: The Structure of Remedial Law* (Oxford, Oxford University Press, 2019)
John Searle, 'Collective Intentions and Actions' in P Cohen, J Morgan, and M Pollack (eds), *Intentions in Communication* (Cambridge, MIT Press, 1990)
JC Shepherd, *The Law of Fiduciaries* (Toronto, Carswell, 1981)
AP Simester, *Fundamentals of Criminal Law: Responsibility, Culpability, and Wrongdoing* (Oxford, Oxford University Press, 2020)
Robert Stevens, *Torts and Rights* (Oxford, Oxford University Press, 2007)
Joseph Story, *Commentaries on Equity Jurisprudence: As Administered in England and America*, vol 2, 7th edn (Boston, Little, Brown and Company, 1853)
Raimo Tuomela, *Social Ontology: Collective Intentionality and Group Agents* (Oxford, Oxford University Press, 2013)
Charlie Webb, *Reason and Restitution: A Theory of Unjust Enrichment* (Oxford, Oxford University Press, 2016)
Celia Wells, *Corporations and Criminal Responsibility*, 2nd edn (Oxford, Oxford University Press, 2001)
Ernest Weinrib, *The Idea of Private Law*, rev edn (Oxford, Oxford University Press, 2012)
—— *Corrective Justice* (Oxford, Oxford University Press, 2012)
Glanville Williams, *Joint Torts and Contributory Negligence* (London, Stevens & Sons Ltd, 1951)

Articles and Chapters

Farrah Ahmed, 'The Delegation Theory of Judicial Review' (2021) 84 *MLR* 772
Armen Alchian and Harold Demsetz, 'Production, Information Costs and Economic Organization' (1972) 62 *American Economic Review* 777
JG Allen, 'The Office of the Crown' (2018) 77 *CLJ* 298
John Armour, 'Companies and Other Associations' in Andrew Burrows (ed), *English Private Law* (Oxford, Oxford University Press, 2013)
Elise Bant, 'Causation and Scope of Liability in Unjust Enrichment' [2009] *Restitution Law Review* 60
Andrew Bartlett, 'Attribution of Contributory Negligence: Agents, Company Directors and Fraudsters' (1998) 114 *LQR* 460
Allen Beever and Charles Rickett, 'Interpretive Legal Theory and the Academic Lawyer' (2005) 68 *MLR* 320
Christine Beuermann, 'Vicarious Liability and Conferred Authority Strict Liability' (2013) 20 *Torts Law Journal* 265
—— 'Tort Law in the Employment Relationship: A Response to the Potential Abuse of an Employer's Authority' (2014) 21 *Torts Law Journal* 169
—— 'Vicarious Liability: A Case Study in the Failure of General Principles?' [2017] *Professional Negligence* 179
Peter Birks, 'Equity in the Modern Law' (1996) 26 *University of Western Australia Law Review* 1
—— 'Definition and Division: A Meditation on Institutes' in Peter Birks (ed), *The Classification of Obligations* (Oxford, Clarendon Press, 1997)
—— 'Receipt' in Peter Birks and Arianna Pretto (eds), *Breach of Trust* (Oxford, Hart Publishing, 2002)
—— 'The Concept of a Civil Wrong' in David G Owen (ed), *The Philosophical Foundations of Tort Law* (Oxford, Oxford University Press, 1996)
Douglas Brodie, 'Enterprise Liability: Justifying Vicarious Liability' (2007) 27 *OJLS* 493

Ian Brown, 'The Significance of General and Special Authority in the Development of the Agent's External Authority in English Law' [2004] *Journal of Business Law* 391
Michael Bryan, 'No Intention to Benefit' in Elise Bant, Kit Barker and Simone Degeling (eds), *Research Handbook on Unjust Enrichment and Restitution* (Cheltenham, Edward Elgar, 2020)
Andrew Burrows, 'Illegality after Patel v Mirza' [2017] *CLP* 55
—— 'A New Dawn for the Law of Illegality' in Sarah Green and Alan Bogg (eds), *Illegality after Patel v Mirza* (Oxford, Hart Publishing, 2018)
—— 'In Defence of Unjust Enrichment' (2019) 78 *CLJ* 521
—— '"At the Expense of the Claimant": A Fresh Look' [2017] *Restitution Law Review* 167
Peter Cane, 'Mens Rea in Tort Law' (2002) 20 *OJLS* 533
Neil Cavanagh, 'Corporate criminal liability: an assessment of the models of fault' (2011) 75 *Journal of Criminal Law* 414
Robert Chambers, 'The End of Knowing Receipt' (2016) 2 *Canadian Journal of Comparative and Contemporary Law* 1
Robert Chambers and James Penner, 'Ignorance' in Simone Degeling and James Edelman (eds), *Unjust Enrichment in Commercial Law* (Sydney, Lawbook Co, 2005)
Winnie Chan and AP Simester, 'Four Functions of Mens Rea' (2011) 70 *CLJ* 381
CMV Clarkson, 'Kicking Corporate Bodies and Danning Their Souls' (1996) 59 *MLR* 557
JC Collier and LS Sealy, 'European Communities Act 1972 – Company Law' (1972) 32 *CLJ* 1
Walter Wheeler Cook, 'Agency by Estoppel' (1905) 5 *Columbia LR* 36
—— 'Agency by Estoppel – A Reply' (1906) 6 *Columbia LR* 34
Michael Conant, 'The Objective Theory of Agency: Apparent Authority and the Estoppel of Apparent Ownership' (1968) 47 *Nebraska LR* 678
Ronald Coase, 'The Nature of the Firm' (1937) 4 *Economica* 386
Tatiana Cutts, 'Materially Identical to Mistaken Payment' (2020) *Canadian Journal of Law & Jurisprudence* 31
—— 'Modern Money Had and Received' (2018) 38 *OJLS* 1
—— 'Unjust Enrichment: What We Owe to Each Other' (2021) 41 *OJLS* 114
Mark D'Souza, 'The Corporate Agent in Criminal Law – An Argument for Comprehensive Identification' (2020) 79 *CLJ* 91
Deborah Demott, 'When is a Principal Charged with an Agent's Knowledge?' (2003) 13 *Duke Journal of Comparative and International Law* 291
Patrick Devlin, 'Fraudulent Misrepresentation: Division of Responsibility between Principal and Agent' (1937) 53 *LQR* 344
John Dewey, 'The Historic Background of Corporate Legal Personality' (1926) 35 *Yale LJ* 655
AV Dicey, 'The Combination Laws as Illustrating the Relation between Law and Public Opinion in England during the 19th Century' (1904) 16 *Harvard LR* 511
FE Dowrick, 'The Relationship of Principal and Agent' (1954) 17 *MLR* 24
James Edelman, 'Equitable Torts' (2002) 10 *Torts Law Journal* 64
—— 'When Do Fiduciary Duties Arise?' (2010) 126 *LQR* 302
—— 'Money Had and Received: Modern Pleading of an Old Count' [2000] *Restitution Law Review* 547
Christopher Essert, 'Legal Powers in Private Law' (2015) 21 *Legal Theory* 136
Eugene Fama, 'Agency Problems and the Theory of the Firm' (1980) 88 *Journal of Political Economy* 288
JH Farrar and DG Powles, 'The Effect of Section 9 of the European Communities Act 1972 on English Company Law' (1973) 36 *MLR* 270
Eilis Ferran, 'Corporate Attribution and the Directing Mind and Will' (2011) 127 *LQR* 239
Paul Finn, 'The Fiduciary Principle' in TG Youdan (ed), *Equity, Fiduciaries and Trusts* (Toronto, Carswell, 1989)
Brent Fisse, 'The Attribution of Criminal Liability to Corporations: A Statutory Model' (1991) 13(3) *Sydney Law Review* 277
Robert Flannigan, 'The Fiduciary Obligation' (1989) 9 *OJLS* 285
Judith Freedman, 'Lord Hoffmann, Tax Law and Principles' in Paul S Davies and Justine Pila (eds), *The Jurisprudence of Lord Hoffmann: A Festschrift in Honour of Lord Leonard Hoffmann* (Oxford, Hart Publishing, 2015)

Nick Friedman, 'Corporations as Moral Agents: Trade-Offs in Criminal Liability and Human Rights for Corporations' (2020) 83 *MLR* 255
Lon Fuller, 'Legal Fictions' (1930) 25 *Illinois LR* 363
John Gardner, 'Can There Be A Written Constitution?' in Leslie Green and Brian Leiter, *Oxford Studies in Philosophy of Law: Volume 1* (Oxford, Oxford University Press, 2011)
WM Geldart, 'Legal Personality' (1911) 27 LQR 90
Jamie Glister, 'Equitable Liability of Corporate Accessories' in Paul S Davies and James Penner (eds), *Equity, Trusts and Commerce* (Oxford, Hart Publishing, 2017)
Paula Giliker, 'Analysing Institutional Liability for Child Sexual Abuse in England and Wales and Australia: Vicarious Liability, Non-Delegable Duties and Statutory Intervention' (2018) 77 *CLJ* 506
Ross Grantham, 'Commentary on Goddard' in Charles Rickett and Ross Grantham (eds), *Corporate Personality in the 20th Century* (Oxford, Hart Publishing, 1998)
Ross Grantham and Charles Rickett, 'Property Rights as a Legally Significant Event (2003) 62 *CLJ* 717
Andrew Halpin, 'The Concept of a Legal Power' (1996) 16 *OJLS* 129
Henry Hansmann and Reinier Kraakman, 'The Essential Role of Organizational Law' (2000) 110 *Yale LJ* 387
BV Harris, 'The "Third Source" of Authority for Government Action' (1992) 108 *LQR* 626
—— 'The "Third Source" of Authority for Government Action Revisited' (2007) 123 *LQR* 225
HLA Hart, 'Definition and Theory in Jurisprudence' in *Essays in Jurisprudence and Philosophy* (Oxford, Oxford University Press, 1983)
Bob Hepple, 'Negligence: The Search for Coherence' [1997] *CLP* 69
Wesley Newcomb Hohfeld, 'Some Fundamental Legal Conceptions as Applied in Judicial Reasoning' (1913) 23 *Yale LJ* 16
—— 'Fundamental Legal Conceptions as Applied in Judicial Reasoning' (1919) 26 *Yale LJ* 710
David Ibbetson, 'Development at Common Law' in Elise Bant, Kit Barker and Simone Degeling (eds), *Research Handbook in Unjust Enrichment and Restitution* (Cheltenham, Edward Elgar, 2020)
Michael C Jensen and William H Meckling, 'Theory of the Firm: Managerial Behavior, Agency Costs and Ownership Structure' (1976) 3 *Journal of Financial Economics* 305
Thomas Krebs, 'Agency Law for Muggles: Why There is No Magic in Agency' in Andrew Burrows and Edwin Peel (eds), *Contract Formation and Parties* (Oxford, Oxford University Press, 2010)
Rachel Leow, 'Attributing Shareholders' Knowledge: Corporate Attribution One Step Further?' [2018] *LMCLQ* 316
—— 'Understanding Agency: A Proxy Power Definition' (2019) 78 *CLJ* 99
—— 'Two Kinds of Agency' (2019) 93 *Supreme Court Law Review* 383
—— 'Attribution and Illegality Again' (2020) 136 *LQR* 181
—— 'Equity's Attribution Rules' (2021) 15 *Journal of Equity* 35
Rachel Leow and Timothy Liau, 'Birksian Themes and Their Impact in England and Singapore: Three Points of Divergence' [2021] *LMCLQ* 350
Timothy Liau, 'Privity: Rights, Standing, and the Road Not Taken' (2021) 41 *OJLS* 803
Ernest Lim, 'A Critique of Corporate Attribution: "Directing Mind and Will" and Corporate Objectives' [2013] *Journal of Business Law* 333
—— 'Attribution in Company Law' (2014) 77 *MLR* 794
—— 'Attribution' in William Day and Sarah Worthington (eds), *Challenging Private Law: Lord Sumption on the Supreme Court* (Oxford, Hart Publishing, 2020)
Ernest Lim and John Lowry, 'Reconsidering the Rule on Shareholders' Exercise of Voting Powers' (2020) *Journal of Business Law* 645
Lars Lindahl and David Reidhav, 'Legal Power: The Basic Definition' (2017) 30 *Ratio Juris* 158
Arthur W Machen Jr, 'Corporate Personality' (1911) 24 *Harvard LR* 253
Ben McFarlane, 'Form and Substance in Equity' in Andrew Robertson and James Goudkamp (eds), *Form and Substance in the Law of Obligations* (Oxford, Hart Publishing, 2019)
Ben McFarlane and Robert Stevens, 'What's Special about Equity? Rights about Rights' in Dennis Klimchuk, Irit Samet and Henry E Smith (eds), *Philosophical Foundations of the Law of Equity* (Oxford, Oxford University Press, 2020)

Charles Mitchell and Jessica Hudson, 'Legal Consequences of the Flawed Exercise of Pension Scheme Powers' in Sinead Agnew, Paul Davies, and Charles Mitchell (eds), *Pensions: Law, Policy and Practice* (Oxford, Hart Publishing, 2020)
Charles Mitchell and Stephen Watterson, 'Remedies for Knowing Receipt' in Charles Mitchell (ed), *Constructive and Resulting Trusts* (Oxford, Hart Publishing, 2010)
JL Montrose, 'The Basis of the Power of an Agent in Cases of Actual and Apparent Authority' (1938) 16 *Can Bar Review* 757
Phillip Morgan, 'Recasting Vicarious Liability' (2012) 71 *CLJ* 615
M Moore, 'Intention as a Marker of Moral Culpability and Legal Punishability' in RA Duff, and S Green, *Philosophical Foundations of Criminal Law* (Oxford, Oxford University Press, 2013)
Wolfram Müller-Freienfels, "Legal Relations in the Law of Agency: Power of Agency and Commercial Certainty" (1964) 13 *Am J Comp L* 193
JW Neyers, 'A Theory of Vicarious Liability (2004) 43 *Alberta LR* 287
Jason Neyers, 'Form and Substance in the Tort of Deceit' in Andrew Robertson and James Goudkamp (eds), *Form and Substance in the Law of Obligations* (Oxford, Hart Publishing, 2019)
Lord Nicholls, 'Knowing Receipt: The Need for a New Landmark' in W R Cornish and others (eds), *Restitution: Past, Present and Future* (Oxford, Hart Publishing, 1999)
Donal Nolan, 'Assumption of Responsibility: Four Questions' [2019] *CLP* 123
Richard C Nolan, 'Controlling Fiduciary Power' (2009) 68 *CLJ* 293
Richard Nolan and Matthew Conaglen, 'Good Faith: What Does it Mean for Fiduciaries and What Does It Tell Us About Them?' in Elise Bant and Matthew Harding (eds), *Exploring Private Law* (Cambridge, Cambridge University Press, 2010)
Jennifer Payne, 'Company Contracts and Directors' Authority' [2010] *LMCLQ* 187
—— 'Corporate Attribution and the Lessons of Meridian' in Paul S Davies and Justine Pila (eds), *The Jurisprudence of Lord Hoffmann: A Festchrift for Leonard Hoffmann* (Oxford, Hart Publishing, 2015)
Jennifer Payne and Dan Prentice, 'Company Contracts and Vitiating Factors Developments in the Law on Directors' Authority' [2005] *LMCLQ* 447
JE Penner, 'Trustees and Agents Behaving Badly: When and How is 'Bad Faith' Relevant?' in Paul Miller and Matthew Harding (eds), *Fiduciaries and Trust: Ethics, Politics, Economics, and Law* (Cambridge, Cambridge University Press, 2020)
Adam Perry, 'The Crown's Administrative Powers' (2015) 131 *LQR* 652
Max Radin, 'The Endless Problem of Corporate Personality' (1932) 32 *Columbia LR* 643
Joseph Raz, 'Voluntary Obligations and Normative Powers' (1972) 46 *Proceedings of the Aristotelian Society* 59
—— 'The Law's Own Virtue' (2019) 39 *OJLS* 1
Francis Reynolds and Tan Cheng-Han, 'Agency Reasoning – A Formula or a Tool?' [2018] *Singapore Journal of Legal Studies* 43
Andrew Robertson and Julia Wang, 'The Assumption of Responsibility' in Kit Barker, Ross Grantham and Warren Swain (eds), *The Law of Misstatements: 50 Years on from Hedley Byrne v Heller* (Oxford, Hart Publishing, 2015)
Phillip Sales, 'Use of Powers for Proper Purposes in Private Law' (2020) 136 *LQR* 384
Irit Samet, 'Proprietary Estoppel and Responsibility for Omissions' (2015) 78 *MLR* 85
AW Scott, 'The Fiduciary Principle' (1949) 37 *California LR* 539
Helen Scott, 'Change and Continuity in the Law of Unjust Enrichment' [2019] *Acta Juridica* 469
LS Sealy, 'Fiduciary Relationships' (1962) 20 *CLJ* 69
Warren A Seavey, 'The Rationale of Agency' (1920) 29 *Yale LJ* 859
Lionel Smith, 'Unjust Enrichment, Property and the Structure of Trusts' (2000) 116 *LQR* 412
—— 'Fiduciary Relationships: Ensuring the Loyal Exercise of Judgement on Behalf of Another' (2014) 130 *LQR* 608
—— 'Parenthood is a Fiduciary Relationship' (2020) 70 *University of Toronto LJ* 395
—— 'Restitution: A New Start?' in Rohan Havelock and Peter Devonshire (eds), *The Impact of Equity and Restitution in Commerce* (Oxford, Hart Publishing, 2019)
Stephen Smith, 'Duties, Liabilities and Damages' (2012) 125 *Harvard Law Review* 1727

—— 'A Duty to Make Restitution' (2013) 26 *Canadian Journal of Law and Jurisprudence* 157
—— 'Duties to Try and Duties to Succeed' in Andrew Dyson, James Goudkamp, and Frederick Wilmot-Smith (eds), *Defences in Tort* (Oxford, Hart Publishing, 2015)
Sandy Steel and Robert Stevens, 'The Secondary Legal Duty to Pay Damages' (2020) 136 *LQR* 283
Robert Stevens, 'Why Do Agents "Drop Out"?' [2005] *LMCLQ* 101
—— 'Vicarious Liability or Vicarious Action?' (2006) 123 *LQR* 30
—— 'Non-Delegable Duties and Vicarious Liability' in Jason Neyers, Erika Chamberlain, and Stephen Pitel (eds) *Emerging Issues in Tort Law* (Oxford, Hart Publishing, 2007)
—— 'The Unjust Enrichment Disaster' (2018) 134 *LQR* 574
—— 'Private Law and the Form of Reasons' in Andrew Robertson and James Goudkamp (eds), *Form and Substance in the Law of Obligations* (Oxford, Hart Publishing, 2019)
GR Sullivan, 'The Attribution of Culpability to Limited Companies' (1996) 55 *CLJ* 515
William Swadling, 'The Nature of 'Knowing Receipt" in Paul S Davies and James Penner (eds), *Equity, Trusts and Commerce* (Oxford, Hart Publishing, 2017)
Warren Swain, 'A Historical Examination of Vicarious Liability: A "Veritable Upas Tree"?' (2019) 78 *CLJ* 640
Benedict Tompkins, 'Restitutionary Liability for Third Party Negligent Statements' [2014] *Restitution Law Review* 61
Sir William Wade, 'The Crown, Ministers and Officials: Legal Status and Liability' in Maurice Sunkin and Sebastian Payne (eds), *The Nature of the Crown: A Legal and Political Analysis* (Oxford, Oxford University Press, 1999)
Susan Watson, 'Conceptual Confusion: Organs, Agents and Identity in the English Courts' (2011) 23 *Singapore Academy of Law Journal* 762
—— 'How the Company Became an Entity: A New Understanding of Corporate Law' [2015] *Journal of Business Law* 120
—— 'The Corporate Legal Person' (2019) 19 *Journal of Corporate Law Studies* 137
Stephen Watterson, 'Agents and Organisations: Attribution Rules in Unjust Enrichment Claim' [2017] *Restitution Law Review* 255
Peter Watts, 'Deeds and the Principals of Authority in Agency Law' (2002) 2 *OUCLJ* 93
—— 'Imputed Knowledge in Restitutionary Claims – Rationales and Rationes' in Simone Degeling and James Edelman (eds), *Unjust Enrichment in Commercial Law* (Sydney, Thomson Reuters, 2008)
—— 'Illegality and Agency Law: Authorising Illegal Action' [2011] *Journal of Business Law* 213
—— 'Principals' Tortious Liability for Agents' Negligent Statements – Is "Authority" Necessary?' (2012) 128 *LQR* 260
—— '"Unjust Enrichment" – the Potion that Induces Well-meaning Sloppiness of Thought' [2016] *Current Legal Problems* 289
—— 'Directors as Agents – Some Aspects of Disputed Territory' in Danny Busch, Laura Macgregor, and Peter Watts (eds), *Agency Law in Commercial Practice* (Oxford, Oxford University Press, 2016)
—— 'Actual Authority: The Requirement for an Agent Honestly to Believe that an Exercise of Power is in the Principal's Interests' [2017] *Journal of Business Law* 269
—— 'The Acts and State of Knowledge of Agents as Factors in Principals' Restitutionary Liability' [2017] *LMCLQ* 386
—— 'Attribution and Limitation' (2018) 134 *LQR* 350
—— 'The Quincecare duty: Misconceived and Misdelivered' [2020] *Journal of Business Law* 403
Ernest Weinrib, 'Correctively Unjust Enrichment' in Robert Chambers, Charles Mitchell, and James Penner (eds), *Philosophical Foundations of the Law of Unjust Enrichment* (Oxford, Oxford University Press, 2009)
Tony Weir, 'Subrogation and Indemnity' (2012) 71 *CLJ* 1
Glanville Williams, 'Vicarious Liability: Tort of the Master or of the Servant?' (1956) 72 *LQR* 522
—— 'Vicarious Liability and the Master's Indemnity' (1957) 20 *MLR* 220
Frederick Wilmot-Smith, 'Should the Payee Pay?' (2017) 37 *OJLS* 844
—— 'Illegality as a Rationing Rule' in Sarah Green and Alan Bogg (eds), *Illegality after Patel v Mirza* (Oxford, Hart Publishing, 2018)

Christian Witting, 'Intra-Corporate Conspiracy: An Intriguing Prospect' (2013) 72 *CLJ* 178
—— 'What are We Doing Here? The Relationship Between Negligence in General and Misstatements in English Law' in Kit Barker, Ross Grantham and Warren Swain (eds), *The Law of Misstatements: 50 Years on from Hedley Byrne v Heller* (Oxford, Hart Publishing, 2015)
M Wolff, 'On the Nature of Legal Persons' (1938) 54 *LQR* 494
Sarah Worthington, 'Corporate Attribution and Agency: Back to Basics' (2017) 133 *LQR* 118
Alison Young, 'Lord Hoffmann and Public Law: TV Dinner or Dining at the Savoy?' in Paul S Davies and Justine Pila (eds), *The Jurisprudence of Lord Hoffmann: A Festschrift in Honour of Lord Leonard Hoffmann* (Oxford, Hart Publishing, 2015)
Benjamin Zipursky, 'Civil Recourse, not Corrective Justice' (2003) 91 *Georgetown LR* 695

Unpublished Works

Joshua Getzler, 'Disciplining Corporation through Tort Liability and Disability' (Law and Finance Workshop paper, University of Oxford, 2010) (unpublished)
Timothy Liau, 'Standing in Private Law' (DPhil thesis, University of Oxford 2020)

Reports

Australian Law Reform Commission, *Final Report: Corporate Criminal Responsibility* (ALRC Report 136, 2020)
Home Office, *Corporate Manslaughter: The Government's Draft Bill for Reform* (Cm 6497, 2005)
Law Commission, *Criminal Law – Involuntary Manslaughter* (CP 135, 25 Feb 1994)
—— *Legislating the Criminal Code: Involuntary Manslaughter* (Law Com No 237, 1996)
—— *Illegal Transactions: The Effect of Illegality on Contract and Trusts Law* (Law Com CP No 154, 1999)
—— *The Illegality Defence in Tort* (Law Com CP No 160, 2001)
—— *The Illegality Defence: A Consultative Report* (Law Com CP No 189, 2009)
—— *The Illegality Defence* (Law Com No 320, 2010)
—— *Corporate Criminal Liability: A Discussion Paper* (9 June 2021)
Ministry of Justice, *Corporate Liability for Economic Crime: Call for Evidence* (Cm 9370, 2017)
Report of the Committee on Company Law Amendment (Cohen Report 1945) (Cmd 6659)
Report of the Company Law Committee (Jenkins Report 1962) (Cmd 1749)

INDEX

www.ingramcontent.com/pod-product-compliance
Ingram Content Group UK Ltd.
Pitfield, Milton Keynes, MK11 3LW, UK
UKHW020249290926
15470UKWH00002B/818

9 781509 941353